# Realms of Meaning

# Learning About Language

General Editors:
Geoffrey Leech and Mick Short, Lancaster University

*Already published:*

**Analysing Sentences**
Noel Burton-Roberts

**Patterns of Spoken English**
Gerald Knowles

**Words and Their Meaning**
Howard Jackson

**An Introduction to Phonology**
Francis Katamba

**Grammar and Meaning**
Howard Jackson

**An Introduction to Sociolinguistics**
Janet Holmes

**Realms of Meaning:
An Introduction to Semantics**
Th. R. Hofmann

**An Introduction to Psycholinguistics**
Danny D. Steinberg

**An Introduction to Spoken Interaction**
Anna-Brita Stenström

**Watching English Change**
Laurie Bauer

# Realms of Meaning
## An Introduction to Semantics

Th. R. Hofmann

Longman
London and New York

**Longman Group Limited,**
Longman House, Burnt Mill,
Harlow, Essex CM20 2JE, England
*and Associated Companies throughout the world.*

*Published in the United States of America*
*by Longman Publishing, New York*

© Th. R. Hofmann 1993

First published 1993
Second impression 1995

ISBN: 0 582 02886–8

**British Library Cataloguing-in-Publication Data**
A catalogue record for this book is available from the British Library

**Library of Congress Cataloging in Publication Data**
Hofmann, Th. R. (Thomas Ronald), 1937–
    Realms of meaning : an introduction to semantics /
    Th. R. Hofmann.
        p.   cm. — (Learning about language)
    Includes bibliographical references and index.
    ISBN 0–582–02886–8
    1. Semantics.   I. Title.   II. Series.
P325.H57   1993
401'.43—dc20                                          92–35281
                                                            CIP

Set by 8V in 11/12pt Bembo

*For*

Thomas Burl

Thomas John

Thomas Reuben

Thomas Takushi

# Contents

## Chapter 15    Afterwords    293

Pasigraphy, writing by meaning. Notable theories of meaning and what is meaning, after all?

# Preface

Because mathematics and science have dominated the realm of intellect this past century, they have influenced our expectations about everything, including language. Thus a word of warning: the meaning of a mathematical symbol is in many respects like a stool — rigid, strictly limited and resting on overt definition(s), with a general understanding that a stool should hold only one body. A natural language word is different in each of these respects, rather more like a mound of earth with no precise edge, no rigidity and no clear definition (a dictionary reports and catalogues the ways a word has been used, more or less accurately). And like a mound, its shape and size are always changing imperceptibly and, depending on circumstances, it may seat varying numbers of bodies. As we shall be treating natural language meaning with a largely scientific approach, we will use the tools of science to explain how natural language manages to have the precision to define the symbols used in science, yet have much greater power in depth and range of things that can be expressed.

## Value

I hope that the material in this book will prove to be of practical value to you, whether or not English is your native language, especially if you expect to be teaching or learning a language. But foreign languages are not the only application, for there are many advantages in being able to use your own language better. Whether in questions of law, where niceties of meaning can break fortunes, or in engineering and the sciences, where the communicative power of a natural language is needed to make discoveries known and to defend one's ideas, a better understanding of what words mean and how they can be used to mean something else will stand nearly all in good stead.

It goes without saying that the principles of meaning are valuable, but theories without practical application tend to be castles made of clouds, and not easily learned by ordinary people. So let me first point out a few aspects of language learning where anyone may expect practical benefit. If you keep these in mind as you read, the benefits will be greater.

One practical use is to help learn a language better and more quickly by picking up meaning accurately from text or conversation, as a child does, without wasting time turning dictionary pages. This can happen because you will learn how to make good guesses, knowing how meaning works and expecting certain common elements of meaning.

Also, in seeing the logic of human language you will be far better prepared to accept the true facts of other languages, instead of trying to squeeze them into the shape of English or into the logic of science and argumentation. Thus, knowing how languages can differ, as well as how meaning works, you will not waste your effort in the impossible goal of understanding one language in terms of another, but can learn only what is useful to learn.

In fact, we will find a few (less than fifty) basic elements of meaning by which a small vocabulary can be multiplied immensely. If you learn ways to express these basic concepts in a foreign language, you can bypass much of the agony of trying to learn all the common words – at least for saying what you want to say. Those other, less necessary words can be learned passively only (much easier!), and upon hearing them repeatedly you will naturally come to use them in speech too.

To be sure, a three- or four-year-old child knows much of this method of learning a language, in the sense that he does it naturally and learns many more words in a year than many language students do. School methods of language teaching often kill this ability or drive it underground. I will be satisfied if this course does nothing more than reawaken the ability you had fifteen or so years ago, when you learned the common words of your native language – with very little work, help or dictionaries.

It is my firm belief that abstract theories with little connection to the real world are like the barren sands of a desert, always shifting, supporting little life. Thus I am pleased to contribute to a link between theory and life – in some respects the ultimate test of a theory. As the abstract theories of nuclear physics became real when applied to building X-ray machines and nuclear reactors (and bombs), so also does linguistics become real if, and only if, it can contribute to some aspects of ordinary life such as the learning of foreign languages, though one hopes, and most likely, in no such dangerous manner. Although the primary subject is English, with some examples from other languages, the lessons learned will contribute greatly to the learning of any language. I have been horrified by the great amount of effort wasted, especially by Japanese students of English, in trying to learn unimportant things, and particularly in their over-use of dictionaries.

## Theories

There is as yet no generally accepted theory of meaning for human language, though there are some popular assumptions that are easily seen to be wrong. Most well-known semantic theories in linguistics are paste-ons to some theory of syntax – how words are arranged into sentences – which are too often adhered to for irrational reasons. Given this state of affairs, we will avoid nearly all theoretical questions and stick to facts that you can observe yourself. If you cannot find what I say is there, you need not accept it on my authority, as I am no angel with a direct pipeline to the truth. In fact, if you find something not convincing, I will appreciate knowing what it is and will send you an answer, if you will send it to me on a postcard, via Longmans, or direct to the address given at the end of this section.

Instead of general theories, we will restrict ourselves here to systems of elements, and explanations of some facts in terms of other facts – things that ought to be included in any general theory of meaning. You can expect that most other books, and many teachers, will have general theories, and may have alternative explanations. If they work, that will simplify your learning, and if they don't, you had better have your argument solid before you disagree with a teacher – and if you write it down (the only way I have found to have confidence in an argument), most teachers will be impressed whether you are right or wrong.

It has been a technique of physics, my intellectual origin if not that of all of science, to avoid philosophical questions and general theories until there is a good understanding (i.e. adequate theories) of specialized areas. Although this can make learning a little harder, still it does provide for learning the facts without preconceptions about the nature of the universe, and will fit in with any theory you or your professors espouse, if that theory is adequate to the breadth and depth of the task. I don't know of any that are, but if you are interested in my conceptions you can take an advance peek at the last part of the last chapter, 'Afterwords'.

## Your second language

I assume that you can speak a second language, or at least have studied one. The more different it is from English, the more you have (or should have) already learned of what we shall see here. The material in this course may not have been learned and is less useful in learning languages that are quite similar, like French or Dutch are with English. The real benefits appear when you face a really different language, like Arabic or Hebrew, Chinese, Indonesian (Malay), Japanese, Hungarian, Turkish, Swahili and so on. As all these languages are becoming more important, you may some day find yourself wanting to know one of them.

If English is a second language for you, do not feel that this book holds little of interest. Most of the facts of English presented here derive directly or indirectly from teaching English to non-natives, from seeing mistakes commonly made and noting how to avoid them. Moreover, it is written in a simple and clear English, a better model for nearly all writing (e.g. reports, essays, news reporting, business letters) than is provided by conversation textbooks or literary works.

Note, however, that the examples are spoken English. This is why they do not begin with capital letters and do make liberal use of contractions. When stress and rhythm are important, as they often are in spoken English, an underline is used to indicate the syllable(s) that receive stress and form the rhythm.

## In-text questions and notes

Questions at the end of each chapter are intended for your
practice, though with some modification they could be used for
testing. The other questions, in the text, are meant as a check for
understanding, and to keep you awake if my story gets boring.
They may be skipped, but I think you will find them interesting
and fun in their own right, as well as a valuable exercise.

Not all of these in-text questions have cut-and-dried
answers, but the basis for answering them should be in the
immediately preceding paragraphs. If necessary, their answers will
be found among the notes at the end, before the exercises.

The notes interspersed with these answers are to provide
more detail on points that may be of interest to some of you but
(in my opinion) are not important to the general principles. I
imagine that good students will read them all, poor students
none, but your teachers may point out those they consider
valuable.

## Organization

In the absence of any unquestionable theory, the chapters have
been written to be read independently of each other, though
connections to other chapters are mentioned. This will allow for
reading chapters selected on the basis of personal interest, often
the best way of learning something well. It also allows the
instructors to follow a different sequence, to skip chapters they
think less important, to supplement selected ones with materials
of their own choosing, and even to substitute some chapters with
material they find more appropriate. Nevertheless, unless they
advise against it, you may find that reading skipped chapters is
useful, and even entertaining.

Nevertheless, I have arranged the chapters in an order that
builds up to an interlocking knowledge of semantic structure.
The selection of materials reflects, unavoidably, the author's
perceptions of what is important and solidly known, but, having
been built up over some years, with other well-known linguists
(T. Kageyama and G. Leech) involved in the selection, provides a
guarantee that no modern directions have been completely
ignored.

In essence, then, this text provides a light description of much of the most modern work in semantics. The substantive work – knowledge about the structure of English and other languages – has been emphasized at the cost of theories, which are always changing (whatever abstract theory is believed today it surely will not be acceptable in ten years' time), and which are in any case hardly relevant to the student of English. For much the same reasons, technical details and terminology are avoided, so students of English literature and of other languages can profit nearly as much as students of linguistics.

*Th. R. Hofmann*
Prefectural University of Kumamoto
2432-1 Kengun-machi
Kumamoto, Japan 862

# Acknowledgements

I, and hopefully many readers, owe thanks to:

Taro Kageyama, who shared the authorship of the predecessor of this work, which benefits greatly from his impeccable scholarship and writing.

Dwight Bolinger, for reading many parts and posing problems while offering unlimited encouragement, Igor Mel'chuk for his comments, and both for providing boundless examples.

Yoshihisa Nakamura and Minoru Ohtsuki, for discussions of difficult problems such as negation and verbal aspect.

Geoffrey Leech, who as a knowledgeable and active researcher in semantics has made the best of all possible editors, not to speak of his encouragement and patience.

Longman, for providing the means to make this book widely available and for the patience to put up with long delays.

Kevin Monahan, who could read this as a bored student might while still being able to identify its problems.

The English students of Kanazawa University, who by stumbling over the rough spots in this text and its predecessor have led to some smoothing of the way. Asking difficult questions often leads to better answers. The students of Toyama, Shimane and Ottawa Universities have also contributed, though not so directly, to an even earlier version.

And perhaps the most vital contribution of all, the various families to which I belong, for tolerating my preoccupation(s) as well as for their comments (especially Anne) and for providing examples of semantics in action.

# List of Semantic Elements and Other Symbols

Throughout the various chapters we will use some very common semantic elements; this is done consistently as far as possible. This list is primarily to provide you with a reference to where they are best defined or explained, and, more usefully, to jog your memory as to what each one means.

You will find it useful, however, to remember and use them in dealing with any foreign language. Firstly, they are fairly universal, being found in nearly every language with apparently identical meanings. Translation between languages is relatively safe at this level; it avoids the pitfalls of translating between words of one language and words of another.*

Secondly, when learning a language, learn as soon as possible how to say and use these elements in that language. Then you will be able to say nearly anything you want to, even if it is in a roundabout way.

More importantly, when you learn a new word in that language, you can learn its meaning in terms of that language, with words that express these elements in that language. Just as translation between two words of two languages leads to many errors, so if you learn the words of a foreign language in terms of your own language you can be fairly confident that you will use them incorrectly. As far as possible, always learn the words of a language in terms of that language; not only will you learn their meanings faster and better, but you will learn to 'think in that language'. Moreover, you can check the meanings that you thereby devise with a native, for accurate responses.

Last and most important, though you will not notice it straight away, is that once you make a habit of using these

---

* Languages differ mostly in other ways, e.g. in how they combine these elements, and in how they classify things in the world like plants, animals, foods, and especially abstract ideas.

elements in thinking about meaning, when you hear (or see) a new word a few times you will often be able to guess its meaning accurately, with no need to look it up in a dictionary. This is what you must eventually learn to do to become good at a language, for this is what everyone can do in their own language. What children under six years old look up words in a dictionary (assuming they can read it)? Yet they learn ten or twenty words every day; they learn much of a language in only a few years. Once you discover how to learn new words this way, you will learn faster and with less effort.

For these reasons, then, you will find it useful to learn these concepts, though the symbols used here are not important. In fact, symbols for semantic elements have not yet been standardized as the chemical elements were standardized a century ago. We have tried to keep to three-letter symbols, capitalizing the first one. In other works, English words in capital letters are commonly used to stand for semantic elements.

Page references before semi-colon are definitional or explanatory, those after it are mentions or uses.

| ELE-MENT | ROUGH MEANING | | TEXT REFERENCE (Page numbers) | NOTES |
|---|---|---|---|---|
| Abl | from, SOURCE, ablative | | 63; 161ff, 205 | |
| (Adr | the addressee | | 66, 64; 98, 125 | = Neg-Spk, Neg-Awa) |
| Adt | adult, mature | | 245f; 227 | |
| (Agnt | agent | | ; 204 | first actant of [Coz]) |
| Aid | help, aid | | 256f | |
| Ami | friend(ship), love | | 237; 257 | |
| Ani | animate | | 232, 306 | moves, eats |
| Apx | near, approximate(ly) | | 105ff, 164ff; | |
| Awa | not close to Spk, Adr | | 62ff; 125, 226 | Dst (Distal) |
| Bcm | become, get | INCHOATIVE | 238; 45, 218, 241, 257 | |
| Cnt | in(side(s)), contents | | 161ff; 85f, 174 | |
| Coz | cause, make | CAUSATIVE | 240; 45, 111, 218 | |
| (Dat | goal | DATIVE | | old name for [Dir]) |
| Dir | direction, goal | (DATIVE) | 161ff; 62ff, 68, 205, 211, 226 | |
| (Dog | canine, dog | | 193 | ad-hoc) |
| (Dst | distal, -ance | | | alternative for [Awa]) |
| (Expr | experiencer | | 83 | a role, see [Stms]) |
| Fct | fact, true | | 99 | |
| Fem | female, (feminine) | | 28; 40, 193, 227ff, 257 | |
| Fut | future | | 126ff; 111 | S<R |
| (Gse | goose, geese | | 29 | ad-hoc) |
| Hav | have, with | ACCOMPANIMENT | 238ff | |
| (Hrs | horse, equine | | 59, 247 | ad-hoc) |
| Hum | person, human | | 40; 73, 232, 257 | |
| Imp | impossible, can't | | 98ff | |
| (Inst | instrument, with | INSTRUMENTAL | 204f | a role) |

| Kno | know(ledge) | | 142; 241, 257 | |
|-----|-----|-----|-----|-----|
| Lng | language | | 257 | |
| Loc | location | LOCATIVE | 61ff; 161ff; 205, 211, 226 | |
| Mnr | manner | | 62ff | |
| Mov | movement, go | | 75 | |
| Msc | male, (masculine) | | 28; 40, 192, 217 | |
| (Mtf | meat-of | | 30 | doubtful) |
| Much | big, much, a lot | | 257 | |
| Nec | necessary, unavoidable, have to | | 99ff; 239 | = Imp-Neg |
| Neg | not | NEGATIVE | 42; 29, 64f, 68, 114, 161ff, 232, 239, 306 | |
| Par | parent of | | 40; 218, 228 | |
| (Patient | | PATIENT, THEME | 204 | a general role) |
| Pls | pleasant, not harsh | | 82f; 42, 44 | |
| (Pres | present tense | | 220 | English form) |
| (Prt | preterite tense | | 126f; 111 | R<S, English tense) |
| Psb | possible, optional | | 98ff | = Neg-Imp |
| Pst | past time | | 99; 110f | E<S |
| Qst | questioning element | | 63; 226 | |
| (Shp | sheep | | 29 | ad-hoc) |
| Sng | single, –ular, unity | | 244; 63f | |
| Spk | (speaker), act of speaking | | 64, 62ff; 70, 97f, 125, 231, 239 | |
| Sps | spouse, married | | 231, 239 | |
| Srf | surface, boundary | | 161ff | |
| (Stms | stimulus | | 83 | a role, see [Expr]) |
| Try | try, attempt | | 257 | |
| Via | by way of | | 164ff | |
| Viv | *vivant*, living | | 232, 306 | |
| Voj | visible object | | 243; 226, 239 | |
| Yng | young | | 28ff; 227f; 217, 257 | |

*One-letter symbols for other elements*
*for temporal and aspectual points in time in tense and aspect*

| S | time of Speaking | 122ff | Spk |
|-----|-----|-----|-----|
| R | time of Reference, viewpoint | 122ff, 140 | |
| (E | time of Event | 122ff | for punctive events) |
| B | time of Beginning of event | 140; 127ff | Bcm |
| F | time of Finish of event | 140ff; 127ff, 280 | Abl, Bcm-Neg |
| x=y | time X is same as Y | 123ff, 144, 152 | |
| x<y | time X is before time Y | 123ff, 145ff | |

*for elements of integrative model*
C     content or comprehension of prior context
K     background, 'encyclopaedic' or 'shared' knowledge

*for types of modal usages*
C     capacity (dynamic): ability and capability
D     deontic: personal (authoritative) and social
E     epistemic

*for (informal) linear representation of meaning*                     *example*
a.b     A and B both describe same thing                     Msc.Hum. Yng
a–b     A 'dominates' B                                                    Neg-happy
a:b     A and B share referent, second actant of A            Dir:Spk
a\b     A and B share referent, first actant of B
*variables*
x y z   referents of nominal phrases X, Y and Z

Items in parentheses are not believed to be real universal semantic elements, for some reason or other. For example, [Adr] is excluded because it is simply [Neg-Spk.Neg-Awa], [Agnt] because it is simply the first actant of [Coz], [Dog] because it classifies what may well not be a universally recognized object, and [Dat] because it is an old name for [Dir].

Examples from given language, and in parentheses discussion about the language.

French:     4, 24, 48ff, 64f, 81f, 90, 124, (130), 139, 145, 165, (181), 190, 219, 231, 280, 283
German:     49, 160, (181)
Dutch:      54
Russian:    (130), 144f, 147, (160), (214), 294
Spanish:    62, 71, 75
Japanese:   4, (49), 62ff, 68ff, 75, 80f, (122), 139, 149, 171, (203, 206, 214, 216), 204f, (214, 216), 226ff, 260, 272, 282, (288), 294
Chinese:    4, (49, 122, 159, 214, 231, 288)
Eskimo:     4, (75), (130), (160), (165), 214
Tagalog:    (130)
Latin:      (160)
Finnish:    (160), (165)
Hungarian:  (160)
Turkish:    (160)
kanji★ (characters used in writing Chinese and in part Japanese, Korean)   166, 272, 293

★ This word comes from Japanese, where it means [character(s) from China] and is thus an appropriate term for the international system.

# CHAPTER 1
# On Entering the Realms

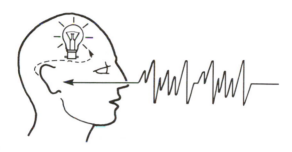

How is it that I get ideas in my head when I hear sounds of my language, but not when I hear sounds of another language?

Humpty Dumpty said to Alice that he could make a word mean exactly what he wanted it to mean; that it was only a question of who was to be the master. Can you? Can he really?

It is no doubt more interesting to talk about the meanings of words and sentences than to try to talk about what meaning is. Nevertheless, it is worth a few words at least, to know where we are going and how to fit things together.

The English verb *to mean* can be used for many things: in just about any case where you can learn something important, F, from something else, X, we can say 'X means F (to you)'. For example, if we can know that it is going to rain from some dark clouds blowing up, it is perfectly natural to say 'Those clouds mean rain.' The optional '(to you)' is used in case you would conclude it but others might not.

what did she mean by winking like that?
that nasal accent means he comes from Chicago.
how she feels means a lot to me.
who do you mean to refer to by that?

who do you mean by 'that guy with an earring'?
what does the word <u>teacher</u> mean?
what do you mean by <u>freedom</u>?

Really, however, we are not so interested in this particular word of English, even if philosophers worry a lot about it. As would-be scientists, we are interested rather in what the world of meaning in language is like, and freely accept that English words might not match that world too closely. The noun *meaning* is closer to our needs, for it cannot be used in all the ways the verb can.

---

Q.  Which of the ways that *to mean* was used above can be paraphrased (i.e. said in a different way) with the word *meaning*? The last, for example, can be paraphrased as 'The meaning of (the word) <u>freedom</u> for me is . . . .'[1]

---

On a most basic level, the meaning that we are interested in is cognitive or **descriptive** meaning: what is communicated when one person tells another something. That is, we are interested in the meaning that can be expressed in language, meaning that describes something. There are also some other things that we can learn by listening to a person, like his social or geographical origins or his emotional state, that we should not want to call meaning. If we heard 'Gimme a cup o' wa'er', we can guess a lot about its speaker – where he comes from as well as the fact that he is thirsty – but all that is hardly his meaning. He did not say he was from London, only that he wanted some water – and he might be an actor putting on a local style of speech. Happily, these other things are seldom subject to much control, so descriptive meaning can usually be distinguished as being easily controlled by all competent speakers. Of course, some people control it less well, but by learning more about it we can all control it better.

---

Q.  Is there any difference between saying, 'She gave me, a man from York, a call' and 'She gave us a call' in a male Yorkshire voice? If I were a New Yorker, would I be lying if I said these, pretending, or what?[2]

---

## Language as a tool

Although we have excluded a lot of things from meaning, there is plenty left. Enough, in fact, to make this one of the most exciting areas in language to study; it is, I believe, much of what makes human beings human, and what allowed us to dominate all other animals so that now they work for us or entertain us. Each type of animal has some special weapon or defence, like running fast or sharp teeth, sharp ears, long claws or a long neck. We humans excel in none of these ways, but we have language.

How is language stronger than claws and teeth and speed? Simple: ten men armed with only stones or clubs can take a tiger or an elephant by surrounding it and coordinating their actions so that several attack its weak spots whenever it attacks one of them. Some animals like dogs or sheep use numbers as a weapon, but in coordinating ourselves we become like a single animal spread out in many different places! This was so effective that even thousands of years ago, the only wild animals that didn't avoid human beings were dead animals.

It used to be said that what distinguished human beings was that they make and use tools. Unfortunately for our pride, however, some types of great apes have been seen to use tools, and even to invent simple ones, and some birds will also do so. Chimpanzee mothers have even been seen in the wild showing their offspring how to use things as tools – but how much can you learn by imitation? Some animals have communication systems, of course, but they are so limited in what they can communicate that linguists refuse to call them languages. The most extensive one known, that of some honey bees, can (apparently) communicate only a location – where some nectar is to be found. Our languages by contrast can communicate apparently anything – locations, emotions, facts, procedures, possibilities, fantasies, lies and many other things.

---

Q.  What is communicated in:
    a dog's bark, whine, snarl?
    a cat's meow, purr, . . .?[3]

---

There is no doubt that human beings are superior to most or all animals in being able to think, but what is thinking? A lot of our thinking is done in our native languages, sort of like talking to ourselves. If we can understand what meanings a language can express, we will be much closer to knowing what thinking is. In any case, it seems doubtful whether we might be any better than other primates in thinking without language.

---

Q.  Might there be something that human language cannot communicate? What? Please tell me about it, if you can.[4]

---

I am not even convinced that we can think much better than the great apes – you or I, that is. What tools have you invented recently? Our languages give us, almost from birth, the refined wisdom of our ancestors. Every useful procedure and tool has a name, and when we learn our first language we learn these names and what to apply them to. The words for concepts that do not prove so useful are normally forgotten in a generation or so.[5] By going on from what our ancestors have learned we have left our primate cousins far behind, for each one of them has to start once again from the beginning. No doubt the chimps have had their geniuses, but their discoveries are always lost when they die.

---

Q.  When you take an elementary course in chemistry, or poetry, or any subject, a lot of your effort goes into learning the specialized vocabulary. What are you really learning?[6]

## Communication

The sort of communication in which we are interested then, is that between two people, one making sounds with his or her mouth (or hand movements in sign language, or pencil marks in written language) and the other listening (or watching or reading). Of course it is not enough simply to make sounds, for if I said 'nǐ dǒng bu-dǒng wǒ suó–shuō-de ì-si?' or 'est-ce que tu comprends tout ce que je dis?' or 'zenbu wakarimasu-ka' or simply 'tukusiviin', you wouldn't have any idea of what I was saying unless you knew some Chinese, French, Japanese and Eskimo respectively. We don't have communication unless the receivers get ideas from the sounds.

Even that is not enough; they must get the right ideas. If I pronounced the sound [hai] in the right way, they might think I was agreeing with them if they thought I was speaking Japanese or Cantonese Chinese, while I might only be greeting them in English. Or I might be saying *ashes* in Japanese or *high* in English. Unless they get the idea I want them to, we don't have good communication. A simple diagram of this is in Fig. 1.1.

Figure 1.1    Diagram of 'good communication'

Communication is successful if the idea they get (the **impact** on them) is the same as what I intended them to get (my **intent**). If they don't match, then we have poor or no communication, and the idea-bulb in the cloud above their heads is dim or completely out. Poor communication is an interesting study in itself − it happens often enough − but it is wisely left until we know what happens in this ideal case of good (i.e. perfect) communication. The meaning that we will study, then, is whatever it is that gets transmitted between people in a case of good communication, i.e. when the intent and the impact are identical.

The study of meaning is exciting, and important, because it concerns the top half of the diagram − the brains of these two people, and the idea floating in the cloud above them. It has been slow to develop, as we don't like cutting into people's brains (don't worry about yours; we shan't touch it) and we can't see ideas or record them for study as we can see lips and tongue, and record the sounds they form. In the last ten years or so we have made machines that can recognize language sounds nearly as well as our ears can do it. It seems unlikely that we shall ever make a machine, however, that can record the ideas, for ideas are not objects. While sounds are not physical objects, at least they are vibrations of objects, but ideas are not even vibrations in the physical world.

## Does meaning really exist?

In trying to be scientific, most linguists avoided theories about meaning until some twenty years ago; it couldn't be shown even to exist. That was unfortunate, however, for it ignored half of communication, the top half of the diagram in Figure 1, and good communication could not be distinguished from no communication. As a result of that prohibition, linguists snuck meaning in between the rules of their grammars, most importantly as *deep* or *logical* structure in transformational grammar. After all, conveying ideas is a primary use of language, and the only obvious one.

There is nothing wrong in studying things we can't see, however, even ghosts or angels if you like. We can't see electricity but we developed meters to measure it, discovered how to control and use it, and it is now an essential of human life in most places. Indeed, most of physics and chemistry deal with things we can't see, but these things exist nevertheless – because we can measure them, control them and use them.

Ideas, and hence meaning, must surely exist because treaties are made of them, and even wars are fought or avoided because of them. The cooperation and coordination by which human beings dominate the world depend on it. What we need for the study of meaning is some method(s) for observing it, for we cannot discover how it works, nor hope to control it, unless we can tell what it is in most circumstances. We shall use various different ways to determine what it is in the chapters to follow, but leave it to the good student to notice what they are.

Words are commonly said to 'have' meanings in ordinary English, and there is surely something the same in **synonyms** like *father – dad – male parent* but totally opposed in **antonyms** such as *quick – slow* and *deep – shallow*. The English word *word* is not very exact (see Exercise question 4), so linguistics now uses a technical term **lexical item**, an item or entry in the **lexicon** or dictionary of the language. As we are concerned with meaning only, we can – and generally will – use the simpler term *word* instead. Remember, however, that a word (or lexical item) is a connection or association between two things, a pronunciation that is different in all these examples, and a 'meaning' that is the same for the synonyms but opposed for each pair of antonyms.

Q. In literate languages, a word also has a standard way of being written, so it can be considered as three associations. However, the written form is almost always closely associated with the pronunciation or with the meaning. Everybody has heard of languages written mostly according to sound, and others written mostly according to meaning; which ones are they? Can you think of some words in English of each type?[7]

Because meaning plays an important part in most of the humanities, many different terms have come to be used for these two parts of words, pronunciation and meaning. In literature they are often called *form* and *content*, while psychology tends to follow an earlier philosophical usage, 'a sign' and 'its referent'. Philosophers, however, now carefully distinguish between *sense* and *referent*, as we shall see shortly, and few would agree with that usage. The most general terms are *expression* and *content* and have the advantages of being systematic and relatively unambiguous. We will adopt these terms here, so **content** is what we commonly speak of as meaning. As it is a technical term, we can make it mean exactly what we want it to without bothering about the vague English term *meaning*.

More specifically, the content of a single word is the **concept** that it associates with its form or expression. Modern psychology has also been exploring concepts, and not just those associated with words. When a form has several different concepts associated with it, we sometimes call them different **senses** or 'readings' (of the word).

The meaning or content of a sentence has a different nature from the content of a word and is often called a **proposition**. If I put several words (or rather their concepts) together, 'Bear bite man', I am saying something, something that can be true or false, something you can react to. If I say merely 'Bear', however, I am not really saying anything at all, unless I fill in the rest of a proposition by pointing to something. Sentence meaning is like an idea plus a bit that indicates what its speaker wants its listener to do with the idea,[8] as we shall see in Chapter 14, while word meaning is a concept. Together we call them **content**, and reserve the term *concept* for the very incomplete sort of content that words have. A proposition is a content that is complete enough to be true or false.

SUPPOSING:

THEN: (1) bear bit man!   (2) man bit bear!   (3) bear bitten by man!

There can be no doubt that sentence meaning exists and is more than just concepts. The content of the second sentence above is very different from the first; it describes a different (and unusual) event, though it contains the very same concepts. Moreover, it is clear that this difference is not simply a matter of arrangement. The order of concepts in the third sentence is like that of the first but it is a **paraphrase** of the second — they have essentially the same descriptive meaning. We will understand propositional (descriptive) content, then, to be whatever it is that makes this third example similar to the second but different from the first.

We conclude that just as words have two parts, an expression part and a content (or meaning) part, sentences also have a content part, and that such a proposition is made out of concepts but not simply by arranging them. This, surprisingly, was not generally understood until about twenty years ago, so it is still relatively unexplored. We shall learn how to observe content and how concepts (word meanings) fit together into sentence meanings, and even how sentence meanings fit together to make paragraphs. In the process we shall even be drawing diagrams of the meanings of words (concepts) and sentences or paragraphs (propositions). This is a big advance, really, for if anyone had suggested, a mere thirty years ago, that this might be possible, most linguists would have said they were 'nuts'.

A word to the wise: although people commonly say that a word **'has' a meaning** in ordinary English, we will avoid that for several reasons. First, we want to avoid the idea that a word is a pronunciation (or spelling) that has a meaning; rather the word or lexical item has two parts, a pronunciation and a meaning. Second, it just won't do to think that a word has a fixed meaning that you can look up in the dictionary. A dictionary does report the literal meaning of a lexical item but there are systematic ways to modify these meanings, such as using them metaphorically. Besides, most words are used with different meanings (intents) nearly every time they are used. Thus linguists generally speak of a word *with* such-and-such a meaning.

Even worse is to think of a sentence as ***having a meaning***. In a specific context it may be possible to identify a meaning for it, but generally a sentence can be used in so many contexts that I think it is almost pointless to try to talk of its ***meaning***. As it is very difficult to imagine all the contexts in which a sentence might be used, it is nearly impossible to grasp its meaning in its full generality. Much safer is to speak of a sentence, or even a word, as *expressing* a certain meaning – in that context.

## Language as a bridge

Let us go back now to the diagram of good communication to see where language was in it. Both people had to be using the same language if they were to share the same idea for a sound, so we can say that it is in both of their heads, though often enough they have slightly different versions of it (dialects or accents) and communication is not so perfect. In the ideal case that they have perfectly identical languages, however, the speaker uses that language to convert the meaning into sound (called ***encoding*** the idea or message) and his or her addressee uses it to recreate the idea (called ***decoding***). The language, then, is a way of associating sounds or forms with contents. We can add it to Figure 1 as a connection between the cloud above their heads and the sound that stretches between the people.

We can see a language, then, as a bridge connecting a realm of sounds and a realm of meanings. When we say that a person can speak a language we mean that they can cross the bridge both ways; from a sound they can get an idea (usually instantaneous, if they are competent), and for an idea they can make up a sound (often harder and, in the case of writing, requiring some time and effort if they want it clear). Part of the reason that speaking and especially writing are harder and slower is that for any idea there are many ways to express it and writers must find one that will give their reader just the meaning they want. If writers do not do their job well, we will not bother to read or to publish their work, so the reader normally has the easier task.

> Speaking makes a ready man; writing makes a careful man.
> (after Sir Francis Bacon)

In talking as well, the speaker can stop and collect his or her thoughts, but the listener can seldom stop, so understanding has to be done as fast as the words arrive. This is one good reason why most studies of meaning concentrate on how to find the content of some expression rather than finding an expression for some content. It is wise to study easier things first.

Sound and ideas are very different. Sound is nothing more than vibrations in the air while content or meaning is – perhaps – vibrations in the mind or 'tremulations on the ether' as D. H. Lawrence put it. It is not surprising that the bridge between them is long and a little unwieldy. For convenience in studying this bridge, linguistics has found it useful – necessary even – to divide it up into sections according to its nature, just as a bridge across the Thames or the Mississippi must be built of different sections, often of several different types. On this basis we can make a sketch of a language (Fig. 1.2).

The labels on the different sections are the parts of linguistics that deal with those sections, and to suggest some historical perspective I have added rough dates (give or take ten years) when that section was most recently at the forefront of linguistic study.

Modern linguistics began with studying sound and this reached a sort of peak early in this century with the creation of the International Phonetic Alphabet. Phonology reached one peak in the early 1940s and a further one in the 1960s. Morphology, the structure of words, began as early as history, reaching a peak in the early 1950s and again in the last few years. Syntax, the structure of sentences, peaked around 1970 but has tended to divide since then into real (surface) syntax and semantics, which has been going strong since that time. It is tempting to see the study of meaning at the forefront now, but recent history is always hard to judge accurately.

The emptiness at the right of the diagram reflects the fact that we still do not know very well what should really be there. The whole area is sometimes called *semantics* but most people today will distinguish **pragmatics**, dealing with how sentences

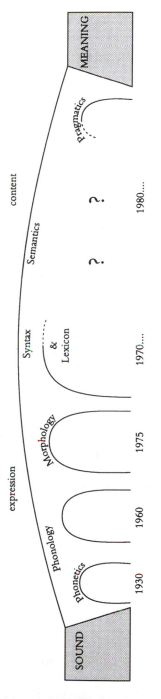

Figure 1.2  Language – a bridge between sound and meaning

are used, even if we have not yet agreed on what this should include. Some, myself included, take it as the relationship between the content of the sentence and its impact on the addressee. Other people may use this same term, pragmatics, for any relation between content and the situation in which a sentence is used.

In logic the term *semantics* is often used for the connections between symbols and the real world, but in linguistics and modern philosophy connections to the real world are put into **reference**, or a recent and more detailed ***model theory***. It is quite standard today (except in some areas of psychology noted earlier) to identify the **referent** of a nominal phrase as some object(s) in the world, or an imaginary world if need be, that it identifies or points to. So in a sentence such as 'Your cat ate my tweety bird', the first two words and the last three point to two objects in the world, their referents.

---

Q.   What is the referent of 'this chapter' in 'This chapter is exciting'?[9]

---

A referent is generally *not* part of the language, and so it cannot be meaning. It is often mistaken for meaning, however, for 'Who do you mean by "the guy with an earring"?' asks what may be better said by 'Who do you mean to **refer to** (or point to) by "the guy with an earring"?' We cannot say that the meaning of that phrase is a certain person. Meaning, often called **sense** in contrast to reference, is what one can understand from the words alone, divorced from the context of use, so it does not change depending on who is speaking; a referent is something that one can point to (refer to) with some words, and it almost always depends on who is speaking, when and where.

## Triangle of Signification

A simple way to keep these notions clear and to cope with other terms that are sometimes used for them is to diagram the relationships between these ideas. As you may already know, the father of modern linguistics, de Saussure, popularized the notion that a word or lexical item is an association between a form and a concept. The collection of them all is called the ***lexicon***, what dictionaries try to describe (Figure 1.3, top section).

form ——————— concept ⋮ in the LEXICON

When several words (or possibly just one, like a name) are used together in a sentence, they may refer to some object in the world, their referent. This makes the ***Triangle of Signification*** below, having a referent in the world but form and concept in language. It used to be popular, to show that referring is not a simple direct relation between words and things. Sometimes we use the term **sense** for the concept here, to keep it distinct from the referent, in the way philosophy had shown long before.

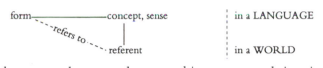

In such a case, where words are used in some actual situation and thus have a referent, they must also have an actual pronunciation, so a complete diagram must have another leg, as below, with labels that derive from L. Hjelmslev.

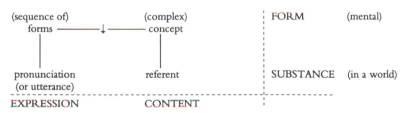

Figure 1.3    Relationships between basic concepts

If we bend the two legs out in the bottom section of Figure 1.3, we get back to the bridge of Figure 1.2, but in this form the parts have clear and systematic labels: the right half is called **content**, the left **expression**; the top two are called **form**, and the bottom two **substance**. The substances (sound and things or actions) exist in the real world or an imaginary world, while the forms above (and the association between them, language) exist only in the minds of people or in a society. Until recently, most of linguistics has been concerned with the upper left-hand corner, the ***form of expression***, which explains, perhaps, why this view of language had not been popular before. It has now been adopted by most theoretical linguists, though many would include a small addition at the centre of the cross-bar to allow ***transformations*** to create the structures of sentences.

Q.   Where do phonology and phonetics fit into this diagram?[10]

In general, then, we shall be concerned with the less explored half of language, especially the *form of content* (upper right, bottom section of Figure 1.3). It is the most interesting part; most everyday arguments about language are about meanings of words and phrases. Because this area has been neglected, however, it has yet to be completely explored, so there are many differences of opinion and not yet a really standard terminology.

Q.   Lawyers and judges spend much of their time arguing about language. In terms of the diagram above, what parts are they arguing about?[11]

Indeed, don't be surprised if your teacher disagrees in small ways from what we say here; he is likely to be right. Knowledge is advancing so fast that the only books that are right up to date don't say much about meaning (or else they would be out of date when published). Here we go right to the forefront, with the result that some relevant facts have been discovered between the writing and the reading of this book. In any case, it is probably not worth reading anything on semantics more than fifteen years old, except for studies on how word meanings change in time (an old study, peaking around 1900) and on some simple structures of meanings of nouns (peaking around 1950).

## Limits of the realms (summary)

We have spent most of this chapter talking about what we shall study and what not, and why. The main subject will be content or descriptive meaning, roughly what is meant by the *meaning* of linguistic expressions: words (i.e. lexical items), phrases, sentences and even paragraphs. We avoid the substance of content, and in particular the referents of phrases, but how the connections are made to worlds and things in them is 'fair game'. In the other direction, we have only passing interest in the linguistic expressions that make up the other half of language, even though it is usually easier to talk about them as we have traditional ways to write them down and standard ways to talk about them.

Because meaning is not easily observed, we have taken a

little effort to show that it really does exist, most objectively based on the fact that some words and phrases have (nearly) the same meaning, synonyms and paraphrases respectively, while other words have opposed meanings, antonyms, or 'opposites' in common language. We have even sketched a simple description of 'good communication' which has the aim of planting a meaning or idea in someone's mind. Towards the end of the book, in Chapter 13, we will see how to extend this conception a little for more ordinary conversations where two or more people interact, by asking questions or even by building an idea together.

Finally, we have identified the meanings of words with concepts, and noted that they are less complete than the meanings of sentences and paragraphs in that they can't be true or false until applied to something. In the chapters to follow we shall proceed to find how to split these concepts into smaller elements of meaning that combine in various ways, just as chemical atoms combine in different ways to make all the substances of the physical world. Then, progressively, we will put them back together to make the meanings of sentences and then show how sentences are used in situations (pragmatics) and combined together.

Some of these areas have standard names, while others have no names at all yet. We will find ourselves bumping into the limits of the known, but will retreat each time after touching them long enough to give some feel of the unknown terrain. I find it all very exciting, because what we are inevitably discussing are the elements of the human mind, the elements of thinking. It is here that linguistics, psychology, logic, philosophy and even anthropology and sociology meet and overlap. Have fun.

## Notes and answers

1. Only the last two, in my opinion.
2. Yes. In the second case he is pretending, but in the first he is lying, or close to it; the lie is submerged in an independent clause, 'a person from York', so it is not an overt lie as it would be if she had not given him a call.
3. My guesses are: (dog) [threat]; [desire]; [fear] respectively. (cat's meow) – any of these, depending on intonation; (purr) [contentedness].
4. I suspect there might be, but how can I tell you what it is? It may not be hopeless, however, if we can develop an 'arithmetic of meanings'.

5. Slang includes the new words that haven't stood the test of time and aren't given scientific definitions. Most of those words fall out of use in five or ten years, partly at least because the old words are more useful or yet newer concepts replace them. If you are criticized for using slang, you can always reply that your generation is casting about for words that better match the new world, but if you write to be read five or ten years later, half-forgotten slang will probably cloud your meaning if not obscure it totally. The same goes for talking to people of other countries or other generations.

6. A specialized vocabulary that expresses the concepts that have proved useful in that subject. By learning what to apply them to, you are learning the significant aspects of the objects and procedures in the subject.

7. Languages with alphabets, e.g. Spanish or even English, write words in a way that relates to their pronunciation, but when we write Arabic numerals, e.g. '11' or '1907', they represent meaning, for the first is not pronounced in any way related to '1' twice, and there are at least four ways to say the second number but only one meaning. Japanese is written partly in this semantic way, but the formulas of mathematics, chemistry and physics are simply this.

   Chinese is not a good example. Although kanji stand for meanings in Chinese, they also stand for pronunciations. That is, they stand for words, and most of them are composed of a tiny element of meaning with a fairly complete indication of pronunciation. In Japanese the link between kanji and pronunciation is more or less broken.

8. The difference between 'You're going to open the window', 'Are you going to open the window?' and 'Open the window', plus indications of the emotion and the relationship between speaker and addressee, as for example in adding '. . . please?' or '. . . damn it!' at the end.

9. Chapter 1 of the book that you are reading this from.

10. Phonetics can be seen as the link between substance and form in expression, and phonology the form-end of that line. The corner that is labelled 'form' there can (and must) be divided into several areas, as may be necessary also for the corner for complexes of concepts.

11. Content, both form and substance: form in 'Is a three-week-old foetus within the definition of a human being and therefore subject to being murdered?', and substance in 'Is he (or is he not) the person who stole my car?'

## Keywords

descriptive/cognitive meaning, content, concept, synonym, antonym, lexical item, referent, pragmatics.

## Further reading

The 'Triangle of Signification' comes from Ogden and Richards, an easy read on semantics up to the breakthrough in the late 1960s, and was clarified in a more scholarly Ullmann.

Ogden, C. K. and Richards, I. A. *The Meaning of Meaning* (1923) London: Routledge.

Ullmann, Stephen *The Principles of Semantics* (1957, 2nd edn). *Semantics: An Introduction to the Science of Meaning* (1962) Oxford: Blackwell. *Précis de sémantique française* (1959, 2nd edn) Bern: Francke.

(Heger added the missing leg (see Baldinger) to arrive at a Hjelmslevian structure. Hjelmslev is not such easy reading, but is provocative.)

Hjelmslev, Louis *Omkring sprogteoriens grundloeggelse* (1943), Copenhagen: Munskgaard. *Prolegomena to a Theory of Language* (1953) *IJAL* Memo 7. (1961) Madison: University of Wisconsin Press.

Baldinger, Kurt *Semantic Theory: Towards a Modern Semantics* (1980), Oxford: Blackwell. *Teoria semantica: Hacia una semantica moderna* (1977, 2nd edn) Madrid: Alcalá.

Black, Max (ed.) *The Importance of Language* (1962) Englewood Cliffs: Prentice-Hall.

Morris, Charles *Signification and Significance: A Study of the Relations of Signs and Values* (1964) Cambridge: MIT Press.

Ogden, C. K. and Richards, I. A. *The Meaning of Meaning* (1923) New York: Harcourt.

Whorf, Benjamin Lee (ed. J. B. Carroll) *Language, Thought and Reality* (1956) New York: Wiley.

## Exercises on entering

1. The idealized model of communication of Figure 1 had one person doing all the talking and the other all the listening.

Some classrooms are like that (if the students are listening), but there are everyday situations that fit this ideal almost perfectly. Can you find two?

2. What are the referents of the following expressions?
   (a) the teacher of this course
   (b) the person who is answering this question
   (c) where you ate lunch last
   (d) a child of your parents

3. In the previous question (a) and (d) might have more than one possible referent.
   (a) Under what conditions could this happen?
   (b) Modify the expressions to allow them to refer to all possible referents.

4. A lexical item, or 'lexeme' as some call it, is any form whose meaning cannot be determined from its parts. It can be longer than a single word; *to put up with*, for example, has three orthographic words (not counting the marker of infinitive forms *to*), but the loss or substitution of any part changes its meaning in unpredictable ways. *Catalogue* is much the same, except that we don't write it as three words, *cat,a,log. On the other hand, *trees* can be divided into *tree*, -s, and its meaning is a logical composition of the meanings of those parts, so it is not a lexical item. How many lexical items are in each of the following expressions? (Do not count grammatical markers like *to* or obligatory verb–suffixes, for they are not lexical and do not carry an independent meaning. The material in < > is given just to help you recognize the intended meaning.)
   (a) nevertheless
   (b) to run <up the hill>
   (c) boys
   (d) watch dog
   (e) to run up <a bill>
   (f) in so far as
   (g) girl-watcher
   (h) hotdog
   (i) to look up <at me>
   (j) to look up <a word>

5. Besides synonyms (words with the same meaning) and antonyms (words with opposite meanings), a word commonly has several **hyponyms**, words that have a more specific or detailed meaning and describe fewer (or at least no more) objects. Thus:

   *dog*         is a hyponym of   *animal*
   *terrier*     is a hyponym of   *dog*
   *fox-terrier* is a hyponym of   *terrier*

   For the following pairs decide which, if either, is a hyponym of the other.

(a) elephant, animal
(b) bird, sparrow
(c) tricycle, bicycle
(d) rabbit, jack-rabbit
(e) saucepan, pan
(f) fly, butterfly
(g) building, house

6. If we arrange under each word all of its hyponyms, we will have a classificatory hierarchy that is embedded in a language. These differ from language to language, as for example Japanese includes worms with insects, and English used to have starfish and porpoises as fish (not with the scientific meaning of *fish*). Try your hand at building up the hierarchy of terms for birds in English, including at least *chicken, eagle, sparrow, duck, hen, hummingbird, chick, ostrich, fowl, owl, penguin, robin, falcon*. You may notice that you want to group some of these together, and if you search hard enough you will probably find names for these groups.

7. Give examples of how the hierarchy of birds of the previous question contains useful knowledge, knowledge that is based on the experience of our ancestors.
   (a) Suppose you discover a useful thing about hens.
   (b) Suppose you want to tell your children which birds are edible.

# CHAPTER 2

# Markedness and Blocking

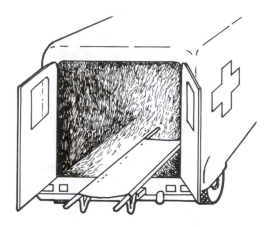

Why is it odd to say ★'a female nurse', while it is reasonable to say 'a male nurse'?

If you point to your thumb and ask 'Is this a finger?' you will probably not get a 'Yes' answer. You can then ask 'How many fingers do you have?' and will almost certainly get an answer of 'Ten'. Is language really so illogical?

Let us begin with a parody of a familiar puzzle.

> One day, John went shopping with his mother. On the way their car was hit by a truck and his mother was killed. John was seriously injured and taken to a hospital in an ambulance. One of the nurses in the emergency room was startled, and cried, 'Oh my God, that's my son!' Who was this nurse?

This puzzle takes advantage of the fact that in our culture nurses are usually women. This assumption, however, contradicts the story that John's mother had just died. When you finally remember that some nurses are men, you can solve the puzzle by identifying the (male) nurse as John's father.

## Marked and unmarked adjectives

In the case of nurses, history and custom have it rather strongly that they are women, so much so that the expression *'a female nurse' sounds strange. This is so because it is **redundant**; it is almost saying [female] twice, for saying *nurse* already implies that. In more linguistic terms we say that being female is **unmarked** (usual, typical, normal) for nurses in our culture, and conversely, being male is a **marked** (unusual, uncommon) state for nurses, so that it is almost necessary to add the modifier *male* to describe a man as a nurse. In everyday language female is the unmarked sex for secretaries, midwives, prostitutes, ballet dancers and house-keepers as well.

The opposite situation, maleness as the unmarked sex, is found in many professions and occupations, including surgeons, pilots, sailors and most jobs whose names end in -*man*, such as *policeman, salesman, postman, fireman*, etc. Feminists in the United States and elsewhere felt that these expressions reflected male chauvinism and have campaigned (with some success) to substitute -*woman* or -*person* for -*man*, as in *policewoman, chairperson* and *freshwoman*. Many institutions now avoid the difficulty by using terms such as police officer, firefighter, etc., rather than resorting to the use of a modifier, such as 'a woman pilot'.[1]

---

Q.  In the last chapter we spoke of lexical items as cultural transmitters. Why are there so many profession names ending in -*man*, and what might their effect be?[2]

---

This notion of markedness is useful for coming to grips with many other phenomena in language. It gives us a clue to understanding, for example, why the first sentence below is odd while the second is fine.

* Jane is an eyed and haired girl.
  Jane is a blue-eyed and long-haired girl.

The adjectives *eyed* and *haired* cannot occur alone but must be combined with expressions like *blue* or *long* to characterize a person. The first sentence was weird (marked by '*', see Exercise question 8) because human beings in the unmarked or normal form have eyes and hair, so it conveys no more information than: 'Jane has eyes and hair', i.e. just about nothing. Because those adjectives do not help you imagine what Jane looks like, they are not reasonable things to say. The second sentence, on the other hand, is informative; not so many girls have blue eyes and long hair, so these adjectives make a useful contribution. They describe how she is different from other girls.

---

Q.  Describe some circumstances where 'Jane is an eyed and haired girl' would be reasonable.[3]

---

Another area where the notion of markedness is helpful is in the pairs of 'opposites' such as *long:short*, *old:young*, *wide:narrow* and *tall:short*. In these pairs, the first member is said to be **positive** and the second **negative**. The way we perceive the world around us, we seem to take positive things as normal or unmarked, and negative things as marked. We can see this most clearly in English in its system of word formation. There are words like *common*, *wise* and *frequent* that are positive but can be turned into negatives by adding a prefix *un-* or *in-* (*uncommon*, *unwise*, *infrequent*). This is the general pattern of English, and the reverse case, i.e. making positives out of negatives with a prefix, is rare.[4] So in pairs like *tall:short* and *old:young*, the first member is regarded as unmarked. This semantic property finds several reflections in English.

Let us first look into questions with *how*. When you ask someone's age or height, you would say,

(a) how <u>old</u>'s your <u>brother</u>?
(b) how <u>tall</u>'s your <u>sister</u>?

(We will use underlines to indicate stress, and will not capitalize the beginnings of examples as a reminder that we are talking about spoken language rather than written language. For the same reason, we will use contractions extensively, as in speaking; they reflect the rhythm and stressing of a sentence. These will become most important in Chapter 3.)

In contrast to the examples above, however, it would be impossible to begin:

(c) ! how <u>young</u>'s your <u>brother</u>?
(d) ! how <u>short</u>'s your <u>sister</u>?

These last two are very unusual, so unusual that the contraction would probably not be used although it is quite normal in the first two. These would be reasonable only if the speaker already knew that your brother, or sister, is young, or short, and wanted to enquire further into the matter. The first two have no such 'presupposition' (we will see this notion again in Chapters 13 and 14) and can be used without knowing anything about your brother. Nothing would be felt amiss with (a) if your brother turned out to be quite young, but the speaker is definitely in the wrong ball park (i.e. he shows complete ignorance) if he asks (c) and gets an answer that your brother is not young.

---

Q. When could you use a sentence like 'How slow can you ride a bicycle?'[5]

---

We have seen, then, that the only normal way to ask the age, height or the like of someone with a question beginning *how* is to use an unmarked adjective. The answers, and in fact any quantification of a simple adjective (i.e. modifying it with a number), can use only the unmarked forms.

> Mount Fuji is 4000 metres high.    *. . . 4000 metres low.
> that train was only 15 metres long.    *. . . 15 metres short.

The same preference for unmarked forms (−Mrk) is found when we turn adjectives into nominal forms (Noml).

| −Mrk | +Mrk | Noml | | −Mrk | +Mrk | Noml |
|------|------|------|---|------|------|------|
| long : | short | – length | | fat : | skinny – | fatness |
| wide : | narrow | – width | | thick : | thin | – thickness |
| deep : | shallow | – depth | | sharp : | dull | – sharpness |

The nouns *length*, *width* and *depth* are related to the unmarked adjectives *long*, *wide* and *deep*, and are used to distinguish the various physical dimensions without implying that the object is actually long, wide or deep. Thus we can say 'What is the length of this train?' or 'What is the width of your street?' but cannot say, without the same sort of presupposition as in the *How*-questions, !'What is the shortness of this train?' or !'What is the narrowness of your street?'. You can find much the same situation in other languages, such as in French where *grandeur* means 'size' in an unmarked sense (e.g. *par ordre de grandeur* 'according to size'), whereas *petitesse* means 'littleness', focusing on the lower end of the size scale.

As we have seen, when we say that a form is 'marked' it usually has an extra semantic element or two. Negative adjectives are marked because they have an extra element [Neg], the semantic element of negation. Unmarked words designate the usual, common or normal case in ordinary life, while marked words are for less common cases.

## The lexicon

In fact, it is a useful rule of thumb in semantics that common words normally have simple and general meanings that allow their use in many situations, while uncommon words generally have complex and specific meanings (see Exercise questions 9–10), although words can be uncommon for other reasons (e.g. the word for snow is not so common in Arabic). Because complex and detailed meanings can be used in only a few cases, we call these words highly marked or **specific**.

The **lexicon** is the collection of all the words or lexical items, i.e. associations between sound and meaning, that a language has. Often one language has a single word for a concept that another language does not, such as the French words *lendemain*, *veille* for [the next day] and [the previous day]. English, on the other hand, manages quite well without these words but has many words for mechanical objects that French finds no need for, such as *typewriter* (Fr: *machine à écrire*).

As new concepts become frequent, we add new words to the lexicon, making new associations between forms and concepts. Most typically we stretch existing words to include the new concepts or adopt ('borrow') forms for them from some other language. Similarly, when a concept becomes very uncommon, a word for it can totally drop out of use, that is, out of the lexicon of the younger speakers, though in a literary language it may remain in the dictionary for many generations. Thus the lexicon is in a constant state of flux, and different people know different words. This could easily make communication very difficult, not knowing what words another person knows, but the concepts in the lexicon, especially those of nouns, are ranged in various structures.

Q.  Although we can and do make personal, private concepts, we must learn the concepts embedded in our native language. What sets these concepts apart from our own private conceptions? What guarantee do we have that they are useful?[6]

One of the most basic types of lexical structure is that of inclusion or hyponymy. We say that *dog* is a **hyponym** of *animal* because the concept of *dog* includes the concept of *animal*. Not only are all dogs animals today, but it is inconceivable to find a dog ever, in any geological era or on any other planet, that is not an animal. This relation of inclusion is also fundamental in other areas. It appears, for example, as the notion of subset in set theory, and all of mathematics is based on set theory. There, we could express this same idea as 'The set of all dogs is a subset of the set of all animals.' Of course, there are other sorts of lexical structure, but we have to leave them for a longer discussion.

Languages differ quite a lot in lexical structure, and because this is not easily perceived, it is one of the hardest parts of a language to learn well. An example of differences in hyponymy is the case of potatoes. For North Americans they are usually classified as starchy foods like bread, rice or noodles that we combine with something else to make a meal, but which you would never mix together. A rice sandwich or noodles with potatoes verges on the inconceivable. In Japan, however, potatoes are classified as vegetables like carrots, cucumbers and the like. This may be reasonable, since they had sweet potatoes (which are vegetable-like) long before they came to eat white potatoes, but in any case they find it reasonable to (and often do) eat potatoes with rice, which seldom fails to shock Americans and leave them feeling uneasy. This is a case where the term *potato* designates the same thing in two languages but fits into their lexical structures in different ways – and, incidentally, it affects how one acts and feels!

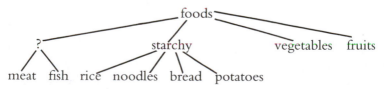

Another example of how languages can differ in lexical

structure can be found in the case of worms. While they are not grouped with anything other than snakes in English, perhaps because of their shape and way of moving, they are clearly different from snakes. The situation is quite different in Japanese, for they fall together with caterpillars under the general heading [insect]. Not only will Japanese people sometimes surprise us in saying 'Look at that insect' while pointing to a worm, but there is one sort here in Japan (from where I am writing) that is poisonous. I am pretty sure it is a type of caterpillar, but Japanese are not very specific on this because of their language, and thus their thinking; they simply avoid touching all long and crawly 'insects'. A potential difference in behaviour that illustrates this difference in perceiving the world is that if speakers of English and Japanese were stranded on an island with no food and managed to bring themselves to eat worms to stay alive, the English speakers would probably try snakes as a slightly less revolting thing to eat, while the Japanese speakers would more likely try 'other sorts of insects'. That thought would never occur to the English speaker, as the idea of snakes would not occur to a Japanese.

In general, every noun or verb in the lexicon is a hyponym of some other word, from the lowest to the highest level. Thus *animal* is a hyponym of *thing*, *dog* is a hyponym of *animal*, *terrier* is a hyponym of *dog*, and some would go on to say that *Fido*, the name of my dog, is a hyponym of *terrier*. At each level a word has (usually) several hyponyms and is itself the hyponym of some other word, except for the highest words like *thing, place, action* which have no words above them. This forms a hierarchical classification embedded in a language, somewhat like the biological taxonomy of species.

Q.   A hyponym is a more specific term as it has an extra element of meaning. Does it apply to fewer or more things?[7]

Viewed in this way, each hyponym can be seen to be marked relative to the higher word, and the whole vocabulary of nouns and verbs can be ranged from the most general (at the top, hyponyms of nothing) to the most specific (at the bottom). General words are known to everyone, while people differ in their knowledge of the more specific words. Thus if communication fails due to differences in vocabulary, it can be easily re-established using more general words instead of their hyponyms.

More commonly, however, by using only general words, communication will never fail on this count, and this is the usual way in conversation, especially as it may take extra time or effort to find a more specific word that fits the situation precisely.

Sometimes a hyponym can be quite as common as the more general term so that we seldom use the general term where we could use the more specific one. A term like *dog* can be said to 'block' the use of the more general term *animal* when it is dogs you are talking about. When a word has only one hyponym, as does *sheep* in the domain of age (*lamb*), this sort of blockage may tend to split the meaning of that word into two. Let us see how this happens.

## Lexical blocking

If you were bitten by a fox-terrier, it would be reasonable to tell your doctor or friends that you had been bitten by a dog. The species of dog that did the biting is almost surely irrelevant, unless of course terriers had something special about their bites, perhaps that they were generally infected with rabies that year. In that case to say that you had been bitten by a terrier would be far more reasonable than saying you had been bitten by a dog.

There is a basic rule of human language that if there is a common word that means just what you want to say, you should use it rather than some more general word. If you saw a cow in my office, you would not be likely to say 'I saw an animal in his office!' That would be a true statement but would suggest to others that you were not sure what sort of animal it was. In a case like this we can say that a word with an appropriate meaning, e.g. *cow*, **blocks** (i.e. prevents the use of) other words, words of more general meaning, and as we shall see later, phrases of several words. In psycholinguistics this is called the 'principle of contrast'. It does not mean that one does or should choose words that are as specific as possible, but only that when one selects a specific word, there is something in that extra meaning that one wants to communicate. It would not be unreasonable, for example, to say you had been bitten by a chihuahua or a Doberman, as their bites are not simply ordinary dog bites.

For this reason, we do not use the word *parent* very often; we are usually talking about one parent or the other, and whether it is a father or a mother is usually relevant, so we mostly use those words. They block *parent* completely except when we are talking about both, or either, or when it is not important whether it is a father or a mother, as in 'a parent–teacher meeting'. If a child says 'One of my parents is coming', we can conclude that he doesn't know which one, or perhaps that he doesn't want to say which.

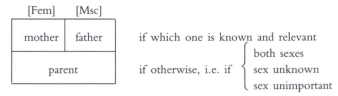

Here, we say that both *father* and *mother* are marked for sex, while *parent* is unmarked. Although it is commonly assumed that language ought to work as in this diagram, this is a fairly unusual case that is commonly found only in the central core of the vocabulary. (Note the use of three-letter symbols for semantic elements that are widespread in human languages, derived usually from an English word that expresses it – 'Fem' and 'Msc' from *FEMinine* and *MaSCuline*, so far.)

---

Q.  Complete this table, using '*' for blanks for which there is no particular term.

| [Msc.X]: | father | son | __ | uncle | gander | _____ | __ |
| [X]: | parent | __ | __ | __ | goose | chicken | cat |
| [Fem.X]: | mother | __ | girl | __ | _____ | hen | __ [8] |

---

More commonly, a general word can seem to have its meaning restricted by being blocked out of certain usages when it has only one or two hyponyms that are commonly used. For example, *lamb* is more restricted than *sheep* as it has an extra semantic element [Yng] (from *YouNG*); that is, it is marked for being young. If you want one, and you won't accept anything but a young one, then you can't ask for it using *sheep* but must use *lamb*. If you really don't care what its age is, or if you don't know, then you must use *sheep*. To call something a lamb is to say not only that it is young but also that its youth is relevant.

---

Q.  Complete the following table for [Yng]. Add another pair or so at the end.

|  | [Yng]: | lamb | chick | kitten ___ | calf ___ | ___ |
| --- | --- | --- | --- | --- | --- | --- |
| without | [Yng]: | sheep | chicken | _____ dog ___ | bear ___ [9] |

We have no special word for sheep that are not young, i.e. [Neg-Yng] (i.e. NEGative in YouNG-ness), so if that is what you want to talk about you will have to make do with the word *sheep* and, if the age is really important, add another word like *adult* or *old*. We can diagram these facts as below, showing that the word *sheep* is **block**ed by *lamb* for sheep which are all young, if their youth is important enough to be mentioned. Otherwise, it is used for groups of sheep of all ages, for sheep of unknown age or whose age(s) is not important – and so for adult sheep too.

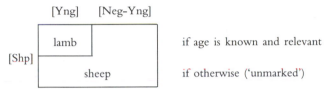

[Shp]  
[Yng]  [Neg-Yng]  
lamb  
sheep  

if age is known and relevant

if otherwise ('unmarked')

This seems quite elementary and obvious, but these blocking relationships sometimes lead people to think that the general word has two meanings. In this case it is clear that we should not say that *sheep* is ambiguous, with two meanings [Shp] (from SHeeP) and [Shp.Neg-Yng] (i.e. SHeeP that are not YouNG), but this is not always obvious.

Similar to the relation between *sheep* and *lamb* is the relation between *goose* and *gander* [male goose]. It is easy to mistake *goose* as having two meanings, a general one (call it [Gse] after GooSE/GeeSE) for groups of mixed sex, or for birds of unknown sex, or when their sex is not relevant though known (as, for example, if you only want to watch it), and another specific meaning [Fem.Gse] for female geese, when it is opposed to *gander* [Msc.Gse]. In fact, you will find just this in the *Oxford Advanced Learner's Dictionary* but not in *The Concise Oxford Dictionary*. It may well be unclear whether people mean only female geese or geese in general when they use *goose*, but that does not mean that this word is ambiguous, any more than the word *dog* is ambiguous, even though one may use it variously for police dogs, pets or poodles. As the chart below shows, *goose* means simply [Gse], and can be used for female geese but not for male one(s) only. In cases like this we can say that the message 'It is a goose' is **vague**: it can be used for different situations, but then almost all messages are vague to some extent.

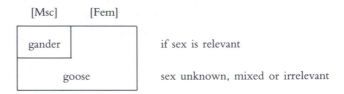

| [Msc] | [Fem] | |
|-------|-------|---|
| gander | | if sex is relevant |
| | goose | sex unknown, mixed or irrelevant |

In more complex situations it may be difficult to see such blocking relationships for what they are. For instance, English has a semantic element [Mtf] for words that designate the MeaT oF some animal, as in *beef, veal, pork*. When there is no special word for the meat, we simply use the name of the animal, such as *chicken, rabbit, whale, oyster*. Thus these marked terms like *pork* block the more general terms like *pig* when talking about cooking or eating them. *Mutton* is the word for [Mtf.Shp] but as there is no word for the meat of a young sheep, we call it *lamb*. Nevertheless, some otherwise good dictionaries give *lamb* two meanings, [young sheep] and [meat of a young sheep]. Of course, if you order mutton in a restaurant you can expect to get the meat of an old sheep. But restaurants tend to serve lamb, the tender succulent meat of a young sheep, and it looks as if *lamb* contrasts with *mutton*, as *veal* (meat of a young cow) does with *beef*. Rather, the word *lamb* is not restricted to live animals, so it serves as well for the meat; it has only a single meaning.

---

Q.   Complete the following table for types of meat.

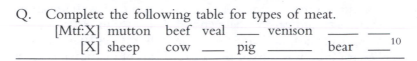

| [Mtf:X] | mutton | beef | veal | ___ | venison | ___ | ___ |
| [X] | sheep | cow | ___ | pig | ___ | bear | ___ |[10]

As we saw in the previous sections, it is very common for one word to differ from another only in having some extra semantic element(s), and the marked word is usually less common. An unusual example is provided in the word *finger*: because of the word *thumb*, its general usage is much less common than its specific usage. We normally take *finger* to designate the four long appendages of the hand, yet we also say that a person has ten fingers and ten toes. Does this mean that *finger* is ambiguous with two meanings, a general one (five fingers on a hand) and a specific one (only four)?

There is no reason to suppose *finger* has any meaning other than [appendage of the hand], parallel to *toe* for the foot. However, there is a special word for that short stubby one, *thumb*, and it naturally blocks *finger* when we talk about thumbs. There is no special word for the other fingers, so we have no choice but to use the general term *finger* for them. Since thumbs are so different from the other fingers, we almost never consider them all together except when counting them. As a result, *finger* is easily mistaken to mean any of the four longer fingers when it actually means any of the five.

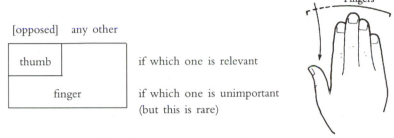

This is like the situation we saw for the word *parent*; it is not used very often as we are usually talking about one parent or the other, and whether it is a father or a mother is usually relevant, so we mostly use those words. The earlier examples, such as *lamb*, *gander*, are the normal case; the specific term(s) do not cover all possible uses of the general terms. Therefore, lexical blocking prevents the use of the general term only in specific circumstances, which, if common, can make it look ambiguous with a general meaning and a specific meaning (for an unblocked specific use).

In discussing the lexicon earlier, we noted that common words have simple meanings that allow them to be used in many cases, while in general, uncommon words are marked with extra elements of meaning that prevent their common use. Actually, to have a word at all implies a fair amount of usage, for words that are not used are usually forgotten in less than a generation, which is why slang seldom gets into the dictionary. The other, less common concepts that are not often important are left to be expressed with complex descriptions (i.e. phrases of two or more words); language is obviously more efficient that way.

Because we give names to the usual case, and make complex descriptions (using several words) for unusual cases, the words a language contains provide a very good indication of what is commonly talked about, or at least what has been commonly talked about in recent generations. For example, Eskimo may have special words for different types of snow but has only one word for all the varieties of blue and green, while Amazon Basin languages can have no words for snow while they have many words for different shades of green. They could still express the concept of [snow], however, as [solid rain], or, if they have a word for [freeze], as [frozen rain].

A word will also block such a descriptive phrase, which is why we cannot say *'the day after today'. The word *tomorrow* has precisely that meaning and must be used if that is what we mean, leaving no opportunity to use that phrase. For the same reason, we would not use *'male cow' unless we couldn't use the word *bull* for some reason, as for example if someone didn't know the word, or if we were trying to explain what it means.

---

Q.   What expressions are blocked by *yesterday, here, boy*?[11]

---

It is a good hint, then, although not proof of a word's meaning, to find a 'missing composition of words' such as in these examples. Thus, because !'to cause X to die' is virtually impossible, it is a good candidate for the meaning of *to kill* X. However, blocking is seldom complete in the general vocabulary outside the core lexicon, as ordinary words commonly have some additional elements of meaning, such as, in this case, that the causing and the dying must be perceived as the same event. If the causing and the dying are separated in time or place, *to kill* can't be used and a more complex description is both possible and necessary. Suppose, for example, that Dirty Dick fixes the sheriff's gun so that it shoots crooked and as a result the sheriff gets shot and dies when he faces down Slow-draw McGraw. We can't say that Dirty Dick killed the sheriff, though he might still be hanged for murder, for he *caused the sheriff to die*. In this case, avoiding a common word implies that it does not adequately describe the situation and only a more general description will do.

## Markedness, blocking and the lexicon (summary)

It is easy to observe that some situations are **marked** – unusual or special in some way. When we speak of a word being marked (relative to some other one), we mean that it has some special or additional element of meaning that the other does not have. Using a marked word when its unmarked counterpart would do as well is appropriate only if that extra element is true and important to the communication, so doing it naturally creates a type of **presupposition**, or assumption that the speaker seems to make. This can confuse a conversation immensely if it is not true. To look at a rusty, tired car and ask 'How new is it?' is a real conversation stopper, though 'How old is it?' can be asked even of a three-day-old one.

While adjectives can often be described as simply marked or not, nouns and verbs often have a whole range from the very general, through various levels of **hyponyms**, down to the most highly marked or very **specific** terms. This hierarchy of lexical items is a major part of the lexical structure of a language, and is learned – at least its higher parts – when one learns the language. It may influence the learner's perceptions and even behaviour, especially the concepts of his or her native language.

Normally, when a word has a meaning that is appropriate to what the speaker wants to say, it must be used if it is known to the addressee (i.e. if it is a common word, or a technical word between specialists). We say it **blocks** other words of more general meanings, as well as complex expressions that have that same meaning. That is, a word such as *father* prevents other words such as *parent* or expressions like 'male parent' from being used when talking about fathers, and a marked word such as *lamb* normally blocks its unmarked counterpart (*sheep*) when it is appropriate, i.e. when we could say 'young sheep'.

## Back to meaning

Lexical blocking cannot apply, of course, if either the speaker or the addressee does not know the word, so it doesn't apply in definitions, as, for example, 'Tomorrow is the day after today' or 'A lamb is a young sheep.' Otherwise, to say something roundabout, avoiding a word which means just that, implies that the speaker means something a little different. To call someone a 'male parent' is to avoid giving him the label *father*, perhaps denying the authority or responsibility of a father, or to reject the associations of family life that this label suggests.

We can ask, with much more understanding now, whether meaning includes those facts that we can conclude from the choices of words someone has made to express an idea. In the case, for instance, of the child who says 'one of my parents' instead of 'my father' or 'my mother', it is unlikely that he or she is trying to say that they don't know which parent, even though this expression does suggest that strongly. Similarly, avoiding a word like *kill* suggests that the speaker sees the causing and the dying as separate events, though that may well not be the intent, and it might even be that they don't know the word *kill*. Because we can only guess why a person has avoided some particular word, we must exclude conclusions (actually guesses) based on its avoidance from meaning (content). Instead, they are merely what one can conclude from one aspect of the expression, word choice – not too different from concluding something about the speaker because they are hesitant in saying something, or, at the other extreme, if they look you straight in the eye as they say it. Not content, but probable conclusions about their thoughts and feelings. In any case, there is usually a variety of reasons why one might not have used a given word (including even that one does not know it), and to decide which, you must usually use all manner of observation such as facial expressions, speed of talking, the situation of talking and so on.

The content of a lexical item, then, is what one does express with it, and not what one expresses by not using some other word(s), either to avoid them or for some other reason. Thus *finger* means [appendage on the hand] and not just one of the longer ones, and when a girl describes someone as a 'friend who is a boy' its content is only that, though the listener may infer that because she is avoiding the word *boyfriend* she doesn't want to admit any special relationship between them. Although what is not said is sometimes more significant than what is said, it is not part of **content** as we shall understand it.

## Notes and answers

1. It is felt today to be in poor taste, and discriminatory, to point out sex gratuitously, particularly of women. The now defunct modifier *lady* as in 'lady lawyer' was clearly negative, adding a meaning (amateur, incompetent) from perhaps fifty years ago or so when women (often those who did not need to work) were not seen as professionals, and sometimes were not.

2. They come from a time when women seldom entered professions, being busy in the home. If this suffix is equated with the word *man* it might well act as a subconscious block

for women to enter those professions, but I don't think they should be equated, as it is pronounced 'mun', as in my name, and I would surely not like to change that to *Hofperson*! An alternative might be to change the suffix to -mun.

3. In a place (or time) where quite a few people do not have eyes or hair. Note that 'seeing people' is a standard term in discussions about blind people.

4. There are some (e.g. *undimmed*, *unfailing*, *unquenchable*) that derive from negative verbs (Chapter 3), *to dim*, *fail*, *quench*.

5. In a competition for riding slowly – or any time that the speaker can assume their addressee wants to ride slowly, even to express annoyance at their slowness (see Chapter 14).

6. They are public concepts shared with all the others of our community. They must be fairly useful, for our society has found them so over the centuries – indeed, they are essentially the distilled wisdom of our ancestors.

7. Fewer; the extra element(s) of meaning restrict its applicability. The extra element is like an additional modifier on a noun.

8. (son) – ★ – daughter; boy – child – girl; (uncle) – ★ – aunt; (gander) – (goose) – ★; cock (or rooster in the USA) – (chicken) – (hen); tom(-cat) – (cat) – ★. Notice that *child* fits with *boy-girl* and not with *son-daughter*. It is commonly used for that too, because we have no common term for it. The word *offspring* has that meaning but is not a countable noun, and you deserve an extra point if you thought of it.

9. (kitten) – cat; pup/puppy – (dog); (calf) – cow; cub – (bear); chick – chicken; whelp or cub – fox; cub (again!) – wolf; calf (again!) – elephant. These repetitions of *cub*, *calf* suggest they have more general meanings, perhaps [Yng.carnivore] and [Yng.herbivore].

10. (veal) – calf; pork – (pig); (venison) – deer; bear – (bear); chicken – chicken; fish – fish; and so on. There are not [Mtf] terms except for the things most commonly eaten when the Normans came to England.

11. 'the day before today', 'the place where I am', 'young male human being'.

## Keywords

positive and negative adjectives, marked, presupposition, hyponym, specific – general, lexicon, (lexical) hierarchy, blocking.

## Further reading

The notion of markedness came from the study of phonology and was applied to semantic phenomena in the 1970s. See Clark and Clark or Lehrer for its extensive application.

Clark, Herbert H. and Clark, E. *Psychology and Language* (1977) NY: Harcourt.
Lehrer, A. 'Markedness and Antonymy' (1985) *Journal of Linguistics* **21**: 397–429.

The lexicon can provide a full course of study by itself; we have barely mentioned some superficial facts. Jackson is a pleasant and readable introduction, especially into the structure and use of dictionaries. The reader is recommended Lehrer or Cruse for a more technical discussion.

Cruse, D. A. *Lexical Semantics* (1986) London: CUP.
Lehrer, Adrienne *Semantic Fields and Lexical Structure* (1974) Amsterdam: North Holland.
Jackson, Howard *Words and Their Meanings* (1988) London: Longmans.

The notion of lexical blocking has appeared only recently, and under different names. In psycholinguistics, Eve Clark has argued strongly for a version wherein no two expressions can have the same meaning, starting from Bolinger. Various attempts have been made to describe it accurately, ranging from most specific to most general: Aranoff, 'morphological blocking', Gruber, 'disjunctive ordering', Hudson, 'priority to the particular', Hofmann, 'lexical blocking', Clark, 'principle of contrast'.

Aranoff, M. 'Potential Words, Actual Words, Productivity and Frequency' (1983) *Proceedings of 13th International Congress of Linguists*.
Bolinger, Dwight *Meaning and Form* (1977) London: Longmans.
Clark, Eve V. 'The Principle of Contrast: A Constraint in Language Learning' in Brian MacWhinney (ed.) *Mechanisms of Language Learning* (1987) Hillsdale, NY: Erlbaum.
Hofmann, Th. R. 'Lexical Blocking – I, II and Restatement' (1982–84) *Journal of the Faculty of Humanities* **5**, **6**, **8**, Toyama, Japan.
Hudson, Richard *Word Grammar* (1983) London: Longmans.

McCawley, James D. 'Conversational Implicature and the Lexicon' in Peter Cole (ed.) *Pragmatics, Syntax and Semantics 3* (1978) NY: Academic Press.


## Exercises with markedness and blocking

1. Determine which member of each following pair is the unmarked one, writing down examples to demonstrate your answer. With the following, use quantifying phrases such as '3 feet (tall)'.
   - (a) high:low
   - (b) shallow:deep
   - (c) long:short
   - (d) thin:thick
   - (e) narrow:wide

   Quantifying phrases do not work with the following, so use *how*-questions to determine which is the unmarked member.
   - (f) many:few
   - (g) little:much
   - (h) seldom:often
   - (i) sharp:blunt
   - (j) stupid:smart
   - (k) large:small
   - (l) heavy:light
   - (m) far:near

2. The noun *length* refers to the general dimension in which the adjectives *long* and *short* describe regions. Find such 'abstract nouns' for the following pairs of adjectives.
   - (a) tall:short
   - (b) thick:thin
   - (c) heavy:light
   - (d) wide:narrow
   - (e) old:young
   - (f) far:near
   - (g) fast:slow
   - (h) clever:stupid
   - (i) broad:narrow
   - (j) hot:cold
   - (k) warm:cool

3. In what contexts would the following sentences be used appropriately?
   - (a) How infrequently do you visit your parents?
   - (b) How slow can you run?
   - (c) This pool is the shallowest of the bunch.

4. When both members of a contrast are equally marked, there is usually a more general term for use if the distinction between them is not appropriate (i.e. if one doesn't know or care which type, and for groups of mixed composition). For example, the term *parent* is the general term for *father:mother*. The relations between these three words can be expressed in a diagram like in the text.

| parent | | sex unmarked |
|--------|--------|------|
| father | mother | sex-specific |

For the following words, give the general term like *parent* in the above diagram.

  (a) grandson:granddaughter  (e) husband:wife
  (b) stallion:mare        (f) arm:leg
  (c) hen:rooster/cock       (g) brother:sister
  (d) ram:ewe                 (a technical term)

In the examples below, one or both of the terms is marked. First identify it and then make a diagram as for parents above, with the unmarked term covering all but one corner of the chart. Be sure to label the rows of the chart.

  (h) bull:cow          (k) actor:actress
  (i) witch:warlock       (l) watch:clock
  (j) lion:lioness       (m) cat:kitten

5. A marked word will block the use of its unmarked counterpart if it is appropriate, but it will also block any other expression meaning the same thing. So while we say 'next week', 'next month' and 'next year', we don't say ⋆'I'll see you next day' because the specific term *tomorrow* has precisely that meaning and blocks any possible use of it. In the following, the expressions in parentheses are not normally used but are instead replaced or blocked by specific words. Give these blocking words.

   (a) last year, last month, last week, (last day)
   (b) this morning, this afternoon, this evening, (this night)
   (c) pale blue, pale green, pale purple, (pale red)
   (d) horse meat, whale meat, dog meat, (pig meat), (cow meat), (sheep meat), (chicken meat)
   (e) to bicycle, to helicopter, to taxi, to jet, (to car), (to aeroplane)

6. English is in rapid change in the area of sex-based terms because of recent disappearance of sex-linked restrictions, and older English has more than we do today. If you don't know th opposite sex terms of the following, look them up in a dictionary. Then say which if either is less marked.

   (a) alumnus   (b) poet      (c) blond     (d) brunet
   (e) witch     (f) toastmaster  (g) mermaid

7. Ordinal numbers (numbers used to show the "order" in a series) are generally formed by adding a suffix -th. There are some exceptions, however, as in *1st, 2nd, 3rd, 5th, 8th, 9th, 12th*. (a) Which of these are merely spelling exceptions, which are phonetic changes, and which are independent words that block a *th*-form? (b) In making ordinals for [21, 22, 23, . . .] does one add the -th to the whole number or to just the last digit (in pronunciation)? And in content, (c) does the meaning change specified by -th apply to the whole number or just to the last digit?

8. It is customary to add an asterisk or "star" before an expression that is impossible, and an exclamation mark before one that is simply very strange and needs some extraordinary context. In semantics, however, nearly any combination of words can be interpreted (see Ch 14 on reinterpretation rules), so "impossible" is more likely to mean just extremely extraordinary. Which judgements ("★", "!" or nothing) should be added to the following expressions? Explain why in each case.
   (a) that bridge is 376 meters short.
   (b) a male goose
   (c) a one-headed person
   (d) a male midwife
   (e) a male policewoman
   (f) a male prince

9. Taking *animal – dog – mongrel* as a good example of words ranging from more general to more specific, explain the relationships between (i) general : specific, (ii) number of meaning elements, (iii) marked : unmarked, and (iv) hyponym : general term.

10. Using the same example again, what is the relation between adding an element of meaning (eg. [Msc]) or a modifier like *white* to some word such as *horse*, and the number of things described (the 'denotation', Ch 10? (b) What happens if the added element does not exclude anything, eg. "a female woman"?

11. An old adage has it that "synonyms don't exist", not perfect synonyms anyhow. What would happen if a pair of words were perfectly synonymous, according to the principle of lexical blocking?

## CHAPTER 3

# Opposites and Negatives

*Tall* is the opposite of *short*, and *long* is the opposite of *short*, right? The opposite of *red* is *blue*, or at least it used to be in the USA fifty years ago, but today, with a better understanding of colour, and colour television, its opposite might be *green*. But in any case, the opposite of *blue* is *yellow*! What has happened, did the colours change?

We say that the opposite of *father* is *mother*, as *wife* is to *husband*. What then is the opposite of *mountain*? Most Japanese would say *sea*, but most Americans would give *valley*!

There are many different kinds of 'opposites'. Before we get confused in their variety, let us call the last examples above 'opposite numbers', after the jargon of spy novels and military usage. What is happening with these can be pretty clear, as in this example where *father*, *mother* and *son* have meanings as below. ([Fem] means [is female], [Msc] means [is male], and [Par] means [is parent of].)

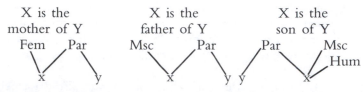

That is, if 'X is the father of Y' has a meaning [X is male and X is a parent of Y] and others similarly, then these 'opposite numbers' are words that differ only in single elements of meaning, like [Msc] and [Fem], which are opposites in a simpler sense that we shall get to directly.

Before we look at the simple oppositions, however, notice how easy it is to pass over hidden aspects of the meaning of a word. We could easily say that *son* is the opposite of *father*, though it is opposite in a different way, namely that the parenthood [Par] relationship is reversed. What is not easily noticed, however, is that *son* is restricted to human beings [Hum] while *father* is not, as indicated in the diagrams. That is, so long as we consider only male human beings, if 'John is the son of Ron' is true, then 'Ron is the father of John' is also true, and vice-versa. When we speak of any other animal, however, to say 'That dog is the father of my dog' is quite reasonable, but it is not possible to say ★'My dog is the son of that dog' – it is simply not English.[1] Thus a son is necessarily human while a father can be any male animal (but see Exercise question 9), even though we cannot perceive this difference directly.

## Antonyms

The first type of opposites in the box at the beginning are called 'gradable antonyms' or simply **antonyms** in linguistics. Antonymous pairs of adjectives like *tall:short* or *deep:shallow* form a scale ranging from very tall to very short, or from very deep to very shallow. These sorts of adjectives are called **gradable** because many gradations are possible, when they are modified by adverbs of degree (AvD) or compared with comparatives (AvC) as below. The highest grade *completely* is possible only with adjectives like *open* which have a limit.

| AvD | AvC |
|---|---|
| (completely Aj) | |
| very Aj ⎫ | |
| quite Aj ⎬ | the most Aj |
| rather/pretty Aj | more Aj than |
| somewhat Aj | as Aj as |
| sort of Aj | less Aj than |
| not so Aj ⎫ | |
| hardly Aj ⎬ | the least Aj |
| not Aj | |

With the gradable pairs like *tall* and *short*, generally one term is

**marked** or special; the marked antonym contains a negative element [Neg] that makes it special.

| unmarked | marked | |
|----------|--------|--|
| tall | short | – [Neg-tall] |
| thick | thin | – [Neg-thick] |
| old | young | – [Neg-old] |
| deep | shallow | – [Neg-deep] |
| happy | happy | – [Neg-happy] |

A neutral question of degree uses the unmarked member of these pairs as in the first two examples following. The lower examples are very unusual (indicated by '!') for they can be used only in special circumstances.

> How old is your brother?   How thick is the paper?
> ! How young is your brother?   ! How thin is the paper?

The second type is unusual because it implies that the speaker already knows that your brother is young and wants only to know how young. This does not happen very often, of course. If the degree is modified by a number, we absolutely must use the unmarked form (the '*' marks an impossible form).

> he is three years old.   it is 3 cm thick.
> * he is three years young.   * it is 3 cm thin.

Q.   Which is the marked adjective in each pair: *high:low*, *new:old*?[2]

There are more complex situations of antonymy (Exercise question 4) that we do not understand very well yet. Antonyms like *hot* and *cold* provide a good example because *warm* and *cool* seem to be intermediate terms forming a four-term scale. These latter two may merely have an additional semantic element [Pls], roughly indicating PLeaSant or not harsh on the senses. They thus block *hot*, *cold* in the pleasant range, leaving them to describe unpleasant temperatures (making it seem like a four-term scale) as well as temperatures where pleasantness is not relevant.

## Complementaries

Not all adjectives are gradable. There are no gradations for more or less of the quality described by the following pairs, so they are called complementary antonyms or simply **complementaries**, or sometimes 'classificatory' in contrast to the gradable 'qualitative' adjectives. It is not English, for example, to say a radio is ★'very off' or ★'more off than the television'. The structure of the meaning of these ungradable adjectives is very simple.

| | | | |
|---|---|---|---|
| off | : on | married | : single/unmarried |
| dead | : alive | male | : female |

These are pairs of words whose meanings are apparently related simply by negation [Neg]; to say that a radio is off is to say that it is not on, and vice-versa, to say a radio is on is to say it is not off. However, although we know that these ungradable binary pairs differ in meaning by a negative [Neg], it is usually hard to know which is the more basic. That is, we cannot be sure which is correct.

off – [Neg-on]          OR?   on – [Neg-off]

With gradable antonyms, the marked number will usually show itself in modification of degree or comparison as we saw above (★'three years young'), but we have not found a way yet to prove markedness for these complementary pairs except when one has a negative prefix as *unmarried* does.

## Antonymous groups

Not all antonyms come in (binary) pairs; they may also form mutually exclusive sets like the colours. To say something is red is to say that it is not green, blue, yellow, orange or any other basic colour. The same is true of every other colour on that level, so together they form an **antonymous group**: to use any one of them excludes all the others of the group. It doesn't, however, exclude a hyponym (Chapter 2), for to say that something is red does not deny it might be crimson, rose or magenta, for example.

The antonyms and complementaries that we saw above, the pairs of adjectives that are directly opposed in meaning, are merely the simplest type of an antonymous group. Adjectives normally form groups with only two members, i.e. pairs, for they commonly designate a simple quality or its absence. Some sets of adjectives, however, divide up a scale into more than two regions, such as *huge-big-small-tiny* or *aged-old-adult-adolescent-young*. There are many adjectives, moreover, where pairing is artificial. For example, *bright* is opposed to *dim* when talking of lights but to *dark* when talking of rooms, and again to *subdued* when talking of colours. This doesn't mean that it is three-ways ambiguous, however, for a single meaning is possible: [causing one to decrease the amount of light entering the eyes] or even the [Neg-Pls] above.

Unlike adjectives, nouns commonly describe complexes of qualities, so they tend to form into larger antonymous groups. North, south, east and west, for example, or animal, vegetable and mineral (dividing up the class of physical objects). This is no doubt why we accept certain nouns as opposites of others, the 'opposite numbers' above, as for Americans *mountain* and *valley* are general terms for major land forms, convex and concave respectively. For the Japanese, who mostly live between mountains and ocean, these notions *mountain*, *ocean* form mutually opposed directions away from living space.

Antonymous groups can have internal structure: north is directly opposed to south just as east is to west. We now accept that red is similarly opposed to green, as blue is to yellow, but not long ago green was accepted in art and physics as a mixture of blue and yellow and the three primary colours were red, yellow and blue. We see here how languages can change their antonymous groupings, and differences between languages here can be surprising. This is an interesting and enjoyable study, as it delves into how different peoples classify the things in the world, but it is complex enough for a chapter or even a book. We touched on it in Chapter 2 and shall see it again later, but let us now return to simpler things.

## Negative prefixes

A number of adjectives in English begin with *un-*. They are always the marked member of an antonymous pair and have a negative meaning. With gradable adjectives *un-* forms negative scales from the middle. This prefix is **productive** as it can be added to any adjective if there is not already a word with that meaning. That is, if there is an adjective, e.g. *good*, there is potentially another adjective, *ungood*, that means roughly [not good], though this particular possibility is blocked (Chapter 2) by the adjective *bad* (except in George Orwell's NewSpeak where that word had been banned).

| common | uncommon | – [Neg-common] |
| wise | unwise | – [Neg-wise] |
| comfortable | uncomfortable | – [Neg-comfortable] |
| intelligent | unintelligent | – [Neg-intelligent] |

---

Q.   What would be antonyms for *grammatical, enchanting, broken, endurable?*[3]

---

The same prefix with a verb is very different and forms yet another type of opposite, called a 'reversative' [reversing the process].

| to tie | to untie |
| to clothe | to unclothe |

These contain a [Neg] but it is hidden away inside their meanings. *To tie* is to put something into a *tied* state, and its reversative *to untie* is to put something into an *untied* or [Neg-tied] state. The adjectives *tied, untied* may thus be semantically simpler than the verbs even though they are derived from the verbs in form or morphology. In Chapter 12 we will see more of this, but for the moment we can take this verbal reversative *un-* to be like the adjectival negative *un-* which always negates an adjective-like meaning, with the addition of a verbal notion, [Bcm] (BeCoMe), so *to untie* means something like [Bcm-untied] or [Bcm-Neg-tied]. There are not many verbs that take this *un-* as a matter of course, but it is a productive prefix in English today, like *re-*; it can be added to almost any verb to designate the opposite direction, often humorously.

> You will have to unlearn your bad habits.
> ! Let's unlight the fire.
> ! They're going to unbuild the temple before rebuilding it.

Another negative prefix is *dis-*, but it is not productive; it occurs only in certain words, for example the adjectives *disingenuous, disinterested* or the verbs *disobey, dislike.* These generally contain a negative element in their meaning, but there seems to be no reliable way of knowing where it is. It is not, in particular, in the first place, where it could be paraphrased with *not.* Compare the meanings of the following words, where [Bcm] means roughly [to become] and [Coz] has a meaning like [to cause].

> to disobey    – [Neg-obey]
> ⎧ to appear     – [Bcm-visible] i.e. [to become visible]
> ⎩ to disappear  – [Bcm-Neg-visible] i.e. [to become invisible]
> ⎧ to enable     – [Coz-Bcm-effective] (to make it become
>                     effective)
> ⎩ to disable    – [Coz-Bcm-Neg-effective]

There is another unproductive prefix for adjectives, *in-* or *iX-*
where X stands for a repetition of a following consonant. It was
productive in Latin and French with a meaning [Neg], and
English adopted so many words from these languages that it is
perceived[4] as a prefix for [Neg] in English too. Nevertheless, we
cannot add it freely to English words, nor can we subtract it in
many cases, so it is not productive either.

> informal       – [Neg-formal]
> inefficient    – [Neg-efficient]
> insubstantial  – [Neg-substantial] = [Neg-Hav-substance]
> illegal        – [Neg-legal]
> immaterial     – [Neg-material] (the Aj, as in a *material object*)

Some examples where only the negative word was adopted into
English:

> inert    – [Neg-active] (cf. *ert)
> insipid  – [Neg-tasty] (cf. *sipid, *sapid)

There is another productive prefix for negation in English, *non-*
with adjectives or nouns, but it is like the external negation
described in the next section and applies to the word concerned,
e.g. *non-normal*, *non-person*, and is used mostly in scientific and
legal contexts.

## Negation in sentences

There are several different ways to negate a sentence, adding *not*
in different places, and they have different effects. Let us consider
in particular three ways to negate an old philosophical example.
(The '\' marks the syllable with the strongest stress and
intonation.)

> The king of France is bald\.
> (a) The king of France isn't bald\.

(b)  It is not true\ that the king of France is bald.
(c)  The king of France is not\ bald.

The word *not* is stressed or emphasized as in (c) when we want to deny completely something that someone else has said or suggested. It may be used simply to emphasize what one has already denied, or it may be equivalent to adding 'It is not true that' in front of the sentence, as in (b). This is sometimes called **external negation**; it stands logically outside a sentence and negates or denies the sentence as it stands, along with any presuppositions or anything else it may have. Much more commonly, as in (a), there is no stress on the negative itself and it leaves the presuppositions of the sentence intact so that if you say (a) to deny the first sentence, you are still admitting (i.e. presupposing) that France has a king. Only (b) or (c) leaves you free to continue, '. . ., for there isn't any king of France'.[5]

When not stressed, sentence negation ordinarily applies to only part of a sentence, and in English it applies to the stressed[6] or 'focused' part, so we can call it 'focused' or **narrow negation**. The part of the meaning to which a negative element applies is called its **scope**. All the rest of the sentence is **presupposed** (accepted or assumed) to be true and appropriate, so the sentences below suggest the questions on the right! Only the last, with emphasized negative (logical negation), denies the whole thing; we can say that its scope is the rest of the sentence.

| | |
|---|---|
| he didn't kiss his wife last night\. | – When did he? |
| he didn't kiss his wife last\ night. | – Which night was it? |
| he didn't kiss his wife\ last night. | – Who was it he kissed? |
| he didn't kiss his\ wife last night. | – Whose wife was it!? |
| he didn't kiss\ his wife last night. | – What did he do to her? |
| he\ didn't kiss his wife last night. | – Who kissed her? |
| he did\n't kiss his wife last night. | – What did happen? |

The way that the scope of syntactic negation is attracted to stress also explains why some English negatives appear to be in the wrong place. In the first example below, he really thinks that she will not come, but the *not* has escaped from *come* and looks as if it has climbed right up into the main sentence from the embedded sentence, so it is sometimes called 'negative raising'. However, it is really just another example of ordinary *not* applying only to stressed words.

he doesn't think she'll come\.    [he thinks she will *not* come]
he does\n't think she'll come.    [it's not true he thinks she
                                   will come]

he doesn't think\ she'll come.    SAME or 'thinking' is not a
                                   good description of it]

In the second example we do not know what he thinks, whether he thinks [she will not come], or whether he simply has no opinion on the matter. The negative applies to the stressed *think* in the third example as a negative ought to. In the first, too, the negative applies to the stressed word, so it seems to jump over the verb *to think* and appears quite illogical if we ignore stress.

On special occasions the scope of a negation can even be a second negative marker, as in 'Finally on the fourth night, he *didn't not\* sleep, but then again, he didn't sleep either.' This can be understood as the second *not* being incorrect; what he did cannot be described as 'not sleeping'. On the other hand, it cannot be described as 'sleeping' either, or else the speaker would have said simply 'He slept' (cf. lexical blocking in Chapter 2). As a result, it says that he was clearly not awake, but what he was doing was not something that we would normally call sleeping – thus, it was sort of like sleeping. Such sentences are hardly common and usually need a strong context, as the example below illustrates, but they show how a language can express things it has no words for.

> John couldn't keep his mind from returning to it again and again, even if he did have his comprehensive exam the next day. In the end, he couldn't study much, but he didn't not study either.

> A: Still not drinking coffee?
> B: I'm not not\ drinking coffee; I had half a cup the other day.

Because the scope of negation plays such an important role in language, various ways have evolved to identify the scope. Spoken English mostly uses stress or emphasis but can also isolate the scope together with the negative at the front of the sentence, as in 'It was*n't his wife\* (that) John kissed last night.' This is common in French: 'Ce n'est pas *sa femme* que Jean a embrassée hier soir.' Some languages commonly use a different case or preposition (often the genitive case or preposition) to identify a nominal as the scope of a negative.

Q.   What is the scope of the negative in the following? And
what presuppositions do they have?
    Reuben won't\ come tomorrow.
    Reuben\ won't come tomorrow.
    Reuben won't come tomorrow\.[7]

Sometimes a sentence is negative because the scope refers to
nothing at all, as in the examples below. Languages have evolved
diverse ways to express this special but common situation.
German and older English use negative determiners (e.g. *kein(e)*,
Eng: *no*) or pronouns like *nothing*, as on the left below, e.g. 'Wir
haben *keine* Banane.' Modern English prefers to express the
negation with the verb, using *any* to mark the nominal in the
scope, as on the right. We can still use the *no*, but because it is
uncommon it is taken to be emphatic, or even [nothing of the
sort], as in the last example.

| | |
|---|---|
| he gave it to *no* one. | = he did*n't* give it to *any*one. [he kept it] |
| I saw *no*thing. | = I did*n't* see *any*thing. (my eyes were closed) |
| we have *no* bananas. | = we do*n't* have *any* bananas. |
| she's *no* lady. | = she's not *any sort of* a lady. |

The *de* in French 'Nous n'avons pas *de* bananes' can be seen as
the same sort of scope marker, but it can also be seen as the
genitive case, which is used in many languages in these
circumstances. Japanese prefers to use a pronoun like *whoever*,
*whatever* with a negative verb, making a meaning structure
something like '*Whichever* banana, we do*n't* have [it]', rather like
the *any* of English. Chinese may do this also, but also likes a
structure like 'We have*n't* a *single* banana', also used for emphasis
in English and French.

Q.   What is the scope of the negative in the following?
    Anne didn't see you put any books there.
    nobody saw Tommy leave.
    He ain't got no time for the likes o' you.[8]

English is odd in using *any* with a negative verb as a substitute for
*no* only to the right of the verb. To the left of the verb (in a
statement), the *no*-form must be used, as follows, so it is common
and not emphatic. As the last examples show, however, *any* is

possible with some modals where it means something like [every], or in a question where it questions existence. Anyone who can find a simple explanation for these various uses of *any* should make it known.

* any bananas aren't ripe yet.      * anybody didn't come.
  no bananas are ripe yet.          nobody came.
* anyone can't do it.
  no one can do it.

  any idiot can do that!      [does] anyone know the answer?

A more common device of language is to combine a negatively marked verb with a negative pronoun, as is standard in French 'Nous n'avons rien' or common in English (non-standard dialects only) 'We don't/ain't got nuthin'.' These are sometimes called 'double negations' and are castigated on the basis that two logical negations cancel each other out, but this is really only a single negation marked in two (or more) places: 'She ain't told nobody nuthing' [it is *not* true that she told *some*body *some*thing]. In fact, it is merely one of the various ways in which languages have evolved to express a negative whose scope designates nothing.


## Double negation with adjectives

In logic, a negation of a negative makes a positive; the two negatives cancel out like two minus signs in arithmetic. This is called **logical negation** and is like adding 'It is not (true) that . . .' before the sentence, so external negation is always a logical negation. On the other hand, a negative embedded in the meaning of an adjective, such as *unhappy*, *short* for example, is more restrictive, so a syntactic negation may not quite cancel it out; the result is usually a weak positive.

he is not unhappy.          [he is sort of happy]
it is not illegal.          [it is vaguely legal]
it is not shallow.          [it is sort of deep]

The reason this happens is that a gradable adjective typically designates the end of a scale, a significant surplus or a deficit of some attribute, rather than ordinary, average degree of that quality. To say simply that someone is tall is to say that they are significantly taller than average (less than 25 per cent of people would qualify, perhaps), and not that they are merely over average height (including 50 per cent of the people) – that is, in terms of the table at the beginning, we would probably not say 'He is tall' if he were only 'sort of' tall or less.

Because a gradable adjective and its antonym are used to describe the two ends of a scale, the parts far enough away from the average to be worthy of remark, they leave a middle ground where neither adjective is very appropriate. This means that scales are commonly divided into three parts in human language, unlike logic which divides a scale into two, the presence and absence of some quality. For example:

| ← positive → (unmarked) | ← neutral → | ← negative → (marked) |
|---|---|---|
| happy | | unhappy |
| deep | | shallow |
| tall | | short |

A negative element in an adjective, then, whether a prefix like *un-* or simply a semantic element as in *short*, changes a description [at the positive end of the scale] effectively into [at the negative (marked) end of the scale]. This kind of negation inside a word can be called '**lexical** negation' for it is quite different from the syntactic (logical) negation of an adjective: everything else but the designated area or all the rest of the scale, including both the neutral and opposite parts. Of course, with complementary antonyms like *true:false*, *on:off* there is little or no middle ground, so syntactic negation with this sort of adjective has nearly the same effect as lexical negation: 'It's not true' means 'It's false' rather than 'It's less than true.'

---

Q.  In uncommon circumstances, the syntactic negation of even a complementary adjective may not imply its lexical negation. When, for example, can a video recorder be not on, without it being off? Or again, what can X be in: 'X is not married, but then again X is not unmarried either.'[9]

---

If we combine narrow negation (i.e. with stress on the adjective, cf. p. 47) with a negative adjective, as in 'He's not short\', then it excludes the negative end of the scale. If the person were tall, however, we would simply say 'He's tall', so if we go to the trouble to use this double negative construction, we must mean something else. That is, the word *tall* blocks this from describing the positive end of the scale. The result is that this complex form means [somewhat tall, but not tall enough to be described as 'tall']. Adjectives usually designate an abundance of some quality, or its lack, leaving the neutral, middle ground that makes double negatives not uncommon.

The same happens with an overtly negative adjective like *unhappy*; 'not unhappy' means [vaguely happy, but not enough to be called 'happy']. Fortunately, perhaps, this form is not written much any more, and you will seldom find it except in older literature and fancy writers. We do use it in speaking, however, where the stress is clear, often to avoid committing ourselves to saying too much.

It is also possible to use logical negation (stressing the *not*) with a negative adjective: 'He's not\ short' or 'He's not\ unhappy.' This gives us the equivalent of 'It is not true that he is short', covering both the middle ground between short and tall as well as the positively tall. The positive area is not blocked in logical negation, making a small but noticeable difference in meaning depending on which is stressed, the (negative) adjective or the negative itself.

| | |
|---|---|
| he's not short\. | ? . . . in fact, he's tall\. |
| he's not\ short. | . . . in fact, he's tall\. |

In writing, of course, we don't normally mark what is stressed, but because English normally spaces out stresses or beats at equal intervals, we usually perceive what is meant by where the stresses in nearby words are, and if not, the writer should rewrite the piece (though italics are sometimes used as a stopgap). This is one reason why, incidentally, it is hard for foreign learners to write understandable English until they learn to speak it with normal rhythm patterns.

## Contraries and contradictories

In an older terminology, a proposition is said to be **contrary** to another if they cannot both be true. Thus if you plan to disagree with what someone else has said, you may begin, 'On the contrary, . . .'. While a proposition and its contrary cannot both be true, they can both be false, so 'She is young' and 'She is old' are contraries; they can't both be true, but they may well both be false. In modern logic we would say that two such propositions are **inconsistent**.[10]

On the other hand, what is normally meant by the 'denial' of a proposition is a logical negation, i.e. adding [Neg] to it, and is technically called its **contradiction**. It is a contrary that is complete; [P] and [Neg-P] cannot both be true (i.e. they are inconsistent), and in addition, they cannot both be false. Thus one of the two must be true and the other false.

It is clear why a proposition can have only one contradiction, but it can have several possible contraries, as we saw with antonymous groups. Anything that is inconsistent with 'It is red' is a contrary, for example 'It is green' or 'It is blue.' Contraries occupied a somewhat special place in traditional Aristotelian logic based on the 'Square of Opposition' (the top row is reversed below to emphasize the important relations). The letters A, E, I and O stand for propositions based on *all, no/none, some, not-all/some . . . not,* as in the examples on the right.

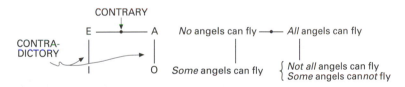

In this arrangement the vertical lines connect contradictories, while the horizontal lines connect contraries. The other relations also have traditional names but are not marked here as they have limited value and follow from these relations. Note, however, that the inconsistency at the top is true only if some of the things exist. If you believe that no angels exist, then the top two propositions are not at all inconsistent.

For reasons not yet entirely clear, there are very few words in language to express concepts of the O-type above. As seen in these examples, we usually have to synthesize that sort of meaning by combining an A-proposition with logical (or external) negation [Neg] that negates the whole proposition, or by an E-proposition with internal negation,[11] as seen in the example above.

In fact, it seems to be a common pattern for lexical words to occur in threes as below with the negative term in the middle.

We shall see this pattern again in logical modality (Chapter 6), but a few examples are:

| 'A' — contrary —'E' — contradictory —'I' | | |
| --- | --- | --- |
| and | nor | or |
| all | none | some |
| most | few | many |
| start | stop | continue |
| require (make) | forbid | permit (let) |
| assert | deny | assent |
| necessary | impossible | possible |
| more than | less than | as much as |

Why words should come in such negative triples is not at all clear, but these relations can help keep clear the differences between words such as *to assent* [not deny] and *to assert* [deny that it is not]. Sometimes a word can be ambiguous between these different arrangements of [Neg] with a negative concept, as in Dutch *laten* [let or make].

## Negation (summary)

We see, then, that negation has many functions in human language. It distinguishes (Chapter 2) the marked antonym from its unmarked counterpart, as well as appearing most generally as the prefix on adjectives *un-*. Not all opposites are antonyms, however, for there are a number of ways that a pair of words can be opposed in meaning.

When [Neg] is used as a free element in a sentence (*not* in English), it seldom negates the whole sentence (**external** negation). What it does negate is called its **scope**. The general English rule is that the scope is the focused or stressed (with strong intonation contour) part of the sentence, though a word like *any* will mark the scope (and the emphasis). What is left unnegated is **presupposed** or accepted to be true, so to negate the whole sentence, presuppositions and all, we must either stress the negative itself, or, less ambiguously in writing, use a construction like 'It is not true that . . .'. We also noted the variety of ways that languages express the situation when the scope is to refer to nothing. The English rule that the scope of *not* automatically applies to an *any* to the right explains why we seldom use *no* today except to the left of the auxiliary verb where *not* or -n't would sit.

In ordinary usage, a gradable adjective and its antonym are contraries. They are not contradictories because they are normally appropriate only when the quality described is significantly different from the average. They can thus leave a neutral ground in the middle of a scale that explains why we sometimes need to use double negation.

There are many, many things to say about negatives, but let us stop here in noting that human language and human language alone has negatives. Negation is notably late and difficult in the limited languages that some animals have been taught, and apparently not found in any naturally occurring non-human language. Human children on the contrary normally have a negative word or two (e.g. *all-gone*, *no*, *don't*) among their first dozen words. Indeed, it is somewhat special to be able to think about what is not here, or not anywhere. While the more intelligent animals, especially chimpanzees, can handle some limited types of abstract thought and communication, probably the most abstract is to think of what is not. Even human children cannot do it for a few years. Out of sight, out of mind.

## Notes and answers

1. Not literal English, anyhow, though it might possibly find a place in poetry, or if one wanted to give some human qualities to the dog.
2. low, new; *'300 feet low', *'two years new'.
3. *ungrammatical, unenchanting, unbroken, unendurable.*
4. The *in-* of *inflammable* did not come from [Neg] but from [Bcm] as in *to inflame*, but it confused many people as being [not flammable] (i.e. safe) and led to enough fires that *flammable* is now used as a warning in many places.
5. A stressed contraction with *-n't*, however, appears to leave the presuppositions intact. 'The king of France is\n't bald' cannot be continued, *'..., for there isn't any king of France'.
6. Commonly a fall ... rise in British varieties of English, which can surround the focus like a pair of parentheses, '(...)'. North American varieties spread the intonation contour over the whole focused sequence.

7. 'Reuben will come tomorrow', 'Reuben', 'tomorrow'. The second has the presupposition that someone else will come, and the 3rd, that he'll come some other time.
8. 'books', '-body' [person], 'time for the likes of you'.
9. When it is broken. X could be a man with a common-law wife, or it might not be a human being – a ghost or a swan, for example.
10. There are various hints that this may be the basic element underlying both negation and logical modality (Chapter 6), but that is another story!
11. Called 'internal' negation because the [Neg] is inside the scope of something else, the *some* here. 'Some angels cannot fly' can be paraphrased 'Speaking of angels, there are *some* (who can*not* fly)' where the parentheses show the scope of *some* with [Neg] inside.

## Keywords

antonym, gradable, complementary, external negation, contradictory, contrary, inconsistent.

## Further reading

Horn's provocatively titled book covers all aspects of negation and is excellent on all of these points. The only other book that is generally recommended is Jespersen's, written without the aid of modern understandings of syntax or semantics. Both are hefty tomes and not to be undertaken lightly.

Horn, Laurence *A Natural History of Negation* (1989) Chicago: UC Press.
Jespersen, Otto *Negation in English and Other Languages* (1917) København: Høst.


●opposites, antonyms.
Hofmann, Th. R. 'The Law of Denotation and Notions of Antonymy' (1981) *Prague Bulletin of Mathematical Linguistics* **36**: 25–46.
Lehrer, A. 'Markedness and Antonymy' (1985) *J. of Linguistics* **21**: 397–429.

Lehrer, Adrienne *Semantic Fields and Lexical Structure* (1974) Amsterdam: North Holland.

Lyons, John *Semantics*, vol. 1 (1977) London: CUP.

•rhythm and stress

Abercrombie, David 'A Phonetician's View of Verse Structure' in *Studies in Phonetics and Linguistics* (1965) London.

Bolinger, Dwight L. 'Pitch Accent and Sentence Rhythm' in *Forms of English: Accent, Morpheme, Order* (1965) Cambridge, Mass.

Halle, Morris and Keyser, S. J. 'Chaucer and the Study of Prosody' (1966) *College English* **28**.3.

Hofmann, Th. R. 'Observations on the Timing of English' (1983) *Memoirs* **12**, Senzoku Gakuen School of Music, Kawasaki, Japan.

## Exercises with negation

1. Give the 'opposites' of the following words.

   (a) dry <of wine>   (e) drunk       (i) obligatory
   (b) hostile         (f) harmful     (j) to persuade
   (c) tender <of meat>(g) flammable   (k) to entangle
   (d) paperback       (h) courageous  (l) coin

2. Give a word that describes the middle part of the following scales.

   (a) rare      – ( ) – well-done       <of meat>
   (b) wet       – ( ) – dry (three answers)
   (c) bad       – ( ) – good            <of behaviour>
   (d) possibly  – ( ) – certainly
   (e) fail      – ( ) – good – excellent <of school marks>
       (three answers)
   (f) cold – cool – ( ) – warm – hot (two answers)

3. Which are the ungradable pairs?

   (a) far:near           (e) mortal:immortal
   (b) finite:infinite    (f) accurate:inaccurate
   (c) generous:stingy    (g) true:false (in logic)
   (d) dangerous:safe

4. Some antonymous pairs lie between the open-ended (gradable) scalar type and the complementary antonym type. One side defines a limit (e.g. *shut*) while the other side has no limit (it is open-ended), like *open*. In 'asymmetric antonyms'

a **degree** modifier like *half, more . . . than* or *relatively* can apply to the open–ended side but not to the limit side.

This door's more open than that one.

\* That door's more shut than this one.

Modifiers of **limits**, like *almost* or *absolutely*, on the contrary, apply only to the limited side:

\* The door's almost open.

The door's almost shut/closed.

(a) Given the facts below, is *not . . . at all* a degree modifier or a limit modifier? How about *slightly, rather, a little bit*?

not open at all            \* not shut at all

(b) Classify the following pairs, whether both sides have limits (complementary antonyms), neither side has (gradable antonyms), or only one side has (asymmetric antonyms), and in this last case, which side has? (Use 'L, G' for limited and gradable respectively.)

|     |     |     |     |
|-----|-----|-----|-----|
| (a) | open–closed | (e) | raw–cooked |
| (b) | tall–short | (f) | sick–healthy |
| (c) | wet–dry | (g) | deep–shallow |
| (d) | true–false | (h) | empty–full |

(c) When opening a package at Christmas, one can easily say 'it is almost open'. How can this be rationalized with the facts above about doors?

5. Add the correct prefix (*in-, im-, il-, ir-*) to the following adjectives.

|     |     |     |     |     |     |
|-----|-----|-----|-----|-----|-----|
| (a) | _rational | (e) | _direct | (i) | _partial |
| (b) | _expensive | (f) | _literate | (j) | _human |
| (c) | _sincere | (g) | _regular | (k) | _frequent |
| (d) | _legitimate | (h) | _mature |     |     |

What is the rule for selecting these prefixes?

(l)   *il-* goes with words beginning with __.

(m)  *ir-* goes with words beginning with __.

(n)  *im-* goes with words beginning with __.

(o)  *in-* goes with words beginning with __.

Now add the correct prefix to the following.

|     |     |     |     |     |     |
|-----|-----|-----|-----|-----|-----|
| (p) | _gratitude | (s) | _tolerable | (v) | _balanced |
| (q) | _justice | (t) | _valid | (w) | _literate |
| (r) | _organic | (u) | _compatible | (x) | _relevant |

6. Explain the difference in meaning for each of the following pairs.

(a)  They are looking for un-British people.

(a') They are looking for non-British people.

  (b)  That is an illegal act.

  (b') That is a non-legal act.

  (c)  Some children are amoral. (*a*- is like *non*-)

  (c') Some children are immoral.

7. Explain the differences in meaning, based on the scope of negation.

  (a)  You cannot accept the scholarship and apply for the assistantship.

  (a') You cannot accept the scholarship or apply for the assistantship.

  (b)  The teacher simply didn't answer.

  (b') The teacher didn't answer simply.

  (c)  A bad student cannot even take the exam.

  (c') A good student can even not take the exam.

  (d)  He didn't marry her, because he loved her.

  (d') He didn't marry her because he loved her.

  (e)  John didn't return home exhausted.

  (e') Exhausted, John didn't return home.

  (f)  Not many of the boys can solve this problem.

  (f') Many of the boys cannot solve this problem.

  (g)  Not all of the boys can solve this problem.

  (g') All of the boys cannot solve this problem.

8. (advanced) The mathematical idea of the **converse** of a relation $R(x,y)$ is another relation $R-1$ with the arguments reversed; $R-1(x,y) = R(y,x)$. For example, 'X is-the-wife-of Y' is the converse of 'Y is-the-husband-of X', for whenever the first is true, the second must be too, and vice-versa (at least in the standard old-fashioned world that English evolved for). Although many relations may seem to be converses at first glance, true converses are rather rare in human language. For instance, [Son] is not the converse of [Father], for 'X is-the-father-of Liza' does not suggest in the slightest 'Liza is-the-son-of X.' Give similar examples to show that each of the following pairs are not converses.

  (a)  master:slave

  (b)  doctor:patient

  (c)  wife:husband (in a homosexual society)

9. In the text, *father* was given a meaning [Msc.Par], though it cannot be used (due to lexical blocking) if a more appropriate word is known. Thus if we are talking about horses [Hrs] and we know the word *sire* as used of horses, we could not say that one horse is the father of another. What, then, is the

meaning of *sire*, and do we need to revise the meaning we assigned to *father* by adding [Neg-Hrs]?

10. As negation is an extremely important concept of human language, it is found in the meanings of a number of concepts. You will find, in fact, when stumped for how to explain a concept, that a negative definition is often easier, and clearer as well. Take *freedom* for example; it is very hard to say what it is but easy to say what it isn't – thus *freedom* means [no restraint]. And *restraint*? [anything that holds one back from an action]. Try your hand with the following concepts.

(a) to survive

(b) to continue

(c) to allow

(d) to remain

# CHAPTER 4

# Deixis

When someone calls for a bit of help, we would normally say 'I'm coming' or 'I'll come in a moment.' A Japanese might say, however, 'Sugu iki-masu' which translates as 'I go in a moment', but he 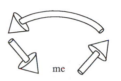 doesn't mean that he is leaving and refusing to help. Many languages use *to go* in some cases where English uses *to come*. So what do these words mean? And why can't we say ★ 'She went here yesterday' in ordinary speech?

Language would be impossible without a speaker and a hearer. It is not hard, then, to see why interesting things happen with words that are related to the speaker and the person he or she is talking to (the **addressee**). This is what linguists call **deixis**. Deictic or 'pointing' words such as *this*, *that* and the like are found in all languages and are very useful for 'referring' to objects around you. You will even see, if you watch yourself or others, that these words are often accompanied by a pointing gesture − with a finger typically, or if that is too impolite, maybe an elbow, or just the eyes.

## This and that

In perhaps every language, deictic words form systems or patterns that are semantic in nature, so semantics often starts in noticing these patterns and realizing that there must be fundamental units of meaning on which these patterns are based. Japanese has one of the more perfect deictic systems, so let us begin there. The central part of the system includes the following demonstrative expressions.

| Pro | Det | Loc | Dir | Mnr | |
|-----|-----|-----|-----|-----|-----|
| kore | kono | koko | kochira | koo | [speaker] |
| sore | sono | soko | sochira | soo | [addressee] |
| are | ano | asoko | achira | aa | [neither] |

with abbreviations: Pro = pronoun (*this one*)
Det = determiner (*this*)
Loc = location (*here*)
Dir = direction (*in this direction*)
Mnr = manner (*in this fashion*)

This loses a lot in translation, but just to show what is lost, and how different languages can be, we would have to translate the table above as follows, even though each word in the original has a quite distinct meaning. Spanish distinguishes the rows better.

| usual English translation | | | | | Spanish | |
|------|------|-------|----------|----------|--------|-------|
| this | this | here | this-way | this-way | este | aquí |
| that | that | there | your-way | your-way | ese | allá |
| that | that | there | that-way | that-way | aquel | allí |

Speakers of Japanese know that the words in the first row belong together, not simply because they all have the same beginning *ko-* in common, but because they describe something related to the location or territory, physical or psychological, of the speaker. This notion is so important in the languages of the world that we should give it a special symbol, [Spk] (SPeaKer).

In a similar way, the words in the second row signal something similarly related to the person being spoken to, the 'addressee', and all begin with *so-* which makes the chart rather perfect. Although this concept is not nearly so universal as we shall see, and there is reason to doubt that it is fundamental, we can make an abbreviation for it too: [Adr] (ADdRessee). The words in the last row all refer to something away from both speaker and addressee, and all begin with *a-*. Let us call it [Awa], meaning roughly that it is 'AWAy', i.e. not close to the participants of the conversation. The systematic nature of these words, then, is shown by breaking them down into 'morphemes', i.e. units of form (pronunciation, plus how they fit together with other units) that have particular meanings. Japanese is near perfect in this area because these units of form match almost one for one with elementary units of meaning, what we can call 'semantic atoms'.

| | FORM | MEANING |
|---|---|---|
| rows | ko- | [Spk] = [close to the speaker] |
| (R) | so- | [Adr] = [close to the addressee]? |
| | a- | [Awa] = [not close to either participant] |
| columns | -re | Pro = pronoun; functions as a noun |
| (C) | -no | Det = determiner; functions with a noun |
| | -ko | [Loc] = place or LOCation |
| | -chira | [Dir] = DIRection |
| | (*long vowel*) | [Mnr] = way or MaNneR of doing something |

Perhaps you have noticed where this system has a flaw; *asoko* is an odd man out with an extra -so- in the middle. By the system laid out in (R) and (C) above, it should be *ako*, and it is in a few dialects. The very fact that we know that *asoko* belongs where we put it, however, means that *asoko* has a meaning of two pieces, [Awa.Loc], and that the table we started with was an arrangement of meanings, not of forms. We should thus add *asoko* to the analytic form-meaning table above.

---

Q.  If you found out that *doko* means [where?], what could you guess for the meaning of *dochira*, and how might one say the Japanese pronoun for [which one?]? Add a row to the table above for [Qst], QueSTion words, and an entry in (R) above.[1]

---

In contrast to this nearly perfect system, English is noticeably less systematic, but the semantic system is still quite clear and appears rather different from Japanese. Beginning from this same arrangement we can again identify semantic elements by labelling the columns and rows, to identify what each means below.

| | Dem.Sg | Dem.Pl | [Tym] | [Loc] | [Abl] |
|---|---|---|---|---|---|
| [Spk] | this | these | now | here | †thence |
| [Neg-Spk] | that | those | then | there | †tthence |
| [Qst] | what | — | when | where | †twhence |

Beginning with the last two columns labelled [Loc] and [Abl] (using the dagger symbol † to indicate 'archaic' or 'out of common use'), we can detect a system in the forms.

|  | FORM | MEANING | |
|---|---|---|---|
| rows | *h-* | [Spk] | = [close to the speaker] |
| (R) | *th-* | [Neg-Spk] | = [not close to the speaker] |
|  | *wh-* | [Qst] | = [more description requested] |
| columns | *-ere* | [Loc] | = [location or place] |
| (C) | *-en* | [Tym] | = [time location] |
|  | *-at* | Dem.Sg | = DEMonstrative and SinGular |
|  | *-ose* | Dem.Pl | = demonstrative and PLural |
|  | †*-ence* | [Abl] | = [from a place], the ABLative case in Latin |

lexical items that block systematic formations:

|  |  |
|---|---|
| *now* | [Spk.Tym] |
| *this* | [Spk.Dem.Sg] |
| *these* | [Spk.Dem.Pl] |

Although we cannot come up with so complete a correspondence between form and meaning for the other words in the English table, still it is obvious that these words form a neat semantic system.[2]

---

Q.   We also have archaic forms like †*thither* [towards here] or [Dir.Spk]. What do you need to add to the (C) part of the table above to explain it, and in so doing, what other forms are created? Did they exist, with the meanings expected?[3]

---

When we compare English and Japanese we do not find a whole lot of similarity, but this is not surprising as they are completely unrelated languages with virtually no influence between them until a century ago. In the rows R expressing different distances, for instance, English has two levels while Japanese has three. This difference is not so large as it appears at first, however, because in both English and Japanese the first level is the same: [close to the speaker], or [Spk]. The only difference, really, is that Japanese like many other languages splits the remaining possibilities, [Neg-Spk], into two distances, [Awa] and [Adr], while English and many other languages do not bother with this split. There are few languages that do anything else.

Like English, French has only two distances but expresses the difference with a suffix *-ci* [Spk] or *-là* [Neg-Spk] behind a noun or pronoun. For example, 'ce livre-ci' meaning [this book] has a structure like 'this book-here', in contrast with 'ce livre-là' [that book]. English does something like this in the dialectal 'this here book' and 'that there book'. Korean and Spanish, on the other hand, make a three-way split as in Japanese.

Because the French suffix is optional, it is not used when distance is not important or relevant, giving French a little more flexibility. In English, we can use *the* instead of a deictic when the distance from the speaker is not relevant, but this may not be possible in discussing several similar things. In that case, we may be forced to use *this* or *that*, perhaps with a metaphorical sense of distance (as in this very sentence).

For pointing back across a paragraph break, a deictic with a noun is much better than *the* (as explained in Chapter 13), so there is a tendency to use deictics to recall a topic. Also, *this* has a greater sense of immediacy or intimateness, while *that* suggests a cool and rational distance for a better perspective. This may be the reason for the American tendency to use *this* in writing where British might prefer *that*, as for example in the word that began this sentence. Japanese, incidentally, tend to use *sono* if distance is not relevant, showing that its meaning is not really [Adr] but rather something like [Neg-Spk.Neg-Awa].

---

Q.  Spanish also uses intermediate terms like *ese* when the referent is not especially close to the addressee (or to the speaker) yet within the range of the conversation. What does this suggest about the element [Adr]?[4]

---

A language can switch between two- and three-way divisions of deictic distance in the course of time. The old terms †*yon*, †*yonder*, as in 'He lives yonder' or '. . . in yon(der) village' show a distance further than in *there* or *that*. English thus seems to have had a time when three deictic distances were used, and Chinese seems to have made a similar change recently; the court language of the Manchu dynasty had three distances, though today the two [Neg.Spk] words *nà*, *nèi* are considered mere variants in pronunciation.

---

Q.  If the meaning of *there* is [Neg.Spk.Loc], what was the meaning of *yonder*?[5]

---

There is something similar in modern English, in the *over* of 'over there' which feels further than just *there*. However, this is not a third distance as it can be used with *here* too, as in 'Come over here, would you?' It only emphasizes the distance inherent in *here* or *there*.

We see, then, that languages commonly employ several levels of 'deictic distance'. One of these is nearly always [Spk], i.e. close to the speaker or the act of speaking. This divides the physical world into two, *here* and *not-here* (i.e. *there*), and appears to be basic in nearly all languages (but see Exercise question 7). *Not-here* [Neg-Spk] is divided in some languages, e.g. Spanish and Japanese, into places away from the conversation [Awa], and [Neg-Awa] for places neither away nor close to the speaker, often just near the addressee. Thus the intermediate level which we called [Adr] seems to be used merely in cases where neither [Spk] nor [Awa] applies.

Although these are easiest to talk about in terms of physical distance, and have their greatest application there, the elements [Spk] and [Awa] may actually have nothing to do with physical distance. The English distinction *now* – *then* – *when* has no more to do with location than *here* – *there* – *where* has to do with time. We can conclude that the meaning of *now* is [Spk.Tym], *here* is [Spk.Loc], and *I* is [Spk.Hum], so that [Spk] must point simply to the event of speaking, its location in space and time.

## Symbols for meanings

By now you have noticed that we are using square brackets [. . .] here to enclose meanings, and elements of meaning or 'semantic atoms' are given three-letter labels. A list of the ones used here is found at the front of the book. There are no standard symbols for them yet, and the most common practice is to use an English word in block capitals to stand for a semantic element. They should not be confused with real English words, however, for they are only labels for semantic elements, discovered by analysing the words of a language as we have done here. Longer elements and uncapitalized words or phrases are used in brackets in this book for their English meanings, without worrying about their exact content.

In the preceding chapter we used diagrams for meanings of *father* and *son*. Although that is perhaps the easiest way to understand the structures of meanings, and we will find it almost essential later on, it is not convenient to use in ordinary text or in a dictionary. Here we have been using a simplified system that works for most simple cases. A dot stands for a logical *and* (as used by some logicians, though '∧' and '&' are more common today), and a hyphen connects an element with a following one that it applies to. We will add a few more such informal but convenient symbols.

## Coming and going

Deixis is not restricted to demonstratives, pronouns and similar sorts of things; most languages have some deictic marking in verbs that describe movement (called 'verbs of motion') like *to come* and *to go*. To be sure that we are dealing in fact with a question of deixis, we can note that it is nearly impossible to say ★'to go here', even though we can easily combine *to go* with any other directional adverb, and *here* can generally be found after any verb of motion except *to go*, as in 'to walk here', 'to ride here', 'to fly here', and so on.

The first hypothesis about the structural meaning of these words was made about twenty years ago: *to come* means [to go here]. This explained at one stroke (a) what *to come* means, (b) why it is difficult to combine *to go* and *here* – use the simpler expression 'come' if that is what you mean – and (c) why it is redundant and thus emphatic to say 'Come here'. Lastly, it also explained (d) why *to come* with any locational expression adds the meaning that the expression designates *here*; 'Come home' implies that the speaker is home, while 'Go home' implies she is not. Or 'They came to Penny Lane' implies that the speaker was at Penny Lane when those people went there.

It was soon discovered, as nice as that hypothesis was, that it didn't always work (first hypotheses are never completely correct), as we can say 'Come to Tokyo next week' even though neither of us is there now. It turns out that *to come* is used if the speaker is at the designated place either now or at the time of the sentence, or even if it is only the addressee who is there, as in 'I'll come to the beach if you will be there.' So English *to come* has a meaning something like [go to: Spk-OR-Adr]. More simple, and logically equivalent, is to state this meaning with negation [Neg] of the element [Awa] we found in Japanese: [to: Neg-Awa], i.e. [go to a place that is not far from Spk]. Thus although English demonstratives are distinguished on the basis of [Spk] or not, the verbs of motion are distinguished on [Awa] or not. Together, they give English three distinctions in distance, like Spanish or Japanese! Roughly, then (see Exercise question 8 for more detail):

to come [Dir:Neg-Awa]          here [Dir:Spk]
to go    [Dir:Awa]             there [Dir:Neg-Spk]

---

| | | |
|---|---|---|
| come | here | [Dir:Neg-Awa.Dir:Spk] = [Dir:Spk] |
| come | there | [Dir:Neg-Awa.Dir:Neg-Spk] = [Dir:Adr] |
| go | there | [Dir:Awa.Dir:Neg-Spk] = [Dir:Awa] |
| *go | here | *[Dir:Awa.Dir:Spk], impossible |

---

Q.  What is the difference between 'Where will he go?' and 'Where will he come (to)?'[6]

---

In **collocation** (possibilities of combination) with *there*, Japanese *kuru, iku* seem to match *to come, to go*; both languages allow the expression *to come there* if it is understood that (at least) the speaker will be at the designated location when the person described is to do his *coming*. Not all languages allow this. Nevertheless, English and Japanese do differ, in a situation like the following. Imagine a wife at home calling her husband in another room for a bit of help. In English he could answer 'I'll come in a second' but a normal Japanese answer would be 'Ima iku-yo' [now go] and not *'Ima kuru-yo' [now come]. It appears, then, that the meaning of *kuru* involves [Dir: Spk] rather than [Dir: Neg-Awa] as *to come* does. That is, a person can 'kuru' only to a place where the speaker is, was or will be, but he can 'come' to a place where either he *or* his addressee is, was or will be.

---

Q.  Under what circumstances can one say 'They came to his house at five p.m.'? And why is it impossible to say *'Let's come to his house'?[7]

---

Languages typically have transitive or 'causative' counterparts for *to come* and *to go*, with parallel possibilities for deictic locations. They are *to bring* and *to take* in English, so it is difficult to say *'take something here', in the same way as *'go here' is difficult. It is used when the speaker and addressee are coming together, or when some third party is coming to either or both. The reason why the contrast between words like *to bring, to take* is normally the same as the contrast between *to come*, *to go* is suggested by the morphemes used in some languages: 'to bring X' in Japanese is 'X-o motte-kuru', while 'to take X' is 'X-o motte-iku', which could also be translated as 'to come, carrying X' and 'to go, carrying X'. The meanings for these causative words in most languages are probably no more than their words for *to come*, *to go* plus some element of carrying or leading.

The way that *come*, *go*, *bring*, *take* are used, then, commonly gives hints about where the speaker is, and in a novel where the addressee's (i.e. the reader's) location is not involved, their use usually adds up to a 'point of view' of the author.

## Extensions

The meanings of *to come* and *to go* also contrast in their non-physical or metaphorical uses. A good example is the difference between the following pairs of sentences.

- (a) the patient's temperature *went* up today.
- (b) the patient's temperature *came* down today.

Sentence (a) means that the temperature went upward, away from normal body temperature, while the second sentence describes its return towards normal; normal is where Spk and Adr are, [Neg-Awa]. In contrast, the sentences below naturally describe a patient who suffers from an unusually low temperature.

- (c) the patient's temperature *went* down today.[8]
- (d) the patient's temperature *came* up again today.

In both cases *go* is interpreted as moving away from a normal state, while *come* suggests a return to a normal state from the abnormal. [Awa], then, can be interpreted as [abnormal state], and [Neg-Awa] is a normal state, i.e. where you and I are.

Extended senses of the causatives *to bring*, *to take* can similarly be understood in the same metaphorical way.

- (a') that medicine really *sent* your patient's temperature skyrocketing,
- (b') but this medicine will *bring* it (back) down.
- (c') that same medicine *took* another patient's temperature down.
- (d') how can we *bring* it (back) up?

This sort of extended use of these verbs (NB: *to send* is like *to take* in meaning but the subject of the sentence does not go with the object sent) is easy to understand from the basic (physical) meanings of *to come* and *to go* involving [Awa], which may be metaphorically extended to represent an abnormal or untypical state.

---

Q.  We can easily say 'That song really *takes* me back to my childhood' and 'The baby's crying *brought* her back to reality.' Why can't we exchange the italicized words?[9]

---

Another sort of extension is the use of *here*, *there* with a map or a diagram (e.g. a stock market index). Touching a place on the map, it is normal to say 'She will *go here* tomorrow', just what we saw earlier to be virtually impossible, and it is difficult to say 'She will go there.' This meaning of *here* must be something like [Loc that Spk is designating], instead of [Loc where Spk is]. It seems that some reinterpretation (as in Chapter 14) of elements like Spk may be necessary, but it may only be that the speaker puts himself figuratively at the place corresponding to the place represented on the map. From this example, incidentally, we can note that although the possibilities of normal collocation give good hints about the meanings of the words, they cannot be accepted uncritically, while the full range of extraordinary collocations can hide the meaning quite thoroughly.

## System in deixis (summary)

English, and perhaps every other language, has systematic arrangements for **deictic** words, which shows again that these words have meanings that can be divided into smaller pieces that we can call 'semantic **atoms**' (provided that they do not need to be further divided). Superficially, the systems of English, Spanish and Japanese are rather different, which is one reason why we can seldom translate them word for word. Nevertheless, when we look closely at the semantic elements underlying these systems we find amazing similarities, and we saw how English can express the same three distances as Japanese deictic elements by combining the [Spk] contrast between *here*, *there* with the [Awa] contrast in *to come*, *to go*.

We have seen several extensions of these contrasts, and have discovered that a word's **collocations**, what it can be combined semantically with, can provide strong indications of its meaning. Alone, however, they are not proof and should not be accepted uncritically.

The similarities in semantic elements suggest the idea that human beings might all have the same ones from which to build words, and at the beginning of this book there is a list of the most common and universal elements. It is reasonable to suspect that we all have the same basic building blocks of articulate thought, for we are all human beings. This concept of universally shared elements is clearly not true for words, however. Languages differ widely even in their central aspects such as deixis for what words they have and what their meanings are. Of course, the words that describe the world must necessarily vary quite a lot; Eskimos live in a world that is very different from that of the Polynesians, so their languages need words for things that don't even exist in the others' world, like snow and coral for instance.

It might be, however, that the same elements can have different meanings. [Awa] in Spanish *aquel, allí* is quite a bit further than [Awa] in Japanese *ano, asoko*. Indeed, it is more or less [out of sight] (see Exercise question 10). So the question arises, are these [Awa]s really the same element interpreted differently in different languages, or are they different elements? In any case, some possibility of reinterpretation seems to be necessary for the metaphoric extensions.

## Notes and answers

1. [Which direction?] for *dochira* and [which one?] is properly *dore*. The new row should be: [Qst] *dore dono doko dochira doo*, and in (R): /do-/ [Qst] = [identification wanted].
2. The spelling hides some more irregularities in pronunciation. All told, the items that block systematic formations are: *nŏw*, *thĭs, thēse, hēre, thăt*. The cross–dialectal diacritics are found in many dictionaries and given precise definition in my 'Showing Pronunciation in the EFL Classroom' (1990), *The Language Teacher*.
3. †*-ither* meaning [toward a place] or [Dir] as in Japanese. Adding *this* creates †*thither*, [towards there] and †*whither* [towards where?] respectively.

4. Either that it is not a real element, and we should use [Neg-Spk.Neg-Awa] instead, or that the tentative interpretation we gave it was wrong.
5. [Awa.Loc], i.e. a place outside the range of the conversation.
6. The first is normal if he is not to come towards the speaker, but the latter presupposes that he will be coming either to the speaker or to his addressee.
7. If the speaker was there at five p.m. Because *let's* includes both the speaker and the addressee, neither can be there, so *to come* is impossible.
8. This could also be used in a (b) case, for *to go* is actually the unmarked (Chapter 2) member of the opposition. However, to do so may seem somewhat cold and clinical as it avoids any suggestion of a normal human temperature.
9. One's childhood is away from here and now, so *to take*, *to go* are reasonable. *To bring* would be possible only if one was there while speaking, as in !'That crazy pill you gave me has brought me back to my childhood.' Conversely, reality is here and now for most of us; *to take* would be possible only for someone who felt he was not there.

## Keywords

deixis/deictic, speaker, addressee/audience, collocation.

## Further reading

• deixis
Clark, Eve 'Normal States and Evaluative Viewpoints' (1974) *Language* **50**: 316–332.
Fillmore, Ch. 'Santa Cruz Lectures on Deixis' (1975) Bloomington, Ind.: Indiana University Linguistics Club.
Lakoff, R. 'Remarks on This and That' (1974) *Papers, Chicago Linguistic Society* **10**: 345–56.
Rauh, Gisa *Essays on Deixis* (1983) Tübingen: Narr.

• metaphor
Lakoff, George *Women, Fire and Other Dangerous Things* (1987) Chicago: UC Press.

## Exercises with deixis

1. The English deictic system can be extended as below.

| | Dem.Sg | Dem.Pl | Loc | Tym | Hum | Reason | Manner |
|---|---|---|---|---|---|---|---|
| Spk | this | these | here | now | (a) | (c) | (e) |
| Neg-Spk | that | those | there | then | (b) | (d) | (f) |
| Qst { | what | (g) | (i) | | when | who | why | how |
| | which | (h) | (j) | | | | |

Give ways of expressing the ideas in (a)–(f). There are several different possibilities for (a) and (b), while (c)–(f) may require more than one word.

The first and second columns contrast in singular (Sg) and plural (Pl), but are there plural forms for the question words (g) and (h)? If not, why do you think there aren't any?

The difference between *what:which* is that *which* asks for a choice out of a limited set of possibilities, while *what* does not itself suggest a limited range of choices. Does *where* express (i) [what place?] or (j) [which place?]? How would you express the other one?

There are several answers for (a) and (b), so we might split that column into [Hum.Sg] (k)–(l) and [Hum.Pl] (m)–(n). What are the forms for (k)–(n)?

2. Which of the following sentences are not semantically well formed? Explain what is wrong with the ones you reject.
   (a) She bought this book here at a discount sale.
   (b) She was given this book there by its author.
   (c) I would like to buy this book you have there.
   (d) I don't want that book you have there.
   (e) I'll come there and meet you at 4.30.
   (f) I'll go and meet you here at 4.30.
   (g) If you will wait there, I'll go and meet you after work.

3. Explain the difference in meaning between each pair of sentences.
   (a) This really is a difficult problem.
   (a') That really is a difficult problem.
   (b) This is a difficult problem you have.
   (b') That is a difficult problem you have.
   (c) Are you going to go to the beach party tomorrow?
   (c') Are you going to come to the beach party tomorrow?
   (d) It's late; I've got to be going home.

(d') It's late; I've got to be coming home.

(e) His schoolwork is coming along nicely this year.

(e') His schoolwork is going along nicely this year.

(f) The plane came down near the lake.

(f') The plane went down near the lake.

**Hints**: Whose problem is it in (a)? Does Spk offer to help in (b)? Is Spk planning on going in (c)? Which one of (d–d') must be said on the telephone? Which of (e–e') would be said by his teacher? Where is Spk in (f–f')?

4. There is usually a fixed order for common conjunctions of words, as for example we say 'ladies and gentlemen' but not ⋆'gentlemen and ladies'. In the following pairs of words, what is the fixed order? Find a general rule.

    (a) this, that   (b) go, come   (c) now, then   (d) there, here

    A different rule is applied (except by children) to the following. Again, which comes first, and why?

    (e) I, you   (f) I, he   (g) you, he

5. The intransitive verb *to come* has many idiomatic expressions in common with its transitive counterpart *to bring*. Combine each pair of sentences together with *to bring*. For example:

    Land is very high-priced.   The question of a new site *came up*.

    → The high price of land *brought up* the question of a new site.

    (a) A pocket-sized word-processor has just come out.
       It is made by a Japanese company.

    (b) We had warm weather this winter.
       The peach trees will come into blossom a week early.

    (c) The prime minister takes long walks in the evening.
       He comes into contact with ordinary people.

    (d) My tests were deplorable.
       It came home to me how lazy I had been all year.

    (e) They excavated the tomb at Ixtapetl.
       New evidence came to light that there was trans-Atlantic commerce even then.

6. Using either *to come* or *to go* as the main verb, form inchoative sentences from the stative descriptions below. That is, make sentences that describe how those states came to be, and add the modifiers on the right for the inchoation.

    (a) Jenkins is raving mad.          + Perf (have . . . -en)

    (b) The schedule is awry.           + yesterday

    (c) My predictions are true!         + again

  (d) The electric mains are dead.
  (e) The party is alive.                        + finally
  (f) Your milk was sour after three hours in the sun.
  (g) The moon was up from four p.m. till noon.

7. Many languages make a deictic distinction between Spk and Neg-Spk, and some languages further subdivide this latter into Awa and Neg-Awa. However, some languages, e.g. Eskimo, appear to take Awa as basic, with a number of deictic words for various aspects of Awa (higher, lower, spread out, localized). How can such a language make the same three-way distinction as in English or Spanish, which Eskimo does for pronouns?

8. In explaining the contrast between *to come, to go*, we brushed over a few things. First, there is an element of movement that we might call [Mov], so that *to go* has a meaning [Mov.Dir:Awa] if semantic structure resembles the order of elements in expression. Second, *here, there* were treated as Loc(ative) elements earlier but need to be prefixed with [Dir:] here. Give the meanings of the following expressions, in this framework.

  (a) come                        (e) come here
  (b) go                          (f) come there
  (c) here                        (g) go there
  (d) there                       (h) *go here (self-contradictory)

9. Based on this, explain why 'Where should I come?' implies the question 'Where will you be?'

10. Both Spanish and Japanese have three–term deictic distinctions, with two words for our *there*: *soko, asoko* in Japanese, and *allá, allí* in Spanish. This doesn't mean, however, that the Japanese and Spanish words are used in the same way, and in fact *allí* is not much used, while its Japanese counterpart *asoko* is quite common. This can be explained by the fact that the range of conversation in Spanish includes everything that is visible to the speaker and the addressee, while it does not extend much beyond the addressee in Japanese. What can you conclude about the universality of semantic elements?

11. Make a chart of systematic deictic elements for your native language, or some language that we haven't discussed. You may expect there to be rows for Spk, Qst and one or two other distances, and columns for Loc, Pro, and possibly also Dem, Dir, Tym. You may need to divide a column into two if there are generally two forms for each place in it, and

decide how the two new columns differ. And any pair of columns that have nearly the same forms should be tested to see if they don't have exactly the same forms and should be coalesced into one.

# CHAPTER 5

# Orientations

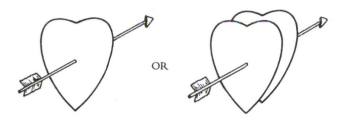

OR

> Do sentences 1 and 2 mean the same thing?
>
> 1. Pinkerton fell in love with his beautiful secretary.
> 2. Pinkerton and his beautiful secretary fell in love.

The main use of language is to talk about the world, but in doing so the facts are usually described from some point of view or another. These orientations give rise to differences in meaning that are sometimes subtle, as above, and sometimes gross. They can also be utilized to say a lot in just a few words.

## Towards speakers, or subjects

Although the example sentences above seem to have the same meaning at first glance, they are different in a significant way. While (2) means that Mr Pinkerton and the secretary love each other, (1) says only that Pinkerton was attracted to the secretary; namely, that there may be (and probably is, as we shall see in Chapter 14) only a one-sided love here. To put it differently, the English expression *to fall in love* describes the mental state of the subject only. In the first case Pinkerton has those feelings, while in the second they both do, as both are mentioned in the subject of the sentence.

*To fall in love* is not alone in having this **subject-oriented** (or 'subject-centred') property. For example, the verb *to meet* includes movement on the part of the subject. It is natural, then, to say the first example following, if the meeting is accidental, but the second is not so reasonable.

> I met your girlfriend in the bookstore.
> ! your girlfriend met me in the bookstore.

This second sentence is unusual because it suggests that the girl came to the speaker as part of a previous arrangement.

---

Q.   In these examples, who is the more affected by the event?
>    I ran into Professor Jones in the Delinquent Tax Office.
>    ! Professor Jones ran into me in the Delinquent Tax Office.[1]

---

Such orientations are common in language. Japanese, for example, is rather rich in this sort of verb. A typical example is Japanese *morau* [receive], which expresses a receiving event from the standpoint of the subject, typically the speaker [Spk]. Although it is normal to say 'Spk-wa Tarō-ni baiku-o moratta' [I received a bike from Tarō], it is impossible to turn this around: *'Tarō-wa Spk-ni baiku-o moratta' [Tarō received a bike from me]. It is possible to use a subject that is not [Spk], e.g. 'Tarō-wa nambaa-wan-o [# 1] moratta' [Tarō got first place], but then it is understood that the speaker is somehow related to or identifies himself with the subject − Tarō might be his brother, for example, or his student. In purely objective writing such as news reporting, a neutral verb without subject-orientation (e.g. *ataeru*) must be used, as in 'Tarō-wa nambaa-wan-o ataerareta'.

In syntax, the most common way to have an orientation towards the object is to make the sentence passive. Although there is nothing wrong with 'I was hit by the boxer', it is quite strange to say ?'The boxer was hit by me.' The problem with this is that the pronoun for the most prominent person in the conversation, the speaker, has been pushed off the stage by *the boxer*, as it were, to where it cannot play a role in syntactic processes. The importance of the subject is shown, for example, by reflexive pronouns like the following which identify with the subject, regardless of what nominal it contains.

> Mary told John about her<u>self</u>.
> ? Mary told John about him<u>self</u>.

> John was told by Mary about himself.
> * John was told by Mary about herself.

This notion of viewpoint or **orientation** is not restricted only to verbs; it is fundamental to understanding what some kinds of adverbial expressions are used to describe, as in these examples.

> John sold that old car to Bill out of kindness.
> Bill bought that old car from John out of kindness.

Q.   In the sentences above, who is being kind?[2]

You might think that *to buy* and *to sell* describe one and the same situation, so that there ought to be no difference in what these sentences mean. If we take a closer look at the adverbial *out of kindness*, however, we find that it was John who was being kind to Bill in the first sentence, and quite the reverse in the second. This sort of adverbial phrase depicts the attitude of the subject of the sentence; it is subject-oriented. Some other adverbial expressions that are similarly subject-oriented are:

| | | |
|---|---|---|
| willingly (un-) | on purpose | carefully |
| reluctantly | in revenge | deliberately |
| gladly | intentionally | |

At the end of a sentence, these describe its 'deep' or 'logical' subject, what would be the subject if the sentence were not passive, so making a sentence passive does not change this connection. The following examples are not very different.

> John hit Billy on purpose.
> Billy was hit by John on purpose.

At the 'centre' of a sentence (i.e. at the special place for adverbs right after the first auxiliary verb), however, the adverbs in the first column can also describe the 'surface' subject, the actual subject of the sentence as it stands. Thus the following examples are ambiguous.

> Sister Mary was reluctantly interviewed by John Knowsey.
> Little Pete was willingly bathed by his elder sister.

These subject-oriented verbs contrast sharply with other, **speaker-oriented** adverbs such as the following:

| frankly | honestly | regrettably |
| hopefully | fortunately | to my sorrow |
| strangely | luckily | to our surprise |

These express the speaker's comments about the sentence. That is, they show his relationship to the **proposition**, the idea discussed.

hopefully, the Tigers will beat the Giants.
hopefully, the Giants will beat the Tigers.

Since *hopefully* can be paraphrased as 'I hope that . . .', the speaker of the first of these examples must be a Tigers fan, and a Giants fan must be the speaker of the second.

There is an important difference, then, between subject-orientation and speaker-orientation. This difference was seen most clearly in sentence adverbs, and we saw besides that some of the subject-oriented ones could be oriented towards the surface subject as well as the logical subject. We shall see these orientations again in Chapter 6, for the 'capacity' modal verbs like *can, dare not* are subject-oriented, while the 'epistemic' modals like *must have* are speaker-oriented. Let us now apply this notion of orientation to requests.

## 'Please, . . .' and '. . ., please'

This notion of orientation is also useful to understand the nature of the word *please*. This adverb is not just a semantically empty marker that adds a polite flavour to requests (in fact, politeness in English – giving freedom of choice to the addressee – is not shown so much by *please* as by 'Could you . . .' or 'Would you . . .'). Rather *please* is a way to note that the action is to benefit the speaker, and that she will be obliged if the request is properly carried out. You can use *please*, then, in requests, pleas and wishes, as in (a) below, but using it in giving suggestions, advice or permission, as in (b) – an error that some foreign learners make – is strange or even weird in English, as the addressee rather than the speaker is to benefit from the action.

(a)  please wash the dishes.                    [a request]
     will you please wash the dishes?           [a strong command!]
     please let me go with you, mummy.          [a plea]

|  |  | please make yourself comfortable. | [an invitation] |
|  |  | a cup of coffee, please. | [an order] |
| (b) | * | why don't you please stay in bed. | [suggestion] |
|  | * | you can please go home now. | [permission] |
|  | * | please add only salt, and fry on a low heat. | [directions on package] |
|  | * | please take two pills when you feel hungry. | [recommendation by doctor] |

These last examples come from English misused in Japan, apparently in imitation of their *doozo* [if you would like], like French *s'il vous plaît*. This is a common polite marker but shows benefit for the addressee, who is the subject in this sort of sentence. In contrast, the use of *please* at the beginning of a sentence is a mark that the speaker is seeking a favour. This is no doubt why it is odd in the (b) examples.

In fact, *please* is very curious. At the end of a sentence, pronounced very long as if it were two syllables, *plea-eese*, it expresses exasperation and is often a form of begging appropriate for people who are in a very weak position, e.g. prisoners, beggars or children. If it is pronounced normally at the end of the sentence, it is quite the opposite, as at the beginning of Shaw's *Major Barbara*: 'Don't repeat my words please.' There it suggests that the speaker is in control, for it expresses his right to ask or even demand the action. If that is not true, using *please* this way can be very insulting. In both cases it expresses a 'push' by the speaker for action, as we shall see shortly for imperative–suffixes in general, but they express very different perceptions of the speaker's status.

| can you let me out, plea-eese? | Spk = prisoner |
| BUT: |
| may I speak with Dr Strange, please. | Spk = caller, to a secretary |
| have some more cake, please. | Spk = the cook or host |
| could you open the door, please? | Spk = the boss! |

This last one, for example, would be quite reasonable if said by my boss; it implies that the speaker wants it and has the right to ask for it. If you said it in my office, I would be insulted and angry, even though it has the softness of using 'Could you . . .'. You could say it, however, if your hands were full, carrying a box of books for me, for you are doing me a favour which gives you (temporarily) extra rights.

---

Q.  From whom would the following be appropriate? Why?
      Please be quiet.   Be quiet, please.
      Be quiet, plea-eese.[3]

---

Whichever way it is used, then, we see that *please* has an orientation towards the speaker, quite unlike Japanese *doozo* or French *s'il vous plaît* which are oriented towards the subject.


## Benefit for subject

Benefit for the subject can also be found in the informal way of speaking: 'have a . . . [Vb]', such as 'have a walk, have a nap, have a drink'. What is the difference, for example, between 'to drink' and 'to have a drink' (*to take* may be more common in North America, as in 'take a walk', where other English speakers commonly use *to have*)?

> she drank some water.
> she had a drink of water.

Besides the difference in style – that the second is colloquial – there is some semantic difference. The second type, with *have a*, implies that the subject enjoyed drinking water; drinking it made her feel better. The same goes for 'have a bit, a chew, a lick', which all suggest something pleasant to eat. On the other hand, the straight and simple sentences like the first have no such suggestion and can be used in any context, whether the subject likes it or not, and whether or not the situation is formal. Thus one can never *'have a drink of poison', though it is quite possible to speak of 'drinking some poison'. The subject orientation is shown by the possibility of saying 'Elvis had a chew of tobacco', even though the speaker doesn't like chewing tobacco (it's horrible, even to smokers like me!).

Incidentally, the best way to remember things like this is to note that *to have a Vb* both is [informal] and indicates [enjoyment by the subject]. The other, **plain** (or 'unmarked', Chapter 2) sentence is used in any other situation. This sort of arrangement, with one special and one plain way to speak, is very common in semantics.

This property of being pleasant to the subject (perhaps the same element as [Pls] in Chapter 3) is thus seen in expressions like 'have a walk, a jog, a stroll, a swim', and in England 'a play' or 'a lie-down'. We see, then, why it is a strange speaker who would say \*'have a work'. In English, work is understood as something unpleasant, and [Neg-Pls] is part of the meaning of that word. 'Have a go at doing this' or 'Have a try' suggests that the subject will enjoy it and thus that it will not be unpleasant. However, this pattern is only for verbs that are masquerading as nouns; real nouns after *to have* do not have this pleasant orientation towards the subject, as in 'have an operation' or 'have a problem'.

## Other orientations

This notion of orientation towards the subject can be extended to the pairs of adjectives on the left below that give problems to most learners of English. The ones that derive from verbs (Vb+), however, form an easy-to-remember system that extends naturally to the plain adjectives (Aj).

|      | [Stms]        | [Expr]        | related Vb  |
| ---- | ------------- | ------------- | ----------- |
| Vb+: | pleasing      | pleased       | to please   |
|      | surprising    | surprised     | to surprise |
|      | distressing   | distressed    | to distress |
| Aj:  | bothersome    | bothered      | to bother   |
|      | delightful    | delighted     | to delight  |
|      | troublesome   | troubled      | to trouble  |
|      | suspicious to | suspicious of | to suspect  |
|      | pleasant      | happy         |             |

Although both types are oriented towards their subjects, they differ greatly in what their subjects can designate. The first of each pair takes a stimulus [Stms] as a subject, the event or the thing that produces the emotion, as in the first example below. Quite to the contrary in the second of each pair, the subject points to the person or animal that receives or experiences [Expr] the emotion, with much the same meaning.

> this news is quite distressing (to me).
> I am quite distressed (at this news).

The difference between these sorts of pairs, then, is that the first is oriented to the object or event that causes the emotion, [Stms], while the second is oriented to the experiencer of it. The proper forms can be easily remembered if they are seen as passive or progressive modifications of the single pattern that English has for such verbs of emotion: the subject is the stimulus [Stms] and the object is the experiencer [Expr].

The examples deriving from a verb (Vb+) and most deriving from an adjective (Aj) have the suffix *-ed* when describing the experiencer, so they look like passive verb forms. They really are passives if *by* is used, as in the second sentence below.

> I am distressed (at this news).    Aj
> I am distressed (by this news).    Passive of 'This news
>                                    distresses me.'

That is, the 'distressed' in the first sentence here is an adjective, while this same word in the second sentence (together with *to be*) marks the passive form of 'This news distresses me.' As the only difference is in the choice of preposition, when the preposition is absent, 'I am distressed', there is no way to tell which it is. Reasonably enough, there is not much difference between these forms; the second, the real passive, describes more the event of receiving or perceiving the emotion, while the first (not a passive form but an adjective) focuses more on the emotion itself and the state of the [Expr]–subject. The true adjectives may also have this *-ed*, as if they were passives, but each goes with a preposition that must be learned, often *at* but sometimes another, as in *bored with* or *interested in*.

On the other hand, the verbal forms oriented towards the [Stms]–subject all have an *-ing* that looks like the progressive suffix (the *-ing* in 'You are read*ing* this now', see Chapter 7), as in the second sentence below. Here, the progressive form depicts clearly the momentary event of receiving the emotion, while the identical adjective describes the emotional state that results.

> this news is distressing (to me).    Aj
> this news is distressing me.         Progressive of 'This news
>                                      distresses me.'

Perhaps the easiest way to remember how to use these pairs, then, is simply to remember that most English verbs that describe emotions ($Vb_{emo}$), such as *to shock, horrify, invigorate, discourage, encourage, soothe, bore, interest, disgust, please, surprise, distress, thrill, intrigue*, take subjects that describe the cause of the emotion [Stms], and the living being [Ani] that experiences [Expr] the emotion is referred to by their objects, encapsulated in the following format. As shown below it, the progressive form (-*ing*) keeps, but the passive form (-*ed/-en*) reverses, the order of the subject and object.

[Stms] Vb$_{emo}$ [Expr.Ani]

Progressive:    [Stms] be Vb$_{emo}$-ing [Expr]
Passive:        [Expr] be Vb$_{emo}$-ed (by [Stms])

The two adjective forms differ from these only in taking a preposition *to* for the experiencer or *at, in, of* or *with* for the stimulus, or no complement at all, and do not have the idea of [momentary] that the true progressive and passive often have with these verbs. Although these are all subject-oriented, the subject can stand for different sorts of things. They gain different orientations because the subject can express different relationships with the verb or adjective, marked by its suffix.

Sometimes, there are even two different orientations through the subject that are possible with the same form of a verb. Compare each pair of sentences below.

1. (a) this river abounds *with* man-eating fish!
   (b) man-eating fish abound *in* this river!
2. (a) your garden is swarming *with* killer bees!
   (b) killer bees are swarming *in* your garden.
3. (a) the fields grow rich *with* grass.
   (b) grass grows rich *in* the fields.
4. (a) the park is littered *with* empty cans.
   (b) empty cans are littered *in* the park.

We know which way to understand this sort of example by the nouns and the prepositions with which they occur. The (a) examples are all oriented towards a container and the things that are there are marked with the preposition *with* after the verb. The (b) examples, on the other hand, are oriented towards the things in the container, leaving the container [Cnt] marked with a preposition of location, *in* (or *on*, etc.) as we shall see more systematically in Chapter 9.

Orientations can be important in yet other ways. In the examples above, if the thing oriented towards is marked definite, we understand it as [all of them/it], so from 4(a) we would expect cans to be found all over the park, not suggested in 4(b). If we add *the* to 2(b) 'The killer bees are swarming in your garden', it changes the meaning from [some] to [all of them], though no such change is induced by adding *the* to 2(a): 'Your garden is swarming with *the* killer bees.' Why this should be so is not yet well understood, but it may well be a general interaction between orientation and the semantic element [Cnt] that relates the container to the contained, for we find the same thing happening in other languages.

We also find it in English when this element [Cnt] relates the object of a verb to a second complement. Notice how the (a) and (b) examples here differ in being complete.

5. (a) he has loaded your truck with my furniture.
   (b) he has loaded my furniture on to your truck.
6. (a) I'm going to spray that wall with red paint.
   (b) I'm going to spray the red paint on to that wall.

5(a) means that your truck is full though I may still have furniture left to carry, while 5(b) says that all my furniture is on your truck, and leaves it open whether there might be space for more.

We see then how the orientation towards the subject can be expanded into various specific orientations, when the subject is used to express specific relationships with the main verb of the sentence. Let us return, then, to the very specific area of speaker and addressee in making requests and other similar speech acts.

## Making requests

Although we can say that *please* adds a polite flavour to a sentence because its use implies that the speaker and the addressee are not too close, we saw above how it can be used to show obligations, weakness or rights of the speaker. What many consider to be real politeness in requests or commands, what we can call 'consideration', is to allow that the addressee has the freedom to do it or not, as they like. We seldom use a bare command like the first example below, then, except for policemen and criminals or soldiers with guns – or if we are in a big hurry, say, to a co-worker, as if something bad will happen unless it is done quickly. In any normal circumstance we will be likely to add at least 'Would/won't you ...' at the beginning, as in the second example, which is an ordinary polite request, or a 'tag', as in the third, which is a bit more familiar.

open the door.
would you open the door?
open the door, would you?

What makes the first example impolite is denying any choice to the addressee, for something he might not want to do. If he can see it is to his benefit, of course, there is no need to offer choice, and it is misleading to add *please* or any other marker to examples such as following.

have a good time!
take your time.
look at this.
enjoy your supper.
make yourself at home.

On the following page is a 'map' or graph of the sorts of expressions we commonly use in adding politeness or strength to a request or command. The different expressions that it makes possible make the request 'tentative' or respectful (in the respect section), lower the speaker, or raise the addressee (the status section), or add force to the request (the 'push' section).

This sort of a 'morpheme order graph'[4] is like a road map with one-way streets (the arrows). You must begin at **start** and find a route to an end on the right. This particular graph has two ends; the upper one is for eliciting permission and the lower one for eliciting action. Each expression is like a village through which you can pass only if the speaker has said that, and is semantically different from the other villages (expressions) that you pass by. Only a few of the meanings are hinted at in the chart, but it will guide you in discovering what the differences are.

Q. Follow the arrows on this graph that give the following expressions. The graph has some numbers added in circles to help show a route (as one describes a route in a Japanese city!). Add these numbers between the words where you find them.
   (a) I wonder if you would be kind enough to open the door?
       perhaps I could trouble you to pass the salt?
       please be so kind as to shut up.
   (b) perhaps I might be allowed to leave for a moment?
       I wonder whether you think I might leave early.
   Which of the above are requests for action, and which requests for permission?[5]

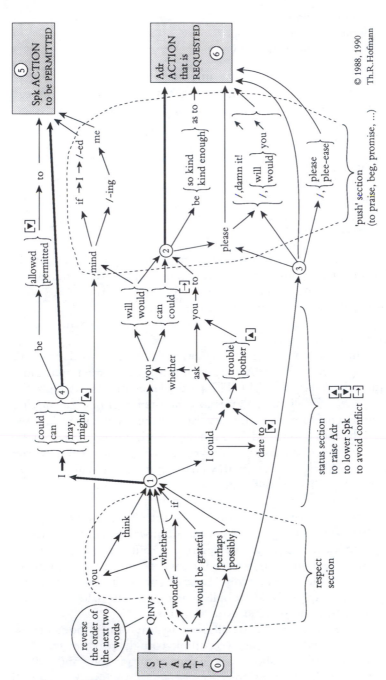

Morpheme order graph for politeness formulas

© 1988, 1990
Th.R. Hofmann

Each choice made in following this map makes possible some words and excludes others, and their meanings in these polite formulas are seldom explained well in dictionaries as they focus on descriptive meaning. Their general types of social or interpersonal meanings are shown by which section each belongs to, but they differ from each other within each section. *Dare to*, for example, lowers the speaker [▼], while *bother you to* raises the addressee [▲], and together they would express a rather large vertical distance. The use of *can/could* to [avoid conflict] [→] escapes the possibility of a direct refusal by the addressee, by allowing her to say that she can't, rather than won't, do it, and using the indirect form of a modal (see Chapter 6) *would*, *could*, *might* instead of the direct form *will*, *can*, *may* is tentative or doubtful and thus deferential, making it easier for the addressee to refuse.

The heavier arrows are the frequently used routes, the highways so to speak, and the language learner will be well advised to stay on them and avoid the byways until she has seen them used a few times. The symbol 'Qinv' means that you will have to make a question with the next two elements (technically they will have an 'inverted' order), so 'Qinv you would' stands for 'Would you . . .?' as in the (c) examples below. The symbol '/ ' means to hold on to that expression for a while; before a suffix it means to attach the suffix to the next verb, while '/, xyz' means to attach the form *xyz* at the end of the sentence ((d) examples).

---

Q.    Trace the derivations of the following in the same graph.[6]

    (c) would you be kind enough to open the door?

        might I be allowed to leave for a moment?

    (d) would you mind me smoking here?

        please open the door, will you?

        open the door, damn it.    (a command)

---

In making requests, suggestions or commands in any language, the relationship between the speaker and the addressee is especially important. Languages thus have ways of expressing the speaker's perception of this relationship, which may be more or less obligatory, and tend to become formulaic. Three general types of non–descriptive meaning are notable in the common English formulas: tentativeness or respect for the other person, his relative status, and the strength with which he is 'pushed' into acceding to the request. The first two, at least, are commonly found in languages and may even, as in older Japanese,[7] be required in all complete sentences.

---

Q.   Why would it be strange to say 'I wonder whether you think you could be so kind as to bum me a cigarette'? What is the longest (reasonable) request you can make with this graph? Is 'Would you please be so kind as to shut the door, damn it?' a request?[8]

---

There are a few other English formulas for cooperative action between speaker and addressee. They do not express much about the relationship between speaker and addressee but do suggest some benefit for the addressee. The last one, however, cannot be used to superiors as it treats the addressee as an equal. To a professor, or a judge, you had better use a request marked for their status, e.g. 'Would it be possible to . . .?'

Offer:        Shall I . . .?
Suggestion:   Why don't you . . .?
              How about /-ing . . .?
Proposal:     Let's . . . .

## Summary

We saw at the beginning that some words have an **orientation** towards the speaker of the sentence while others are oriented towards the subject. This was especially clear for sentence adverbs, but we also looked at words that imply benefit to the speaker (*please*) and others imputing benefit to the subject ('have a —' and Fr: *s'il vous plaît*). Later we saw that orientation towards the subject can multiply into many special orientations because the subject itself can express various types of relations between the nominal and the verb that will be expanded in Chapter 11. In one pattern at which we looked closely, the subject relation could designate [Stms], that which triggers an emotion, or [Expr], that which experiences the emotion.

Lastly we saw how requests and allied ventures are commonly marked for aspects of the relationship between speaker and addressee, in a sense oriented to both. These politeness formulas generally take, however, the addressee as the subject, so we remain with two basic orientations, towards the speaker and towards the subject.

## Notes and answers

1. The subject in both cases: the speaker in the first sentence and the professor in the second. (NB: *to bump into, to run into* <*a person*> are often used for [to meet], in North America at least, despite their basic meanings, for their aspect of [accidental, unplanned] and thus surprise for the subject. *To meet* is often used this way too but is unmarked for intentionality.)
2. The subject in both cases: John in the first sentence and Bill in the second.
3. One student to another; the librarian to a student; a student with an exam coming up, to his room-mates. The first is a (strong) simple request, the second by a person who has the right to tell the other, and the third is begging.
4. Technically, a 'morpheme order graph', a close (linguistic) relative to a 'finite state machine' that you may meet in studying computers or mathematics.
5. (a) (0) I wonder if (1) you would (2) be kind enough to (6) open the door? (0) Perhaps (1) I could trouble you to (2)(6) pass the salt? (0)(3) Please be so kind as to (6) shut up. (b) (0) Perhaps (1) I might (4) be allowed to (5) leave for a moment? (0) I wonder whether you think (1) I might (5) leave early. Actions requested in (a), permission requested in (b).
6. (c) (0) Qinv (1) you would (2) be kind enough to (6) open the door. (0) Qinv (1) I might (4) be allowed to (5) leave for a moment. (d) (0) Qinv (1) you would mind /-ing me (5) smoke here. (0)(3) please /,will-you (6) open the door. (0)(3) /,damn-it (6) open the door.
7. Younger Japanese pay much less attention to the marking of status, but respect or 'distance' between speaker and addressee remains obligatory in every complete sentence.
8. It is very tentative (two tentative markers − it must be a stranger who looks impressive) and then 'pushes' him to 'bum' (slang for *to lend*) a cigarette. The longest I have found is: 'I wonder whether you think I could dare to ask whether you

could please be kind enough as to. . . .' It is so 'pushy', though superficially polite, that I hesitate to call it a request.

## Keywords

subject, adverbs, politeness.

## Further reading

Kuno, Susumu *Functional syntax* (1987) Chicago: UC Press.
Jackendoff, Ray *Semantic Interpretation in Generative Grammar* (1972) Cambridge, Mass.: MIT Press, Chapter 5.
Wierzbicka, A. 'Why Can You Have a Drink When You Can't Have an Eat?' (1982) *Language* **58**: 753–99.

• politeness
Brown, P. and Levinson, S. 'Universals in Language Usage: Politeness Phenomena' (1978) in Goody, E. (ed.), *Questions and Politeness: Strategies in Social Interaction.*
Goffman, Erving *Relations in Public* (1971) New York: Basic Books.
Haverkate, Henk *Speech Acts, Speakers and Hearers* (1984) Amsterdam: Benjamins.
Kageyama, T. and Hofmann, Th. R. 'Please, Please, Plea-eese' (1986) *The Rising Generation* 132.8: 372.
Leech, Geoffrey *Principles of Pragmatics* (1983) London: Longman.

## Exercises with orientations

1. Determine whether the following adverbs are oriented towards the subject of the sentence, its speaker, or ambiguously, to either. Make an example for each one.

    (a) secretly            (e) thankfully
    (b) honestly           (f) with a little luck
    (c) understandably    (g) luckily
    (d) miserably

2. Explain the difference in meaning between each pair of sentences.
   (a) Sadly, Bill declined the teacher's generous offer.
   (a') Bill declined the teacher's generous offer sadly.
   (b) After shopping, his daughter counted the change correctly.
   (b') After shopping, his daughter correctly counted the change.
   (c) The medic unwillingly examined the late patient.
   (c') The late patient was unwillingly examined by the medic.

3. Explain (expand) the meaning of the adverb in the following examples and then decide which role (e.g. deep subject, Spk, etc.) it describes. For example, 'Janet tripped me accidentally' says that it was an accident [not intentional] on Janet's part, and the adverb describes the subject (both deep and surface) of the sentence.
   (a) Did Bob hit Abdul intentionally?
   (b) Was Abdul hit by Pierre intentionally?
   (c) Did Taro get himself hit by Pierre intentionally?
   (d) Frankly, his new book is trash.
   (e) Frankly, is his new book trash?
   (f) Seriously, are you going to marry an actress?
   (g) She was stabbed accidentally.
   (h) Hopefully, we will both be recommended for promotion.

4. With a future event, *will* depicts a Spk-prediction, while the present tense shows that the event is already accepted as a fact (see Chapter 7). Based on the answers in (1), which of the following are strange, and why?
   (a) Luckily, he arrives tomorrow.
   (b) With a little luck, he arrives tomorrow.
   (c) With a little luck, he will arrive tomorrow.

5. Supposing you are a university student, which of the following requests could you use to: (1) the professor whose office it is, (2) a passer-by, (3) a new student that is coming with you, if: (A) your hands are full carrying things (for the professor), (B) you merely want to go in, (C) the professor has just said 'Come in' but it seems locked? (Make a table with '1A, 1A, 3A, 1B, 2B . . .' across the top, using '+,−' for possible and impossible.)
   (a) Could you open the door\, please.
   (b) Open the door\.
   (c) Please open the door\.
   (d) Please open the door/.

   (e) Could you open the door\?
   (f) Could you open the door/?
6. Explain why the following examples are strange.
   (a) Can I use your pen a moment? *Yes, please.
   (b) *Shall I please open the door for you?
   (c) *Have a bite of this overcooked steak, will you?
   (d) *Could I dare to ask you to sit down, please?
   (e) !I wonder if I might dare to ask you to be so kind as to sit down.
7. Add a suffix to the indicated adjectives to make reasonable sentences.
   (a) I'm glad that your new tutor is such a (delight__) person.
   (b) Mr Thatcher is annoyed with his (trouble__) colleague in the office next to his.
   (c) He doesn't seem to feel (regret__) at all for what he did.
   (d) Clark Kent received my valentine with a (surprise__) look.
   (e) The audience began to fall asleep listening to the (tire__) speech.
   (f) The lecturer seemed to be rather (bore__) with it all.
   (g) Father nodded his approval with a (please__) look on his face.
8. Correct the errors in the following sentences.
   (a) *The bride was blushing at the embarrassed questions the reporters kept asking.
   (b) *She was in total despair at the unsatisfied results of her experiment.
   (c) They are crying for help! *We've got to save those dangerous girls.
   (d) *You must have been very painful when you had that tooth out.
9. As with the example 'The garden swarms with bees' and 'Bees swarm in the garden', locatives can often change places with another actant. As you no doubt noted, the locative preposition is always lost in subject position, and it commonly goes in object position as well. For the following, make such exchanges, supplying a missing preposition if need be.
   (a) The librarian piled up huge books on the front desk.
   (b) My mother spread the table with her best tablecloth.
   (c) The room filled with smoke.
   (d) Our cheers echoed for five minutes in the vast stadium.
   (e) Our job is to clear the road of snow as soon as possible.
   (f) Classical citations are sprinkled throughout his new book.

# CHAPTER 6

# Modal Verbs

'You may not [do it]' denies a request 'May I do that?', but to deny 'He may have come' it won't do to say 'He may not have [come]' for both these might be true. Instead, we must say 'He can't have come' or 'He must not have come.' That does not mean, however, that either *can* or *may* has the same meaning as *must*. How are these words related?

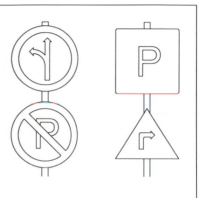

Then again, what are the differences in saying the following?

| | |
|---|---|
| I shall leave tomorrow. | I am going to leave tomorrow. |
| I will leave tomorrow. | I am leaving tomorrow. |
| I am to leave tomorrow. | I leave tomorrow. |

English has a group of words called '**modal** verbs' or just **modals** – *can, may, shall, will, must* and some others – that have a special place in English syntax. Often it is not at all easy to decide which modal to use in a given context, or if any one should be used. Although they are easy and natural for people who have grown up speaking English, books and books have been written about their meanings and when to use them, and still foreigners seldom get them right. Linguists and grammarians have even been known to fight over what they mean, so although we will find some simple explanations, you should not be surprised to find others, especially in older books.

One simple but deceptive fact is that the first four of these modals have an alternative or 'indirect' form that is used in reporting what someone said or thought (or when talking about an impossible situation — as in the question following), as shown in the equivalences below. The other modals lack a special form for this, so either the same form is used or it must be replaced by a word that is not a modal.

$$
\text{he} \left\{ \begin{array}{l} \text{said} \\ \text{thought} \\ \text{wondered} \end{array} \right\} , \text{'I} \left\{ \begin{array}{l} \text{can} \\ \text{may} \\ \text{shall} \\ \text{will} \end{array} \right\} \text{go'.} \longleftrightarrow \text{he} \left\{ \begin{array}{l} \text{said that} \\ \text{thought that} \\ \text{wondered if} \end{array} \right\} \text{he} \left\{ \begin{array}{l} \text{could} \\ \text{might} \\ \text{should} \\ \text{would} \end{array} \right\} \text{go.}
$$

Q.   These indirect forms are also used for the 'counterfactual subjunctive' that expresses doubt or non-belief of the situation described. What are the forms needed to put *can*, *may*, *shall*, *will*, *must* in non-factual frames such as 'If you __ come, everything would work out' or 'I wish that you __ come'?[1]

These 'indirect' forms used to be called 'preterite' or 'past', but that was deceptive. Other preterite forms in the language are freely used for past time events but these forms can be used that way only in a few specific uses. Except for *could* and some special cases, modal forms depict present possibilities, obligations, conclusions or whatever. As a result, these underused forms such as *should, might* have been put to new uses, and with other changes that have occurred there is no longer any simple way to describe the meanings of the English modals.

In fact, many attempts have been made to find central or basic meanings for each modal that can explain their common and effortless use. Other studies end up with three or four meanings for each modal. Most recent work has tried to explain the variations of meaning for each modal on the pragmatic factors of Chapter 14, but may not be helpful in deciding which meaning a modal has in a given context, or which one to use when. A useful description lies between these extremes, where we can find some system mixed with some evolutionary remnants.

Having identified the 'indirect' forms used for reported speech and non-factual situations, we can put them aside to concentrate on the heart of the problem. A second step to simplify our study of modals is to recognize that some special idioms include modals, such as the following polite formulas seen in Chapter 5. (Here the indirect forms are used for tentative, doubtful and thus deferential proposals.) These can also be left aside, for their effective meanings are most accurately described by the circumstances when these formulas are used.

|  | --- offers ---- | ----------- requests ----------- | |
|---|---|---|---|
|  |  | *(plain)* | *(conflict - avoiding)* |
| *(plain)* | Shall I ... ? | Will you ... ? | Can you ... ? |
| *(tentative)* | Should I ... ? | Would you ... ? | Could you ... ? |


## Future

First, in the area of most confusion, are *shall* and *will*; how is future expressed in English, and what do these words mean? Ask a dozen experts and you'll get a dozen answers, if not more. In speaking, fortunately, we don't have much of a problem. We use *(be) going to*, commonly pronounced something like *gŏnna* for simple future, and the contraction __'ll to depict one event as later than another. Neither is appropriate to formal writing, however.

Another simple fact is that when it is emphasized, *shall* has a meaning something like [the speaker (Spk) promises/vows that . . .]. For example, when the Japanese pushed MacArthur out of the Philippines, his 'I shall return' meant that if he did not return, his honour and self-pride would be seriously wounded if not utterly destroyed. Although it is rare, if anyone ever says to you 'You SHALL\ finish it' I would recommend doing so – the speaker's honour is bound to that goal, and non-compliance will doubtless lead to a serious breach in your relationship. On the other hand, the indirect form of this modal, *should*, is now a common way to say that the subject has an obligation to do something – what we once used *ought to* for. We shall have to put this off for a bit, however, for it is not simply a marker of future time.

For the simple future in writing, where contractions like __'ll and *going to* feel too much like speaking, most people in North America use *will*, but the old British rule of using *shall* if the speaker is the subject ([Spk]: *I* or *we*) is still alive in the Commonwealth, among careful writers at least. In general, writers use *shall* this way when they want to impress their readers but not if they want to be friendly.

In a general way, *will* marks a prediction by the speaker while *shall* expresses his guarantee or promise, so that this British rule is simply: 'One should not merely predict his own actions as if he can't be sure of what his body will do, but rather he should promise them. Conversely, one will wisely avoid promising others' actions.' If you are careful not to use these modals except where you could predict or promise, you can be pretty sure that no mistakes will be made.

In contrast to these, the '*going-to*-future' is not a prediction or a promise but a self-assured statement, so an official weather forecast could hardly say 'It is going to rain this afternoon' – unless it is already starting to rain. Because it expresses so much confidence, we cannot use it except for things we are completely sure of, like 'We are all going to die some day.' The things that we can be this sure of are mostly things that are just about to happen, as in 'I'm going to leave', so *(be) going to* usually functions as a near-future if there is no indication to the contrary. As in speaking, *will* is more and more reserved for placing the time of an event at a specified time (R of the next chapter, SLR), though it has some special uses.[2] The other ways to express future time will have to be left to Chapter 7 on time and tense.

## Capacity modals

The **capacity** or 'dynamic' modals are easiest, and seldom give problems. First, for physical or mental capacity we normally use *can, can't, have to* or *need to*. These last two are really ordinary verbs for they take *to* afterwards and 'agree' with the subject by ending with *-s* for singular subjects other than [Spk] or [Adr] (i.e. for [Sng.Awa] subjects).

[Psb] this little pig *can* eat roast beef.    I *can* lift a car.
[Imp] this little pig *can't* fly.                   I *can't* get there by five.
[Nec] this little pig *has to* eat something. I *need to* breathe.

These describe the physical or mental capacities of the subject of the sentence (they are 'subject-oriented' as described in Chapter 5), and so we can label them **ability** modals. *Can* is used for an action that is **possible** [Psb], while *can't, cannot, can not* are used for something that is **impossible** [Imp]. If, however, some action is **necessary** [Nec] for the subject, we use *need to* or *have to*. These facts can be summarized as in the left column of the table below, put in a logical order. In these ability usages there is no proper modal for the [Nec] cases, so I have put usual expressions (verbs with *to*) in parentheses.

| ABILITY | plain | [Pst] or [Neg-Fct] |
|---|---|---|
| [Nec] | (need to, have to) | (had to) |
| [Psb] | can | could |
| [Imp] | can't, cannot, can not | could not, couldn't |

The column on the right is for past time [Pst] as in Chapter 7, e.g. 'I could solve the problem yesterday', or for the non-factual [Neg-Fct] that we saw above, e.g. 'If I could fly, I could be there on time', as well as in reported speech. In simple statements, then, the plain forms on the left are for events at any time except in the past, i.e. present, future[3] or always, as in 'I can finish this now', 'I can leave in a half-hour' and 'I can read.'

An important point here is that *could* (like *can*) does not suggest that the action was carried out but only that the possibility was there. In fact, it is seldom used with a specific action except in the negative, for it would suggest that the action did not take place. If the event did in fact happen, we would not say *could* but *did*. This is why we do not say ★'I could have a good time at their party yesterday' if a good time was had. Rather we would use a factual statement, 'I had a good time at their party', showing that the speaker both could and did have a good time.

Although *to be able to* is a fairly accurate paraphrase of *can* in most circumstances, using it to describe a past action uncovers a clear difference; 'was able to do X' implies that X was done though with some effort probably, while 'could do X' says only that it was possible, and with a specific action, implies that X was not done.

---

Q. Which of the following can take *could, was able to*?
The day the water level went down,
(a) my mongoose __ cross the river and find many snakes.
(b) I __ cross the river without a boat, but I didn't even go out.[4]

---

We do not speak of psychological or emotional capacity very much today, but in older times it was more common to distinguish it from ability using **capability** modals, as in these examples.

> he *dare not* show his face here again.
> she *can't help* dream*ing* of what she'll do with her prize money.

The first describes a person who has too much fear to do something, while the second depicts one who is unable to resist doing something. There is no special form other than *can* for saying that one has the capability of acting, so this usage can be charted as below. The */-ing* is in the chart to indicate that the next verb must have an *-ing* suffix, as in the second example.

| CAPABILITY | [Neg-Pst] | [Pst] or [Neg-Fct] |
|---|---|---|
| [Nec] | can't help /-ing | couldn't help /-ing |
| [Psb] | can | could |
| [Imp] | dare not | dared not |

The negative marker, *not* or *-n't*, must be part of the lexical items for [Imp] and [Nec] in these cases, for positive forms like ★'He dare come here' or ★'She can help dreaming of it' are meaningless. Questions, however, are like negative sentences in many respects, even without a negative marker, so seemingly positive forms are possible in questions.

> how dare he show his face here?
> can he really help dreaming?

However, *dare* is now quite rare as a modal (but alive and well as a verb, with *to* following it), and indeed all these capability uses are no longer common. Of course, the modal *can* is common for it is also used to express ability.

---

Q.  As we saw in Chapter 3, negatives take *any* instead of *some* for an indefinite complement, as in 'She isn't engaged to anyone/★someone.' What about *can't help /-ing*, as in 'I can't help loving ___'? Is it negative or positive semantically?[5]

---

Together with the ability modals, these capability modals form the group of capacity modals, sometimes called 'dynamic'. They may describe what is possible [Psb] for the subject, *can*, as well as what is impossible [Imp], *can't*, or necessary [Nec], *have to*. If either of these latter is due to a lack of spiritual or emotional capacity, then we can use the capability modals *dare not, can't help* to mark that.

## Logical modality

Both kinds of capacity modality, ability and capability, as well as the other linguistic types of modality to follow, show the same contrasts in the vertical dimension in these tables, the difference between necessary [Nec], possible [Psb] and impossible [Imp]. Possibility and necessity are favourite notions of logic, symbolized with □ and ◇ respectively, and are studied formally as 'modal logic'. As we saw in Chapter 3, human languages typically have a third term, impossibility [Imp] in the case of modals, where the relations between these three logical notions can be stated:

Psb = Neg-Imp          Nec = Imp-Neg

Q. Both [Psb] and [Nec] are defined here in terms of [Imp], but as [Imp] is seldom used in logic, how can the relation between [Psb] and [Nec] be stated directly? (Assume that if A = Neg-B, then B = Neg-A.)[6]

Possibility and impossibility [Psb] and [Imp] are contradictory (Chapter 3); if one is true the other is false, and vice-versa. Thus to say 'It is *not true* [Neg] that she *can* [Psb] solve that problem' implies that 'She *can't* [Imp] solve it', and vice-versa, to say it is *not true* that you *can't* get top marks implies saying that you *can* get them. On the other hand, [Nec] and [Imp] are contraries; they cannot be true at the same time but both might be false. As noted in Chapter 3, this is also called 'internal negation' for the negative marker is inside the scope of the modal (unlike the previous case of 'external' negation), and this sometimes makes for difficult examples. To say 'He *dare not* [Imp] *not* [Neg] study' is to say that 'He *can't help* [Nec] studying' and vice-versa, 'She *can't help not-*answering' (i.e. remaining silent) implies 'She *dare not* answer.' These relations can be represented as below with impossibility as the central notion.

      contradictory           contrary
Psb ←——————→ Imp ←——————→ Nec

A more practical way to look at these relations is as a continuum ranging from 100 per cent [Nec] at the top, down to 0 per cent [Imp] at the bottom. We will continue to use this arrangement in this chapter, for there are some intermediate terms that we shall see later.

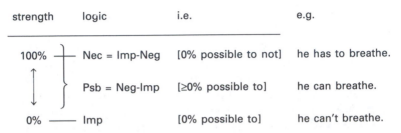

| strength | logic | i.e. | e.g. |
|---|---|---|---|
| 100% | Nec = Imp-Neg | [0% possible to not] | he has to breathe. |
| | Psb = Neg-Imp | [≥0% possible to] | he can breathe. |
| 0% | Imp | [0% possible to] | he can't breathe. |

These notions [Nec:Psb:Imp] are used in this chapter whenever these interrelations hold. The percentages on the left represent a notion of 'strength' of the modal, where both 0 per cent and 100 per cent make 'strong' statements but *can* for example is 'weak'. In some cases they can be interpreted as probability, as in the generic modals to follow.

We can call this vertical dimension 'logical modality', for it is important in the study of logic and languages do not differ significantly in it. Let us then return to 'linguistic modality', the modal contrasts that are not logical modality but cross-classify with it. Here languages show significant differences and similarities.

## Generic modals and *used to*

In English there is a **generic** modality, not used so often but nevertheless a very natural way to express general characteristics, and mastered by few foreigners. These depict something that happens generally or characteristically and are often used to express the speaker's annoyance, as in most of the examples below. So for habits, present or past, we can use expressions like the first or fourth examples below.

(1) I'*ll* spend the whole night, often enough, getting a program to run.
(2) When I lived in Toyama, it *would* often snow 1 metre in a day.
(3) Late in April, the cherry blossoms *would* all open beautifully.

(4) When I was young, she *would* always nag me to finish my homework.

(5) She *can* talk your ears off, if you don't watch out.

(6) She was in great pain and *could* get angry over the smallest thing.

We can often perceive a force of will with these modals but it is not always present, as examples (2) and (3) show, for nature has no will. Rather, these generic modals show that the speaker is affected emotionally, as the third example demonstrates well; it could be said by someone who likes cherry blossoms or, sarcastically, by one who dislikes the mess their petals will make. Of course, with human subjects we naturally assume that it must be wilful (fourth example) or habitual (fifth) on their part, to affect us so much, but it need not be so (sixth). The emotion does not have to be annoyance, as, for instance, we can say 'My mother *would* forgive and forget, whenever I did something wrong.'

This generic use of *would* has long been recognized, but its parallel *will* has escaped equal attention because *will* has so many uses, though it is sometimes called a *will* of insistence. Finding *can* is more surprising, but it belongs here as its negative is not *can't* but *won't*, as you will see if you deny the main clause in (5) or (6). Putting these facts into the sort of matrix that we found useful with capacity modals, we have:

| GENERIC | [Neg-Pst] | [Pst] | equivalent adverbs |
|---------|-----------|-------|--------------------|
| [Nec] | will | would | normally |
| [Psb] | can | could | sporadically |
| [Imp] | will not | would not | abnormally |

Q.    What are the negatives of (5), (6) and 'He can get so engrossed that he forgets to eat'? Generally two negatives are possible, one without a modal and the other with a generic modal. Can you explain the difference?[7]

It is often difficult to distinguish *will* of prediction from this *will* expressing characteristic nature, for what is characteristic but [predictable in general]? When it is stressed, or in the past, or with negative, the difference becomes clearer, or again in special circumstances such as 'Oil will float on water' or 'Boys will be boys', where a prediction of these facts would be pointless. Similarly this *can* is often difficult to distinguish from a capacity *can,* but it functions much like generic *will (would)* except that the action described is sporadic and thus not predictable, but characteristic nevertheless. In fact, it can be substituted for *will (would) often* with little change in meaning, as in (1) and (2), but it cannot be used in (4) because of the *always,* and this notion [always] cannot fit with this generic *can.* In any case, *can* and *will not* are contradictories in these generic uses, quite unlike other uses of these words.

The expression *used to* is quite different from this generic *would.* It simply means [past durative] – it 'endured' for a long time in the past – as in the examples below. Generic *would,* on the other hand, is [past characteristic], so the action must have been repeated many times. This is why it cannot replace *used to* in the examples on the left but can in the examples on the right if a (far) past time adverb is added.

| | |
|---|---|
| the garage used to be over there. | they used to study together. |
| there used to be trees here. | he used to sing dirty songs. |
| she used to like older men. | I used to smoke cigarettes. |
| this stream used to flow past my house. | |

If the action is not something that cannot continue indefinitely, as in the examples on the right, we automatically reinterpret a durative (see Chapter 7) to include many repetitions. In these cases, *used to* comes to have a meaning similar to the generic *would* but still has no suggestion of [characteristic nature], nor of annoyance, as in 'Clive used to type many pages a day when he was writing his thesis.'


## Deontic modals

We also use modals commonly to describe what is expected or demanded of us. These are **deontic** modals. The ones in the following examples depict what the speaker [Spk] or someone else makes impossible, possible or necessary for the subject.

| | |
|---|---|
| You *may* leave immediately. | You *shall* leave immediately. |

*May* is not used very much any more in this meaning, for it depicts possibility that derives from the speaker's authority. Most people use *can* instead of *may* as we prefer not to talk about authority in these democratic and egalitarian times, so even if the speaker permits X to do Y, still we would normally say 'X can Y' and use 'X may Y' only when we want to note the authority of the speaker (e.g. a teacher or a judge). Today, *may* is used mostly as an epistemic modal (to follow shortly), or as a humble formula to request permission: 'May I . . .?' Using *may* in a question suggests the reply 'You may . . .' and therefore acknowledges the authority of the person who is to give permission.

We mentioned at the beginning that 'X shall Y' expresses something like a vow or an undertaking by the speaker that X will do Y, especially if the *shall* is emphasized. It thus belongs here with these personal deontic modals.

| PERSONAL DEONTIC | authority | | promise |
| | [Spk] | [unmarked] | [Spk] |
| --- | --- | --- | --- |
| [Nec] | —— | (have to) | shall |
| [Psb] | may | can | (can) |
| [Imp] | may not | can not | shall not |

Perhaps the most common use of these today is in formally written laws and rules where the law is Spk, e.g. 'Bars *may not* serve minors, and *shall* display this fact prominently.'

Distinct from these authoritative or Spk-oriented deontic modals above, another type of deontic modal derives its force from society. Society, morality and customs make certain things obligatory, other things possible or forbidden. We have many words in this area that express finer distinctions, so we need to expand the scale of logical modality with [Apx] for [ApProXimately] or [nearly].

| You | must | arrive early. | [Nec] |
| | should | | [Apx-Nec] also: ought to |
| | can | | [Psb] |
| | shouldn't | | [Apx-Imp] also: ought not (to) |
| | must not | | [Imp] |

The effect of this expansion is that the [Apx-Nec] terms, *should* or older *ought to*, roughly [more or less necessary] or [nearly necessary], allow for exceptions if there is an excuse or a reason. That is, it is like the extreme [necessary] except that it is not so extreme. This same tolerance for exceptions is found in [Apx-Imp]. By lexical blocking (Chapter 2), [Nec] and [Imp] are left with no tolerance at all for exceptions, so *must not* is not only stronger than *should not* but is also a stronger prohibition than *may not* for this has no [Apx-Imp] contrasting term. However, the force behind these social deontics is not the speaker – he or she denies any responsibility for the stricture – but rather some aspect(s) of society, so it may well be easier to violate a *must not* in front of its speaker.

---

Q.   Given the glosses for [Apx] above, and the meaning of [Psb] from 1 per cent to 100 per cent, what might the meaning of [Apx-Psb] be? Can you find a word with this meaning?[8]

---

In English-speaking cultures there are not many occasions for telling people that they absolutely must, or must not, do something, so *should* and *should not* are much more common, and *must* is commonly found only in connecting ideas, as in 'If you want to get a good job, you *must* study hard.' Here the *if*-clause gives the source or basis from which *must* derives its force, and the other 'social' deontic modals also function this way, especially *should, ought to.*

SOCIAL DEONTIC (Aj)

| | | | |
|---|---|---|---|
| [Nec] | must | (have to)[9] | |
| [Apx-Nec] | should | ought to | supposed to |
| [Psb] | *can* | | |
| [Apx-Imp] | should not | ought not (to) | not supposed to |
| [Imp] | must not, mustn't | | |

In fact, a simple 'You must' is appropriate only if the requirement is irresistible – for example if someone has a gun pointing at the subject's head – so it is a very good way to get people angry. Be careful about using this deontic *must* with anyone other than yourself as subject! Much safer is to use *should* or its modern adjectival equivalent *(be) supposed to*, pronounced rather like *spōsta*. If you do want to say that you will force the action, *had better* is more normal; it warns of danger in non-compliance. The forms with *ought* are like *should*, except that they add some element of moral obligation or duty as the source of the command, and are thus less used than formerly.

In a polite formal context, however, *should* is too weak to show sincerity in an invitation, so *must* is often used to express an 'irresistible' suggestion, as in 'You must have some of this cake I made.' It is also useful to a child to whom you cannot give a command – 'You mustn't do that' – for it attributes the prohibition to someone other than oneself, besides telling him that he can't resist it.

## Generality, and a problem

You have no doubt noticed that *can* is used for [Psb] for all the modalities so far, except when we desire to recognize the authority of the speaker (*may*). This is precisely right; the meaning of *can* is simply [Psb], while the meaning of *may* is [Psb.Spk:permits] (it is possible and the speaker permits it). The different tables above do not represent separate meanings for *can*; they are only ranges of usage and *can* has a general meaning that applies across this broad range.

In contrast to this, *can't* does not have such a broad range of usage; it is not used for capability and social deontic types of meanings. Below we shall see that it can, however, be used for epistemic modals, while *can* cannot. Together, these facts suggest that *can't* is not the negative of *can*, for it has a distinctly different range of usage. This might justify Shaw's custom of dropping the apostrophe in *can't*, if it is simply an independent word today. But is it? Perhaps *can't* is not used in those meanings because it is blocked by *dare not* and *mustn't*.[10] On a superficial view of the situation, *can't* is not the negative of *can*. Nevertheless, we can perhaps explain the gaps in both their ranges of usage as blockage by other lexical items. Until an indisputable answer emerges clearly, take your own choice (and look for that answer!)

## Time marking

Most modals have an alternative, 'indirect' form, as we noted at the beginning, used in reporting (without quoting) a modality that was expressed at an earlier time. It is also used to mark non-factual clauses, saying what one believes not to be true, e.g. 'He wishes that he *could/would/might* buy a yacht tomorrow.' We saw in the tables for capacity and generic modality that these indirect forms are also used for past abilities, capabilities and characteristics.

In the tables for the deontic modals, however, as in the epistemic modals to follow, those indirect forms are not used

because these modals generally describe obligations and possibilities that exist at present. In the case of rights or duties (i.e.
*may*, *should*, *must*), these possibilities are about future actions:
one's present rights or duties to do something in the future.
Permission, for example, is almost always for something to
follow. However, some of the social deontic modals (e.g. *should*,
*ought* but not *must*) can be marked for a past obligation (usually
not carried out, else we have little call to talk about it) by using
perfective, i.e. *have* with the past participle of the following verb.
On the other hand, there are preterite forms for *have to*, *be
supposed to*, *can*, so we use them. For all these social deontic
modals, a duty or right to do something at the moment is marked
by using progressive, *to be* with the present participle (*-ing*) of the
verb, leaving the commonest case, the future action, with no
special mark.

> you *should have* finished yesterday.
> you *ought to have* completed it on time.
> he *had to* go to Alaska.
> he *was supposed to* meet me there.
> * he *must have* sung yesterday; why didn't he?
>
> I really *must be* going now.
> he *ought to be* studying now; where has he gone off to?
> you*'re not supposed to* sing tomorrow.
> * you *shouldn't be going to* sing tomorrow.

---

Q.   Why can't the excluded (*) examples be used? How can you
express these ideas?[11]

---

## Epistemic modals

While the capacity and deontic modals have a subject orientation,
describing what is necessary, possible or impossible for the subject
of the sentence, the **epistemic** modals can be seen as logic-
oriented (sometimes called 'alethic'). We noted in passing that the
social deontic modals are often used to connect propositions.
These epistemic modals seem to be totally devoted to that end,
often when the other proposition is expressed as an independent

sentence. So, in the example below, the two sentences express the idea that the modalized sentence is a necessary conclusion from the other, whatever order they are said in.

> John's umbrella is wet. It *must* be raining.
> It *must* be raining. John's umbrella is wet.

Similarly, showing a conclusion of possibility and a conclusion of impossibility:

> It *may* be raining. It's awfully dark out.
> It *can't* be raining. There's not a cloud in the sky.

The listener must find with which other proposition to connect the modalized clause. This is obvious if the two clauses are punctuated together as a single sentence, but if not the listener must decide which of the neighbouring sentences it connects with, or, as sometimes happens, what unsaid piece of information the speaker intends it to be connected with. In greeting an out-of-town guest with 'You *must* be tired and hungry', for example, the speaker is tacitly recognizing a long journey that is the cause of fatigue and hunger. Such unspoken propositions are quite real (see Chapter 14), enough for the guest to reply, 'Oh no, we stayed overnight in the next town', explaining that it was not a long journey after all.

The relationships between ideas are so important that there is a very complete range of epistemic modals in English. Note that the adverbial expressions of possibility (AvP) on the right are fairly close synonyms except that they don't include the idea that the truth or probability of the sentence rests on other ideas present.

| EPISTEMIC | factive | non-factive | rough meaning | AvP |
|---|---|---|---|---|
| [Nec] | must | (have to) | [certain] | surely |
| [Apx-Nec] | | should | [quite probable] | probably |
| | may well | could well | [quite possible] | likely |
| [Psb] | may | could | [possible] | maybe, perhaps |
| | might | | [vaguely possible] | possibly |
| [Apx-Imp] | | shouldn't | [improbable] | probably not |
| [Imp] | must not | can't, couldn't | [impossible] | surely not |
| | | | | |
| [Neg-Nec] | may not | need not | [not certain] | |

Adding an epistemic modal is a common way for the speaker to relieve himself of responsibility for the truth of a proposition. For example, 'She *must* be sleeping' cannot be used if the speaker has direct information as to what she is doing. Rather, it indicates that the speaker does not know by direct experience that she is sleeping but is inferring it from some other facts, perhaps the time and the fact that she doesn't answer her telephone. He is responsible only for the logic and perhaps for a good selection of facts (usually provided). Indeed, the non-factive modals can report a logical deduction from reasonable facts even when they contradict one's beliefs or observation, as for example the *can't* in the novelist's classic 'You *can't* be here; I saw you off on the flight to Istanbul!' The factive modals cannot be used this way: *'You *must not* be here; I saw you off on the flight to Helsinki!' These factive modals express the speaker's belief that the modalized proposition is in fact true.

An epistemic modal is also commonly used to tell the listener that there is some unspoken assumption and to force him to find it, as, for example, if I said here and now, 'You *must* love semantics by now.' To understand how this is a logical conclusion, you must supply what I left unsaid – perhaps 'I am such a good writer' and/or 'Semantics is by nature lots of fun.' In this way one can make a covert comment, often in jest, and if that comment is nasty or wrong, the speaker cannot be held responsible for saying it.

---

Q.   What are the missing assumptions in the following?
      it *must* be going to rain; I forgot my umbrella.
      he *can't* be asleep. It's only midnight.
      you *shouldn't* be studying – there aren't any exams yet.
      he *may well* have gone hang-gliding. The final exam is tomorrow.[12]

---

The epistemic modals mark the application of logic at the time of speaking, so like the deontic modals they are independent of tense and instead use the following 'aspects' to show when an event happens.

| | | |
|---|---|---|
| be going to | | – future time [Fut] |
| be -ing | (progressive) | – present (and some types of future) |
| have -en | (perfect) | – past time [Pst] |

The first examples below show how this is done for events. However, as shown in the second set of examples, a present state does not take a progressive marker (as we shall see again in Chapter 7), and for some unknown reason, future states are difficult to express naturally.

|  | [Pst]: | he *must have* sung yesterday. |
|---|---|---|
| events: |  | he *must be* singing now. |
|  | [Fut]: | he *must be going to* sing tomorrow. |

|  | [Pst]: | he *must have* liked singing a lot in those days. |
|---|---|---|
| states: |  | he *must* be rather tired now. |
|  | [Fut]: { | ? he *must be going to* feel happy tomorrow. |
|  |  | * he *must (be going to)* be tired tomorrow. |

There is some variation in epistemic usage.[13] This is a standard usage but do not be astonished if you meet other uses, especially in factivity. British linguists commonly report *can* alongside *could* here, but this is primarily in questions and, as we have noted, questions can be formed from negative modals in dropping the *not*. In fact, ordinary questions exchanging the subject and the modal verb are notably uncommon for epistemic modals and tend to be 'echoic': they are seldom used except to question what the addressee has just said, as for example 'He must have cheated on his exam' is questioned by 'Must he?'


## Connections

Before we leave modals, let us note the similarity of these epistemic modals (MoE) with the social deontic modals (MoD) and with other elements of language. The table below shows the parallels with 'quantifiers' (Qnt) and adverbs of frequency (AvF) on the right side. These seven degrees of 'strength' range from [Nec] down to [Imp] and are found in many guises in most languages, though specific words may well be missing (as in MoD, and especially for the capacity modals) for intermediate terms. The quantifiers (Chapter 3) provide the most complete scale in most languages.

|         | MoD        | MoE             | AvF             | Qnt         |
|---------|------------|-----------------|-----------------|-------------|
| [Nec]     | must       | must            | always          | all, every  |
| [Apx-Nec] | should     | should          | usually         | most        |
|         | —          | may/could well  | often           | many, much  |
| [Psb]     | can        | may             | sometimes       | some        |
|         | —          | might           | occasionally    | a few       |
| [Apx-Imp] | should not | should not      | seldom, rarely  | few         |
| [Imp]     | must not   | must not, can't | never           | none, no    |

The parallel of epistemic modals with quantifiers (Qnt) and adverbs of frequency (AvF) above is obvious in this table, and this same scale appeared in adverbs of possibility (*certainly, probably, likely, maybe, possibly, not/hardly likely, certainly not*) as we saw in the epistemic table. It seems obvious why these adverbs (probability, and frequency above) should be related to the quantifiers if they express a quantification of probability and frequency respectively. Apparently, grades of modality are quantifiable in this same way.

Earlier, we gave the deontic modals (MoD) only five grades of logical modality, which makes gaps in this table. However, these missing modals are perhaps not so missing after all. Some people use *ought to* and *ought not (to)*, and others use *sposta* and *not sposta* in these slots, and it is not easy to determine exactly how strong their meanings are. In any case, *ought* is fairly weak, suggesting even that the action is hardly necessary.

In the first two and last two rows of the table above, the total parallel between *must* and *should* and their negatives suggests that there are only two lexical items here, strong and weak respectively, that can be used either deontically or epistemically. These usages have sometimes been described as a difference in objectivity: the MoD are generally 'objective' statements about rights and duties while the MoE report 'subjective' judgements.

## English modal verbs

Natural languages have three basic **logical** modal concepts: [Nec] necessary, [Psb] possible, and [Imp] impossible, the first two of which are defined and given symbols in logic. Although they were discovered there first for the epistemic and then later for the deontic modalities, they are quite a bit more general than how they are described in elementary logic texts, as we have found them pervading the whole modal system. There is a fourth modal idea, [Neg–Nec] or the logically equivalent [Psb–Neg], and an old form that can be used for this idea, *need not*, with most varieties of modality. It is uncommon today, however, and *don't have to* is used in its place. For epistemic modality, this idea is more precisely expressed with *may not* or *might not* [Psb–Neg].

The big division in English **linguistic** modality is between the epistemic ones which relate propositions one to another, and the others which generally have some subject-orientation. For these others, capacity and deontic modals, *can* can always be used for possibility but impossibility has different forms for different meanings.

Note also that *should* expresses either logical or deontic near-necessity (i.e. necessity with the possibility of exceptions), as *must* does for absolute necessity of either type, though of course, absolute deontic necessity is not a common idea to express these days, in the English-speaking democracies at least, nor is the authority of *may*.

Last, although the modals are very natural in English and may even be seen to be central, there seems to be a growing tendency to create and use substitutes for them, in speaking at least; most of these substitutes feel somewhat informal in writing. The following are standard non-modal ways of expressing modal ideas, and each has a common (assimilated) way of pronunciation different from how it would be pronounced as two words.

| Substitute | Modal | Relaxed pronunciation |
| --- | --- | --- |
| used to | for would (generic) | he ūsta study. |
| have to | for must (deontic especially) | he hǎsta study. |
| have got to | less formal form of *have to* | he's gǒtta study. |
| be supposed to | for ought-to, should (deontic) | he's spōsta study. |
| be going to | for shall, will (future) | he's gǒnna study. |

Perhaps the English modal system has become too complex and our speech is leading the way to a new system. If so, you can expect some new paraphrastic forms in your lifetime.

## Notes and answers

1. could, might, should, would, had to.

2. a 'military' use:  You *will* capture Hill 264 at 0800.
   a use showing force of will: I *will\* do it.
   a pure predictive use:  And that'*ll* be Tower Bridge, I suppose.

3. A future possibility, however, cannot be described with *can*; *to be able to* is needed: 'As of now, I *can't* go tomorrow, but I *will be able to* go by this evening!'

4. *was able to, could.*

5. It acts like a positive, not a negative, in taking *some*, so although it is negative in form, it is apparently not in meaning.

6. Nec = Neg-Psb-Neg or Psb = Neg-Nec-Neg.

7. (5) She won't/doesn't talk your ears off, even when you don't watch out. (6) . . . but she wouldn't get angry over small things. He won't get/never gets so engrossed. . . . Non-modal expressions report factual observations while the modalized expressions describe a characteristic or the nature of the subject (inferred from observations).

8. Perhaps 0 to 100 per cent, a totally useless concept as it excludes nothing and is nearly identical to [Psb]. I can't imagine any words that say nothing because they allow everything.

9. *Have* can change to *have got* when speaking informally, so this *have to* is often pronounced *'ve gotta*, written *'ve got to*.

10. These must be lexical items and thus have the power to block, as their negative elements are not free and their denials are entirely different words.

11. See previous paragraph. He had to sing yesterday. You shouldn't sing tomorrow.

12. It rains whenever I forget my umbrella. He never sleeps before midnight. You seldom study except before exams. He often relaxes himself before exams.

13. The status of *must* may not yet be fixed for English as a whole, for some people, myself included, find it perfectly reasonable in 'My keys *must\* be here; they can't just walk away – but they're not\ here!' For these people, *must* is non-factive with locations, not committing one to the truth of the proposition. Others find this example to be inconsistent, showing that *must* is factive for them. Because *must not* is factive, those others speak in a more systematic way but have no way to express the idea that 'all facts and logic dictate the contrary of what we know', as in this example, unless *have to* can be used. For me, however, this is factive.

## Keywords

possibility, necessity, epistemic, deontic, capacity/dynamic, generic.

## Further reading

Modal verbs are a perennial concern of linguistic theory, and there are dissimilar ways to treat them.

Coates, Jennifer *Semantics of the Modal Auxiliaries* (1983) London: Croom Helm.

Hofmann, Th. R. 'Modality in English and Other Languages' (1979) *Papers in Linguistics* **12**: 1–37.

Palmer, Frank R. *Modality and the English Modals* (1979) London: Longmans.

Leech, Geoffrey *Meaning and the English Verb* (1971, 1987) London: Longmans.

Wierzbicka, A. 'The Semantics of Modality' (1987) *Folia Linguistica* **21**, 25–43.

Debate is active and continuing in the area of English modals, see Bolinger's recent article on *may, can*:

Bolinger, D. '7 on *May* and *can* +1' (1989) *Journal of Pragmatics* **13**: 1–23.

## Exercises with modal verbs

1. Explain the different interpretations (epistemic, deontic, etc.) possible for each of the following.

   (a) It can't be done.  (e) She can swim for hours.

   (b) He may go.  (f) You won't do it again.

   (c) Anne should be singing.(g) Pete can't come before 3.00.

   (d) He must be back home.

2. Recall that the question forms following have special uses and can be made more polite (tentative, distant) by using their indirect forms (ending with *-ould*).

   shall I . . .?  [do you want me to . . .?] (an offer)

   will/can you . . .?  [I want to . . .] (a request)

   can/may I . . .?  [I want your permission to . . .]

What, then, are the ambiguities with the following?

   (a) Will you go tomorrow?

   (b) Should I open the window?

   (c) Could you answer the question?

3. Show the differences in meaning when the indicated words are exchanged by providing paraphrases in English.

   (a) Smoking (may/can) damage your health.

   (b) The nurse (has to/must) take his temperature at midnight.

   (c) Tom and Mary have to (study/be studying) now.

   (d) Sorry, I (must/should/ought to) leave now.

   (e) You (shall/will) finish it before you leave.

4. Correct the errors (if any) in the following sentences.

   (a) My homework looked hard, but I could finish it in an hour.

   (b) I ran and ran, and could barely catch the train.

   (c) When he came to Japan for the first time, he couldn't use chopsticks.

   (d) (at a hamburger shop) I like to have two burgers and a coffee.

   (e) (at a party) My wife baked this cake. You may have some.

5. What is strange about the following sentences?

   (a) *You shall finish it if you want.

   (b) *He can be going to sing tomorrow.

   (c) *There would be a church on that corner when I was a child.

6. Give the direct denials, i.e. contradictories (e.g. *all:not-all, some:none*), of the following sentences.

   (a) He might have gone.

   (b) You mustn't sit there.

   (c) It might not rain tomorrow.

   (d) You've got to be kidding.

   (e) They can't have got there yet.

7. Give the opposites (contraries, e.g. *all:none, many:few*) of the sentences in (6).

8. Complete the short answers to the questions below, using modal verbs wherever possible.

   (a) Do you have to work on Saturdays?

      No, we __.

   (b) Hadn't/Shouldn't we better ask John to come?

      Yes, we __.

      ('shouldn't we better' appears to be a more modern and polite way in North America to say 'hadn't we better')

   (c) Shouldn't we report this to the police?
      Yes, I think we __.
   (d) (to teacher) May I leave now?
      No, you __.
   (e) May I use your phone a moment?
      Yes, __.
   (f) (to someone with hands full) Shall I open the door for you?
      Yes, __.
   (g) No, __.

9. When speaking to someone higher and distant, e.g. a clerk to a customer or guest in an expensive hotel, we often avoid modals and use more explicit paraphrases without *you*, as well as avoiding simple 'yes' and 'no'. Complete these answers.
   (a) Can I smoke here?
      I'm sorry, sir, but __.
   (b) Could you book me for next week?
      One moment, I'll see if __.
   (c) Do you have to come with me to my room?
      I'm sorry, but __.
   (d) Should I leave my key when I go out?
      Of course, sir, __.

10. In the following examples, insert a supportive or emphatic (consistent if not redundant) adverb from among: *possibly, probably, certainly.*
   (a) The rumour cannot __ be true.
   (b) What Becky said might __ be right.
   (c) It must __ be surprising to you!
   (d) __, he may not come.
   (e) John should __ have left home by now.
   (f) Tom __ may not come!

11. In the following examples of word play, what is the unspoken assumption that is needed to make sense of the sequence? The whole point of saying things like this is to communicate this hidden idea without actually saying it.
   (a) Sheba can't be sleeping. It's only midnight.
   (b) He shouldn't be studying – there aren't any exams yet.
   (c) The road might be open; it didn't snow very much.
   (d) It must be going to rain; I forgot my umbrella.

12. (advanced, for native speakers) The COBUILD grammar recognizes a sense of *couldn't* to express unwillingness, because the subject is 'afraid, embarrassed or disgusted' or the act is 'unfair or morally wrong' (§4.204)

I couldn't possibly go out now.
I couldn't let him touch me.
I couldn't leave her to cope on her own.
I couldn't take your last cigarette.

(a) If you are a native speaker, what forms can be used to show the subject is not afraid, embarrassed or disgusted, or if the act is not unfair or morally wrong?

(b) And what for an act that it would be unfair or morally wrong not to do, or that the subject would be afraid, embarrassed or disgusted not to do?

In §4.203, *can't* is mentioned for when the subject has strong feelings that prevent him from doing something.

I cannot leave everything for him.
I can't give you up.

As the reasons for *couldn't* are parallel 'strong feelings':

(c) Are there forms for possibility and necessity parallel to the indirect forms of (a) and (b)? What are they?

If you know the answers to the above:

(d) Can you fit these modals in with the capacity modals that are mentioned in the text, or do we need an additional table for 'new capability' modals, taking these meanings to be simply the expression of capability?

# CHAPTER 7

# Time: Tense and Aspect

---

Non-native speakers can easily make mistakes like:

* Take this medicine after you *ATE* dinner.

English-speakers, on the other hand, tend to make the reverse error, [Take this medicine after you *EAT* dinner], which sounds just as silly in other languages. Where do these mistakes come from?

---

One of the harder things about learning English well is knowing when to use the preterite tense (also called the past tense, a name that misleads many) and when to use the perfect aspect. That is, which of the following should one use in a given circumstance?

    he *has broken* the record.    [simple perfect]
    he *broke* the record.         [simple preterite]

Few languages force you to choose between two such forms, so just about everybody who learns English has problems with them. Happily, a recently discovered answer seems pretty simple, and if it is right, English students should not have any more trouble. The **preterite** form is used when there is a definite or specific time in mind − or if there is an adverbial specifying the time. Otherwise, if there is no special time in mind, or if the exact time is not important, then the **perfect** is the form to use.

Chapters of text, and even whole books, have been written about the perfect, but this has given us little more than a list of different ways to use it, such as:

| | | |
|---|---|---|
| Experiential: | I've never seen a ghost. | (when is not important) |
| Present relevance: | we've learned this already. | (when is not important) |
| Hot news: | the Prime Minister's been shot! | (exactly when is not known) |

These all share the idea that exactly when the event took place is either not known or not relevant. It is natural, for example, in asking whether someone has had some experience, to ask only that, and not to complicate the issue with the question of when. Or, in telling others of something important that has just happened, not to let the time of the event distract from its importance. The simple question 'Is the time unknown or unimportant?' is nearly all you need to remember in describing past events; if yes, use the perfect, otherwise use the preterite. Because the perfect de-emphasizes the time, it throws more emphasis on the action, with some interesting by-products found in Exercise question 1 at the end of the chapter.

---

Q.   Why can't we use a time adverb in a sentence like 'I have seen the President yesterday'?[1]

---

Interestingly, the question to ask for choosing between perfect and preterite is almost the same question as for when to use the definite article *the*: 'Is the identity of the thing known and important?'

   put it on *the* table.     put it on *a* table.

When we use a definite article, as in the first example, we have a 'definite' or specific table in mind, and the definite article indicates that the person we are talking to can and should identify which one we have in mind. If instead we use the indefinite article, as in the second example, we either don't have any particular table in mind or we really don't care which one. Like the perfect, an indefinite article throws emphasis on the qualities described by the noun.

   In a very real sense, then, the preterite is like *the* or like a definite time adverb, 'at **the** time', while a simple perfect is like 'at **some** time', not referring to any specific time. This is why you cannot use a preterite like 'I saw Anne climbing Mount Fuji' unless it is relevant when it happened. If it is, the preterite must be used.

   The language learner's rule, 'Answer in the same form as the question', will usually keep one out of trouble, but we can see here that it is not infallible. A question in the perfect can (and must) be answered in the preterite if an adverbial indicating time is added.

A    have you been to Tasmania?
B    * yes, I have been there last year.
      yes, I was there just last year.
C    have you seen my car key [recently]?
D1     yes, I saw it on the table.
D2   !! yes, I have [seen it].
D3     no, I haven't [seen it].
D4     yes, I have . . . but I don't remember where.

In fact, to answer a question like C's according to that simple rule, as in D's second answer, could well be perceived as deliberately obscure; as C clearly wants his key, and D saw it, D could surely say where he saw it, which requires the preterite as it was at a specific time. The negative answer, however, should use a perfect form, for the not-seeing did not happen at any specific time. The perfect form in (D4) is natural as the speaker clearly does not remember when as well as where.

## Tense and aspect

The area of semantics from which this discovery comes is the semantics of tense and aspect. In principle, **tense** shows when an event happens: before now ('happen*ED*'), right now ('*IS* happen*ING*'), after now ('*WILL* happen') or even all the time ('happen*S*'). Many languages, however, do not have a special form for future events; we have a variety of ways to indicate future in English, the modal *will* being only one of them.

Other aspects of when something happens are called (not surprisingly) **aspect** – for example, whether an action is continuing, completed, iterative, intermittent, or other possibilities that will occupy Chapter 8. In English we have two syntactic aspects called **perfect** and **progressive**.

| it HAS growN cold. | perfect | |
| it IS snowING now. | progressive | syntactic in English |
| it USED TO snow in November. | durative (past) | |
| it is STARTing TO snow now. | inceptive | |
| it STOPped snowING at 2:00. | terminative | |
| it snows OFF AND ON these days. | intermittent | |

it may KEEP ON snowing for a week.   continuative
he fell down OVER AND OVER again.   (re)iterative

Most, perhaps all, languages make it obligatory to say something about when an event happens, and this obligatory marker often plays an important role in the syntax of the language. In English, for example, the word *not* and short adverbs (Av) are normally placed just after the auxiliary verb that carries tense (Ts), as in the examples below; and it is this same verb that appears at the beginning of a question. Technically it is sometimes called the 'tense-carrier', but we will take it as a location, the 'centre' of an English sentence, for it can be empty, as in the last example.

| (Ts) | (Av) | |
|------|------|---|
| he can | | sing it well. |
| he has | not | sung it in church. |
| he is | often | singing it. |
| he has | really | been singing opera recently. |
| he | already | sings quite well |

These obligatory markers are usually called 'tense' in syntax, even if they do not specify the time relative to now, like Japanese *-ta* or Chinese *-le* for prior events. For semantics, however, **tense** is the indication of time, relative to the moment of speaking, before now, now, or after now. This is often taken to be the time of the event, but as we shall see shortly, English for one does not mark that but uses tense to locate a reference time.

There are many theories about tense and aspect, but the simplest and yet probably the most adequate basis to explain what each form means, and thus also when each can be used, was put together some forty years ago in a text on logic! It is sometimes called an SER system because it uses the three points in time below, S, E and R, and describes a meaning in terms of the two relationships between them, S:R (tense) and R:E (aspect).

S = the moment of Speaking
R = a time of Reference       > Tense
E = the time of the Event     > Aspect

It was not too clear at first exactly what the R stood for, but the system works quite well if we let R stand for the time indicated by an adverb, if there is one.

He didn't come to class yesterday. He couldn't get up.
He had stayed up too late [the night before].

In this example, 'yesterday' describes R in the first sentence. Of course, many sentences do not have an adverbial of time, like the second and third sentences, but there is still an R, unmentioned though it may be, and we take it from the preceding sentence, so R = 'yesterday' for them too. We could add 'the night before [then]' to the third sentence, making its R = 'the night before yesterday'.

---

Q.   The third sentence of the example above might be said 'He stayed up too late the night before.' What effect does that have on the smoothness and flow of the paragraph? Why?[2]

---

The **preterite** puts the R before the S [R<S], so it goes naturally with past time adverbs but not with present or future time adverbs. The **perfect**, on the other hand, puts the E before the R [E<R], so it shows an event E to be past without a past time adverb, and in fact does not go with past time adverbs. You cannot, for example, say 'I haven't eaten breakfast this morning' unless it is still morning. After noon, we say 'I didn't eat breakfast this morning.'

In this chapter we will find that the relation [X<Y], i.e. [X is before Y], is nearly all that is needed to explain the tenses and aspects of English, in combination with temporal notions like S, E and R above. The symbol '<' can also be understood as [is less than] in arithmetic, if we take those temporal notions to be times on a clock, or dates on a calendar.

The crux of this explanation is that if the terms of either relationship, S:R or R:E, are not specifically indicated to be different, e.g. by some grammatical marker like preterite or perfect, or by a time adverb that sets R to some other time, then they are left pointing to the same time.[3] With this, the temporal differences between the perfect and the preterite become crystal clear, with or without the parenthesized adverbs below.

| he has sung (now). | E | R = S | |
|---|---|---|---|
| R | | $\longrightarrow$ | $[E < R \cdot R = S]$ |
| | sing | [now] | |

| he sang (yesterday). | E = R | S | |
|---|---|---|---|
| R | | $\longrightarrow$ | $[E = R \cdot R < S]$ |
| | sing | [now] | |
| | [yesterday] | | |

These may seem quite similar, and indeed there is not all that much difference in positive sentences. When the sentence is negative (or interrogative), however, there is a world of difference.

he hasn't sung (yet) · ──────────────── R = S ──→ [Neg-(E < R) · R = S]

/s̶i̶n̶g̶/ s̶i̶n̶g̶/ s̶i̶n̶g̶/ [now]

he didn't sing (yesterday). ──────── E = R ──── S ──→ [Neg-(E = R) · R < S]
R

/s̶i̶n̶g̶/ [now]

[yesterday]

When these markers are combined in the same clause, we have the preterite perfect. The perfect places the event E at some time earlier than the specified time R that is placed in the past by the preterite.

he had sung when I came. ── E ─── R ─── S ──→ [E < R. R < S]
└──R──┘
sing come [now]

It works almost like magic, doesn't it? Most languages don't make this contrast. The 'past' marker *avoir . . . -é* in spoken French shows simple E is at or before R, so it is an aspect semantically and not a tense. This is why many foreigners use the English preterite as in the examples in the box at the beginning of the chapter; the medicine is to be taken **after** the eating of dinner, even though that eating is a future event. A more accurate translation might be 'Take this medicine after you *have eaten* dinner', a present perfect form. However, the perfect is not obligatory in English, and as it simply repeats what *after* expresses overtly we more commonly simply say, '. . . after you *eat* dinner'.

## Not past

Because the syntax of English forces us to choose between the preterite or not in a simple sentence, grammars often say that the choice of tense is obligatory and that any sentence that is not preterite is in the 'present tense'. This term, however, does not have any special connection to the present time, i.e. the moment of speaking S, and really means only [not-preterite]. This so-called 'present tense' is commonly used for future events that are taken as assumed facts, such as 'My plane leaves at 9:10.' It can also be used for past events if no time is mentioned, as in the 'present' perfects we have already seen, or in a special form called the 'historical present', often used to add vividness to a recounting of a memorable experience, such as the following.

> I'm in this bank, y'know? An' this mafia-type walks in and hauls out this sawed-off shotgun and yells that everybody should lie down.

This sort of blow-by-blow reporting does not use tense or aspect (i.e. 'simple present tense'), for the events happen faster than it takes to describe them. It is common in sports broadcasting: 'He hits the Champ . . . He hits him again . . . He lands a good one on his chin', as well as the progressive, 'Oh, the Champ is falling!' needed if the event is longer than the description, as we shall see shortly.

Having such a wide range of use — past, present and future — this 'present tense' has no meaning itself and we will not speak of it further in the realm of semantics. In word formation it is real enough to appear as the suffix /-s/ on a verb, but only if the subject is singular and not 'personal', i.e. not [Spk] or [Adr], the [Awa] of Chapter 4.

For future events R is after S, so of course preterite [R<S] is impossible. The modal auxiliary verbs *shall* and *will*, as well as deontic *must*, have [S<R] as part of their meanings, so they naturally go only with future time adverbs:

$$\text{he will sing (tomorrow).} \quad \underset{\substack{\text{R} \qquad \text{[now]} \quad \text{sing}}}{\xrightarrow{\hspace{0.5cm}\text{S} \qquad \text{R} = \text{E}\hspace{0.5cm}}} \quad [S < R \cdot R = E]$$

The so-called future perfect, a perfect with one of these modals (*will* especially), puts the E before the R because it is perfect, and the R after the S. However, it is left open whether the E is before or after the S.

$$\text{he will have eaten when we arrive.} \quad \underset{\substack{\text{[now]} \quad \text{arrive}}}{\xrightarrow{\hspace{0.5cm}\text{S} \qquad\qquad \text{R}\hspace{0.5cm}}} \quad [S < R \cdot E < R]$$

$$?\leftarrow E \rightarrow ?$$

$$\text{(maybe already)} \quad \text{eat} \quad \text{(maybe not yet)}$$

---

Q.  How can SER theory explain the impossibility of *'He will surely come yesterday'?[4]

---

As we noted above, the only temporal fact that English requires in a clause is whether or not R is in the past, using preterite (or not). In particular, we don't need to mark an event explicitly as future, especially if there is a future adverb in that sentence or a preceding one to specify the R. There are thus many ways to express near future events (left) and fewer with far future events (right).

| | |
|---|---|
| he comes tomorrow. | ! he comes five years from now. |
| he will come tomorrow. | he will come five years from now. |
| he is going to come tomorrow. | ! he is going to come five years from now. |
| he is coming tomorrow. | ! he is coming five years from now. |
| he plans to come tomorrow. | he plans to come five years from now. |
| he is to come tomorrow. | he is to come five years from now. |

The first sentence is quite normal if the event is already a fact, as for example if there is a schedule and it is a fact that he is marked down for tomorrow. If it is not a fact for the speaker, he would use the second or third, *will* typically suggesting a prediction and *going to* expressing sureness, as explained in Chapter 6. One is seldom so sure of something so far in the future,[5] so *will* or some more specific relationship to the event such as *plan to* is normal for 'five years from now'. The last, *be to* is similar to this, suggesting a plan or a schedule, but unlike the first 'simple present' it is not accepted as a fact.

---

Q.   Most of these 'future' forms can be combined with preterite, e.g. 'He was to come tomorrow', so they are only 'relative futures' that place the event after the reference time, [R<E]. Which ones cannot? Of the ones that can, do they necessarily imply that the projected event has been cancelled?[6]

---

For this same reason, we don't add anything to show futurity [S<R] in an adverbial clause; if it limits a future sentence, then it must also be future and there is no need to say so − so why bother? The parallel past time sentences are different, because English forces us to choose between preterite [Prt] or not for every clause without a modal verb (Chapter 6).

| time | Main clause | Adverbial clause that limits it | |
| --- | --- | --- | --- |
| [future] | she will come | when I get hungry. | no [Fut] |
| | | * when I will get hungry. | *[Fut1] |
| | | * when I'm going to get hungry. | *[Fut2] |
| [past] | she came | * when I get hungry. | *[Neg-Prt] |
| | | when I got hungry. | [Prt] |

Because an English sentence about the future nearly always has a marker of future, unless it is seen as a fact, it looks as if a *will* has been deleted in the first adverbial clause above. This is where we get the old rule 'Don't use *will* in an adverbial clause.' More accurate is 'Don't mark the future (*will*, *shall* OR *be going to*) in an adverbial clause if it is clearly future', or even 'Be lazy; don't mark the future unless you need to.' In fact, *will* can be used in *if*-clauses when it is expressing more than simply the future, meaning [the subject is willing to], as in 'We'll be done in an hour if everybody *will* help.'

Q.  Sometimes this absence of *will* is called *will*-deletion in syntax, but we saw several reasons why it is not a syntactic process. Can you find them (in the last three paragraphs)?[7]

## Progressive aspect

This SER system seems to answer a lot of questions and guides us away from common errors. It really looks too good to be true, and in fact it has an assumption that limits its application: that the event happens at a single moment, E. When we are a long way away from something it seems as if it happened all at once, like the moment when you were born, and this SER system works quite well. When the event is close at hand, however, like reading this sentence, its beginning 'B' can be significantly different from its finish 'F'. The original notion E has to be replaced by B and F to deal with extended aspects, but then it is adequate for many more things, as we shall see below and in the next chapter.

Rather unusual among the languages of the world, English has a **progressive** aspect that puts R in between B and F, with the result that the event is presented as sp    out with its beginning before, and its finish after, the reference time R, which is often the moment of speaking, S, as in the examples below.

he is singing (now). ———— S = R ————▶[B < R < F · R = S]

               R            B —— sing —— F

he was singing then. ——— R ——— S ———▶[B < R ≤ F · R < S]

          R     B—sing—F? ········· F?

When R is not the same as S, as in the second example, the event is spread out about that time but there is no indication of whether it is going on at the time of speaking (like the case with the future perfect). This is why we put two Fs with question marks in that diagram; diagrams cannot show clearly what things are left unexpressed in language.

For events that are taking place right now, it is difficult not to distinguish the beginning from the finish, and English has a special rule for simple sentences that makes using the progressive obligatory for on-going events: 'Use at least one marker, tense or aspect, unless none is possible.' Things that are going on at the moment of speaking, S, cannot be marked with preterite, perfect or future markers, so they must instead be described with the progressive, even though the progressive is not required in any other situation. This also means that if a sentence is not marked for any tense or aspect at all, it must be because the progressive is inappropriate, along with all the other markers. That is, the event is (1) not restricted to the past, where we would use the preterite or perfect, and moreover, either (2) the event is completed faster than its description as we saw above, or (3a) it is not yet begun, that is, B is not before S, or else (3b) there is no finish time F. The first three examples below illustrate these latter possibilities.

he sings tomorrow.     (3a)——— S ——— R ——▶

he knows the answer.   (3b)——— S = R ——▶

                        B — know ——▶   (no F)

he doesn't wear shoes. (3b)——— S = R ——▶

                     — not-wear ——▶  (no F, no B)

he isn't wearing shoes.      ——— S = R ——▶

                    B — not-wear—F

he is singing tomorrow.    —— S —— R ——▶

      —R—          B? —— B?—sing–F

Notice how the third example suggests that he never wears shoes as there is no finish F to his not wearing shoes. By contrast, the addition of the progressive in the fourth makes the lack of shoes temporary, as is reasonable for anyone in bed, or in a Japanese house. A small thing like progressive markers with verbs of wearing can make a big difference in the implications one can draw from it. Sometimes it seems as if the nature of the progressive is an action while the non-progressive is a state, but these feelings can be explained as derivative of the formal meaning of progressive.

---

Q.    The progressive places R before the finish F of an event, but does it imply that the event continued to its finish in sentences like 'She was drowning when the lifeguard saw her' or 'I was doing my homework when the lights went out'? When the event has no inherent point of completion, as in 'I was walking yesterday at noon', what does F point to?[8]

---

The first and last of the examples above were future, because of the adverbs, but they describe the event very differently. The first one is a fact; it is sure in the mind of the speaker, so this form tends to be used only for scheduled events. On the other hand, the last is also a near future, for it describes an event as if it has already begun; the preparations for singing tomorrow are under way. This difference is clearer in a relatively distant future, as below.

> our professor goes to Hyderabad next year.
> my girlfriend is joining a safari in Kenya next March.

The professor and some organization in India have made an agreement; there is no escaping – his going next year is taken as a fact. My friend's going to Kenya, however, is not a fact, but she has already begun her trip, in her mind at least if not in actually buying clothes, tickets, and so on. Similarly, because a simple progressive with a future action puts the beginning before R, which is also the time of speaking, it can be used only for events that can be planned, so we do not normally say * 'He is having an accident tomorrow' or ! 'He is getting arrested next week.' By using it, as in this last example, we suggest that the subject is somehow planning the event or has set things in motion to end up there.

A point worth remembering here is that languages treat the future quite distinctively. Some languages have a future tense, e.g. Tagalog in the Philippines, and it is fair to include Russian and French, while others like Eskimo have a near future form, a far future form and so on. English does neither of these but has many expressions that imply a future action. *Will* is for predictions, *must* for inescapable events, *should* for probable events; the progressive is for things begun, to be finished after R, hence for future events already begun, while simple verbs (the so-called 'present tense') are for states of affairs without a finish point F, and for events not yet begun but already fact.

Since this revised SER model does not have an E any more, the meaning of perfect must be revised, and it turns out that perfect places the end F of the event before the R.

he had sung by 5:00. ————— R — S ➔

R    B– sing –F

If there is an adverbially expressed limit to an event, as in 'He has walked (for) 6 miles' or '. . . (for) an hour' or even '. . . all of his life', then the F of the perfect points to that limit. So 'He has walked 6 miles' does not suggest that the walking has stopped, though it may have. Rather it describes a situation where 6 miles of walking is finished. If we then add progressive, as in 'He has been walking for an hour', it specifically denies that the basic action, walking, has finished, only that an hour's worth is finished.[9]

We do not need to go into this complexity, however (but see Exercise question 1), to see how tense and aspect work in language. It is worth noting that modals like *must*, *should*, *can't* and *might* cannot be used with the preterite, so the perfect [F < R] is used here to place the event before the time of the modal, with the *have* commonly pronounced as [ə] or [əv], as in:

he must have come yesterday.
she couldn't have seen me.


## Summary

Based on this SER sort of system, we see how language grabs hold of an event in a jointed way like an arm: the **reference time**, R, is like an elbow, not very useful in itself but lending a great flexibility to the system. R is positioned relative to S by **tense**, as the elbow is set relative to the shoulder. The **time** of the **event**, E, is then located relative to R by **aspect** much as the hand is located relative to the elbow. In the refined system, B and F stand for the times of the **beginning** and **finish** of the event, like the thumb and little finger.

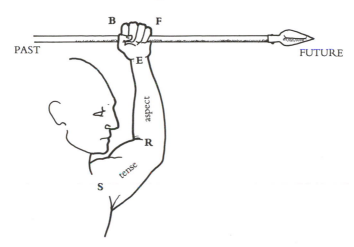

In the case of English, we have a **preterite** tense that must be used in a clause if the event is described as happening at a specific time in the past. If the time is unknown or if it is not important enough to add, then a simple **perfect** can be used instead. Instead of a **future** tense, English provides a number of ways to mark a future event that differ in how the speaker feels towards the projected event, ranging from **prediction** or **promise** to descriptions of it as already begun or sure to happen, and even no marker at all for facts already established in a schedule. Our syntactic system provides specially for two aspects: the **perfect** that locates the event some time before the reference time R, and a **progressive** that locates R in the midst of the event. This latter must be used if it is possible for things to be happening at the moment of speaking (R = S), perhaps because it is difficult not to distinguish the beginning B and the finish F of an event in progress.

Taking /-ed, /-en, /-ing to indicate that the following verb is a preterite, a past participle or a present participle form, we can summarize these forms and their meanings ([a < b] stands for [a is earlier than b]) as:

| usual names | form | | meaning |
|---|---|---|---|
| preterite, 'past' | */-ed* | — | [R < S] |
| perfect | *have /-en* | — | [F < R] |
| progressive, extended | *be /-ing* | — | [B < R ≤ F] |
| futures | *will*, . . . | — | [S < R] |

The 'aspectual points' B and F are also important in identifying aspectual classes of verbs in English and other languages as well as differences between languages. We will meet them again in Chapter 8, where it will become clear that F stands for the 'finish' or 'completion' of the event, and not simply when it ends. The notion R, a reference time associated with the time adverb if there is one, will also be used again there.

## Note for further exploration

Although we have been taking the temporal points R, B and F as times on the clock, or dates on the calendar, there is some evidence that they are really 'relativized' to the time of speaking, S. That is, the time of speaking is subtracted from the other times to make relativized times (marked with primes):

$$B' = B - S \qquad F' = F - S \qquad R' = R - S$$

Because $S' = S - S = 0$, all past time is negative and all future time is positive. With these relativized times, an event far away in past or future looks punctive as $B'$ and $F'$ are nearly the same − both large numbers, either negative (past) or positive (future) − while an on-going event has a negative $B'$ and a positive $F'$ which are always quite distinct. In any case, all our formulas stand unmodified, either for clock times or for relativized times, except that $S'$ can be replaced by zero in the relativized versions making, e.g., the preterite simply [R' < 0].

## Answers and notes

1. If that adverb is used, the time is important enough to mention so preterite is more appropriate than perfect.
2. If 'the night before' is taken as a new R, it is simply past, so a simple preterite is appropriate. However, this breaks the

continuity of the paragraph because it changes the time of reference; the speaker suddenly takes on a new viewpoint.

3. This sort of 'background presumption' is now studied in a new field called 'default logic'.

4. *Yesterday* puts R < S but *will* puts S < R, so there is a contradiction in the time of the action.

5. Except for astronomical events, of course, where we can say 'Halle's comet returns in 2016.'

6. First and second. Except for the fourth, no; they can be continued, '. . . but I don't know whether he will'.

7. Futures without any marker are quite normal if they are facts, as in 'I teach at 3:05 tomorrow', which is what *if-* or *when-* clauses are all about anyhow, [if/when it becomes a fact that . . .]. Second, *will* is possible if an *if*-clause. Alternatively, you can say that *will*, when it does not mean [willing], has a meaning of prediction, but the meaning of an adverbial clause is not [if/when you predict . . .].

8. Apparently not; we hope that the lifeguard saved her, and I probably didn't finish my homework in the dark. To the time when the action stopped.

9. Continuing at least in the mind of the speaker, in spite of temporary interruptions, interruptions that might possibly become permanent.

## Keywords

preterite, past, tense, aspect, perfect, progressive, reference time.

## Further reading

Tense and aspect have often been a proving ground for theories or approaches to linguistics, but Leech provides a well-rounded introduction without too much influence from a theory. Reichenbach originated the systematic descriptions of tenses and aspects extended here and Bull brought it into linguistics. Different approaches can be found in the others. Hirtle provides a good introduction to a very different sort of explanation and Prior is yet another approach.

Bull, William *Time, Tense and the Verb* (1968) Berkeley: University of California Press.

Comrie, Bernard *Aspect: An Introduction to the Study of Verbal Aspect and Related Problems* (1976) London: CUP.

Dahl, Osten *Tense and Aspect Systems* (1985) Oxford: Blackwell.

Hirtle, Walter H. *Time, Aspect and the Verb* (1975) Québec: Presses de l'Université Laval.

Hofmann, Th. R. 'Expression of Time Relations in English' (1980) *Memoirs* **3**.2: 175–201, Matsue, Japan: Shimane University.

Hopper, Paul *Tense-Aspect: Between Semantics and Pragmatics* (1982) Amsterdam: Benjamins.

Hornstein, N. *As Time Goes By* (1990).

Joos, Martin *The English Verb* (1964) Madison: University of Wisconsin Press.

Leech, Geoffrey *Meaning and the English Verb* (1971, 1987) London: Longman.

Prior, A. N. *Time and Modality* (1957) OUP.

Reichenbach, Hans *Elements of Symbolic Logic* (1947) London: Macmillan.

Verkuyl, H. J. *On the Compositional Nature of the Aspects* (1972) Dordrecht: Reidel.

## Exercises with tense and aspect marking

1. Adding a perfect marker (*have*, -en) adds a meaning [F < R], so it is naturally used if the completion of an event is more important than the time it happened, as at the beginning of this chapter. If the precise nature of the action is also not important, e.g. 'Where did you get that crazy tie?', then the marked nature of perfect – focusing on the completion of the event – is not appropriate and we use the preterite. Which of each pair following is better to use in a joke?

   (a) 1. Where've you stolen that tie (from)?
       2. Where'd you steal that tie?
           (*'d* is a [spoken] lax form of *did* here.)
   (b) 1. Look what the cat dragged in!
       2. Look what the cat's dragged in!
           (*'s* is a lax form of *has*.)

   Anything done to or by a person from history is finished so there is little need to point out its completedness, and the perfect is not commonly used unless the person is still alive. Which form is most reasonable for the following? Explain your choice ('**' marks a difficult one).

- (c) Peter the Great (began/has begun) many improvements in Russia.
- (d) This year's Nobel Prize winner (taught/has taught) here for three years.
- (e) The Beatles (gave/have given) three concerts in Prague.
- (f) The President of the USA (was/has been) a native son, always. **
- (g) (at a funeral) This man (travelled/has travelled) in many places and (is/has) now embark(ing/ed) on his best journey. **
- (h) The Holy Roman Empire (was/has been) destroyed.
- (i) — (same as (h)) — and cannot be recreated again in the EC. **

A covert way to suggest that the subject was changed by some event is to use perfect as it emphasizes the completion of the event (verb + complement). From this, it can also suggest that the subject is less eminent than the complements of the verb.

- (j) The Prime Minister (visited/has visited) Chernobyl.
- (k) Chernobyl (was visited/has been visited by) the Prime Minister.
- (l) The Queen (visited/has visited) my flower-arranging class.

2. Correct the errors in tense and aspect or the adverb to make them compatible.
- (a) * That girl and I know each other since childhood.
- (b) * Could you wait until I will come back?
- (c) * Young people don't read serious books recently.
- (d) * Do you know what time the sun is rising on your birthday?
- (e) * I'm surprised that he has finished that assignment for only two hours.
- (f) * Do you think it is raining tomorrow?

3. The unusual examples below would be reasonable in special circumstances or in a different world. Give an example of such a special circumstance (i.e. who could say it, when) and then as generally as possible give what the critical aspects of such special circumstances are.
- (a) Bob is getting sick this afternoon.
- (b) Cleopatra has visited Rome many times.
- (c) Fred is finishing his homework next week.

    (d) It rains tomorrow at 3:15 a.m.

    (e) Mitterand visited Shanghai at least once.

    (f) This bridge has been walked under by your dog.

4. Put the indicated verbs into a plausible tense and aspect.

    (a) The thieves (already run away) when the police arrived.

    (b) Christmas (fall) on a Thursday this year.

    (c) I've got a reservation at that good Chinese restaurant. I (take) Lena there tonight. (Spk hasn't asked her yet)

    (d) (same as (c), but she has accepted the invitation)

    (e) We're late. The concert will probably (end) before we get there.

    (f) I (think) of going to Trinidad with my family this year.

    (g) Look at those clouds! It (start) raining in a few minutes.

    (h) He (lose) money since he took up Mahjong and doesn't have much left.

5. Explain the differences between the following pairs of sentences.

    (a)   They've been to Africa for two months.

    (a')  They've gone to Africa for two months.

    (b)   Akiko always cooks breakfast when I get up.

    (b')  Akiko is always cooking breakfast when I get up.

    (c)   The last train leaves at 0.36 a.m.

    (c')  The last train is going to leave at 0.36 a.m.

    (c'') The last train is leaving at 0.36 a.m.

    (d)   My brother lives in New York.

    (d')  My brother is living in New York.

    (e)   That girl is very friendly.

    (e')  That girl is being very friendly.

    (f)   That actress will have another baby.

    (f')  That actress is going to have another baby.

    (f'') That actress is having another baby.

    (g)   I smell her perfume.

    (g')  I'm smelling her perfume.

    (h)   John always uses my dictionary.

    (h')  John is always using my dictionary.

    (i)   I know a man that always gives his grandson expensive toys.

    (i')  I know a man that is always giving his grandson expensive toys.

    (j)   I wonder if you can lend me some money for a few days.

    (j')  I am wondering if you can lend me some money for a few days.

(k)   The pilot announced that we will fly at 4000 metres.

(k')   The pilot announced that we will be flying at 4000 metres.

(l)   (I'll) see you! [farewell]

(l')   (I'll) be seeing you! [farewell]

(m)   Who has drunk my orange juice?

(m')   Who has been drinking my orange juice?

(n)   We will land at Schiphol in ten minutes.

(n')   We will be landing at Schiphol in ten minutes.

6. (hard) To make the time-graphs that are clearer than the arithmetical description of the temporal aspects of a sentence, start with a time-arrow pointing to the right, the future. S, the moment of speaking, can be put somewhere near the middle, and R, generally fixed by a time-adverb, can be added to its left if the sentence is past or to the right if the sentence if marked future. (If there is no time adverb or indication of tense (i.e. 'present' tense), then the R is probably at S.)

If there is more than one clause, there will probably be several Bs and Fs, so use a subscript '0' for the main clause B − F, and '1' for those of a subordinate clause. Or, alternatively, use no mark for the main clause end-points and a prime (') for the subordinate clauses, or use a separate line for each event as done here. B is by definition before F, so the events of these clauses will appear as short lines connecting a B and an F. For clarity I suggest putting the main clause event above the time-arrow, and the subordinate clause event line below.

For example, take 'Lena said she would wait' which is equivalent to 'Lena said "I will wait"' (beware of verbs that are preterite because a dominated verb is). The first of the two verbs *say*, *wait* is before now ($R_0 < S$) and the second is after that ($R_0 < R_1$):

say:          $B_0$–$F_0$

————$R_0$————————S———→

wait:                 $B_1$?————$F_1$?

(The '?' shows that we don't really know whether the waiting has begun or has ended − their relation to S is not expressed.)

Make time-graphs for the following.

(a) I thought that Anne would refuse.

(b) She came and ate supper, and left.

(c) She came just when I began eating.

7. (for advanced students) When an event is limited, as in 'run (for) 20 km' or 'sing for ten minutes', it is this limited amount (call it F') that ends at R, and the action itself may continue.

This can be diagrammed as:

He has been singing ten minutes (already).

```
───────────────────R = S───→
      B──sing──?–?–?
      B──10mn──F
```

Make time-diagrams for the following, including the time limitation.

(a) Vic had drunk eight bottles by noon.

(b) The film will have been showing for fifteen minutes when we arrive.

(c) Tom had eaten before he left.

# CHAPTER 8

# Limits to Events

While direct translations are sometimes strange or even contradictory, they may be quite reasonable in their language of origin. Why?

(1)  \* I woke my father up at six o'clock, but he didn't wake up.

(1')  I *tried to* wake up my father at six o'clock, but he didn't wake up.

(2)  \* I am coming to Japan since 1979.

(2')  I *have been in* Japan since 1979. OR: I *came to* Japan *in* 1979.

In the following, English needs an extra element to be comprehensible.

(3)  \* it was last summer that I knew him.

(3')  it was last summer that I *got to* know him.

(4)  ! I am here for three hours. « (Fr) je *suis* ici depuis trois heures.

(4')  I *have been* here *for* three hours.

In contrast to this, English does not tolerate a progressive that some languages require. Where do these differences come from?

(5)  \* are [you] knowing him? « (Jp) kare-ga shitteimasu-ka.

(5')  do you know him?

The differences illustrated above between the English ways of saying things and the ways that they may be expressed in various other languages result from the **aspectual** properties of their respective verbs. The term 'aspect' is commonly used for time-relations that are not 'tense' (i.e. not past, present and future), but, as we saw in Chapter 7, these aspects turned out to be concerned with showing the beginnings and ends of events. The verbs themselves, as well as adjectives and even nouns, may or may not include beginnings or ends. Here we look at these aspectual properties of verbs and how adverbial phrases can add limits to the events depicted.

If you have not yet read Chapter 7, it might help to look at its conclusion at least, as the notion F for the time of the finish or end of an event will get a lot of use here, as well as B, the time of its beginning. The perfect and the progressive related these to R, the 'reference' time pointed to by a time adverb in the sentence, so they interact with the aspectual meanings of verbs.

## States and stativity

A **state** is a condition or a changeless event without any inherent end, like *to be tall* or *to resemble (someone)*. Although a state has not always been, nor need it continue for ever, it is continuing when we consider it, with no apparent change. A state does not have a natural point of termination, that is, it does not progress towards a time of being finished, F. This is why the progressive (*be -ing*) cannot be used easily with states – part of its meaning is that the time of reference (R) is before the finish (F), i.e. that the event is not finished at R.

> * he is being tall.
> * she was being very intelligent.
> * I am being very hungry, aren't you?

Most adjectives and nouns are essentially stative in this sense, for it takes no effort to continue being what one is. However, not all adjectives are necessarily stative; *to be polite* or *silly* can be so contrary to one's nature that it takes a force of will to continue being so. If so, we can use the progressive to bring out their temporariness, as in the following.

> he's being silly.
> she was being extra stupid yesterday.

The progressive used with an adjective, then, really adds limits to the state, showing that it is quite temporary. If, on the other hand, a state is more or less permanent, that is for example if a person is silly by nature, we could not use the example above but must avoid the progressive, as in the first example following.

he's silly.
he's silly today.

Of course, the progressive is not the only way to limit a state. A time adverb will do just as well. Thus the last example is as effective as the first one for saying that it is a temporary state.

In fact, as adjectives hardly ever occur with the progressive, it has come to take on an additional flavour of wilfulness or **volition** when used with an adjective. Thus, while it might be reasonable on a summer evening to say the first following, the second is impossible because it attributes a quality of life to the sky.

the sky is red this evening.
* the sky is being red this evening.

---

Q.   What would it mean to say 'He is being suspicious'?[1]

---

The progressive puts limits in time on verbs also, so 'He is singing' speaks of a period of singing, already begun, yet to be completed. Comparing the examples that follow, it is clear that the speaker of the first does not expect that her good singing will last.

she is singing well.
she sings well.

Because verbs usually describe processes, with ends that follow their beginnings as surely as day follows night, using the progressive is normal and seldom adds a sense of volition to the description of an event. A number of verbs in English do describe situations without inherent ends, however, like *to resemble*, *to believe* and *to know*. This last one means [have information or knowledge], and once you know something we do not expect that to end at any given time, if at all. Such verbs are called **stative** verbs, for they are rather like ordinary adjectives in describing a state. We generally speak of these verbs as being incompatible with a progressive, as in * 'You are knowing me well', but in special circumstances a progressive can be used, and again it can add a volitional flavour, such as can be found in the second example below[2] (the 'belief' is deliberate, for the sake of an argument perhaps). It seems that if the progressive forces a finish on to some description that includes no inherent end, a notion of volition may be added, in English at least.

(1)     I believe your theory.
(2)   ! I am believing your theory.
(3)     I am believing this theory more and more
(4)     I see some elephants across the lake.
(5)   * I am seeing some elephants across the lake.
(6)     I am seeing halos around everything.

There are other special circumstances that can lead to using the progressive with a stative verb. For instance, the second example above can also be understood as [gradually, step by step]; it thereby has a definite end — when you completely believe it. If such a modifier is added, as in (3), the progressive becomes normal and even preferred.

Another circumstance where the progressive fits with a stative verb is in (6). Here, the natural interpretation is that the speaker thinks it is a temporary state, as in telling his doctor that his eyes are doing strange things, hoping that he will be able to cure them.

Q.   What does 'I am suspecting him' mean?[3]

This is a special semantic feature of some of the perception verbs, *to see, hear, feel, taste, smell*. They are called stative because, in ordinary circumstances (5), the progressive is quite strange or even impossible with them. Perhaps this is because they are semantic modifications of *to know*. Like the first pattern following, their meanings all include [Kno], and they differ by specifying the source of the knowledge. Thus we can conceive of the meaning of *to see*, for example, as something like [to know by seeing].

they know that she is coming.
they see that she is coming.     [know it using the eyes]
they hear that she is coming.    [know it using the ears]

To see a person is not of course to know a great deal about her, but it does mean that one knows something about her, where she is and what she is doing, if nothing else. We can see why these verbs do not take the progressive easily. The meaning of *to see* contrasts sharply with *to look at* or *to watch*, which mean, respectively, [to direct the eyes at] (without necessarily seeing or knowing anything) and [to keep the eyes on] something. These latter verbs naturally take the progressive.

she is looking at an elephant.
she is watching an elephant.

---

Q.  What is the change in the meaning of *to see* in an example
    like 'I see what you mean' or 'I see, I see!' where it is an
    informal way to say [I know]?[4]

---

Thus we see that most verbs are not stative; they can take the
progressive easily because their meanings include a beginning and
an end, and even (Chapter 7) require it when used about
something happening at the moment. The stative verbs and most
adjectives, however, do not have inherent completions (they lack
an F), so the use of the progressive is definitely unusual and adds
some special meaning (in adding the F), often a volitional aspect.
They can also add, with stative verbs at least, a sense of [gradually
increasing] or [strictly temporary]. Thus the following are normal,
in spite of the general impossibility of the progressive with
statives.

I am seeing Renaissance museums this year.
They are believing me more and more.

## Volition

Though it is not technically an aspect (not referring to B or F),
**volition** is related to non-stative, for not only does the
progressive add it sometimes, but our world is one in which
nearly everything that is done volitionally, that is by free choice
of our wills, is temporary in nature. On the other hand, states are
inherently involuntary, as are processes we cannot control,
including many body functions and most of the processes of
nature like growing, dying or being born. A standard way to test
whether or not a verb is [volitional] is whether or not it can be
commanded. One cannot choose whether or not to die, for
example, so it is generally very strange to command someone to
do it. However, it is possible to try to command just about any
process, especially if emotionally involved; for example, a farmer
in a dry spell might say 'Rain, damn it!'

    English does not have a systematic contrast between verbs in
terms of volition, but this aspect of meaning does play a role in
understanding. Many verbs are understood non-volitionally in a

neutral context, but an adverb that refers to the subject's will adds a component of volition to the sentence that overrides any hint of being involuntary. For instance, *to breathe* depicts an involuntary act if not modified, but if we find it in a context with *deliberately*, the breathing described is under some wilful control, as in 'He was deliberately breathing slowly and softly.' The verb *to try* is little more than volition, as in 'He is trying to breathe', which of course wipes out any trace of non-volition in a following verb that is dominated by it.

## Punctive and durative – perfective and imperfective

Contrary to the stative nature of most adjectives and perhaps all nouns, verbs commonly depict events that have beginnings and ends. If the end must follow on the heels of the beginning, we call the verb *punctive* [as in the word *puncture*) or 'punctual'. Sometimes the term 'punctive' is restricted to the verbs in the first column below, where, conceptually at least, B = F. It is quite hard to imagine a circumstance where the progressive could be used with them, e.g. ★ 'Finally, he is recognizing me.' If on the other hand the end is necessarily long after the beginning, the verb is called *durative* (like the words *duration*, *during*).

| PUNCTIVE | | DURATIVE |
|---|---|---|
| to notice | to explode | to endure |
| to recognize | to hit | to last |
| to arrive | to begin | to study |
| to find | to wake up | to grow |

Most verbs lie between the two extremes, but in Slavic languages like Russian, verbs tend to pair off, the punctive ones (called **perfective**) often being formed from the **imperfective** ones by adding a prefix (often *po-*, but *na-* in the example below). A special feature of Russian tense is that because the perfective ones are so short, a simple 'present' tense (i.e. [not past]) comes to have a future meaning with them. Beware the word *perfective*, however, for the English 'perfect' is quite different, putting the end F of the action before R.

| imperfective (durative) | perfective (punctive) |
| --- | --- |
| ПИСАТЬ | НАПИСАТЬ |
| pisat' [write] | na-pisat' [write (it) down] |
| ГОВОРИТЬ | СКАЗАТЬ |
| govorit' [talk a while] | skazat' [say (it)] |

Some of the differences in English verbs can be understood in these terms. For example, *to learn* <*a fact*> is rather punctive, while *to study*, *to learn about* are durative.

|                      |                                |
| -------------------- | ------------------------------ |
|   to learn a fact    | ! to study a fact              |
| ? to learn chemistry |   to study chemistry           |
|                      |   to learn about one's ancestors |

Another common problem for foreign students of English, how to use *to tell* and how to distinguish it from *to speak*, *to talk*, *to say*, is partly resolved by remembering that it has essentially the same meaning as *to teach*, [to cause someone to know something] (as in Chapter 12), but it is commonly punctive, or nearly instantaneous, while *to teach* is durative. Naturally, you can only **tell** a person your telephone number; to **teach** it to him would imply that he is so stupid that it will take a long time! *To talk* is similarly durative, so it would be quite unusual to ! 'talk about your telephone number'. *To tell* and *to talk* have no direct relation, then, to *to speak* which involves the mouth but not necessarily ideas, or to *to say* which involves making public what one believes or pretends to. Speaking can be long or short, but *to say* is rather punctive.

Literary French has two past tense forms, the *imparfait* (-ait) for durative events meaning basically [not finished at R in the past] or [R < S·B < R < F], and the *passé simple* (-a) for cases where duration is not important, but since it is past it is seen as finished, or [F = R < S]. This distinction is not so common in other languages, at least as an obligatory choice, and is no longer current in spoken French. English has the optional *used to* to express [past durative] when it is important. In addition, the English progressive can be seen to add durativity, with any tense, when something else happens during that period for example, but, as we saw with statives, it also adds temporariness. Because *used to* does not locate some other event within the period of action, however, it is quite different from the progressive, though the past durative of French can be translated as either, depending on the circumstance.

We do have one syntactic expression of durative in English,

though it is not used very often: repeating a verb, adverb or adjective in the predicate twice (or three times for emphasis) with *and* between.

> she swam and swam (and swam).
> the road grew bumpier and bumpier and bumpier.
> she got more and more (and more) beautiful.

## Iterative and generic

When the progressive is used with a punctive verb, time can be really slowed down, for the beginning of the event must be before, and the end after, the moment we are looking at ([B < R <F], Chapter 7). For this reason, as in the examples below, it has sometimes been called the 'expanded tense'. The shot in the first example below is a moment in the jumping, but the second example describes a very short glance.

> I was jumping over the fence when the shot rang out.
> the firecracker was exploding when she glanced at him.

Instead of stretching the event, the punctive verb may be reinterpreted **iteratively**, that is, that it happened repeatedly, and it is the B and F of the whole series of repetitions that the progressive describes. This usually needs a plural subject or object, as in the following.

> the firecrackers were exploding when she kissed him.
> I was jumping 2 metres [jumps] when the new athletic coach was hired.

If there are enough firecrackers in this example, the kiss can be almost leisurely, but because kisses generally take more time than explosions, it is very hard to interpret this without adding the notion of iteration. It need not be so, however, if an explosion is one that takes more time, as 'She kissed Agent 007 while the island was exploding.' We can conclude that the progressive does not itself express iteration but that this notion is added in interpreting a sentence that would be hard to imagine otherwise.

   In fact, any verb in the so-called present tense without progressive is normally interpreted in this iterative sense (unless it is stative, of course); as a rule in English there should be some modification of a verb (e.g. past, progressive, perfect, future) if at all possible. If none is used, then all of these must be impossible, giving a meaning [not restricted to the past or future, nor limited in time]. These cases are called 'gnomic' or **generic**, as in the examples below, but can readily be seen as merely stative interpretations (without F) of events that are not commonly thought of as stative.

> he studies mathematics.  she drives a Mercedes.
>
> girls give valentines to boys in Japan.  it rains a lot in Oregon.

The imperfective (durative) verbs of Russian that designate movement, e.g. [walk, ride, fly, go, come], typically have two forms, one for a single movement as ЛЕТЕТБ *letet'* [to fly to (somewhere)], called 'definite', and the other for more than one simple movement, e.g. *letat'* [to fly], called 'indefinite', for round trips, often, or just wandering by air. These latter are iterative verbs, and we might see Russian as applying the distinction of singular:plural (i.e. non-iterative: iterative) to these verbs as well as to nouns.

Although iteration is not realized in terms of different verbs in English, it is important none the less because it is easy to detect [happening not just once] and appears in a number of different circumstances. We saw one such case in Chapter 6 with the generic modals. These modals mark characteristic actions of the subject, so 'He'*ll* get drunk on Saturday night and spend the night in jail, but he'*ll* always be a good father the next morning' describes a particular characteristic of his. But we cannot usually speak of a characteristic without it happening many times (but check out the second example below), so these usually imply an iterative action, also called 'habitual'. Indeed, its preterite form *would* is commonly recognized as habitual or iterative, as in 'He'*d* sneak out at night and howl at the moon.' With inanimate subjects, however, it is difficult to call these habitual, for habits (in English) are restricted to animates and even the feeling of happening repeatedly can disappear, especially when stating a general rule about the world, such as in the first examples below.

> oil will float on water.
>
> this motor'll overheat if you idle it too long.
>
> pigs'll eat anything.
>
> boys will be boys.
>
> Tommy'd cry when he heard 'no'.

These examples describe characteristics of the subject, and iterativity is perceptible if the subject is a singular count noun. When the subject designates an animal, human or otherwise, we can further perceive it as a habit.

Nor is *used to* in 'She used to eat crackers in the bathtub', an iterative (or habitual) marker, for it goes well with events that happened only once, as in 'An old oak tree used to be in the front yard', as we saw in Chapter 6. It simply marks a long duration and is interpreted as [repeatedly] and even [habitual], if we assume the event (*eating crackers*) to be short, and if the subject is animate. If, however, it was a *hamster* that was eating crackers in the bathtub (no water, of course), then it might have been a fairly continuous thing and the feeling of iterativity can fall away.

Iterative interpretations, then, are fairly common when the aspect(s) expressed in the verb conflict with those expressed by the auxiliary. Other than this, English may have no way of expressing iterative notions except overtly with an adverb like *repeatedly* or *over and over (and over) again*.

## Types of verbs

The 'perfect aspect' focuses on the end of the action, [F < R]; it indicates the event finished at or before whatever time is specified, R. Many English verbs themselves focus on the end-point or finish F of the action, unlike parallel verbs in some other languages. These **accomplishment** verbs, like the examples following, depict an action that includes the end-point, so they cannot be used with the preterite tense unless the activity they depict was successfully accomplished.

| | | |
|---|---|---|
| to give | to learn | to teach |
| to wake up | to persuade | to lift |

This is why the examples below are utter contradictions, although in some languages they are quite reasonable. In Japanese, for example, the word for [to bribe], wairo-wo okuru, means only [to go through the motions of giving a bribe], effectively [to try to bribe], and doesn't include anything about the completion of the exchange, whether or not it was accomplished. We can say that such words don't include a completion or finish point F.

Whether or not the meaning of a word includes F can be important if you don't want to be seen talking nonsense.

* I bribed the mayor, but she refused to accept the bribe.
* he started the motor, but it was too cold to start.

In the same way, *to persuade X to Vb* includes that [X agrees to Vb in the end], whereas the Japanese translation *settoku-suru* describes only the process of talking, arguing or begging, without implying any attainment of the purpose, X's agreement to Vb.

In these examples, the English verbs denote actions plus the accomplishment of their end-points, while their Japanese counterparts describe only the actions. This difference does not hold for all verbs, however. For example, both *to offer* and its Japanese counterpart describe merely the act of offering without implying that the offer is actually accepted. Conversely, some Japanese verbs involve end-points while their English translations do not. As important as it may be, however, this is one aspect of meaning that is seldom indicated in dictionaries.

Often, *up* can be added in English to reinforce this **completive** aspect that accomplishment verbs have, whether or not it is completed. The first example following may or may not be completive, though it would normally be taken to have been completed. In the second, the *for*-phrase defines an end [ten minutes afterwards] which is completed, so the beer is probably not finished. In the last, the beer is surely gone because the *up* suggests that the action of 'drinking my beer' is complete and finished. The combination of them both, last, is 'unsemantic' – it is impossible to get a coherent meaning from it.

(1)    he drank my beer.
(2)    he drank my beer for ten minutes.
(3)    he drank up my beer.
(4)  * he drank up my beer for ten minutes.

The progressive, however, locates the end or finish of the event depicted after the time of reference, so it expressed the lack of completion of the event, even if there is an indication of completive such as *up*. In 'He was drinking up her beer when she came back from the loo', his intent was to drink it all but hadn't when she returned.

Q.  A completive *up* combines freely with verbs that are not
    committed to having or lacking an end-point, defining an F
    at the point where the action cannot be continued further.
    What, then, do the following mean?[5]

    **she cut up the cake.**
    **he fixed up his car.**

    Really novel combinations are possible. What could the
    following mean?

    **I am going to search up something to eat.**
    **he wanted to paint up his bike with weird designs.**

The completive aspect, like many other aspects, is a characteristic
of a predicate or the event depicted. Many verbs are not
inherently completive but, like *to drink*, are interpreted as
completive or not depending on whether a complement of the
verb is limited; 'to drink a glass of sherry' is clearly completive,
while 'to drink sherry' is not. Thus it is really predicates, verbs
plus their complements, that we may call completive, as 'to climb
a mountain' has a finish F when you get to the top, but 'to climb
mountains' does not as there is always another mountain to
climb. However, as a general rule, a specific event in the past is
interpreted in English to be finished and closed unless there is
some indication to the contrary.

Some verbs like *to win, to arrive at* force a completive
interpretation in spite of indefinite objects. They are called
**achievement** verbs as they focus almost entirely on the
completion of some activity. Because these verbs depict
something that happens at a moment in time, they are the
extreme of punctive verbs and seem like they really ought not go
with the progressive at all.

The real world is not mathematically pure, however, for if
you look at the smallest point with a magnifying glass you will see
it has width, and progressive does that with achievement verbs. It
is easy to say 'She is arriving at the top of the mountain', if
watching with a telescope. A mountain top does not have a
specific edge around it that one crosses in an instant, and even if
it did it would still take some time between when her head
crosses that line and when her feet cross it. Nevertheless, these

time expansions are often less likely than some reinterpretation, as in 'I am winning!' This is not likely thought (or yelled) as one crosses the finish line but well before, meaning that the event of winning has already begun: [I am well ahead and sure to win]. A verb like *to find* has nearly the same meaning as *to look for*, differing primarily in being an achievement verb, so ! 'I am finding a buried treasure' is very strange unless the speaker is sure of succeeding, as she might in 'I am finding some chalk for the teacher.'

---

Q.   Most would-be achievement verbs seem to have two ways of interpretation, as the instantaneous event itself or as the process leading up to that event. Use the progressive to decide which if any of these candidates cannot have the latter interpretation.[6]

| win <competition> | arrive at <loc> | reach <loc> |
| start <activity> | finish <activity> | stop <action> |
| die | be born | find <thing> |

---

These achievement verbs may in fact be nothing more than an end-point F, lacking a beginning B for the event. This would explain not only why they are conceived as being instantaneous but also why the progressive has two interpretations with them. Because the progressive locates the reference time between B and F, it adds a B to these verbs. It thus forces them to take on some duration, between B and F, or else the B is interpreted as the beginning when the achievement end-point became assured.

Many verbs are **activity** verbs; the events they depict do not progress towards some point of completion so their meanings do not include an F and they are ambivalent as to whether or not the action is completed. In 'She swam and swam' or 'She swam for two hours' the verb *to swim* describes an action that could be continued indefinitely. They go naturally with the progressive, but unless limited somehow, the perfect can only depict an experience in the indefinite past, a bit strange with an ordinary verb: ! 'She has drunk.' Adding a limited object with a measure like 'a cup of tea' or 'her tea' makes these completive, so it makes accomplishments – 'She has drunk her tea' – out of these activities. The perfect, then, merely says that the F (of some recent event) is before the present, and is quite normal. Vague measures like *some* or the 'have a Vb' in 'have a swim' make for vague Fs, but the perfect is still quite possible.

| no F | vague F | specific F |
|------|---------|------------|
| drink | drink some tea | drink a cup of tea |
| swim | have a swim | swim 2 miles |

## Adverbs for limits

Adverbs, as in 'across the river', can also imply a limit or F; the complex action of swimming-across-the-river cannot go on for ever because the adverb sets up an explicit goal and the action is finished when the other side of the river is reached. Similarly an adverb of duration such as 'for L', where L is some length of time, makes a limit at $F = B+L$. Thus 'She swam for thirty minutes' has an $F = B+30mn$. However, one cannot say 'I swam across the river for thirty minutes' because there are two goals, the other side of the river and thirty minutes of swimming. One of them is sure to be satisfied before the other – unless, of course, it is a narrow river that you swim across back and forth for the thirty minutes (an iterative reinterpretation) or a very wide river, as in 'I had swum across the Amazon for fifteen minutes when some piranhas started following me and my water-wings burst.' In both these cases the time limit clearly overrides the limit in space.

Q.   It is quite possible to say 'He swam across the Mississippi in fifteen minutes', so 'in L' does not provide a time limit as 'for L' does. What, then, is its meaning in terms of F, B and L? Use the '<' [earlier than] of Chapter 7.[7]

Most temporal expressions describe the beginning B or the finish F of an event, so they interact with the aspects of verbs and auxiliary elements. Some of the more obvious ones for a time-point T are as follows, using '=' for [the same time as], and, as in Chapter 7, '<' for [before]. If we take these notions R, B, F and T as clock times or as days on the calendar, we can take '<' as [is less than] and use elementary arithmetic to describe the relationships they express. ('≤' then stands for 'less than or equal'.)

| from T | — | $[B = T]$ | he paddled northward from 8 a.m. |
| before T | — | $[F < T]$ | he sang two songs before 3:00. |
| since T | — | $[B \leq T \cdot R \leq F]$ | he has spoken Arabic since 1984. |

'At T' is not quite so simple; it can designate the beginning of an activity, as in 'He sang at three o'clock', but is not so precise as *from*, allowing that it might be a bit after three when he actually started singing. We might thus represent it approximately as $[B \cong T]$, or $[Apx-(B = T)]$, cf. Chapter 9. However, it also designates the end of an achievement, e.g. 'He won at 3:15', and tries to cover both end and beginning for an accomplishment. This is not hard, given that it is only approximate, for punctive actions like 'He drew a circle at 3:30', but next to impossible with durative actions like ★ 'He climbed a mountain at 3:45.'

---

Q.  What are the likely meanings for the following:[8]

| | | |
|---|---|---|
| (un)til T | [    ] | he paddled till noon. |
| after T | [    ] | he drinks after supper? |

---

The T in most of these phrases can also be described with a clause, as in 'before she came' or 'before he has eaten'. As a general rule of English, the R of the main clause and the R' of this sort of adverbial clause are the same, which is why a time location can be expressed indifferently in either clause, as the 'on Tuesday' is in 'He was singing __ before she came __'. It also explains that either both or neither of the clauses are preterite.

Other adverbial phrases describe the length L of time taken between the beginning and the end of the action, F–B. The difference between *for* and *in* is small but can be important, as we saw in swimming across the Amazon. While 'for L' depicts a continuation until L is past, i.e. until the time B + L at least, 'in L' says it is finished by that time.

| | | |
|---|---|---|
| for L | $[F \geq B + L]$ | he has swum for three hours. |
| (with)in L | $[F \leq B + L]$ | he has swum there in three hours. |

Because a *for*-phrase specifies the length of time L, and creates an F or a B, it goes naturally with an activity verb to make an accomplishment, but it would impose an extra limit on an accomplishment. Sentences like ★ 'He has swum 2 km for three hours' are impossible, for a single accomplishment can't have two goals. On the other hand, a *within*-phrase does not define an F but needs one, so it is natural only with accomplishments and makes nonsense with activities: ★ 'He has swum in three hours.'

Of course, explaining these meanings with elementary bits of arithmetic (and the nasty looking formulas) does not mean that we do arithmetic in our heads while we talk. We could explain all these meanings with graphs as we did with time and tense, and that is probably a little closer to how we actually create and understand sentences. Graphs, however, are harder to print and are always specific for the relations between any times included in them, even though sentences often leave some relations unspecified. Exercise question 6 of Chapter 7 shows how to make graphs that are easier than formulas for most to understand, even if they are not always so accurate.

## Aspect of events

We have seen now how the times of the beginning and end of an event are usually important in grasping well what a sentence means, and, of course, in making sentences that will mean what you want them to. As languages (e.g. English and Japanese) can be significantly different in how they handle these 'aspects', successful language learning requires a sensitivity to them. Fortunately, there are only two basic elements to note: what is the beginning (B) and what is the end (F) of the event, if it has one at all. This finish (F) is the point at which an event is complete and finished, when it cannot be continued further. It is quite important in English, not only in using completive verbs and predicates but also in the perfect and progressive auxiliaries (as in Chapter 7), as well as many adverbial expressions of time. The table below summarizes how F distinguishes aspectual classes of verbs.

| Meanings | Aspects | Examples |
|---|---|---|
| [F soon after B] | punctive, punctual | to explode, tell |
| [F long after B] | durative | to endure, teach |
| [has F] | completive | to find, decide |
| [F, B for series] | iterative | to talk and talk and talk |

| Characteristics | Verb Classes | Examples |
|---|---|---|
| [no F] | stative | to know, resemble |
| [F] if quantified | activity | to walk, swim, teach |
| inherent [F] | accomplishment, telic | to decide, draw a circle |
| [F] only | achievement | to win, realize |

Volitional [the subject wills it] is not considered an aspect in this technical sense as it is not defined in terms of B or F. We have seen, however, that both it and the iterative aspect are involved in reinterpretation forced by interactions of the B and F of a verb with its auxiliaries and adverbial phrases.

English seems to concentrate on the finishing of an event and has many **achievement** verbs that include the F. Other languages such as Japanese may well do the opposite, concentrating on the beginning of an event. Some languages like the Slavic ones (e.g. Russian, Polish) try to do both, having typically two verb forms for each concept, one including an F and the other without. Languages typically have their own specific way, then, of describing the end-points of events, and direct translations can sometimes make strange sentences or even impossible ideas.

Prepositional phrases can be used to make the limits of an event as specific as desired, but as with modals and other areas where a language includes some aspects of meaning in the choice of word or grammatical structure, these totally explicit ways may be harsh or artificial. They should be used to supplement the choices offered by the grammar of the language, not to replace or to override them. Although that may be comprehensible, it will likely be confusing and hard to understand.

## Answers and notes

1. That [he is suspicious] but that this state of affairs is temporary and probably deliberate.
2. When examples like (2) are used without this special meaning, i.e. instead of (1) as often found in India and elsewhere, they are simply errors, as is (5).
3. That [I suspect him], but there is something temporary about it; it hasn't yet reached its final state. Perhaps it is my duty as police commissioner (though I don't believe in his guilt), or that my suspicions are growing.
4. The [using the eyes] drops off (or else it becomes [using the mind's eye]).
5. She cut it until there was no part of the cake uncut. There was no part of his car left unfixed.
   I am going to get [completive] something to eat, by searching,

i.e. I am going to *find* something to eat. He wanted to cover his bike with weird designs.

6. *To be born, to stop* seem difficult to me, but with a time adverbial, e.g. 'in ten minutes', they are possible. But see Chapter 7 on the progressive used with reference to future time.

7. 'in L' means [F < B + L), or as (F–B) is the length of time taken, [F–B < L].

8. '(un)til T' — [T = F]. 'after T' — [T < B].

## Keywords

stative, volition, punctive, durative, (im)perfective, iterative, generic/gnomic, activity, accomplishment, achievement.

## Further reading

Aspect markers were mostly included in the previous chapter; here we are concerned more with aspectual differences inherent in verbs. Vendler is the source of much modern work and of the distinctions in action, achievement and accomplishment. Comrie is a more rounded discussion.

Comrie, Bernard *Aspect: An Introduction to the Study of Verbal Aspect and Related Problems* (1976) London: CUP.

Friedrich, P. *On Aspect Theory and Homeric Aspect* (1974) Bloomington: Indiana University Press (*IJAL Memoir* **25**).

Lyons, John *Semantics II* (1977) London: CUP, § 15.6.

Mel'chuk, Igor *Cours de morphologie générale*, vol. II (in press) Montréal: Presses de l'Université de Montréal.

Vendler, Z. 'Verbs and Times' (1967, revd edn) pp. 97–121 in Zeno Vendler (ed.) *Linguistics in Philosophy*, Ithaca: Cornell University Press.

## Exercises with verbal limits

1. In each pair of examples, one has a problem with aspect. Say which and explain what is strange about it.
    (a) They are tasting the imported wine now.
    (a') This Austrian wine is tasting a little too dry.

(b)  Princess Anne is having beautiful eyes.

(b')  Princess Anne is having a piano lesson.

(c)  Pine trees are surrounding the house.

(c')  The police are surrounding the house.

(d)  She is smelling the perfume.

(d')  I am smelling that something is burning.

(e)  This bucket is holding 2 gallons of water.

(e')  She is holding a canary in her left hand.

2.  Correct errors and infelicitous aspects by revising the verbs in the following.

(a)  * I learned English very hard, but I still can't speak it.

(b)  * Get up and wear your clothes quickly!

(c)  ? Please receive this gift from my parents.

(d)  ? What club are you going to belong to when you enter university?

(e)  ? You are not supposed to ride a motorcycle without putting a helmet on.

(f)  * One of our students drowned in the pond, but luckily a passer-by saved him.

(g)  * I saw into the room to learn who was there.

(h)  Achoo! Darn it, * I seem to have had a cold.

(i)  * I counted how many people were in the hall, but there were so many that I couldn't count them all.

(j)  * The nurse fed the baby some nice warm milk, but he wouldn't drink it.

(k)  * Reuben knew the secret just as he arrived.

(l)  ? I generally read a book when I get on a train.

(m)  * Please be careful not to fall the cups and glasses.

3.  Recast the following states with inchoative (Bcm) verb forms, so as to describe how the state came about. Some adjectives have different inchoative forms depending on what is collocated with them. You may add an adverb at the end of a sentence to make it 'feel better' since English avoids ending a sentence with a verb.

(a) The sky was dark.          (e) He was tired out.

(b) His responses were soft.   (f) The weather is warm.

(c) My belief was strong.      (g) She was upstairs.

(d) He was strong.             (h) Her problems are big.

4.  Inchoative verbs are often used in a transitive form with a subject that 'causes' [Coz] the change. In the following, replace the stative adjectives or verbs with such transitive verbs and add a purpose-clause. For example, 'The room is dark' →

'They darkened the room (in order) to show some slides.'

(a) This road is wide.     (f) Gambling is legal in New Jersey.

(b) Her skirt is short.     (g) The foreign exchange rate is stable.

(c) My knife is sharp.      (h) The boy knows how to read those kanji.

(d) Our library is large.   (i) A special envoy went to Prague.

(e) His answer is simple.   (j) Carol intends to marry the artist.

5. Add an expression such as 'for ___ minutes/hours' or 'in ___ minutes/hours' to the following examples.

   (a) I was drinking with my old friends (    ).

   (b) We reached the top of Mount Fuji (    ).

   (c) Ms Potavova ran 1000 metres (    ).

   (d) Anne practises the piano (    ) every day.

   (e) Becky cleaned the huge living room (    ) 10 minutes!

6. Say whether or not there is a defined end F for the actions that take *for* and the ones that take *in*. If *for* is used instead of *in*, what is the resulting change in interpretation?

7. Explain the difference in meaning of the following pairs of sentences.

   (a) Why aren't you quiet?

   (a') Why don't you be quiet?

   (b) The hungry boy ate for two minutes.

   (b') The hungry boy ate in two minutes.

   (c) Bill gave a jump at the noise.

   (c') Bill made a jump to escape from the car.

   (d) Patricia gave a big cry of pain.

   (d') Patricia had a big cry over her loss.

   (e) Reuben gave Marie a threatening look.

   (e') Reuben took a close look at Marie.

8. Although 'He decided' and 'He will decide' are completive, 'He was deciding' and 'He will be deciding' are not. Explain why the progressive aspect modification (Chapter 7) destroys the completive aspect of a verb.

9. Recall that Slavic verbs tend to form perfective and imperfective pairs. Explain in more detail why a perfective verb [B = F] with the present tense endings cannot have a present meaning and thus comes to depict a future event.

# CHAPTER 9

# Prepositions

In many languages prepositions are used to show aspects of
location of an event – whether something happened, for
example, in, on, at or near my house. English has a rather
extensive set of such prepositions and uses them to carry meaning
for which other languages commonly use nouns or verbs. In
Chinese, for example, we would not watch television in the
kitchen but 'at the kitchen's inside'. English uses prepositions so
much that we might even call it a 'prepositional language'. Here
we will break down some of this complexity, and in the process
find semantic elements that play important roles in most if not all
languages.

 As with the arrays of deictic markers in Chapter 4, the way
the meanings of English prepositions break down into elementary
meanings shows again that many words can be decomposed into
semantic elements. In fact, English prepositions are so extensive
that there is probably no other way to learn them – to list all the
possible uses of each one in a dictionary would be nearly endless,
and almost useless for most language learners.

Although we shall be concerned primarily with prepositions in English, a great many languages are like Japanese and use postpositions instead. These are nearly the same as prepositions except that they are after (*post-*) the nominal instead of before it as *pre*positions are. The only other difference is that there is no stopping between a noun and a postposition.[1] After a preposition, however, one may well need to stop and think of what nouns or adjectives to say next, and languages that use prepositions generally allow this by treating them as separatable words.

| Jpn: | kare-ga | suupa-*ni* | terehon-sita. |
| Eng: | he | | telephon-ed *to* the supermarket. |
| Grm: | er hat d*en* | Markt | telephonier-t. |

Besides prepositions and postpositions, the only other common way to show a noun's function is with 'case' as in German above, Latin, Russian and Old English (*I:me, he:him* are remnants of a complete case system). These are like postpositions except that instead of being behind the whole nominal phrase they are generally suffixed on to the nouns and adjectives in the nominal. Worse, for the foreign learner at least, is that they often have different forms for various genders, as well as for nouns and adjectives. This is not necessary, however. Languages such as Finnish, Eskimo, Hungarian and Turkish have easily learned cases.

What is true of prepositions, then, is roughly true of postpositions and cases, and in fact, cases often double up with prepositions, just as prepositions like *to* can double up with other prepositions, in e.g., *into, on to*.

## Showing locations and limits of events

Prepositions are also commonly used in referring to things by their locations, as in 'the book *on* the table' or 'the ride *to* Banbury Cross'. In English, as in most languages, these same prepositions are used for showing where something happened. It is easiest to begin here where the prepositions can combine with elementary verbs like *to be, to go* to make simple sentences whose meanings can be explored in detail. The table below gives an array of these basic prepositions.

|       | [Loc] | [Dir]  | [Abl]    | [Neg-Loc]  |
|-------|-------|--------|----------|------------|
| [Cnt] | in    | into   | out of   | outside of |
| [Srf] | on    | on to  | off (of) | off (of)   |
| [Ǫ]   | at    | to     | from     | away from  |

The locative prepositions [Loc] in the first column are used to describe the location of something by means of some object (*at*), or as being on its surface (*on*), or being inside it (*in*). It is hard to give a meaning to *at* that is as specific, for it is the 'unmarked' term (Chapter 2), used when neither of the others is appropriate. We represent these aspects vertically as in the table with:

| [Cnt] | the inside of or 'the CoNTents of' | he waited in the car. |
| [Srf] | the SuRFace of                     | he waited on the car. |
| [Ǫ]   | plain or 'unmarked' relation        | he waited at the car. |

Anyone who knows English must know, unconsciously at least, the relationships in the table. The relationship between the first two columns is transparent; add a *to* for the second column – except that an *at*, which has little meaning anyhow, gets dropped in the process. The columns are often named by the names of the Latin cases used for them, but that differs only in using 'Dative' instead of 'Dir' that we needed in Chapter 4, and [Neg-Loc] which means essentially [not at that location].

| [Loc] | LOCative or LOCation                         | at the car   |
| [Dir] | DIRection, also called 'goal' (Latin 'dative') | to the car   |
| [Abl] | ABLative (Latin), also called 'source'        | from the car |

[Dir] and [Abl] describe movements so they occur with verbs of motion (*to go* is the basic one) or they impute motion to a neutral verb like *to drink*, as in 'He was drinking continuously from Miami to Havana.' In contrast, [Loc] and [Neg-Loc] are not motional so they go with *to be* instead of *to go*, and depict movements only if used with a verb like *to put*, *to jump* that implies some movement.

---

Q. The complex preposition *off (of)* is the same for [Abl] and [Neg-Loc]. How is this ambiguity resolved in ordinary sentences like 'He walked off (of) the bridge' [Abl] and 'He stayed off (of) the bridge' [Neg-Loc]?[2]

---

Foreign students of English will have noticed the parallels in usage between the rows: [Cnt] (from Chapter 4) *in, into, out,* [Srf] *on, on to, off,* and [Loc] *at, to, from.* For nouns that name spaces like *a room, a hole,* Cnt-prepositions are necessary, while the Srf-type are obligatory for surfaces like *a face, a side* of three-dimensional objects as well as lines in a two-dimensional drawing such as *circle, river, route.* Similarly, the *at*-type of preposition is needed with nouns that designate a point, like *a corner, a location,* but it is also used for things that don't have surfaces or insides, like *the end, an entrance.* Because this *at*-type is also used when the precise relationship in space is not important, e.g. 'He waited at the cabin' (inside or outside is not important), we take it to be the basic preposition of location [Loc], without any other semantic component. As the others have two components of meaning, roughly *in* [Loc:Cnt], *on* [Loc:Srf], we can use the symbol for 'nothing', Ⓠ, for *at* [Loc.Ⓠ] to have a label for that row in the chart as well as describe its unmarked nature.

| NAMING: | spaces | surfaces | lines | points |
|---|---|---|---|---|
| USE: | in [Cnt] | on [Srf] | on [Srf] | at [Ⓠ] |
| e.g. | a room<br>a hole<br>a cave | a face<br>a side<br>a plane | a circle<br>a trail<br>a boundary | a place<br>an intersection<br>a beginning |

These usages are quite systematic but a little different for two- and three-dimensional objects. This can be summarized simply as:

| for: | two-dimensional<br>figures | three-dimensional<br>objects |
|---|---|---|
| [Srf] boundary: | a line | a surface |
| [Cnt] enclosed: | surrounded by a line | surrounded by surface |
| [Ⓠ] | aspects of location not important | |

The only thing that is difficult here is learning what English considers to be the name of a surface. For instance, *lawns* or *lakes* – who would guess them to be surfaces? Apparently English treats them as such, and when seen from afar they do seem so. Many nouns can be used in several ways, of course, like *centre.* When used with *at* it is the point exactly in the middle, but when used with *in* it designates a vague area around that point. Another example is the word *corner*. When used to designate a part of a room, we must use *in* as it names a space. For the corner of a brick or a table, of course, we would use 'at the corner', for this sort of corner is a point. Other languages may have different nouns for these rather different sorts of corners. Japanese, for example, has a special word *sumi* for concave corners that you can be 'in', as opposed to *kado* for corners that you can be 'at'.

Another example is a big city. Although Chicago is perhaps 36 km (20 miles) long from north to south, without counting the suburbs, it is only a point on a map of North America, so we would use *at* if we only changed aeroplanes there. If we leave the airport, however, and go into the city, we cannot avoid realizing how vast it is and there is no way we can say anything but *in*, because we are surrounded by it. That is why 'stopping *in* Tokyo' suggests a few days' stay there, at least, while 'stopping *at* Tokyo' implies not more than a few hours there.

In a similar way, when we talk about where someone lives, Americans may think of a map. There, a street is only a line, effectively a boundary between two areas, so we would say 'He lives *on* such-and-such a street.' In England, however, urban streets tend to be enclosed by buildings, so one likely lives *in* such-and-such a street in England. If Americans (or British) consider the street as a place to play, however, we are surrounded by the street, so we are playing '*in* the street'. Again, if we park a car there and go in to see our friend, we would probably say it was parked '*on* the street', being at the edge or boundary of the street. However, if it pretty well blocked the street, then '*in* the street' would be appropriate. This is like '*in* the way' where the 'way' [the space needed to pass through] is filled more or less, in contrast to '*on* the way' where the 'way' is like a line, the route that we follow on a map.

The nice thing, and the important point here, is that whichever preposition is right with a given noun for location, the corresponding [Dir] preposition is appropriate to designate motion to that place, the goal.[3] This means that we have to learn only what preposition goes with what noun (with what meaning) for the locative prepositions; selecting a goal preposition is the same. Since we use *on* with a bus (apparently it was once an open surface like an open-back truck), we will use *on to* for entering a bus. The same goes for the source [Abl] prepositions, so of course we use *off (of)* for leaving a bus. You may notice that we often drop the *to* and the *of* if the motion is clear (i.e. expressed in the choice of verb), so most common is 'get *on* the bus' and 'get *off* the bus'. We shall see why below.

## More of these basic prepositions

The principle, and the applications of, the table of prepositions above, as well as the equivalent divisions of prepositional meanings into semantic atoms, is known to most people who have studied the English language. It is, however, only part of the more extensive system that English has, including another column [Via],[4] meaning roughly [by way of], and another row [Apx], meaning something like [APproXimately] or [in the near vicinity].

|  | [Loc] | [Dir] | [Abl] | [Neg-Loc] | [Via] |
|---|---|---|---|---|---|
| [Cnt] | in | into | out of | out(side) of | through |
| [Srf] | on | on to | off (of) | off (of) | across |
| [∅] | at | to | from | ? away from | past |
| [Apx] | near | towards | away from | ? away from | by |

The [Via] prepositions have the same distinctions as [Loc] and other prepositions, so we use *through* when *in* is appropriate for [Loc], *across* if *on* is right, and *past* to gain the vagueness that goes with *at*. Thus we go *through* a tunnel because if we stopped midway we would be *in* it, and we go *through* a field for the same reason, even though this might seem illogical at first blush. We cannot go *through* a bridge but *across* it, for stopping midway we are *on* it, not *in* it. An athletics field, unlike a wheat field such as the one we were just going through, is something that one plays *on*, so naturally one runs *across* it but not *through* it! On your way to school you might go *past* the police station, just as you might stop *at* it, or you might go *by* it if you merely get near it. Of course, whether you stop at the police station or just near it is a matter of perception, and your feelings towards the police. To use an [Apx] preposition suggests that you are sensitive to the nearness of the police station, while using *at* implies that the exact nature of the location is not relevant, to the speaker at least.

Nothing could be simpler, almost. When people learn English well, they need to learn these semantic atoms, [Cnt] and

[Srf], and what nouns they go with. Then choosing between all these prepositions is not difficult, because a language is basically systematic. If it were not, we could not understand sentences we had never heard before.

---

Q. Since we say 'He's in love' for a particular state of mind, what ought we to say for leaving that state of mind?[5]

---

Even here, however, there are special cases. Countries, for example, are lived *in* but one does not 'go into' a country. In ordinary speech we commonly go *to* a country, and leave it at that. In legal terms, to be sure, one *enters* a country, with this same idea of [Cnt] reappearing.

What do these semantic elements mean? [Via] means something like [from one side to the other], but not many languages have special prepositions or cases for it though Eskimo and Finnish do. On the other hand, many languages seem to have these same contrasts [Cnt], [Srf] and [Ø], though they are used in slightly different ways and may not show up as prepositions at all. Japanese, for example, uses ordinary nouns for them, while Chinese uses noun-like suffixes. English uses nouns too, for the less frequent notions, e.g. 'in/at/to the back of', 'on/to the right of', and so on. The element [Apx] is also not often expressed in prepositions in other languages, though of course the idea can always be expressed with words meaning [nearly], [almost] or [approximately] when it is important. The choice of preposition carries a great deal of meaning in English, more than in any other language I know of. Look at French, for example:

| FRENCH: | [Loc] | [Dir] | [Abl] | [Neg-Loc] | [Via] |
|---------|-------|-------|-------|-----------|-------|
| [Cnt] | dans | dans | de | (en)dehors(de) | par |
| [Srf] | sur | sur | de | (en)dehors(de) | par |
| [Ø] | à | à | de | | par |
| [Apx] | près de | vers | de | | près de |

French depends far less on prepositions. The distinction between [Loc] and [Dir] is mostly shown in the choice of verb, and the choice of the noun expresses the differences between [Cnt], [Srf], etc. for the last three columns. And the notion [Via] is usually expressed with a verb *traverser* or *passer*. Even simpler is Chinese:

| *prepositions* | | | | *noun suffixes* | | | |
|---|---|---|---|---|---|---|---|
| [Loc] | zài | 在 | | [Cnt] | -li | 里 | （裏） |
| [Dat] | dào | 倒 | | [Srf] | -shang | 上 | |
| [Abl] | cóng | 从 | （從） | [∅] | -∅ | | |

Q.  We saw earlier that different prepositions with the same noun could focus on different aspects of that noun. What are the different meanings between 'in back of', 'in the back of', 'at the back of'?[6]

The similarity, or identity, of Chinese and English in these basic distinctions [Cnt, Srf, ∅] is not simply a matter of finding in Chinese what is in English; these are the only noun suffixes in Chinese (besides ones for plural and possessive). As we find these distinctions in other languages as well, it seems to imply that they are fundamental to human language even though they are logically rather incomplete.

## Strong, weak and adverbial forms

There is yet another distinctive aspect found in the wealth of English prepositions. Some prepositions attract the beat of the rhythm of the sentence, so they are stressed or emphasized. We can call them 'emphatic' or **strong** prepositions; they are used when the relationship described by the preposition is important to the message. When it is not, we use a **weak** preposition which does not get a stress and so gets squeezed between words that do have beats in the rhythm of the sentence. Thus although the examples below describe the same events, they throw quite a different light on to the action depicted. In the first example the relationship [inside] is not important to the message, and little would be lost if the listener didn't hear it due to someone coughing, say. In the second, however, this relationship is indicated to be important because the speaker chose the strong preposition. This suggests that the subject has taken some effort to get in.

> then he got in the bus.     she crawled in the cupboard.
> then he got inside the bus.     she crawled into the cupboard.

Differences in stress parallel these differences in importance. The first example above is most naturally stressed on *got*, *bus*, but because *inside* takes a stress–beat itself in the second examples, it tends to take away stress from something else, mostly likely the verb as it is nearby. As you know from the chapter on negation, if you read it carefully that is, the rhythm of a sentence points out which words are important and can have major effects on the meaning of a negative sentence (and questions are the same), so the choosing between a strong preposition and its weak counterpart not only indicates whether you think the relationship depicted is important, but it can occasionally be very important to understanding the rest of the sentence.

We can divide the table of prepositions above into two tables, one for weak and the other for strong forms. Not all the prepositional concepts have two forms; the [Via] ones generally do not, nor do the unmarked [Q] ones. We can see, however, why English has many prepositions that translate the same way in other languages. Other languages express their differences in other ways.

|  |  | [Loc] | [Dir] | [Abl] | [Via] |
|---|---|---|---|---|---|
| Weak: | [Cnt] | in | in | out (of) | through |
|  | [Srf] | on | on | off (of) | across |
|  | [Q] | at | to | from | by |
|  | [Apx] | near, by | towards, for | away from | by |
| Strong: | [Cnt] | inside | into | out from | through |
|  | [Srf] | on | on to | off of | across |
|  | [Q] | at | to | from | past, by way of |
|  | [Apx] | near | towards | away from | by, near |

These weak prepositions are used somewhat like the 'weak forms' of pronouns like *him*, *his*, *her* when they lose their /h/ and are not vital to the meaning of the sentence. They throw off stress to neighbouring words, and tell the reader or listener that the relationship is not important, though it is true. As a consequence they are often pronounced unclearly, especially *at* and *to* (commonly with a schwa). None the less, they can be stressed in speaking, which then makes them equivalent to the strong varieties. The greatest use of strong forms, then, is in writing, where the choice between strong and weak forms indicates the relative importance of the relationship, as well as hinting at the intended stress pattern.

---

Q.  What preposition can you use to de–emphasize the locational aspect in the following?

> the fish floated inside the tank.
> the fish swam out from the tank.[7]

There are also some related adverbial forms, similar to both strong and weak forms. To be sure, these are adverbs in syntax only; semantically they contain a pronoun like *there* or *it*, and like such pronouns they need antecedents, as in 'It was an old house; no one was *inside*. A flagpole was in the garden with a bench *nearby*. He stayed *away* and watched as some people walked *by*.'

> Q.  Add pronouns to make prepositional phrases out of the italicized adverbs in the examples just given. Note other changes needed.[8]

| ADVERB: | [Loc] | [Dir] | [Abl] | [Neg-Loc] | [Via] |
|---|---|---|---|---|---|
| [Cnt] | inside | in(side) | out | outside | through |
| [Srf] | — | on | off | off | across |
| [Ø] | — | — | off | — | by |
| [Apx] | nearby | — | away | away | past |

## Other locational prepositions

The rest of the prepositions that show aspects of location are much less differentiated, often with the same forms for [Loc], [Dat] and [Via] forms; only the [Abl] forms are systematically different, adding a *from* before. Even the strong varieties are largely the same. A '#' marks lexical forms that block the systematic forms.

| [Loc] | [Dir] | [Abl] | [Via] | STRONG: |
|---|---|---|---|---|
| above | above | from above | # over | above |
| below | below | from below | # under | # beneath, underneath |
| beside | # up to | from beside | # along | # next to |
| outside | outside | from outside | outside | outside |
| behind | behind | from behind | behind | behind |
| away from | away from | — | — | away from |

There are two strong forms for *below*; *underneath* is more common in North America while *beneath* is perhaps more common in England.

There is more than meets the eye in such a chart; *beside* for example seems to have a narrower meaning than *up to*, and in fact it does have a narrower range of usage. For an object with a front, like a house or a person, there is an older preposition *before* or a newer (complex) preposition *in front of* that designates a location close to the front, like *behind* for the area close to the back. When these are applicable, i.e. with objects that have fronts, they block (as we saw in Chapter 2) *beside*, restricting it to the right and left sides. This restriction leaves it with a narrower range of usage than *up to*, which applies to any side of an object. This narrowed range of usage is so real, however, that we might speak of *beside* having a more specific 'effective meaning' [to the right or left of] when used with an object that has a front. Of course, if there is no specific front, a lake or a tree for example, *up to* is simply the [Dir] equivalent of *beside*.

Not shown in the chart above, *before* is more commonly used with moving objects, e.g. a horse, as in 'He walked before the horse', but *after* contrasts with *behind*, being further away, or even just following the same route. If a time is seen as a thing coming from the future and moving by you towards the past, the use of *before*, *after* with times (below) can be seen as similar.

These are not all the locative prepositions for there are also complexes of several words that function as single prepositions, much as case languages like German or Russian will combine prepositions with different cases for additional relations. Many of these complexes in English are based on a preposition with a noun, followed by another preposition. They often violate the rules of modern English syntax, and even where they do not, changing a word destroys them. Some examples are:

**on top of, in front of, at the side of, next to**

Not all spatial aspects, then, have different prepositions for strong and weak uses, and many of these prepositions are not possible at all in the adverbial use. This means that these possibilities exist in English, unlike most other languages, but that we have not (yet?) pressed words into filling all the available slots. Moreover, there is occasionally more than one strong form for a single slot, as we saw with *under*, which may be a dialectal difference. Again, for *in* there are two strong forms, *inside*, *within*, but the second is not so common in North America. Where a form exists in two or more slots, e.g. *on*, *by*, and the plain [Ø] ones, it is not thereby ambiguous, of course, but has a more general meaning.

## Prepositions for time . . .

Some of the prepositions that show aspects of an event's location are also used to show its temporal aspects, forming adverbials of time. This is fairly systematic: we use *at* with moments in time (what we can describe with hours and minutes), and *in* with periods of time.

| | | |
|---|---|---|
| at 3:00 | in the afternoon | in December |
| at midnight | in the third week of December | in winter |

However, *on* is used with days, with or without a part specified: '*on* the 24th of December' or '*on* the afternoon of the 24th'. However, *on* and *in* are not often expressed with specific days or times close to now, as we shall see shortly.

The other prepositions of time aspect are not difficult to use or understand, and we can give them meanings in terms of the beginning (B) and the completion or finish (F) of an event, as used for the aspectual auxiliaries and the verbal aspects in Chapters 7 and 8. The time T here can be expressed in hours, or as a specific time (often expressed as an event, such as 'before breakfast' or 'before leaving').[9]

| | | | | |
|---|---|---|---|---|
| before T | — | $[R < T]$ | after T— | $[T \leq B]$ |
| till T | — | $[F = T]$ | from T— | $[T = B]$ |
| | | past T —— $[B \leq T \leq F]$ | | |
| | | since T —— $[B = T \cdot R \leq F]$ | | |

Like the prepositions that describe spatial relationships, these prepositions also have weak and strong forms as on the left below, so to emphasize someone's arrival before five minutes have passed, one can use '*within* five minutes'. The contrast between the strong and weak forms is clearer in these time prepositions; one simply cannot stress a weak form to make the equivalent of a strong form. Even emphasized, '*in* five minutes' still means $[F \leq S+5m]$, with the $\leq$ remaining unimportant, suggesting close to or even slightly beyond the five-minute limit. On the right are the special prepositions used in telling the time, as in 'It's fifteen (minutes) __ three (o'clock)'; their weak forms are different and are used only in this pattern.

| WEAK | STRONG |
|------|--------|
| at | — |
| in | within |
| by | before |
| after | after |
| till | until |
| from | from |
| past | past |
| since | since |

*for telling time*

| WEAK | STRONG |
|------|--------|
| to, till, of | before |
| past | after |

> Q. Which two of these prepositions are not found with locational uses in the earlier discussion? Can you make sentences using them as locationals? How is each unusual?[10]

These prepositions used for aspects of events include several of the prepositions used for aspects of location, and the ones that can function either way (*in, at, from, to, past*) can be seen as [Loc], [Abl], [Dat] and [Via] analogues in time. However, the meanings of these five, as well as the others, can be given more accurately in terms of the beginning (B) and finish (F) of an action. The prepositions that are used for both time and location, then, are simply ambiguous; a general meaning covering both uses accurately cannot be given as B and F cannot be applied to locations except in the special case of a route from X to Y, where the X and Y define a B and an F.

## . . . and for causality

Several of these prepositions can also be used to express causal [Coz] connections between clauses. It is easy to mistake a fact [B comes after A] for [A causes B] and English includes a number of prepositions that have taken on causal meanings. Prepositions (or the like) in other languages commonly have similar double uses, locative and causal. Beware, however, that their causal usages appear often enough to be slightly different to the English ones. In Japanese, for instance, X-*kara* has a locative use [from X], but with a clause it means [after X] or [because of X]. In the collection of English prepositions below that are used as clause connectors, 'S' stands for a (subordinate) clause, and '/-ing' indicates that the verb must be in a gerundive form. VP stands for such a clause less its subject.

| Adverbial frame | Type | Example |
| --- | --- | --- |
| since S | cause | she stayed in since it was raining. |
| for NP | purpose | he went on the Haj for his soul's sake. |
| from /-ing S | source | I learned it from his singing. |
| in /-ing S | simultaneous | he meets many in travelling about. |
| by (way of) /-ing VP | means | she learned German by listening to the radio. |
| through /-ing VP | means | he did it through concentrating intensely. |
| out of /-ing VP | cause | he returned it out of being kind. |

Q.   In most of these, a simple noun that depicts an action can appear instead of the clause. Make examples.[11]

I am doubtful if unitary meanings can be proposed for these words that can adequately explain both their temporal and causal uses, but this is an interesting place to see the sort of problems one can encounter. Assuming that the meanings of temporal prepositions are expressed clearly and precisely in terms of B, F and T, then we need to find some equally clear way to describe causal relations, and in terms that will correspond to B, F and T if possible. That would make the problem fairly easy, but getting a good grasp on causal relations is not so easy. The terms in the table − cause, means, purpose and simultaneity − are incurably vague, though quite meaningful. Worse, their assignment to specific clause connectors is more intuitive than scientific.

What we would need to make such a hypothesis, then, are some objective tests (my intuitions or yours cannot be trusted for such a vague area of meaning) to decide whether a given connector is of one meaning type or another, and the classes of meanings for which we can thus test should be parallel to the temporal notions. Almost surely they will clarify the types of causality in the table, so they will have serious philosophical consequences and might even resolve some philosophical disputes about causality. Good luck; those problems date back more than 2000 years – as long as philosophy has existed. Even if you don't solve the linguistic problem, you could contribute to philosophy, or vice-versa.

## The case of the missing preposition

The prepositions *at* and *to*, being the basic prepositions of location and motion, don't carry much meaning, and what little they do have can usually be filled in from context. It is not surprising, then, that they may disappear with certain nouns that are both common and specific. In looking at deixis (Chapter 4), we called *here*, *there*, *where* [Loc]-prepositions, as in 'He is here', but they are also used with a [Dat] meaning, as in 'Come here!' It is probably correct to say that there is a *to* missing from the latter, and an *at* in the former. The missing prepositions can reappear under strong emphasis, 'Come in here!', and the same disappearing act happens with *home*, as in the following.

|  | example | regular parallel |
|---|---|---|
| no preposition: | *home* is where the heart is. | *my house* is . . . |
| overt preposition: | he stays away from *home*. | . . . away from *his house*. |
| missing *at*: | he must be __ *home*. | . . . at *his house*. |
| missing *to*: | he's gone __ *home*. | . . . to *his house*. |

With time, too, *at* is never expressed with *now* or *then*, and *on* is generally dropped with names of days. Besides, *in* is never expressed if followed immediately by a time demonstrative, *next*, *last*, *this*.

| always dropped | optionally dropped |
|---|---|
| tomorrow | (on) Tuesday |
| next week | (on) December 24th |
| now | (on) the night of the 29th of February. |

This non-appearance of elementary prepositions with specific and common nouns of time or location is not uncommon in languages. It may be only a matter of efficiency; why say what can be guessed anyway? If English didn't require a subject and verb for a statement, predictable pronouns and verbs could be dropped too, as subjects are in Spanish, and as we sometimes do in informal letter writing: 'Have been having a good time!'

## Generic forms

We can use some prepositions in special ways in English when we are not referring to a specific piece of the world but only the general idea. As cars take [Cnt] prepositions, we should and do say, 'She went to the party *in* a dirty taxi', talking about a specific piece of the world that was a taxi and was dirty. When talking about taxis in general, however – not about a particular taxi that was either clean or dirty, but about transport – and all we want to say is that she didn't drive her car or ride a bicycle, we could say 'She went to the party *by* taxi.' The preposition *by* is used for all types of transport in generic form, without an article.

> by bicycle      by bus      by tram
> by (aero)plane  by ship  ! by floater

These show that the speaker is not interested in the physical object that served as the means of transport, but only in the fact it was that type of transport. The last example shows how we can suggest a new type of transport.

---

Q.  What is unusual about ! 'We went to the library by skateboard'? Can you propose a circumstance in which it might be used?[12]

---

Another special generic preposition is *at* for standard periods of activity – the units into which a day is divided. They serve to specify location, as in answer to 'Where is he?', and except for 'at home' they also specify a time, somewhat general though it may be, as in answer to 'When will you see her? – At church, Sunday.' Similar to locational prepositions, this *at* is replaced by *to* or *from* with a verb of motion, without losing the generic sense. However, this is apparently a fixed paradigm or set of contrasts, for other equally reasonable expressions are not possible: ★ 'at playground', ★'at midnight snack'.

> at school  at work    at play    at home
> at church  at prayer  at lunch

---

Q.  There are more of these phrases related to meals. Give three.[13]

---

In a similar way, *in* can also be used generically, usually expressing why someone is not available. Notably, these phrases do not drop the *to* of *into* but the *in*, for weak [Dat]: 'We went to bed.' (The examples on the right are rare in North America in this generic usage without an article; a generic *the* is used instead – 'He's in *the* hospital' like 'He's at *the* dentist', even though no specific hospital or dentist is known or intended.)

in bed      in court    in hospital      in university
in school   in church   in conference

One last odd group of generic uses describes a special type of activity. These phrases take *on* for both [Loc] and [Dat] but *off* for [Abl] with the first two.

on duty   on guard   on strike   on trial


## English prepositions

Prepositions (or something similar) are necessary first and foremost to limit the event depicted by a verb, in space and in time, by combining with a nominal that refers to the limits. Among the locative ones are some that describe movement – [Dat], [Abl] and [Via] for towards, away from and past some place – and others that do not, [Loc] and its opposite [Neg-Loc], merely locating the event.

Like many European languages, English cross-multiplies these with relative locations, [Cnt] for inside the bounds of something, [Srf] for on its boundary, [Apx] for near the object, and nothing at all [Q] when the relative location is not important. This makes a full table of prepositions, which requires some learning. Moreover, English along with other languages can sometimes be hard to outguess as to which of these relative locations is appropriate in a given situation. Fortunately, not only do the elements of each row or column have similar meanings, but they are used in much the same way.

English goes on to provide a number of alternative prepositions that differ in whether they attract stress and indicate that the relationship is important (the 'strong forms'), or reject stress and show that the relationship expressed is not very important. These contrasts can be quite important when writing English, for they provide hints of which words in the sentence are stressed, and this can affect the meaning of the sentence in important ways. It is especially through words like these that the writer of English controls the rhythm that is necessary for understanding. It shows the logic of the speaker or writer, as well as what is important in the message.

## Answers and notes

1. Languages with postpositions generally have a small fixed set of them, such as Japanese with seven basic ones (*ga, o, ni, de, kara, made, no*), so there is no need to stop to decide which one to use.
2. *to stay* is not a verb of movement, while *to walk* is; the verbs show the motion or its absence.
3. [Dir] is really [Bcm-Loc], if you have already read Chapter 12, as [Abl] is probably [Bcm-Neg-Loc]. The horizontal distinctions are then:
   Loc : Bcm-Loc : Bcm-Neg-Loc : Neg-Loc : Via
   and [Via] below is suspiciously outside the pattern.
4. [Via] has no standard name yet. It is called 'vialis' in Eskimo linguistics but 'translative' in Finnish linguistics and occasionally 'route' or 'path' in English. *Via* is Latin for *route*.
5. 'He got/fell out of love' (*to fall* is more common than *to get*, *to become* for unfortunate states like sickness, e.g. 'He fell ill', as in 'in disrepute', 'on hard times', and . . . 'in love'!)
6. [behind] = [outside, beyond the back of]; [inside, in the back part of]; [just at the back].
7. *in, out of*
8. '. . . No one was inside *it*. A flagpole was in the garden with a bench near __ *it*. He stayed away FROM *it* and watched as some people walked by *it* (or *him*!).' A *by* was dropped and a *from* was added.
9. If a period of time P (e.g. *day, month*) is used with the preposition *in*, then T in the meanings is roughly 'some T during that P'.
10. *till, since.* 'I will sleep till Athens', 'You have been sleeping since Dubai.' These are normal in an aeroplane, being understood 'till we get to Athens' or 'since we left Dubai'. Actually, any noun that marks a time will do, such as *birth*, *marriage*, and an ordinary noun can be forced to take on a temporal meaning this way: 'I won't leave till three kisses.'
11. None for *since* or *from* without changing their meanings, as in 'since the rain' (temporal sense only), 'from road construc-

tion' (locative sense). Then, 'in travel' or 'in his travels', 'by (intensive) study', 'through concentration', 'out of kindness'.

12. The suggestion that skateboards are a mode of transport, not playthings. Suppose motorized skateboards became common and had right of way over cars. . . .

13. 'at breakfast', 'at dinner', 'at supper', 'at tea', but not ★ 'at coffee (break)'.


## Keywords

locative, directional/goal, ablative/source; surface, contents; weak and strong prepositions.


## Further reading

Bennett, D. C. *Spatial and Temporal Uses of English Prepositions* (1975) London: Longman.

The distinction between strong and weak forms is now standard for pronouns and some other function words. See Ladefoged or Knowles. The rhythm structure of 'stress-timed' languages such as English is much less well understood, but see references to Chapter 3 (negation).

Knowles, Gerald *Patterns of Spoken English* (1987) London, Longman.

Ladefoged, Peter *A Course in Phonetics* (1982) New York: Harcourt.


## Exercises with prepositions

1. Explain the differences in meaning between the following pairs.
   - (a)  She crawled under the table.
   - (a')  She crawled underneath the table.
   - (b)  He sat on the chair.
   - (b')  He sat in the chair.
   - (c)  The ball should be placed at the middle of the court.
   - (c')  The ball should be placed in the middle of the court.
   - (d)  We walked up to the river.
   - (d')  We walked to the river.

(e)  How's life treating you in Singapore?

(e')  How's life treating you over in Singapore?

2.  Choose more suitable prepositions for the following. Also try to find an interpretation for each as they stand.

(a)  He stood in the chair.

(b)  Liz waited for me in the corner of 55th and Broadway.

(c)  Where have you been in?!

(d)  We walked along the bridge.

(e)  He waited for her by the bow as the ship finally left port.

(f)  When she got there, she didn't walk right on.

3.  Find real-life situations that the following would describe reasonably.

(a)  He poured the coffee on the cup.

(b)  He crawled under the street.

(c)  Anne walked over towards Peter.

(d)  She dropped the penny at the cup.

(e)  They talked through the park and on to Harrods.

(f)  She waited for me in the corner of Byron and Leech Streets.

(g)  I'll wait for you inside the chair.

4.  Select as many of the following prepositions as will fit in each of the following sentences. Explain the meaning of strange choices.

on, at, in, by

(a)  We got __ the taxi.

(b)  Reuben threw __ the towel.

(c)  Can you carry it __ a barge?

(d)  I'll be waiting for you __ the park.

(e)  I'll be waiting for you __ Rideau Street and Cumberland Avenue.

5.  What are the differences of meaning in the following?

(a)   He threw a ball to the boy.

(a')   He threw a ball at the boy.

(a'')   He threw a ball towards the boy.

(b)   The dog barked at me.

(b')   ? The dog barked to me.

(c)   She walked for three hours towards the centre of town.

(c')   She walked for three hours, to the centre of town.

(d)   He jumped on to the table.

(d')   He jumped on the table.

(d'')   He jumped over the table.

(e)   There is something on the wall.

    (e')  There is something above the wall.

    (e'') There is something over the wall.

        (in a train)

    (f)   He stood all the way to his destination/the main terminal.

    (f')  He stood as far as Eustace Street/* the main terminal.

6. The [Dir] and [Abl] prepositions can generally drop their second part, for use as anaphoric adverbs, if the 'goal' or 'source' is known, as in the following.

    he got in. = [he got into it]

    he walked on. = [he walked on to it] (perhaps a stage)

    he jumped out. = [he jumped out of it]

    he fell off. = [he fell off of it]

However, we cannot say ⋆ 'He crawled to' even if it is known where he crawled to.

    (a)  Why not? (Hint: what is it that generally drops in these adverbial forms?)

    (b)  What do we say for this meaning: [he crawled to it/that place]?

Nor can we say ⋆ 'It flew from'.

    (c)  Why?

    (d)  What do we say instead?

7. The [Neg–Loc] *away from* is listed with '?' for both [not at] and [not near].

    (a)  Is there any difference between these concepts?

    (b)  If so, which is correct, if either?

8. The anaphoric adverbial form for *before* is *beforehand* with the *-hand* dropped colloquially, as in 'Lisa came at 6:30 but I had left five minutes before(hand).'

    (a)  What are adverbial forms for *after*? Give an example.

    (b)  What about the other temporal prepositions (*within/in, until/till, from, past, since*)? Examples!

# CHAPTER 10

# Reference and Predication

'A tall lanky scholar from Manchuria' surely has more meaning than 'a scholar', but the people who fit that description will be fewer in number. What is the relation between meaning and things described?

What happens if you name your son 'Sue' or your pencil 'Matilda'? I had a male cat once that I named 'Shea' pronounced like *sea*, *Lea*, but no one could say 'Shea's washing himself.' Why?

One of the more obvious facts of language is that some pieces of a sentence **refer to** or point to pieces of the world. For example, in the sentence 'The previous sentence ends with a full stop' the first nominal phrase 'The previous sentence' points to the first sentence in this paragraph, and 'a full stop' effectively points to a little round dot just before the beginning of this sentence. Reference like this, i.e. connections between parts of a sentence and pieces of the world, has been largely left to philosophy, from which most of the basics derive, but linguistics has an increasing interest for several reasons.

First, the forms a language uses sometimes depend critically on whether or not two nominals refer to the same thing (**co-reference**). The sentences below differ in this respect.

Jean-Pierre saw him.     Jean-Pierre saw himself.

In the second, the *himself* refers to the same person that *Jean-Pierre* does, while in the first, *him* refers to someone else. The French pronoun *se/soi*, like the German *sich*, has no meaning other than [identical referent as the subject]. in fact, the [Awa] ('third person') pronouns like *he* and *she* are short nominals that are coreferential with some earlier 'antecedent'. Also, in English as in many languages, an otherwise obligatory object may be dropped (i.e. left unexpressed) if it refers to something that was just mentioned, so while *to finish* requires mention of what is finished, if it has been mentioned recently enough it needs no re-mention, as in 'He was singing Aïda in the bathtub when I left. I don't know if he has finished ___ or not.'

This last example, you may have noticed, did not refer to a physical object but to the action of singing, and not everyone would call this a case of reference. It is, however, an important fact of language which would block much communication if not known. This brings us to a second reason why linguistics must consider reference; philosophy has been concerned primarily with an idealized concept of language − consistent with its use in logical or philosophical arguments. Real human language is much broader, and much richer, than the ideal languages of philosophical logic.

## Not meaning

It is not hard to imagine that meaning is little more than what the words refer to, and many early theories of meaning were based on this idea. Although only a nominal phrase like 'my striped cat' can refer to objects in an obvious way, it is an easy step to suppose that *cat* refers to, or **denotes**, all the cats in the world (the **denotation** of the word *cat*), *striped* to all the striped things, and *my* to all the things that belong to me, so that the referent of this phrase is the object or objects that belong to all three denotations, which is of course just my striped cat.

This sort of explanation gets a little fuzzy around the edges if we try to consider what is in the denotations that are supposed to be meanings. Consider all the cats in the world. Does that include, for example, the yet unborn cats? And, of course, the cats that have already died — even millions of years ago — all the way back to when their ancestors were not cats? This seems a little implausible, for I find it very hard to imagine this set of all cats, even though I must know quite well the meaning of *cat* and can use it effortlessly in communication.

The problem becomes worse for a phrase like 'my big cat', for *big* is supposed to refer to all big things. That must include elephants, mountains and many other big things but would not likely include any cats (unless you are including lions and tigers as cats). Unfortunately for this viewpoint, a gradable adjective (Chapter 3) like *big* has a comparative meaning. A big cat is big relative to other cats and a small elephant is smaller than most elephants, so a small elephant can still be bigger than a big cat (even including lions). Treating meaning as denotation can never give a meaning to most adjectives, because their denotations cannot be determined without knowing what noun they are used with.

---

Q.   Does the interpretation of a modifying adjective depend on the noun or on the concept modified? Consider 'short basketball player', 'short person who plays basketball'.[1]

---

These denotational theories also require a bit of abstraction, for transitive verbs like *to love* must refer to something presumably all the acts or feelings of love between two or more people (let's not worry about dogs or gods). If that isn't difficult enough to conceptualize, then what does a sentence refer to? A standard answer is to say it refers to Truth just in case it is true. This may leave you feeling unsatisfied, however, for all true sentences refer to the same thing, Truth incarnate, so they all have the same 'meaning'. Indeed, if meaning is what we use language to communicate (Chapter 1), then it must be something different from the Truth that a sentence refers to, as we normally assume that one is talking truth. It is rather what is said, i.e. the way one manages to refer to Truth, that conveys meaning, and denotational theories provide no insights on that.

The 'extensional' languages constructed in logic have this sort of nature for they deal only with **extensions**, sets of objects that are denoted by symbols — mathematically sharpened denotations. Their worst feature is that if two expressions refer to the same thing, then they have the same meaning. This was bad enough for sentences referring to Truth, but even at the heart of reference it is missing the point to say that the following expressions have the same meaning when they happen to refer to the same person.

the guy in the front row that's wearing a tie
the only student who took notes yesterday

While these may refer to the same person, on some occasion, and thus have the same extension, extension is not what we understand by meaning.

A more classical example is that both 'a unicorn' and 'a cyclops' refer to nothing at all, so they refer to the same thing and must have the same meaning. But this is obviously not right. A recent refurbishing of this type of theory is to consider possible worlds that differ in some way from the one we live in. In some of those worlds, there are unicorns and cyclops, so the denotation of *unicorn*, all the unicorns in all the possible worlds, is different from the denotation of *cyclops*. The notion of 'possible world' has other uses that you may see if you study more semantics, but it doesn't solve this problem very well, for 'square circles' denotes nothing at all in all possible worlds, and so does 'round triangles'. Since they don't have the same meaning, however, that sort of theory will have to extend denotations to include impossible worlds as well, and we don't know yet where that will lead to.[2]

For the simple case of cats, as for more complex cases, the denotations or extensions are sets of objects. Sets are well loved in mathematics, precisely because nothing gets in the way of deciding whether or not something is in a set. They fail us for the same reason, however; it may be difficult to decide just what to count as a cat, going way back to when cats were hardly cats yet. When we extend denotations to possible worlds we will have harder cases, for a creature just like a cat but having two pairs of ears in a world where all the animals evolved with two sets of ears might well qualify for being a cat – or can it? With all such hard cases, we need some way to decide if something is a cat. We need, in mathematical terms, a 'selector' for the set, i.e. a rule for selecting what is in the set and what is not.

This, however, is just what the meaning of *cat* is, a way of deciding whether or not something is a cat. If I say 'X is a cat' I mean that it passes the test(s) for cathood, and 'a round square' is something that passes the test for roundness as well as the test for squarity. Thus, if you hear me say 'X is a cat' you will know that X passes, in my opinion at least, the test(s) for cathood. Thus we must abandon extensional theories with their wild and woolly denotations, and treat descriptive meaning as criteria or tests that an object may or may not pass. This is thus an **intensional** viewpoint, as 'intensional' is anything that is not extensional.

As an example, for something to be a cat it must be a mammal of an appropriately small size (tests 1 and 2), have a longish tail that twitches when it is concentrating (test 3), have eyes and ears of certain shapes (tests 4 and 5), not make sounds other than meowing, hissing, etc., and many other tests of which I am hardly conscious. Unlike set theory, these tests are not crisp and precise but often have blurry boundaries, which is why the extensional denotations are inevitably fuzzy. For instance, although floppy ears may disqualify an applicant for cathood, how close must ears be to triangular to count as reasonable cat-ears? Nearly all of the tests have large grey areas, so there might well be things, on another planet perhaps, that are more or less cats, and the set of all cats is irremediably fuzzy, so fuzzy in fact that it is essentially uncognizable.

Thus the meanings of most words is intensional, though one could say that pronouns have primarily extensional meanings in so far as they point to something in the world. In fact, languages commonly distinguish between extensional and intensional statements. Consider the two following, only the second of which is true.

> all human beings have two legs.
> human beings have two legs.

The first, called a 'universal' statement, is not true, as there are always a few people that have lost a leg, or who were born without legs. Such facts do not negate the second, however, because it apparently does not talk about things in the world. Rather it seems to say that it is of the nature of human beings to have two legs, and that could still be true if there were only a few humans left and they had all lost a leg. Thus it is called a 'generic' sentence and appears to be a direct expression of general beliefs about the world, rather than of facts about the world. We can thus say that it has only an intensional meaning, while the first is at least partly extensional; facts about the world can disprove it. A truly universal statement (the first is something more than that), e.g. 'Every human being has six legs', is automatically true if there are no human beings left, regardless of the number of legs or other appendages that are predicated.

## Law of denotation

Denotation is clearly not meaning but the projection of meaning into a world. Because of this, it can sometimes be a useful way of attacking the meaning of a troublesome word or phrase. We know that a butterfly is not a fly, but if I proposed a meaning for *butterfly* that was simply the meaning of *fly* plus something else, denotation can be used to prove me wrong. Because there is something that is a butterfly but not a fly, i.e. the denotation of *butterfly*, the set of all butterflies, is not totally contained in the denotation of *fly*, then the meaning of *butterfly* cannot be the meaning of *fly* plus some more.

If two concepts C and C' differ only in that one of them, C', contains additional features, then the denotation of C' must be contained in the denotation of C, or equivalently, if the denotations (D, D') are not related by a relation of inclusion (technically a 'subset, proper or improper'), then the correspond-ing concepts (C, C') differ by something more than some additional restriction. So, in the case above, the meaning of *butterfly* cannot be [Hfl.X], with [Hfl] for the meaning of (*house*) *fly*.

if C' ⇒ C then D' ⊆ D

e.g.    if [cat] ⇒ [Ani] then D(cat) ⊆ D(Ani)

Q.  Determine which if either of the denotations of the following pairs includes the other. Consider only the real world as we know it.[3]

cat:animal          animal:thing          cat:black cat
cat:visible cat     cat:invisible cat

Nevertheless a denotational inclusion is no more than a suggestion that the concepts might be related by additional restrictions. For instance, the fact that the class of 'portable video recorders' is included in the set of 'things made in Japan' (supposing it were true) does not imply that the meaning of portable video recorder is [Made-in-Japan.X]; we could easily start making some in Thailand and they would still be portable video recorders. So the fact that human beings are bipeds without feathers does no more than suggest, and wrongly so, that [featherless. biped] might be the meaning of *human*. That may be an adequate definition in an extensional language, as in our world there are no featherless bipeds that aren't human, but if someone grew a few feathers due to a genetic mistake, that would not disqualify him from enjoying all the rights and obligations that other human beings have, and we would surely call him human, strange one though he be.

It does follow, however, that if two words or expressions have the same meaning, they must have the same denotations, so if we can show a difference in denotations, i.e. if there is something that is one but not the other, then the expressions cannot be synonymous. This is all obvious in some sense, but unless it is stated clearly, the relationships can provide some confusion.

## How to refer – to a single (group of) individual(s)

The denotation of a word includes anything to which one can refer with the word, so we come to the real linguistic act, referring. How is it that a piece of language, a referring phrase if you will, can point to a piece of the world? To understand this, let us step back a moment to see how people can refer to something. If you want to say something about the hamburger on my desk, you must refer to it. How?

In simple cases you can point. If what you want to refer to is close by, you can point to it, and if you can pick it up you can refer to it by waving it about as you say what you want to say about it. Take an apple in a shop, hold it up and say 'Rotten!' and you will no doubt insult the shopkeeper. Perhaps this way of referring reflects a stage of pre-language, but it won't work for things far away – I may not be able to decide which bird on the TV antenna you are pointing to – or for things out of sight, and especially for invisible things like the sound of a mosquito.

Thus at some point in human evolution we discovered that we could refer to many more things by simply describing them. Instead of touching or pointing to the apple, you can mutter 'The apple in the lower right-hand corner of this bin is rotten', to the same effect. This refers to the same apple because it describes something as being an apple (it passes the test for applehood) and being at the specified location. With this technique of describing the referent, we can refer to things we can't see, as in 'the girl who is absent today', or things that are difficult to point to, such as 'this university'.

Ordinary reference, then, is accomplished by making a description of what is to be referred to, that is complete enough to allow the addressee to find the referent. In English like many other languages a marker is added to this description to tell the addressee that they should find a unique thing (or a unique group of things, if plural) according to the description supplied, which is the referent. This is the prime function of *the* and definite articles in general. Demonstratives like *this*, *that* do this too, with an added note on how far the referent is from the speaker, or rather from the act of speaking as we saw in Chapter 4. In many cases this additional bit of information will allow a much simpler description, often merely a noun.

Of course, the descriptions used in referring to something are never complete descriptions, because a complete description is never needed, and probably never possible anyhow. In fact, it need not even be a very accurate description, for its only purpose is to guide the addressee to finding what is being referred to. Describing any distinctive characteristic of the intended referent will usually do, as for example 'Wellington' could easily be used to refer to a patient who thinks of himself as the conqueror of Napoleon.

## Descriptions

When we refer to something using only language, we must give a description of that thing. We must describe it enough for the addressee to know what we are referring to. Descriptions are thus very central to referring without gestures. However, they are even more important to the main show, saying something about the thing referred to, which is why we bothered to refer to the thing in the first place.

If you want to tell me that the coffee is very hot, you can refer to the coffee by pointing to it, or by describing it sufficiently, and then describing its hotness. You might say 'Yeaou!' with a grimace to warn me off taking a gulp, or more in English you might say 'Toooo hot', or even 'Too hot to drink'. The exclamation plus grimace doesn't tell me much, only that I might feel the same way if I drink it. Is it too hot or is it too strong, or might it be burnt? To be more specific, you might add an open mouth, tongue out, with a pant. These non-linguistic acts describe your reactions or my probable reactions.

Human language allows more informative communication, namely describing the thing, not just human reactions to it. Thus the word 'hot' described it, in one aspect that you thought significant enough to bother to communicate to me, and the word 'tooo' mixed a notion of [extremely] with your emotion about the matter. 'Too hot to drink' was a more precise description, basically: [its temperature was above the point that you (I? human beings?) can drink it]. You could have been more precise, of course, with 'Too hot for me to drink' or even '56°C', but such precision is not worth the effort if you are only trying to warn me not to gulp it down.

The point here is that we communicate information by describing something. Descriptions are not only important in referring to an object, event or fact, but they are the essence of saying something about it. If you want to communicate where you live, then you have to describe that location by a route from a known point, or a set of coordinates, or some way. Or if you want to tell me that your car is faster than mine, you may describe both our cars in their aspect of speed. Again, these are not complete descriptions and often less complete than descriptions used in reference, for here you are selecting only some particular aspect(s) of the object that you want to communicate to me. The real object may indeed be very different to what one might imagine having heard only a selected aspect of it described, so before you put your money down it is often wise to look at the real thing.

Language has often been seen as 'representing' the world because pieces of it can refer to pieces of the world. 'General Semantics' was based on the lesson that although a map represents a territory, the territory is different from the map, and similarly the world is different from how it is represented in language. Its main lesson was not to perceive something according to the label it carries; all of the following expressions, for example, might refer to the same person, but one's reactions naturally vary greatly depending on which description is given to him.

a father      a company president      a thief      a dupe

This understates the case, however. Representation is a systematic and complete description of some aspect(s) of a subject and is thus rather more than what language normally provides, for a speaker commonly gives only descriptions of selected facts; a verbal description is rather less than a map, for a map can be trusted in some respects, say distance and angle. Language is so flexible that it is seldom used to give more than a few selected facts, and what is left out of the selection may well be more important (to you perhaps) than what is included. Ask any victim of fraud.

## Predicative – attributive

Descriptions are used in referring but are as well the essence of saying something, i.e. **predicating** something about the thing(s) referred to. These two ways of using descriptions are called attributive and predicative.

In an ordinary nominal phrase, a noun or an adjective is put there to tell the listener what thing or things are being talked about. They give attributes of the thing, so we say that such an adjective is used **attributively**. For these, the speaker is not responsible for their accuracy or truth so long as they adequately identify the thing. For example, in a desert where the only plant visible is a single, fairly large cactus, one could refer to it, half in joke, as 'that huge tree over there'. Because it is the only thing with even a mild resemblance to a tree, this rather inaccurate description still adequately identifies it. Attributive uses, then, function to help the addressee identify something but not to say anything about it. Accordingly they need not be very accurate.

On the other hand, a noun or adjective after *to be* is used **predicatively** and may be called a 'predicate adjective' or 'predicate noun' in grammar. In a question it is this that is questioned, and in a statement this is what is asserted; the speaker is responsible for the truth and accuracy of predicated adjectives or nouns. A speaker could not possibly point to that same cactus and say 'That is a huge tree' without risking being thought to have had too much sun.

---

Q.  In what circumstances would it be appropriate to say each of the following?[4]

　　　that statue is a cat.
　　　that is a statue of a cat.
　　　that cat is a statue.

---

Besides *to be*, there are other copular verbs such as *to become, to appear* or even *to grow into*, and their complements are also predicative.

> he became *a sailor*.
> he grew into *a handsome young man*.

In grammar these nominals are called predicative because they are part of the 'grammatical predicate' of the sentence (roughly everything except the subject), and they are not grammatical objects. A deeper reason is that these descriptions do not function to refer to something. There is no sailor (no Davy Jones, e.g.) that he physically invaded, or that he became as an actor might become King Lear. Put another way, in 'He saw a sailor' there are two distinct people being talked about, him and the sailor, but in the example above there is only one, referred to with *he* and described in a later stage by 'a sailor'. Rather, these predicated nominals function to impart information.

In fact, predicative nominals may be slightly different from ordinary nominals in some languages. French, for example, would not use *un* in such a case, because it is not referring to anyone: 'Il est devenu Ø matelot.' In English, even, the indefinite *a/an* is not normal if a predicate nominal describes a unique function or job title such as president or sheriff, so it is difficult with *to become*, *to elect*.

> he was elected president.    * he was elected a president.

Language, and life, can be tricky, however. *To elect* can also take a direct object, and the same word *president* can be used to refer to someone whom they elected. Then, of course, the *a/an* is needed: 'They elected a president' – we cannot say * 'They elected president'.

---

Q.  Which type of relative clause is attributive, and which predicative?
   (a) RESTRICTIVE: 'My wife who lives in Teheran called last night.'
   (b) INDEPENDENT/APPOSITIVE: 'My wife, who lives in Hong Kong, called last night.'
   Which example presupposes that I have more than one wife?[5]

---

Adjectives are called predicative when they function to communicate some information rather than identify a referent, i.e.

when the description they make is supposed to be new information for the addressee. Otherwise, when they describe something for the purpose of helping the addressee find it – i.e. in referring to something – they are attributive. There are a few adjectives in English which are predicative only (mostly beginning with a-). Some have related attributive forms, but there are only a couple of ordinary adjectives that can be used attributively only, though most numbers (one, two, etc.) are used only in an attributive position in modern English.

| attributive | predicative |
|---|---|
| sleeping, gaping, blazing lone | asleep, agape, ablaze, alone |
| many, most, two, three | awake, aware, aloft, astir, afoot legion, numberless |

Thus, the ordinary uses of an adjective, as in the first row below, are somewhat restricted for these cases. This appears to be a grammatical distinction in modern English, however, for the left two columns are semantically alike.

| attributive uses | predicative uses | |
|---|---|---|
| | as attribute | as predication |
| a tired man | a man who is tired | the man is tired. |
| a *lone* man | a man who is alone | the man is alone. |
| | * a man who is lone. | * the man is lone. |
| * an awake man | a man who is awake | the man is awake. |

We see this same contrast, between attributive and predicative, in other chapters here. It parallels, for example, the difference between 'old information' and 'new information' in Chapter 13. In addition, attributive adjectives are generally understood to be 'presupposed' (Chapter 2) while predicative adjectives or nouns are predicated. In general, the terms *attributive* and *predicative* are used mostly in syntax on the basis of the sentence's structure, while in philosophy 'to *predicate* D of something' is to use the description embedded in D in a non-referential way, usually as the point of a statement.

The main function of *to be* is to mark what is predicated, i.e.

the predicate of a sentence, but a nominal after it is not always used predicatively as it is in 'He is *a smart fellow*.' It may also be used referentially in its own right, as in 'The boy over there is *the boy you were talking about*.' The copula *to be* can then be called **equative** as there is an equating of the referents of the two nominals here; what is asserted is the fact that they both refer to the same thing. It is clear, however, that English and many other languages treat this as simply a predicative nominal that is definite, while the non-equative uses of *to be* have either an indefinite or no determiner.

Although we have been careful to avoid speaking of reference by a noun, it is a tradition to speak of nouns referring to things. Latin (and many other languages) did not have articles like *the*, so it seemed as if nouns could refer to things. In languages with articles, however, it is clear that the article is the essential referring element, and the noun serves only as a more or less detailed description. In particular, the definite *the* indicates that a particular referent is intended and should be identified, while an indefinite *a* shows that the identity of the referent is not important, if known, and *any* says that the addressee is free to choose one as she likes. Of course, names and pronouns are usually complete nominals in themselves, and therefore can refer without additional markers.

## Names

Meanings are often associated with names. For example, *Reginald* means [kingly], and my name *Hofmann* is a word that no reasonable German dictionary can do without, meaning [courtier] in German, or again, *Chicago* means something like [swampy place] in Illinois, the Algonquin language of the previous inhabitants of the area. These meanings, however valid they might be in their languages of origin, are not the meanings of the names as we use them today. *Washington* is not a town where people wash things, and we cannot point to a swamp saying 'That's a Chicago.'

None the less, names are not devoid of descriptive meaning. Most English speakers would feel I had done something wrong if I named my son 'Sue'.[6] We normally say that *Reginald* is a boy's name, *Sue* a girl's name. What this means is that they include a bit of descriptive meaning: [Msc] and [Fem] respectively. This includes metaphoric extensions, whereby hurricanes, ships and vehicles are often treated as [Fem]. In the same way, I can't name my son *Rover* and it would be odd to call my dog *Ronald*. A name like *Rover* must then have a descriptive meaning, roughly [Dog], while *Ronald* must have a descriptive meaning [Msc.Hum]. Some names, however, are possible for animals, as is *Daisy* for a cow.

The main function of names, however, is to distinguish one individual from another. They are thus called 'indexical' for they function as index or serial numbers. They are, however, quite different from index numbers, for they are seldom if ever completely unique. Individuals are 'given' names, and these names are useful because not many individuals have the same name. It is unlikely that there will be two Reginalds in the same class, and if there are I can distinguish them by adding their family names.

In fact, although in some contexts a name may apply to more than one individual, and even though both the speaker and the addressee would recognize this if pointed out, names are nevertheless normally used as if they were unique in reference. We can easily speak of Thatcher doing this and that, as if there were only one Thatcher. In this, names are like nominals beginning with *the*: their use implies that the speaker is referring to a unique individual and thinks that the addressee can identify which with the description given. We might even be annoyed if someone asked which Thatcher we meant: 'Oh, come now, you know who I mean!' Thus a name like *Lena* has a meaning something like [the girl whom you know called 'Lena']. Indeed, a number of names still retain an overt *the*, as in *the White House*, *the Great Lakes*, *the Levant*, *the Magreb*, *the Hague*, *the Bronx*, *the Strand* and even *the Ginza* in Tokyo.

The use of names as uniquely referring words, even though they do not refer uniquely, has led philosophy into the assumption that unique names are possible. One may add other names, and some combinations like 'Avran Noam Chomsky' may indeed be unique, but we are seldom in a position to know whether or not they are. The point, however, is that it is not important in human language whether or not the name has in fact a unique referent.

---

Q.  To save the notion of a unique name, philosophers sometimes propose adding the date and place of birth to make a complex unique name, as do many legal forms.

> What are some circumstances in which even a very unusual name like 'Thomas Takushi Hofmann, born in Tokyo on 16 Oct 1986' might not be unique?[7]

Because names designate individuals, they can be used as ordinary nouns to describe another individual as similar to the one named. Thus 'He's a real Winston Churchill' or 'She's the Mother Theresa of the Andes.' The addition of a determiner (e.g. *a, the, this*) deprives it of its inherent definiteness, rendering it simply descriptive. Its meaning is then something like [having the noted distinctive characteristics of the person referred to by that name].

## Non-singular reference

So far, we have been considering simple cases of referring to single individual objects (or, in the plural, single groups of objects) called '**singular** reference'. When we move away from these examples where the addressee is to identify the referent, things can become a good bit more complex. There are several topics that deserve mention, if only to provide a taste of the problems involved – generic reference, indefinite reference, quantification – all areas of active research in philosophy and linguistics.

**Generics** do not really refer to something in the world, as we saw above with the sentence 'Human beings have two legs.' Some people would see this as reference, however, and the referent of 'human beings' as whatever it is that lies behind its use. As this appears to be a concept, these people take referents to include concepts of a special kind.

English has a wealth of generic forms. Most languages make do with one or two. The three types with different articles have different possibilities of collocation.

elephants
|      | | |
|---|---|---|
| . . . are found in South Asia. | . . . have many offspring. | * . . . love two other elephants. |

the elephant
|      | | |
|---|---|---|
| . . . is found in Africa. | * . . . has many offspring. | * . . . loves two other elephants. |

an elephant
|      | | |
|---|---|---|
| * . . . is found in East Asia. | . . . has many offspring. | . . . loves two other elephants. |

These minor differences in what can be predicated of these generic nominals suggest some small differences in meaning. They can be largely explained by taking 'elephants in general', 'the species of elephant' and 'any member of the elephant species' as paraphrases of these three generics.

**Indefinite reference** is a curious middle ground strewn with holes for the unwary. In general, using an indefinite article *a/an* or a number without a definite determiner (and there is good reason to believe that *a/an* is no more than a 'weak' or unstressed form of *one*) is an indication that the addressee need not find a referent in the world. There may in fact be a referent, as in '*An apple* fell out of your sleeve, Madam', and such an indefinite is called **specific**. Or there may be a whole slew of different referents, as in 'I eat *an egg* every morning.' Or there may not in fact be any referent at all, for a fisherman eyeing a lake of unfulfilled promise may say, 'I'm going to catch a fish today, so help me!' These are called **non-specific**, as even the speaker does not know the identity of the referent, or even if it exists. These tend to correlate with time, as reports of past events usually entail specific objects while the future is ever uncertain, but 'Becky plans to marry *a Swede*' is ambiguous on just this point, specific if it is continued 'She thinks *he's* wonderful' but unspecific with '. . . but she hasn't met *any* yet'.

---

Q.   Explain the ambiguity in 'Every evening a heron flies over the castle.'[8]

---

Definite nominals exhibit both possibilities, for in saying '*Smith's murderer* was crazy' after his trial, there is a specific referent the addressee is meant to find. On the other hand, if it were uttered by a Hercule Poirot hot on his trail, we and he do not know who Smith's murderer is (or are, if it turns out that there were two or more involved). In fact, we do not even know if such a murderer exists – suppose for example that it turns out that Smith was not murdered but in fact committed suicide in an ingenious way so as to throw suspicion on his enemy.

Thus, although a simple conception of definiteness is that it is an indication for the addressee to find the object referred to in the world, in fact we may not have enough information to do that. In an appropriate situation, however, we are willing to accept such 'incompleted definite reference' on the understanding that we will be able to find the unique referent when we know a bit more. Giving a label to an unknown, as X or Y in algebra, is a useful technique of investigation in science, medicine and mathematics, as in detective stories, if we don't forget that a label (like 'Smith's murderer') might prove to have been misguided.

Once an indefinitely marked nominal introduces a referent into a discourse (sometimes called **discourse referents**, to distinguish them from real referents in a world), it can be referred to as if it were unique and identified, with a pronoun like *it* or a definite nominal. Curiously enough, this applies to unspecific referents as well, so the hopeful fisherman can continue, '. . . and when I catch *it*, I'm going to fry *it* with butter'. One way to explain this is to say that he builds a world in his mind wherein he has caught the fish, and he is referring in his continuation to the fish in that world. However, we can also refer to the collection of unspecific referents with a plural, as the egg-eater could well continue, 'I wonder if *they* raise my blood cholesterol very much.'

---

Q.  What is the referent of *them* in 'Each child brought his favourite toy to school, and the teacher put *them* in a box for the morning'?[9]

---

**Quantification** is setting a number or quantity to some class of objects, and is intimately involved in reference, for any act of reference into the world (whether or not completed) involves a specific quantity. To refer to some water, for example, one must refer to some quantity of it, which involves not only a number but also a measure.

> this glass of water    this pool of water    this drop of water

A noun in English that needs a measure when quantified or used in reference is called a 'mass' noun, and they include most substances and many abstract words like *furniture*, *apparatus*, *clothing*, *cattle*. In many languages of the world, essentially all nouns are of this sort, so that the noun alone is generic in force. European languages, by contrast, build a 'unit measure' into most common nouns that have some natural unit (e.g. *pencil*, *person*, *pot*) and use some other device to indicate generic interpretations when needed.

These aspects of quantification have only recently come under the scrutiny of philosophy and linguistics. Study on quantification has been restricted to interesting problems involving universal (*all, each, every*) and existential (*a, some*) quantifiers, which have occupied philosophers since Plato and before. Natural languages usually also include non-existential quantifiers like *none* and English has a very special one, *any*, that has a special relationship with negation (Chapter 3). In fact, these three types of quantification are interdefinable with negation (see Chapter 6, as logical modality has these same contrasts), so it may be that semantic structure has only one such quantifier, but it is not clear which one it is. Natural language also has 'approximative quantifiers' corresponding to *none, all* in *few, most* as well as some odd ones like *many, only*. My preferred solution is both radical and not generally acceptable yet, but whatever solution we do find must apply to all these words, as well as to quantification in general.

## Reference

We can **refer**, i.e. identify or select, something so that it can be talked about with some elementary gestures if the thing (or a representation of it) is visible and near to hand. Otherwise we must use a nominal phrase to describe the referent and tell the addressee that we are referring to something. In special cases – names and pronouns – a single word is a complete nominal, but in languages that use articles it is always the whole nominal that selects the object. In such a language, the noun functions as a description, and the article or 'determiner' guides the reference.

As we now use the term, **reference** is not meaning but rather selecting an object or objects by means of meaning, though other uses of this term exist (Chapter 1). When the selection of the object(s) in the world is complete, philosophers speak of **singular** reference, but when it is halted at the level of meaning because it refers to some unspecified member or members of a class, we have **general** reference. *Extension*, and the older *denotation*, include everything to which a word or expression can refer.

The semantic distinction between **predicative** and **equative** uses of a nominal lies in whether it is used to describe an individual already identified or to refer to an individual that is claimed to be the same individual that was already identified. In distinction to these two uses, an adjective (usually) is called **attributive** when it is used only to help select the individual being referred to, but **predicative** when it describes an individual already identified. These and related terms are also used in other ways (e.g. see the term 'predicate' in Chapter 11), due to the independent evolution of grammar, logic and philosophy.

A referring nominal selects a referent in a world, but the world is often enough not the real world that we live in. Each piece of fiction makes up its own world which may be more or less like the real world we know, and these worlds may be quite detailed, as is that of Sherlock Holmes for example. Nominals in a work of fiction refer to parts of those invented worlds. There are also mythological worlds populated with gods and wondrous beasts, and even mathematics can be seen to be a discussion of the nature of constructed worlds that contain numbers or other abstract objects, worlds that are created by axioms. If we pursue this direction, we soon see scientific theories as descriptions of idealized worlds that match our physical world in a few relevant aspects.

## Answers and notes

1. It depends on the noun, apparently; these expressions imply people of different heights, even though they are conceptually synonymous. Note that 'basketball player' is a (complex) noun for these purposes.
2. Presumably to a place where we can find Russell's self-contradictory set of all sets that don't contain themselves, and other impossible things.
3. The smaller denotation is found in, respectively: *cat*, *animal*, *black cat*. Both *cat* and *visible cat* have the same denotation, so either is included (in the mathematical sense) in the other; *invisible cat* designates nothing, and (mathematically again) nothing or the null set is included in any set.
4. The first identifies something that seems to be a statue and says that it is really a cat, and the third is just the reverse of this. The second is straightforward, that the thing designated is a statue with the shape of a cat.
5. Restrictive relatives are attributive, and since this example might help you identify which wife I am talking about, it implies I have more than one wife. Independent relative clauses give extra information, information not needed to

identify the person or thing, so they are predicated and the speaker is responsible for their being true; they are effectively mini-statements embedded, in this case, in the sentence 'My wife lives in Hong Kong.'

6. There was a popular song by Johnny Cash in the 1970s, 'A Boy Named Sue'. You should listen to it a couple of times; it is a quite interesting story.

7. Tokyo is a big place, and someone else might have chosen that same name, as unusual as it may be. It would be even possible in the same hospital, on the same day.

8. (Specific) the same heron each evening – maybe it lives nearby. (Unspecific) perhaps a different heron – probably the speaker does not know if it is one and the same heron, or a different one sometimes.

9. The collection of toys that the children brought.

## Keywords

to refer, referent, denotation/extension, intension; predicative, attributive; (in)definite, generic, indefinite reference, antecedent.

## Further reading

Most modern work on reference begins from Frege.

Frege, G. 'Über Sinn und Bedeutung' (1892) *Zeitschrift für Philosophie und Philosophische Kritik* **100**: 25–50. 'On Sense and Reference' (1960) in P. T. Geach and M. Black, *Translations*, Oxford: Blackwell. (1974) in F. Zabeeh *et al.*, *Readings in Semantics*, Urbana: University of Illinois Press.

Geach, P. T. *Reference and Generality* (1962) Ithaca: Cornell University Press.

Denotation, extension and intension are found in most elementary texts on logic. Hofmann provides a formalization of the relation between them.

Hofmann, Th. R. 'Law of Denotation and Notions of Antonymy' (1981) *Prague Bulletin of Mathematical Linguistics* **36**: 25–46.

Korzybski developed the notions of 'general semantics' in the first half of this century, and his major disciple, S. Hayakawa, carried them into the latter half, applying them as president of the San Francisco State University, and later in the US Senate. The latter's books are very readable, and are available in popular editions.

Korzybski, A. *Science and Sanity* (1933) Lancaster: Science.
Hayakawa, S. *Language in Thought and Action* (1941) New York: Harcourt.

## Exercises in reference

1.  What are the referents of the expressions in parentheses, if you were to say these sentences right now?
    (a)  (my mother) is healthy now.
    (b)  I would like to meet the author of (this book).
    (c)  I would like to meet (the author of this book).
    (d)  what has become of (the tricycle I had when I was a child)?
    (e)  when will (you) come back?
    (f)  the answer to (this question) is easy.
    (g)  what is (the answer to this question)?!
    (h)  (the circle around g.) is not easy to see.
    (i)  (everybody) is crazy except me.
2.  When do the phrases in parentheses in the following have the same referents?
    (a)  (he) studied (himself) in the mirror.
    (b)  (Clive) watched (him) take the fish out of the can.
    (c)  the instructor is (the smartest guy in the room) and (the oldest person) as well.
    (d)  (I) am (Professor Glaston).
3.  Consider the phrases 'The person in the front of the classroom, who does all the talking here' and 'the person who teaches this course'.
    (a)  These do not have the same meaning, do they?
    (b)  Describe a circumstance where they refer to different people.
    (c)  How do they manage to refer to the same person, when they do?
4.  In the following pairs, first which has the smaller denotation and then which the more specific or detailed meaning?
    (a)  cat : animal

    (b) black cat : cat

    (c) stray black cat : black cat

    (d) mother : female

    (e) mother : female mother

    (f) person : featherless person

    (g) square triangle : round square

    (h) square triangle : triangle

5. In a phrase like the subject of '*The industrious Chinese* dominate South-East Asian business', the adjective *industrious* can be predicative as well as attributive, so such a sentence is ambiguous.

    (a) Paraphase the two meanings of this phrase using restrictive and independent relative clauses.

    (b) Who is excluded in each of the meanings?

6. The antecedent of a pronoun, definite nominal or other referring expression is generally the nearest preceding nominal that refers to the same thing. What, then, is the antecedent of the expressions following in italics? (Because an antecedent is necessarily a piece of the discourse, the answers to this question are not always satisfying!)

    (a) John built a chair and gave *it* to me.

    (b) Marie saw a golden apple and told me about *it.*

    (c) Tommy ate half of an apple and then gave *it* to me.

    (d) he cut off a quarter of the ap e and gave *it* to me.

    (e) each pupil brought an apple a d placed *it* on the teacher's desk.

    (f) After school she gave half of *them* to the other teachers . . .

    (g) . . . and ate *the rest of them.*

    (h) Pete's going to catch some fish and I'm going to cook *'em.*

7. Now describe, from the information in the contexts, the referents of the indicated expressions in the preceding question. (Here you are not restricted to the precise words used, so describe them accurately.)

8. Although English does not have any marker for specificity and many referring phrases can be taken as specific or unspecific, the circumstances may allow only one interpretation. Identify which each of the indicated nominals is, or if it is ambiguous.

    (a) I got upset over *a trivial matter* this morning.

    (b) *an electron* was emitted.

    (c) Rudolph is going to throw *an egg* at me!

    (d) *an apple* a day keeps the doctor away.

    (e) she drank *a glass of water.*

  (f)  *the first person here* should turn on the lights.
  (g)  I saw *the dog that bit you.*
  (h)  you may not know *the answer to this problem.*
  (i)  can you tell me *the way to the stadium?*
  (j)  *the apple you eat every day* won't keep ghosts away.
  (k)  they buried *the hatchet.*
  (l)  *someone* called and asked for you.
  (m) if *someone* calls, tell 'em I'm out.
  (n)  did *someone* call?

9. In a sentence with several quantifiers, like 'Everyone loves someone', there can be two radically different interpretations:
  [there is *some*one that *every*one loves]
  [for *every* single person, there is *some*body that he/she loves]

This difference is usually explained as a difference in order of quantifiers, the universal *every* and the existential *some*. There is also the difference in specific and non-specific *some*one to take account of.

  In the following, the continuations force one or another reading.

  (a) Which ones have the existential quantifier dominant, as in the first example, and which the universal quantifier dominant?

  (b) Which have a specific interpretation for the *someone*, which a non-specific interpretation?

  (1) everyone loves someone, and she's getting an Oscar next week.

  (2) for a while, everyone is crazy about someone, and then a new idol comes along.

  (3) everyone loves someone; at least their mother.

  (4) everyone falls in love with someone, but it seldom lasts a lifetime.

# CHAPTER 11

# Words to Sentences

Suppose you become a teacher of English as a second language and your students make weird responses (indicated by *) like these ones. How do you explain what is wrong?

(1) Did you see Mary? — * Yes, I saw yesterday.

(2) I have a good dictionary. — * Will you lend (to) me?

(3) What did the tired old lady do? — * She put her heavy bag.

Although the starred sentences above are quite reasonable when translated into Japanese, for instance, they do not make sense in English. Many English verbs need the right number of objects, and they do not have them in these sentences. Their Japanese translations are fine because one can omit objects (and even subjects) rather freely, as in many languages. In the first example, *to see* is a **strictly transitive** verb; it requires an overt object, as in 'I saw her yesterday.' As it stands, sentence (1) sounds as if the speaker was looking at yesterday, not at Mary! In the other examples, *to lend* and *to put* each relate three things and one is left guessing what the missing item might be. One could guess correctly in (2) but (3) gives no hint; we must add a direction like 'on (to) the bench' or even just 'down' before it can be understood.

We will begin with a few examples from Japanese, because it is very different from most European languages on this point yet it is typical of a rather common type of language.

## What type?

These examples show that we have to specify for each verb how many and what kinds of phrases it can or must go hand in hand with – technically called the 'valency' of the verb. With the (strictly) transitive verb *to kill*, as in 'John killed a snake' for example, we need to indicate that it goes with a killer (**agent**, here *John*) and the 'killee', the one that gets killed (**patient**, here a *snake*). In this same vein, for a double transitive verb *to lend*, as in example (2) above, we must specify three things: Agent (*you*), Patient ('your dictionary') and Goal (*me*).

Notions like agent, patient, goal and a few others of the same sort are useful not only for analysing English verbs but also for bringing out otherwise hidden differences between languages. Compare the following English and Japanese sentences, for example.

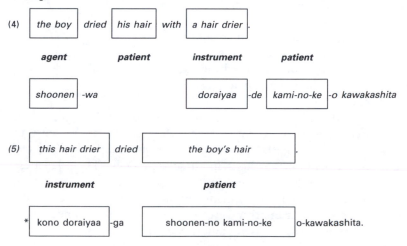

While the agent 'the boy' can be expressed as subject in both English and Japanese, the instrument 'a hair drier' cannot be the subject of *kawakasu* [to make dry] in Japanese. In English, however, an instrument can generally be used as a subject if it is specific enough (note the words *this, his* in the examples to follow). So sentences such as the following cannot be translated directly into Japanese.

> this key opens that door.
> his revolver killed the gangster.

We might suppose that translations of these are bad because inanimate things cannot be subjects in Japanese, but this explanation will not do; in sentences like 'The hair dried' ('Kami-no ke-ga kawaita') or 'The door opened', inanimate subjects are not bad at all. What is important, then, is not whether the subject is human or inanimate, but whether or not it is an instrument. English can have instrument as well as agent or patient subjects, but Japanese does not allow instruments as subjects.

---

Q. *To open* is more than commonly flexible as to which semantic role can fill the subject position: agent (a), instrument (i) or patient (p). Not all combinations are possible; we have seen [pV] and [iVp] (V standing for the verb and auxiliaries), and 'The janitor opened the door with his key' would be [aVp with i]. Make at least three more, including the passive [p was V-ed by a].[1]

---

It is not enough, though, to specify just the **semantic roles** (sometimes called 'thematic roles') as we have done so far. We also have to show how these roles are expressed in sentences, which is largely a matter of general rules in each language. In English, for example, the agent has priority to fill the subject position if there is an agent, leaving the patient to be a direct object and an instrument to be realized with a preposition *with*. In contrast, an agent in Japanese generally shows up with a postposition (like a preposition but behind the nominal instead of in front) *-wa* or *-ga*, patient with *-o*, and instrument with *-de*. Other regular patterns (see Chapter 9) include:

|  |  | English | Japanese |
|---|---|---|---|
| Goal: | [Dir] | to | -ni |
| Source: | [Abl] | from | -kara |
| Location: | [Loc] | in, on, at | -ni, -de |

Life would be easier (though perhaps more boring) if things were just this simple, but we do find exceptional cases from time to time. In English we have *to be dependent ON* as the opposite of *to be independent OF*, and *to equal* without any preposition but with the same meaning as *to be equal TO*. It is not unusual for a preposition next to the verb to disappear, and such idiosyncrasies often cause mistakes for foreign learners, so by and large each verb must be learned with the prepositions that can go with it. The French, and people speaking many other languages, tend to use 'broken' English – ★ 'He wants to marry *with* you' like their 'Il veux se marier *avec* toi' instead of the normal English 'He wants to marry you' – and the Japanese tend to say ★ 'I entered *into* the room', as in their language, instead of 'I entered the room.' Conversely, English-speaking people learning Japanese can easily say the equivalent of 'to obey an order' instead of 'to obey *to* an order' which is the only way to say it in Japanese.

Another point learners of foreign languages need to be careful about is that some verbs may require subject and object in an unusual way. For instance, 'X gives Y to Z' and 'Z gets Y from X' have nearly the same meaning but the first takes a source as a subject while the second takes a goal. Similarly for objects, 'John loaded the hay on to my truck' has a patient (the thing that moves, here 'the hay') as the direct object, while 'John loaded my truck with the hay' takes the goal (where it moves to, 'my truck' here) as the direct object. (Cf. Chapter 5 on orientations.)

To sum up, semantic roles provide a convenient way of describing important parts of the meanings of sentences. What is important here is that sentence meanings can be tackled from the verbs; the verb is the semantic centre of a sentence to which the subject, object and other expressions are connected.

## Prepositions for semantic roles

Prepositions – or something similar like the 'cases' in Latin, German or Russian or the 'postpositions' in Japanese, Turkish, Indian languages and many others – are needed in a language to relate more than one or two nominals to a verb. If there were no prepositions in examples like the following, we could never be sure who did what to whom with what. Most prepositions have systematic meanings that allow us to understand sentences such as the following example (Ø stands here for no preposition at all).

> the Bedouin sold Ø: a slave-girl TO: Lawrence IN: his tent FOR: a camel WITH: a devious suggestion.

Many languages are like English and Chinese. The relationships of two nominals with which a verb connects can be identified by putting one before and the other after the verb without any preposition (Ø:). Many other languages are like Japanese; with the verb at the end of the sentence, they need a postposition for each nominal, though in informal speech we can drop the one right before the verb.

| ame-Ø hutteiru. | [Ø: rain is-falling] | '[i]t's rainin'.' |
| hottotii-Ø chodai. | [give Ø: hot-tea] | 'gimme a cuppa.' |

Many, perhaps most languages have their nominal phrases **before** the verb, as in the Japanese example following. English and most European languages have their nominal phrases **after** the verb, with a special one, the subject, in front of the verb, as in its translation following. Typical of verb–final languages, the order of Japanese is quite the reverse of the English, if we put the English subject (nominal N3) between N4 and N2. Languages of the world tend to follow this order, either forward or backward, with minor variations like English putting the subject in front. Chinese is like Japanese, except that it generally puts the direct object after the verb, so it looks like English when a sentence has only two nominals.

| kinoo-Ø | koen-DE | boku-WA | Mari-san-TO | | tomodati-NI | at-ta. |
|---|---|---|---|---|---|---|
| N1 | N2 | N3 | N4 | -& | N4' | V -ed |

| I | met | Ø: Mary | AND: her friend | | IN: the park | Ø: yesterday. |
|---|---|---|---|---|---|---|
| N3 | V-ed | N4 | &- N4' | (N3) | N2 | N1 |

Chinese: N1 N2 N3 V-le N4 and-N4' or: N1 N3 N2 V-le N4 and-N4'

It is usually possible in English, however, to move one nominal or adverb to a position in front of the subject, as in the first example following, but moving it out of its normal position, marked by (t), in this way has a special meaning – something like picking it up and waving it around while you talk. Not something you should do very often, and it is not at all like putting it in front in Japanese, where it quite normally sits.

> yesterday, I saw Mary on a bicycle in the park (t).
> * yesterday, in the park, I saw Mary on a bicycle (t) (t).

Much worse is to put two nominals in front of the subject, as in the second example, which is just about impossible in English. Because many languages have most or all nominals in front of the verb, this is a common 'stylistic' error for people who speak languages like Japanese.

## Underlying order

In spite of the great diversity in arrangements of words in the languages of the world, there are surprising similarities. First, topics and subjects tend to come first in most languages, and question markers commonly come last. More important for us, however, is that the sequence of the other elements that make up a clause is much the same all over the world, though some languages are quite the reverse of others. This basic clause structure has attracted much attention as it is somewhat semantic in nature and nearly universal.

---

Q.   In the following spoken questions, what are (a) the topics, and (b) the indicators of question?[2]

John\/, you saw him in the park\, didn't you/?
you're coming to my party with Rebecca on Saturday\, eh/?
Reuben didn't sell his own/ car?
and as for Tommy\, you haven't even seen him\, have you/?

---

At one end of the clause is the nucleus, as we see again in Chapter 14, the main verb, with its 'accoutrements' (aspect markers, negation, modals and tense in roughly this order) between it and the actual end. Moving away from the verb towards the other end we find another universal tendency: the object, indirect object, required prepositional phrases, general phrases of time, location, and finally at the other end of the sentence are the adverbial phrases of reason or conditions. In the example above, we saw that Japanese and a vast number of other languages called 'OV languages' because the object is before the verb) finish at the verb end, with negation, modals and tense afterwards. Neutral Latin sentences tended to be in this OV order, finishing at the verb end, though they could be easily rearranged to show emphasis. Most European languages today are more like English (VO), beginning at the verb end (with tense, aspect and negation before), not counting the subject, of course. German, however, is basically OV, as seen clearly in subordinate clauses (main clauses have special features in most languages).

Q.  In the examples in the preceding question, identify the 'basic clause elements' for each example. (Put verb suffixes before the verbs to which they attach, as in Chapters 7, 8.)[3]

These strong tendencies have led many to suspect that this order is a basic of human semantic structure, and to explain the order of words in various languages as minor deviations from it. Alternatively, we can simply take the main verb as the semantic centre of the sentence, so all the nominal and adverbial phrases are related to it on one side, while negation, aspect, modality and tense are stuck to it on the other. Then the basic sense of these orderings follow quite naturally: express what is on the one hand first, then the verb centre, and then what is in the other hand.

Although we will talk of prepositions, because English uses prepositions almost exclusively (though there are some remnants of case in *he, him,* etc.), we could as well be talking of grammatical cases in Latin or Russian. They serve the same semantic functions and act much the same way as prepositions, except that they are suffixes to words, commonly all the major words of a phrase. Then again, many languages use 'postpositions', like case suffixes, but suffixed after the whole phrase, like a preposition is prefixed to the whole phrase. English has one, the possessive - *'s.* It clearly belongs to a whole phrase, such as 'the king of England' in 'The little mouse crawled under *the king of England's* hat', for what it crawled under was not a king who reigned over England's hat, but a hat that belonged to the king of England. It looks a bit illogical at first glance, but if you remember that - *'s* is a postposition, it is quite logical after all.

Most languages use only prepositions or only postpositions, but English, being the bastard language (Germanic + Romance) that it is, has a little of everything all nicely jumbled together. Grammatical cases are a little limiting, for it is nigh on impossible to add a new case to a language if the need arises. And while prepositions are seldom adopted from other languages, it does happen, like the *via* from Latin, and they can be created if usage demands it; *in spite of* seems to be a single semantic word today (cf. *despite*), and *be.neath, a.round* might have been created in this fashion. From this limitation, case-using languages tend to combine cases with prepositions to make complex prepositions, which is why one must learn what prepositions 'govern' what cases in German, Russian or Latin.

## Semantic structure

To show the semantic structure of a proposition, we must put the verb, or a symbol for the meaning of it and any prepositions it requires, in a prominent place. In this way we can represent propositional meanings on the basis of what expressions each verb requires. For example, since the transitive verb *to kill* relates two things (agent and patient), we can write [Kill(x,y)] as on the left below. The order of x before y is important because [Kill(y,x)] means quite a different thing. 'Our cat killed a mouse' has a meaning quite different from 'A mouse killed our cat.'

*To kill* is a transitive verb, so it relates two things and is called a '2-place relation'. There are also 'double-transitive' verbs that relate three things, like *to give* as in 'John gave the book to Mary', or equivalently, 'John gave Mary the book.' We call these three-place relations, as they have three **places** for things to fit in, [Give(x,y,z)]. If we fill in only two places of a 3-place relation, it either makes no sense at all, as in ⋆ 'John gave a postage stamp' that leaves us with a semantic hole – 'Whom [did he give it to]?' – or sometimes we have a standard way to fill in the hole, as in 'John gave $50' (to some charity) or 'John gave his life' (to some good cause).

Equally it is nonsense to specify three things to be related by a 2-place relation, as in ⋆ 'Our cat killed a mouse Anne', though here again English gives us a possibility of interpreting certain overfillings like ? 'John killed Mary a snake', which could mean something like [John killed a snake *for* Mary], though these are usually weird out of context. In general, then, every time you learn a verb in a foreign language (as you did in your own language), you must also learn how many places it needs to make a proposition (i.e. something that can be true or false). This is not only useful to make sentences that are easily understood, but it is necessary, even, merely to know when a sentence is overfilled or lacking something and thus in need of some creative reinterpretation (cf. Chapter 14).

Besides these 2- and 3-place relations, there are also many words that have only one place, but since these do not *relate* things together it is perhaps better to call them all **predicators**.[4]

Both verbs and adjectives are predicators, as in the examples below (*is* marks an adjective).

| 1-place | 2-place | 3-place |
|---|---|---|
| X is beautiful | X is similar to Y | X lends Y to Z (= X lends Z Y) |
| X is bad | X is better than Y | X compares Y with Z |
| X falls | X sees Y | X puts Y on Z |

Q.   Add at least three items to each column in the above table.[5]

'Intransitive' verbs are 1-place predicators; it takes only one thing to fill them up – to make a proposition – and more makes nonsense. So 'My dog died' is complete – it can be true or false – while ★'My dog died my cat' is utter nonsense. Most adjectives are 'intransitive' in this way, but a few need a second place filled. Comparative adjectives always need a second place filled if it is not clear from the context what is to fill it.[6] 'Transitive' verbs are in principle 2- (or 3-) place relations. English does not match logic very well, however, since many transitive verbs can be used with certain unspecific objects left unfilled if the filler has been recently mentioned in the context, as in 'Have you heard the news? – Yes, Bill *told me* Ⓟ' (but not ★'Yes, Bill *told* Ⓟ it'). Moreover, there are many 2-place relations that are expressed with 'intransitive' verbs plus an adverbial phrase. Without an adverbial addition, such as on the right below, they are incomplete, unless the context explains the missing direction or location.

| 'intransitive' | adverbial expressions for second place | | type |
|---|---|---|---|
| he looked | ..at the peak. | ..in(to) the box. | Dir |
| he went | ..away. | ..to the station. | Dir |
| she put it | ..on the table. | ..in the hole. | Dir |
| she lives | ..here. | ..in Rio. | Loc |

None the less, the number of places a predicator has is sometimes the only difference between words, as in the examples following. The 2-place predicates on the right have entirely different meanings from the one-place predicates on the left.

| | |
|---|---|
| he *runs* well. | he *runs* this factory well. |
| he *lives*. [is alive] | he *lives* in Bournemouth. [resides] |
| the light is *on*. | the light is *on* the table. |
| he *died*. | he *dyed* his socks. |

When counting the places of a predicator, we generally do not include locations like 'at my house' or times like 'on Tuesday' as place-fillers because there is still a complete proposition even without these additions, and because they can be added to nearly any proposition. Even excluding them, you will find verbs being used with up to four or five places filled in English, e.g. 'John bought Mary – a motorcycle – for Christmas – with his bonus.' Adverbial phrases that can combine with any sentence, then, are not considered as places required by a verb, so 'because he liked her' does not count as a place. However, any phrase that is required with a given verb is counted as a place for that verb, so '(in) Mambai' counts as a place with *to reside*, for we cannot say simply *'He resides', and with *to live* when it has that same meaning, but not with *to change* as in 'He changed planes in Mambai.' Interestingly enough, Japanese uses different postpositions for these two cases, though not many other languages do.

Sentential complements like 'to go' or 'that he go' count as nominals; *to want* and *anxious* are 2-place predicators in each of the following examples. Note that a preposition needed with a nominal object often disappears with a sentential complement.

|  |  |
|---|---|
| she wants to go. | she is anxious to go. |
| she wants him to go. | she is anxious for him to go. |
| *she wants that he go. | she is anxious that he go. |
| she wants it. | she is anxious *about* it. |
|  | she is anxious about his going. |

Though there are some minor questions, the fact that each predicator requires a specific number of places to be filled is beyond doubt. Having too few places forces the addressee to pick a filler from context, while having too many forces him to interpret the extra ones in some way or other. If he cannot do these reinterpretations for lack of an adequate context, the sentence is anomalous. But because many common words have alternative meanings depending on how many places they have, this automatic selection of word meaning takes precedence over such reinterpretations, and knowing the number of places is indispensable for finding the right meaning.

Q.  How many places are needed for the main verbs in the following? Also identify what fills each place.[7]

Lisa *promised* Reuben a new bicycle yesterday.
He *wanted* to ride it to Chicago.

Some argue that there are 0-place predicators as well, as in 'It rained.' While the *it* looks like it refers to something, it seems impossible to replace it with any meaningful words, like *the clouds* or *God* (two actual proposals that were rejected). The *it* appears to be a semantically empty element that is used to satisfy the grammatical requirement that English sentences have subjects, even when there is nothing to put there. We are inclined to accept this hypothesis, for with weather adjectives like *rainy, cloudy, foggy, muggy*, this empty *it* can be replaced by an adverbial of time or location without a noticeable difference in meaning, as below.

it is rainy in *New Zealand* in *the early summer.*
- *New Zealand* is rainy in *the early summer.*
- *the early summer* is rainy in *New Zealand.*

The last two examples make *rainy* look like it takes one place, but this is impossible for the virtually synonymous first example has that empty *it*. These hypothesized 0-place predicators, typically descriptions of weather, form another small unresolved corner of semantics and have exceptional patterns of grammar in most languages.

## If sentences are real, when are they 'complete'?

The notion of a 'complete sentence' in English grammar is based on this notion of having all the required places filled, except that English teachers tend to be fussy about what one can pick up from context to supply a filler. On the other hand, some modern notions that sentences are not found in conversation overlook the fact that to make sense, all the places of a predicator must be filled in the mind of the addressee. The parties to a conversation, however, may fill each other's places, and may leave places unfilled for the other to fill. As they are often mutually understood without expression – by empathy, eye movements, facial expression or whatever – they produce transcripts or recordings with many incomplete sentences. Full sentences reappear automatically when only one party does the talking, as for example a disc jockey on radio, especially when the listener(s) can't be seen.

The notion of sentence has at least one other important

aspect. At the end of a sentence, each pronoun and each place previously unfilled needs to have something to refer to. The end of a sentence is thus an indicator to addressees that they should fill up all semantic gaps from the context before going on.

Thus sentences do exist, because most languages are organized around predicators, and predicators need their places filled to be interpreted. When they are all filled, the sentence is complete. Some languages like Eskimo, however, are organized talking around a referent, so one can continue indefinitely by adding more comments (each one a predicator with one place unfilled) about that referent. The notion of sentence doesn't apply very well to these languages unless we call each comment, often only a single word and seldom more than three or four words, a sentence (with one place unfilled). A feel for this organization can be had with this example:

> man – yesterday-coming – tea-drink-wanted – seal-hunter – big – . . . .
> [The man that came yesterday wanted to drink some tea. he was a seal-hunter and quite a big man . . . .]

## To be or no to be

You may have noticed that *to be* got lost when we talked about the semantics of adjectives. This is because it has no descriptive content and serves only to help show the syntactic structure of sentences as well as carry tense and mark off the predicate (see below). Indeed, it is not used with adjectives in many languages if it is not needed to carry tense. In Chinese and Eskimo, for example, it is not bothered with at all, Russian uses it only for preterite or future, and Japanese uses it only when respect for the addressee is to be shown (their verbs, but not adjectives, have special forms for respect).

With nouns, too, *to be* expresses no descriptive content, as in 'Motorcycles are rolling death traps', and it is seldom expressed in Russian unless tense needs to be expressed. Thus we generally accept today that nouns are predicators too, and in fact, nouns are now sometimes divided into 1–place, intransitive ones and 2–place, transitive ones, sometimes called 'relational nouns', as in the table below.

| 1-place (intransitive) | 2-place (relational, transitive) |
|---|---|
| X is a boy | X is Y's father |
| X is a doctor | X is the president of Y |
| X is a question | X is the answer to Y |

In some languages, relational nouns form a syntactic class called 'inalienable nouns' for they cannot be used without someone or something to possess them. You cannot, for example, be a president without having an organization or a country to be president of! Like with verbs and comparative adjectives, English does not require one to re-mention the filler of the second place if it is clear from the context: 'While I was at the Yokohama Computer Co., the president [of . . .] spilled coffee all over me.'

Q.  Add three nouns to each column in the table above, considering words like *secretary*, *meaning*, *sheriff*, *sergeant*, *professor*, *ounce*.[8]

Nouns, then, resemble verbs and adjectives in the structure of their meanings. Two examples are as follows.

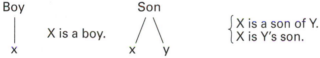

(These examples give only the general structure; we will see later how [Boy(x)] and [Son(x,y)], like most verbs, can be split apart into smaller semantic elements.)

We have seen that verbs, adjectives and now nouns are **predicators** in semantics. Even prepositions can be predicators, as in 'It is in the bag', or 'He put it in the bag', as they obviously relate a nominal 'the bag' to something else. Is everything a predicator? – No, only **lexical** words – words whose meanings can be explained in a dictionary – are predicators. (We speak of the 'lexicon' in linguistics to distinguish that part of a language from the various dictionaries that try to describe it.) The small words whose usage simply cannot be explained in a dictionary are called 'function words' or 'grammatical words' and they are typically not predicators. For example, *to be* completely disappears in the semantics of describing relationships (not too surprisingly given that its usage varies so much from language to language), and pronouns are like the variables x and y in the diagram above.

Although *to be* has no descriptive meaning, it does do something. First, it expresses tense, which English nouns and adjectives cannot do (adjectives are inflected for tense in some languages, Japanese for instance), and tense can be important. The present tense 'is small' and 'is a boy' are quite different from the past 'was small' and 'was a boy'. Second, tense indicates that the following noun or adjective is 'predicated', not merely 'attributive'. It thus identifies what is being said – asserted, questioned, proposed or whatever – as opposed to what is being used to identify what you are talking about, a fundamental difference explained in Chapter 10.

## Sentence meaning

**Variables** like x and y in the meanings of words (predicators, that is) are 'semantic holes' which must be filled in to make a proposition, so when words combine to make a complete sentence, all the variables should disappear. A complete sentence like 'A boy killed a snake' means roughly [there are two things, one is a boy, the other is a snake, and the first one killed the second]. It is clear how to diagram this meaning, as 'Y is a snake' must have the same structure of meaning as 'X is a boy' and we already know how to handle 'X is a boy' and 'X kills Y'. These three separate parts are conjoined together (with [.])[9] on the left, but they should be put together as on the right, for the sentence stands for a unitary and coherent idea. The symbol of conjunction can then be dropped with the understanding that everything is conjoined if not indicated otherwise.

When all the xs are connected together, we add a special symbol ∃ (from logic, a backward E meaning [there is] or [there exists]) to show that the 'hole' it stood for is filled in. There is no further use for variables like x and y in sentence meaning; they serve on the left only to connect the right things together (so that it is the boy who is killing the snake and not vice-versa), but they are needed in logic.

Because logic does not use diagrams, these xs and ys must be kept even for sentence meanings and must be 'bound' by a 'quantifier' such as ∃. Also, a symbol for conjunction is necessary, as are the parentheses.[10] This makes a notation that is too complex to use easily; the simplest way the diagrams above can be represented in usual logical notation is:

$$\exists x \exists y \ (Boy(x) \cdot Kill(x,y) \cdot Snake(y))$$

This can be translated symbol by symbol into English as: 'There is something, call it X, and there is another thing, call it Y, such that X is a boy, X kills Y, and Y is a snake.' Symbolic logics also commonly use an upside-down A, for a quantifier [$\forall$x], to translate 'every X' or 'for any X'. It is equivalent, however, to [Neg-$\exists$x-Neg].

The meanings for many nouns are based on conjunction, for example *boy*: 'He is a boy' has the same meaning as 'He is masculine, he is human and he is young', so in semantic terms this becomes:

$$Boy(x) \quad == \quad Msc(x) \cdot Hum(x) \cdot Yng(x)$$

Boy      ==      Msc  Hum  Yng

x                        x

We can now substitute this for [boy] in the structure of 'A boy killed a snake' above to get:

$$\exists x \exists y \ (Kill(x,y) \cdot Msc(x) \cdot Hum(x) \cdot Yng(x) \cdot Snake(y))$$

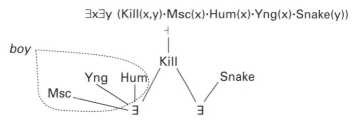

We saw above that the predicated part of a proposition – the part that the speaker wants to say – must be distinguished from the attributive parts – the descriptions used to allow the listener to identify the objects involved. Although the final word has not yet been said about this, and no distinction is possible in standard logical notations, we can make do by adding a special symbol (⊣) from logic that means roughly [assert]. The parts of the descriptive content that are not under this symbol are attributive, serving to help the listener identify the things that the predication is about as explained in chapter 10.

This is perhaps the simplest system that is adequate for

writing down the descriptive content of a sentence (that is, those parts of its meaning that describe something), and although the formulas used in logic are still the most standard way, we will generally use the equivalent diagram for sentence meaning because it is much easier to see the important elements. So far, these diagrams do not seem to say much more than how the words are related to each other, but they are really the key for further semantic progress. This tool will help us to take apart the meanings of most words. For example, besides a notion [dead], *to kill* has two basic elements, causative [Coz] and inchoative [Bcm], that play important and extensive roles in most languages, as we shall see in Chapter 12. It will become much clearer how meanings in different languages are much the same, and how words differ from language to language mostly in combining the same meaning elements in different ways.

## Word meaning, sentence meaning

The meaning of a word can be given adequately only when it is provided with **variables** (in a sentence frame) showing what **places** need to be filled before it can make a predication that could be true or false. These variables are needed to show how those other things relate to each other in its meaning, as for example *parent* and *child* express the same meaning with the variables reversed: 'X is Y's parent' has a meaning [Par(x,y)], while 'X is Y's child' is [Par(y,x)]. At the same time, including these variables will force us to note what preposition (if any) is needed for each place. The units for which the **lexicon** gives meanings are thus seen to be strings of one or more (syntactic) words such as the following. For English, as for most languages, we can shorten a full sentence frame to a verbal frame, as in these examples, where 'X' is reserved for the subject filler.

| | | |
|---|---|---|
| to marry Y | to depend on Y | to be independent of Y |
| to look at Y | to look Y up | to look in on Y |

An important by-product of including variables along with prepositions or other necessary elements is that it prevents us from trying to find a general meaning for *look* in the examples above. As we shall see in Chapter 12, there are three different lexical items or 'semantic words' including *look* here, just as *to overlook*, roughly [pass over (a fault) without note], includes *look*.

It is not hard to find the meaning for each one of such a series, but there need not be, and often is not, a general meaning uniting them that is specific enough to explain when each is used.

Languages may differ in what places are needed with any particular concept, but they differ most in what preposition is needed with each place and which ones must be expressed. French is generally more strict about expressing everything, while English is comparatively lax; many verbs allow one place to go unmentioned if its filler is obvious and not a specific object.

Eng:     I watched Ⓥ while he wrote Ⓥ.
Fr:       je l'ai regardé pendant qu'il l'écrivait.
   * j'ai regardé pendant qu'il écrivait.

Not all verbs do this, however; *to put, to give* for example tolerate no missing elements to be filled in from context. Both Chinese and Japanese, on the other hand, allow anything to be left unmentioned, even a subject phrase, so long as it is specific in the context, but must mention it if it is general. This is rather the reverse of the English rule to mention it when it is specific but leave it unmentioned if general, as in the first two examples following. Many English verbs further allow particular fillers (always general concepts) to be left unexpressed, as in the second two examples.

he eats well.              [he eats good *food*] or [he eats *food* well]
he is writing now.         [he is writing *something* now]
he writes often.           [he writes *letters* often]
he is drinking too much. [he is drinking too much *alcohol*]

The variables in lexical items disappear, however, when words are put together to make a sentence as they do in semantic graphs. In the equivalent logical notation, more standard and more commonly used, they cannot be dropped but must instead be '**bound**' by a **quantifier** such as ∃. In making a complete sentence, the semantic 'holes' that these variables represent can be filled in by pronouns that point or refer to an object, or can be erased by describing the object with attributive expressions.

A **proposition**, then, is the 'predication' of some **predicator** such as a verb or a predicative noun or adjective which has all its places filled. It can be asserted, as in a declarative statement, or it can be questioned, or there are other possibilities that we shall look at in Chapter 14.

The relations of the place-fillers to their predicator, such as 'agent', 'patient' and 'instrument', include many others, and although languages share much in this domain, they also differ quite significantly as to what relations their grammars express. Prepositions (or, equivalently, cases or postpositions) are the usual way to distinguish these relations within a language, so the lexical items that one must learn to use one's native or other language must include these prepositions. Usually, however, there are some rules that give good guidance for the choice of preposition, but there are few if any languages without many exceptional verbs.

We thus saw that meanings are associated with verbs (or other words) together with the required prepositions and variables for the places that need to be filled in to make a proposition. Using these variables leads naturally to including the needed prepositions, as well as to distinguishing different lexical items that contain a word in common.

## Answers and notes

1. [aVp]: 'The janitor opened my door'; [p was V-ed]: 'The door was opened'; [p was V-ed by a]: 'The door was opened by the janitor'; [p was V-ed with i]: 'The door was opened with a key'; [p was V-ed by a with i]: 'The door was opened by the janitor with his key.'

2. Topics: *John, you, Reuben, Tommy*. Question markers: 'didn't you', 'eh', 'have you' and (in all) rising intonation at the end. (Questions are also common with falling intonation – 'Did you come?'; 'Where to?')

3. Saw [Prt-see] – John – in the park (Sj: you). Pres-Prog-come – to my party – with Rebecca – on Saturday (Sj: you). Prt-Neg-sell – R's own car (Sj: Reuben). Perf Neg see Tommy (Sj: you).

4. 'Properties' or 'attributes' (1-place) and 'relations' (two, three or more places) are commonly gathered together as 'predicates' in modern logic, but this term *predicate* is also used in linguistics to mean roughly a sentence without its subject, so it is probably wise to avoid it.

5. (1) is tall, is interesting, dances; (2) is tired of, pushes, is taller than; (3) give, lend, tell. I would reject *borrow/steal Y from Z* as the 'from Z' is not needed to make a proposition; 'John borrowed that car' can be true or false without further ado.

6. 'Grammar' as taught in schools insists that comparatives always need their second place expressed. However, many English verbs can leave unexpressed certain nominal objects, and comparative adjectives can too. To express it is obviously unnecessary in a sentence like 'Tom was quite tall, but Bill was even *taller.*'

7. *To promise*: two – 'Reuben', 'a new bicycle'. *To want*: one – 'to ride it to Chicago'.

8. Sergeant, driver, secretary; sheriff of Y, meaning of Y (!), solution to Y, doctor of Y, ounce of Y. Professor (and secretary) can be either.

9. We are using '·' for conjunction (following Russell and Quine) instead of the more common '&' or '∧', because in the semantics of human language, conjunction appears to be the basic relation between predicators and is almost omnipresent. For these same reasons, it is not represented by an overt symbol in semantic diagrams. Even standard (linear) logical formulae are considerably easier to read with a visually small symbol for conjunction.

10. Parentheses are needed in linear formulas to associate predicators into groups, not illustrated here, and are also commonly used to separate variables from predicators.

## Keywords

(in)transitive, semantic roles/cases, places/actants, function/grammatical words, proposition, quantifier.

## Further reading

Dillon provides an easy introduction to case theory as part of an alternative introduction, and Fillmore is a good read besides being the foundation for most of the work on semantic roles.

Anderson, John M. *The Grammar of Case: Towards a Localistic Theory* (1971) London: CUP.

Clark, Herbert H. *Semantics and Comprehension* (1976) Mouton.

Dillon, George L. *Introduction to Contemporary Linguistic Semantics* (1977) Englewood Cliffs: Prentice-Hall.

Fillmore, Ch. 'The Case for Case' (1968) in Emmon Bach and

R. T. Harms (eds) *Universals in Linguistic Theory*, New York: Holt.

Hofmann, Th. R. *Description sémantique et dynamique du discours* (1978) Grenoble: Université scientifique et medicale. Diss. (1979) Ann Arbor: University Microfilms.

McCawley, J. 'English as a VSO Language' (1970) *Language* **46**: 286–99.

Mel'chuk, I. *Dependency Syntax: Theory and Practice* (1988) Albany: SUNY Press (Chapters 1 and 2).

Tesnière, Lucien *Eléments de syntaxe structurale* (1969, 2nd edn) Paris: Klincksieck.

Welke, Klaus M. *Einführung in die Valenz- und Kasustheorie* (1988) Leipzig: Bibliographisches Institut.

## Exercises with sentence meaning

1. While verbs like *to break* simply require a patient as in 'I broke the cup', verbs like *to hit* can be used not only that way – 'I hit his arm' – but can alternatively be used with the possessor as a patient (object) and the rest as a locative, as in 'I hit him in the arm.'

   (a) Which of the following are like *to hit* and which Loc-preposition does each take? Which are like *to break*?

   pat, bend, strike, fold, grasp, shatter, slap, stroke, grab, kiss, shoot, kick, seize, bite, burn, tear.

   (b) What distinguishes the *hit*-group from the *break*-group?

2. In what circumstances could you say 'I hit his arm' but not 'I hit him in the arm'? What, then, is the special meaning associated with this special form?

3. Correct the errors in the following sentences.

   (a) * They congratulated their son's graduation from university.

   (b) * Cambridge lost Oxford in this year's match.

   (c) * I will be very glad if you will kindly help this difficult assignment of mine.

   (d) * I should like to thank the generous assistance of all my friends.

   (e) * The young singer engaged with her manager who is more than twenty years older than she is.

   (f) * I want to trip to Greece with my friends before we graduate university.

(g) * In such a case, we are supposed to ask permission to our teacher.

(h) * Max failed the course for he never attended to classes.

(i) * She reminded an important appointment just as she was leaving.

(j) * I was stepped my foot in the bus this morning and it still hurts.

4. Which verb collocates best in the following examples?

   (a) I (ate/drank) the soup with a golden spoon.
   (b) He (ate/drank) the soup from a wooden cup.
   (c) The minority representatives (gave/made/put) a special request of the mayor.
   (d) They (gave/made/put) a difficult question to the mayor.
   (e) The mayor failed to (give/make/put) a clear answer.
   (f) How many foreign languages can you (say/speak/talk/tell)?
   (g) The prime minister didn't (say/speak/talk/tell) a single word.
   (h) The minister (said/spoke/talked/told) that he would resign.
   (i) John didn't (say/speak/talk/tell) anything about the accident to his father.
   (j) The lecturer (said/spoke/talked/told) about pollution in Antarctica.

5. There are two general ways to express an indirect object in English:

   (A) Fred gave a box of chocolates to Susie. Vb NP1 prep NP2
   (B) Fred gave Susie a box of chocolates.   Vb NP2 NP1

(a) Which of the following A-types can be changed into B-types?

   (1) The stewardess brought a glass of orange juice to me.
   (2) Joan knitted a warm sweater for her boyfriend.
   (3) Arthur borrowed $50 from his mother-in-law.
   (4) The nurse sang a beautiful lullaby for the little boy.
   (5) The policeman showed an old picture to Henry.
   (6) The students compared the old map with the new one.
   (7) They blamed the accident on the pilot.

(b) In the changes that are possible, what preposition(s) can be lost?

(c) Not all occurrences of these prepositions allow such a change. Of the following, which do? What is the general rule?

   (1) I sent a package to my uncle.
   (2) I sent the package to San Francisco.

    (3) Carol cooked a good dinner for her husband.

    (4) Carol cooked a good dinner for the picnic.

    (5) The catcher threw the ball to the fence.

    (6) The catcher threw the ball to me.

(d) Not only does the nature of the indirect object limit this, but also the nature of the verb. Which of the following allow it?

    (1) They told nothing to me.

    (2) They said nothing to me.

    (3) The teacher assigned a lot of homework to the bully.

    (4) Mr Green dedicated his new book to his kindergarten teacher.

    (5) The orphan addressed his letter to the President.

    (6) The workers suggested a new plan to their boss.

(e) Find five verbs that allow, and five more that do not allow, this sort of rearrangement.

6. Gradable adjectives (see Chapter 3) have only one syntactic place to fill in their 'absolute' form, e.g. 'X is tall.'

(a) How many places do the comparative (*taller*) and superlative forms (*tallest*) require? Give examples with variables (X,Y,Z) and fleshed-out examples that are natural and not incomplete.

(b) Unlike these forms, the absolute form can be accompanied by a *for*-phrase, e.g. 'Dick is tall for a footballer.' What might we suppose to be the meaning of 'X is tall for a Y'?

(c) In 'X is a tall man and Y is a tall boy', X is no doubt taller than Y. What does this imply about the meanings of absolute forms?

7. Many intransitive verbs can be easily transitivized in English, almost without notice. Add an agent to make the following verbs transitive.

    (a) The water has been running for fifteen minutes.

    (b) Your aeroplane is flying over Sicily by now.

    (c) My coffee is boiling!

    (d) That car is turning off the main road.

8. We can even make transitive verbs out of some nouns, e.g. 'She mothers him too much.' Make examples with minimal subject and object that use these nouns as transitive verbs. What do they mean?

    (a) father

    (b) daughter

    (c) sweet-little-thing

    (d) chocolate-bar

    (e) coffee

Can you see a pattern in the meanings of the ones that derive from relational nouns, and of the ones that derive from intransitive nouns? Which one doesn't fit these patterns, and how can it be explained?

9. We can also detransitivize verbs easily in English by dropping general or generic nominals. What are the missing nouns in the following?

    (a) He is eating; can you call later?

    (b) Let's go drinking.

    (c) Sorry, we gave already.

    (d) Don't tickle me when I'm drinking.

We can also drop a definite nominal, as in the following. What is the missing nominal?

    (e) This road is slippery; shall I drive?

    (f) John's washing tonight.

# CHAPTER 12

# Word Meanings

The division of the meanings of words into smaller units of meaning is one of the most successful areas of modern semantics, and turns out to be useful for language learning, for most of the elementary units of meaning of one language are found in other languages. We can call these elementary units of meaning 'semantic **atoms**', for like atoms in chemistry that combine together into molecules, they combine together into tight clusters that can be called 'concepts' or word meanings. Of course, when atoms combine in chemistry the result may have a quite different nature; two gases, hydrogen (H) and oxygen (O), combine to form a liquid, water ($H_2O$). We seldom find such big differences in semantics, but like chemical atoms each semantic atom can combine only with a certain number of things, and a combination can act quite differently from its constituent parts.

There is no known way to prove that a given semantic atom could not be divided into still smaller units, but the ones we will talk about here do not appear to be further divisible. Chemistry had to wait a hundred years before it could be seen why atoms could not be further split into smaller atoms, and perhaps some day we will have such an explanation for semantic atoms.

Some words naturally fit into patterns based on their meanings. In Chapter 4 we saw how deictic words usually form semantic patterns, and also discovered that the meanings of words can be divided or 'analysed' into smaller pieces. This is quite clear in the case of Japanese, where the morphological structures of the deictic words make a pattern.

|         | [Ø]  | [Voj][1] | [Dir]  | [Loc] |     | [Loc] |
|---------|------|----------|--------|-------|-----|-------|
| [Spk]   | kono | kore     | kotira | koko  | ... |       |
| [Ø]     | sono | sore     | sotira | soko  | ... |       |
| [Awa]   | ano  | are      | atira  | *ako  | ... | asoko |
| [Qst]   | dono | dore     | dotira | doko  | ... |       |

This is a perfect pattern but for one flaw. One potential word does not exist, *ako, and there is one extra word that does not fit in, asoko. It is tempting to say that this extra word fills the empty slot, but does it? Indeed it does, for it is used precisely as the word *ako would be used if it existed; it has precisely that meaning. This means its meaning can be divided into two parts, one like the a- in ano, are, and another like the -ko in soko, doko, even though it has three parts, a-so-ko, in pronunciation. Pieces of meaning do not commonly match pieces of pronunciation below the level of words. The example of deictic markers in Japanese is exceptional in the neatness that sound (almost) matches meaning.

In English prepositions we again found a table that cross-classified aspects of location (Cnt–Srf–Ø–Apx) with Loc, Dir, Abl, Via and Neg-Loc. Even though the forms of the prepositions did not share very much, we had to conclude that each was divisible into two pieces of meaning, one from each group. Here we will look at other patterns that are not quite so obvious but can nevertheless be seen easily.

## Conjunctive meanings

Tables like the above show that each of its words has two components of meaning. These elements are commonly put

together by a conjunction like *and* that we symbolize with a dot
(·). Now compare another such table as on the left below, with
some possible meanings on the right.

| man | boy | [Msc·Adt] | [Msc·Yng] |
|-----|-----|-----------|-----------|
| woman | girl | [Fem·Adt] | [Fem·Yng] |

It is clear that [Msc] stands for male and [Fem] for female, [Adt]
for adult and [Yng] for young. This table is too short to prove
that these atoms are significant in English, but it is easy to expand
it to the right or downward, as follows.

| man | boy | father | stallion | ram | bull | ... | ... | [Msc] |
|-----|-----|--------|----------|-----|------|-----|-----|-------|
| woman | girl | mother | mare | ewe | cow | ... | ... | [Fem] |
| chicken | chick | | | | | | | |
| cat | kitten | | | RIGHTWARD | $\longrightarrow$ | | | |
| dog | puppy | | | | | | | |
| horse | colt | DOWNWARD | | | | | | |
| ... | ... | | $\downarrow$ | | | | | |
| ... | ... | | | | | | | |
| [Adt] | [Yng] | | | | | | | |

---

Q.   Find at least two more pairs in each direction![2]

---

Because these extensions are limited only by one's knowledge of
English, it is clear that the elements which they contrast are part
of English. Moreover, we happen to have words in English for
[Msc], [Fem], [Adt] and [Yng], the ones given in the paragraph
above. With a moment's thought you will see that they play
important roles in any language you know, though they may
combine in different ways. In Japanese, for instance, [Yng] is
often expressed by a prefix *ko-*, as below, and this is a good
example to show that what one language does by word-choice
(English expresses [Yng] by choosing a different word), another
language may do with a prefix or a suffix.

| [Yng·X]: | koneko [kitten] | koinu [puppy] | kouma [colt] | koguma [cub] |
|----------|-----------------|---------------|--------------|--------------|
| [X]: | neko [cat] | inu [dog] | uma [horse] | kuma [bear] |

This Japanese example brings out what we might have missed in
the English examples. Except for the first two examples, the
leftmost column is not [Adt] but only the lack of [Yng]; the Yng-
term is the marked term (Chapter 2) and the other is used for
adults or when age is not relevant, as seen in 'A kitten is a young

*cat.*' Indeed, one can hardly say 'A cat is an old kitten' for it is not true; all kittens are cats, but not all cats are kittens. Further use for [Adt] will be found, however, in Question 1.

This sort of combination of semantic atoms by conjunction is extremely common, though there are not so many words whose meanings can be described completely in this way. Until quite recently it was the only way we knew for combining meanings, and 'structural' semantics was unable to progress beyond these words. The table below, for example, suggested that there are two more atoms, [Par] and [Ofs] (PARent and OFfSpring).

| father | son | — | [Msc.Par] | [Msc.Ofs]? |
| mother | daughter | — | [Fem.Par] | [Fem.Ofs]? |

This is not so, however, for [Ofs] is just the reverse of [Par]; if X is a child of Y, then it must be that Y is a parent of X, and vice-versa, if X is a parent of Y, then Y is a child of X. This is an inescapable fact and is part of English; if you don't realize it, you will not be able to speak English adequately (or any other language, for it is undoubtedly found in all languages). There is, then, only one new atom here, [Par], which is combined in two different ways.

To show the difference between *child* and *parent*, we need to use 'X' and 'Y' as in the preceding paragraph, and the standard way is to use parentheses, as with relations in mathematics or logic.

| X is a parent of Y; | X is Y's parent; | Y is X's child | — [Par(x,y)] |
| X is a child of Y; | X is Y's child; | Y is X's parent | — [Par(y,x)] |

The x and y in the parentheses are sometimes called the **actants** of the relation [Par], and which one is first is usually important. Because of this, the meaning of any word can be given only in a sentence frame, with Xs and Ys like above. Properly, we should go back and revise all the meanings of all the words we have talked about, adding one or two variables as needed.

---

Q. While we have been using [Spk, Awa] without actants, that was a simplification that we should now do away with. What actant structure do they have? And how might you paraphrase them in English?[3]

---

When you go back and revise the meanings of words studied previously, you will notice that some words like *father* have two actants, 'X is the father of Y', for no one can be a father without there being a Y. Other words like *man* have only one actant, for a person is a man (or not) independently of what other people are around him. While *man* describes a person, *father* describes one side of a **relationship** between two people. This makes sentences like the first example following strange, unless Y is clear from the context as in the other examples.

> ? I see *a/the father* walking down the street.
> I see *my/Pete's father* walking down the street.
> that must be *the father* of the kid that just played.
> I see *a father* chasing his kid.

As we saw in Chapter 11, many verbs need two (or more) actants, like 'X hits Y', 'X jumps Y' or 'X sees Y', but some, like 'X flies' or 'X breathes', take only one. Most adjectives and nouns, on the other hand, take only one actant, which is why we did not need to include the actants to give the meanings of the simple words in the early chapters. If, however, there is only one actant, then there is no way to reverse the meaning as *parent-of* can be reversed. We must allow this reversal to provide the true relationships between people described by the words below. Even the single-actant atoms like [Msc] must be specified for which person is male. *Father* is not the reverse of *son*, because these words mark different people as male, and also, as we noted in Chapter 3, *son* is restricted to human beings.

> X is the father of Y   —   [Par(x,y).Msc(x)]
> X is a son of Y         —   [Par(y,x).Msc(x).Hum(x)]
> X is the mother of Y —   [Par(x,y).Fem(x)]
> X is a daughter of Y —   [Par(y,x).Fem(x).Hum(x)]

The meaning of '*X is a grandfather of Y*' and thus the meaning of *grandfather* can be described in this same way. It is [Par(x,z).Par(x,y).Msc(x)], 'X is male, and X is a parent of Z, and Z is a parent of Y.' We needed to add a new person Z here, to express the idea of 'a parent of a parent', and indeed, you cannot call someone your grandfather unless there is someone linking you and him, midway between. This sort of meaning is not as complex as it looks. It is the relational notation of mathematics that makes it complex. When we use the diagrams that cut out the useless symbols, you will see that it is much simpler.

Msc       Par       Par
 \  /  \  /  \
   x       ∃       y

With these three semantic atoms, [Msc], [Fem] and [Par], the meanings of all the words of kinship (fathers and mothers, brothers and sisters, aunts and uncles, grandchildren, cousins, and so on) can be specified exactly. This one atom [Par] multiplies the number of words that we can give the meanings of! Nice work, eh? Take a break (after this question) – you deserve it!

---

Q. What is the meaning for *sister*, i.e. what is the meaning of 'X is Y's sister'? Once you have that, suggest how it might be modified to give the meaning of *stepsister*, based on the fact that Y's stepsister is a sister who shares only one parent with Y instead of the usual two.[4]

---

Before you take your break, notice that we must add one more semantic element, [Sps(x,y)] for [X is a/the spouse of Y], to give the meanings of *wife*, *husband*. This combines with [Par, Msc, Fem] to give all the meanings of the terms for in-laws, including the two meanings of *brother-in-law*.

X is a brother-in-law of Y

[∃z∃w Msc(x)·Par(z,x)·Par(z,w)·Sps(w,y)] OR

[∃z∃w Msc(x)·Sps(x,w)·Par(z,w)·Par(z,y)]

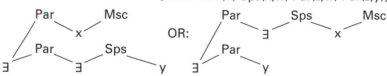

Also, for languages like French or Chinese that distinguish [younger brother] from [elder brother], e.g. French *aîné*, *cadet*, we need another semantic element because there are different words for them, as well as elder and younger sisters, uncles who are older or younger than one's parent and so on. Of course, we shall need it for English too, if only to give the meaning of *elder*, which suggests that it might be the same element as in *younger*, *older*. In any case, we see that languages differ a lot in what semantic elements they combine into words, but they use pretty much the same basic elements.

## Vocabulary and more vocabulary

It is useful here to distinguish the central words of a language, the words that it is very hard to get along without, from the much less common and less useful words that belong mostly in technical discussions. Although there is really a gradation between these two extremes with words that are more or less central, we can speak of the extremes as two separate vocabularies, the **core** vocabulary that contains the words used every day, and the **peripheral** vocabulary, the innumerable words that one uses only infrequently.

The meaning of a core word is described more or less completely by an arrangement of semantic atoms, but the more peripheral a word is, the more likely it is that its meaning is only partly explained by systematic elements. Typically, there are large gaps in the meanings of peripheral words that are filled in with images of experiences, as in the words *deer, antelope, gazelle*. These are basically peripheral words, though *deer* is relatively more central than the others which could be described as types of deer. Few people other than biologists could explain the differences between these animals, and many would be not at all sure, on meeting one of them, which word should be applied to it. The only meaning of *gazelle* that I know, other than that it is like a deer, is a vague memory of pictures that I have seen. This is normal; people commonly use words without knowing all the precise details of their meanings. Sometimes I have fun asking Japanese people what the difference is between *akamatsu* and *kuromatsu* ([red-pine] and [black-pine]), as well known in Japan as *deer* and *antelope* are to us, and you would be surprised at some of the answers I get – even male and female. No, it is not that one is red and the other is black, or even that one is slightly blacker.

Human language is not a scientific notation; you do not need to know precisely what something is to talk about it, and it is seldom useful to try to learn precisely what a peripheral word in a foreign language means. In your own language, you know only roughly what peripheral words mean, so surely that is all one needs for a second language.

The semantic atoms we have seen so far are extremely useful, but there are a number more that are just as common, such as [Ani], animate, and [Viv], living or alive. Something that is animate but not human, [Ani.Neg-Hum], is what we mean by *animal*, while something that is human but not animate, [Neg-

Ani.Hum], is presumably a ghost, a spirit or a god. Classificatory atoms like these form part of the meaning of nearly every noun, and enter into verbs also.

Except for the core nouns this chapter began with, nouns are largely peripheral, which is why new ones can be adopted so easily from other languages. Let us get to the real core of a language, then, its verbs, whose meanings can be described almost completely in terms of semantic atoms. Before that, however, we must make a short survey of what we are doing.

## Not by words alone

Early on, we naively pursued the meanings of words floating free of any context. One can do this with some success if the words fit into a table, as at the beginning of this chapter, but even there we found it was necessary to include variables like X and Y for words like *father* that describe relationships. In fact this is always necessary, for words don't really have a perceivable meaning, or even a substantial existence, until they are used in a sentence. It might be worth rereading the latter part of Chapter 1 if this is not obvious.

Sentences carry the sort of meaning that we can study by looking at what they conflict with and what they entail. *To teach* includes the completion (F) of *to learn* as we cannot say ★ 'I taught him how to solve those problems but he didn't learn it.' When we can do this for words, it is only that we have learned to supply subconsciously the missing sentence frame. Those missing sentence elements are necessary to convince anyone else, or even to have confidence in what seems obvious. You know immediately that *cat* is a hyponym of *animal*, but you can't convince anyone who disagrees with you unless you recast this as a relation between sentences; 'X is a cat' entails 'X is an animal' or 'Everything that is a cat is an animal, in all conceivable worlds.'

Similarly, 'W is an antonym of V' is merely a short way of saying that 'X is W' is inconsistent with 'X is V', when they are both direct hyponyms of the same general term, that is, when both 'X is V' and 'X is W' imply 'X is GT' for some general term, GT. There is, of course, nothing wrong with a short cut if it saves you time and is not likely to lead you astray. It *is* a short cut, however, and not always reliable, so we must keep in mind what method to use when the short cut doesn't work. In point of fact, this proper full route – using complete sentence frames – became known in linguistics only a few decades ago, and skipping it has sometimes led to confusion.

The only adequate way to study the meaning of a word is to put it in a sentence frame, in a predicative position. It must be in a predicative position (Chapter 9) because only there is its speaker obliged to respect all the details of its meaning. In attributive use, a word may be used rather loosely, for its purpose there is only to help the addressee identify some referent in the area of discourse. There should, of course, be as little else in the sentence frame as is possible, to get at the meaning of that word alone, so we need only add *is* for nouns and adjectives, and a suffix -*s* to verbs, plus, without fail, as many variables as are absolutely needed for the mini-sentence to be complete. The demonstratives *this*, *that* are quite good as variables for they have little meaning themselves, but as they can't be used alone for human beings, pronouns will sometimes be necessary. It is enough to write X, Y, etc., but read them as *this*, *he*, etc.

---

Q.   Make up sentence frames for the adjectives *hot*, *taller*, *like*, the nouns *boy*, *son*, *secretary*, and the verbs *to like*, *to live*, *to go*.[5]

---

Many abstract nouns may require *has* instead of *is*, as in 'X has compassion' but it is usually easier to study the equivalent adjectival form, 'X is compassionate.' I know when I see a compassionate act, though I would be hard put to say what compassion was. Indeed, some abstracts like *beauty* are shockingly vague in this form: 'X has beauty.' A lot of philosophical effort has been wasted on questions like 'What *IS* beauty?' or even 'What has beauty?' when a nearly equivalent 'What is beautiful?' is much easier to answer in general, and it is easy to accept that each person can answer this in a different way. (It is not that these mini-sentences are inherently vague, but rather that they are so transparent that they show up the fuzziness in a concept like beauty.) Using sentence frames, then, often suggests an easier route to understanding the meaning of abstract concepts, as well as being necessary for words that relate several things.

## Evidence for word meanings (linguistic concepts)

We thus have a ready way to resolve questions about what a word means, whether or not two words are (descriptively) synonymous, and so on. If you want to say that two words have different meanings, you must be able to point out an object or situation – in some imaginary world if need be – that one but not the other word could be used to describe. Conversely, to say that two expressions have the same meaning is to say that in any conceivable world, whatever can be accurately described by one is equally accurately described by the other.

When we put a word in a sentence frame to examine its meaning, the frame should have as little as possible of its own meaning if we are to see the meaning of the word itself. The most neutral frames for this sort of testing are the following, using pointing to establish what object is being referred to.

that is (a) ____.       for nouns and adjectives (a/an for count nouns)

he/it is ____ing . . . $\Big\}$ for verbs (. . . for required complements)
  he/it ____s . . .

An attributive frame like 'That __ is . . .' gives poor results, for here words need be used only accurately enough to distinguish an intended referent from other possible referents (Chapter 10), and that depends on what else happens to be in the environment.

Although children may be doing something like this in saying 'See the book' or the like, this sort of overt experimental testing is unusual in linguistics. There is another way to test a hypothesized meaning that is often as reliable: to construct a sentence so that it negates one of the supposed components of the concept. If indeed it is a component of the concept, or can be derived from one, then the constructed sentence should be impossible. For example, *to assassinate* has four important components of meaning: [(1) to kill a (2) politically prominent (3) person for (4) political purpose]. To show them, we can construct sentences that negate each in turn.

(1) * although the Generalissimo was assassinated, he didn't die.
(2) * they plan to assassinate Joe Bloke's daughter-in-law.
(3) * they assassinated the gift panda from China.
(4) * the Swedish prime minister was accidentally assassinated by a pickpocket.

Because each of these is semantically impossible (syntactic impossibility doesn't count), we can be fairly confident that *to assassinate* has these components of meaning. This method requires a bit of ingenuity[6] to make good sentences but is far faster than to go about pointing to a wide range of things or pictures saying 'This is a __' or 'He assassinated her.'

Because people can and do use a concept like *to assassinate* in a way that excludes the example sentences above, we can say that they know its meaning to be as we hypothesize, even though few would be able to identify which details are relevant in labelling something as an assassination. Indeed, language users are not conscious of and often cannot bring to consciousness what the components of a concept are. With some training and experience with the common atomic concepts and the ways they combine, however, you will find that you can fairly directly break a complex concept into more elemental ones. At least for experienced people, a proposed analysis can sometimes 'ring true' or not. Of course, such intuitions cannot be trusted; they must be checked out and verified, at least with contradictory examples as in (1) to (4) above.

This method of self-contradictory examples can run into difficulties because we automatically (very quickly and totally unconsciously) try to find another possible interpretation if anything close to a contradiction arises, as explained in Chapter 13. If the word being studied is ambiguous, and many are in some aspect(s), it may be very difficult to get a contradiction by negating a component of only one meaning; the other meaning of the word will almost totally exclude the intended meaning and the contradiction. A perceived contradiction is thus an unresolvable contradiction and indicates a real conflict of semantic elements in all common meanings of the word. Another problem is that the contradiction may derive not directly from a component of the word's meaning but from something it entails, especially in the case of an ambiguous word when different meanings both entail something in common.

In any case, so long as we have the more tedious method to fall back upon to resolve difficult cases, and even to verify this method, we can usually profit by using it. Where it works, this method provides reliable evidence that is quick and easy to verify by asking others, and it is ideal for demonstrating a point in a linguistic paper. Rather than asking readers to trust in your honesty and ability to apply strict experimental procedures and statistics, they can see the proof directly.

We have been assuming here that everyone concerned has the same meaning for a word that we are trying to get at, so the linguist can work on his own dialect if he can guard against infecting the data with what he wants to be true. That is not always so easy, so crucial points should be verified by asking the same sorts of questions of disinterested parties. In addition, some words, e.g. *rubber, to knock up,* have different meanings in different dialects, so actual surveys of users of a language may be called for in certain cases. Usually, however, a few sentences that negate components will be enough when several people from another dialect agree that they are contradictory.

What to do for a dead language, or an older form of English that no one speaks any more? Perhaps the most efficient way is to learn the language well and then ask questions as above of yourself. However, one seldom learns a second language well enough to be confident of the answers needed, and in any case one must guard against infecting the data with one's desires. If others have also learned it, as many learn Latin, the results will be much more reliable, but it will still be a second language to all and different answers will likely arise. The most reliable method here is to fall back upon what was once named 'Semantic Axiom No. 1', that the meaning of an unknown word or expression must be taken to be the least meaning that will explain what each sentence that contains it means, where that can be determined from context. There are problems in applying this sometimes, especially for rare words, but it appears to be the only thing we have to go on for a really extinct language.

## Domination

Until very recently, semantics was unable to describe the meanings of verbs; like the relational nouns above (e.g. *father*), verbs typically have several actants, so we could not describe their meanings until we discovered that the sentence frames with X and Y were necessary. Once this was done, the meanings of verbs began to fall apart like a picture puzzle, and we discovered another type of relation between semantic atoms.

Let us begin with the element for love and friendship, [Ami], which is pretty sure to be a semantic atom. [Ami(x,y)] is the meaning of 'X likes Y', which is quite different from 'Y likes X', [Ami(y,x)]. 'I like you' doesn't necessarily entail 'You like me.' It is obvious, isn't it, that these different meanings, the reverse of each other, must be represented by reversing the actants, as with *parent-of* and *child-of*. But what is obvious today escaped the best of thinkers for hundreds of years – the best that could be managed was [+Ami] for the Y; as is typical of a basic discovery, the people who came before it seem rather stupid, even though they were not.

---

Q.   Go back over the words to which meanings have been assigned so far in this chapter (from 'Conjunctive meanings' on) and diagram their meaning structures in this fashion, in the margin of the page if you like. Don't forget that X (and maybe Y) is absolutely necessary for a definition. They have sometimes been left out to make it easier to understand, but put them back in.[7]

---

The element [Hav(x,y)] similarly describes a relation between two objects, roughly what is common to the meanings of 'X has Y', 'X borrows Y' [to have temporarily] and 'X owns Y' [to have, legally at least]. The meaning of 'X gets Y' is quite similar, for the meaning of *to get Y* is simply to have Y afterwards but not before; you cannot 'get' a car unless you don't have it before but have it afterwards, and vice-versa.

This element of [not before but yes afterwards] is a basic building block of word meaning in nearly all languages and has a name, the **inchoative**. We will symbolize it as [Bcm] after the English word *BeCoMe*; you will see that it is the difference between the first and second rows of words below, and in many many more examples, perhaps every verb (Vb) that depicts movement or change.

| Vb: | have Y | know Y | wear Y | not have Y | be at Y |
|---|---|---|---|---|---|
| Bcm-Vb: | get Y | learn Y | put Y on | lose Y | go to Y[8] |

| Aj: | red | dark | bright | long | dead | big | small |
|---|---|---|---|---|---|---|---|
| Bcm-Aj: | redden | darken | brighten | lengthen | die | grow | shrink |

In the latter examples with adjectives (Aj), [Bcm-Aj] means [to become more Aj] if the adjective is gradable, e.g. *big*, *bigger* (Chapter 3), but [to become Aj] if it is not gradable, e.g. *dead*, *\*deader*. The first few of these show that English sometimes uses an inchoative suffix *-en* with an adjective, but these are relatively few; the systematic way in modern English to express inchoation is by using *to get* or *to become*. However, for many adjectives describing an unpleasant state, *to fall* is possible instead – 'to fall ill, to fall into ruin, to fall into disrepute, to fall in love'(!).

This atom of inchoation talks about the whole predication; in syntactic terms it 'dominates' the proposition. 'He gets a car' is the inchoation of 'He has a car', so its actant is filled by that proposition: [Bcm(Hav(h,c))]. This may seem unreasonable at first, for *he* is the subject of *to get*, but it is not he or the car that is changing, only the relationship between them, [Hav].

There are a few too many parentheses in [Bcm(Hav(h,c))] for easy reading, however, especially when we combine in a few more elements. Let us thus define an abbreviation [-] for predicators that take a single actant filled by another predicator, [Bcm-Hav(h,c)], useful for a predicator like [Bcm] that dominates another predicator. We have already been using it informally for [Neg]. This will also allow us to say informally that a verb like *to get* has a meaning of simply [Bcm-Hav].

If you try combining this very fundamental atom [Bcm] with the atoms we started out with, you will notice that the expression 'X had a baby' is usually understood as [Prt-Bcm-Par(x,z)], somewhat like 'X became a mother/father', and that 'X goes from P' has a meaning [Bcm-Neg-Loc(x,p)]. This is similar to one meaning of *to lose*, [Bcm-Neg-Hav(x,y).Voj(y)].

---

Q.  Recall [Sps(x,y)] – 'X is the spouse of Y' or 'X and Y are married.' What, then, are the meanings of 'X marries Y'; 'X gets divorced from Y'?[9]

---

This way of connecting atoms, with a line downward from one to the other (or with parentheses or a hyphen), is quite different from the conjunction connection [.] found in all the example words in the first few pages of this chapter. In contrast to those 'conjunctive' meanings, we can call this a relation of **domination**, as one predicator dominates or subordinates another. Knowing about it (it wasn't discovered until about 1965), we can begin to pick apart the meanings of most verbs.

These elements can combine in interesting ways. To lack something is to need it but not to have it, so we can pick apart the meaning of a sentence frame 'X lacks Y' along this line as 'X needs (to have) Y' and 'X does not have Y', understanding that the parenthesized 'to have' that is optional in English is a real semantic element. If we take *to need to* as something like *must*, i.e. [Nec] (Chapter 6), then we can roughly specify these meanings as:

Nec(Hav(x,y)).Neg(Hav(x,y))
or shorter, with the hyphen abbreviation:
Nec-Hav(x,y).Neg-Hav(x,y)

Even this short form is unnecessarily complex and can be simplified by using diagrams like the ones for sentences in Chapter 11. We thus use downward lines in place of parentheses (or hyphens), and the [.] for the conjunctive connections is dropped with the understanding that all predicators with nothing above them are conjoined. The order of the actants is still vital, so the first one must be kept to the left of the second. This yields the disjoint diagrams at left below for *to lack*. However, the xs and ys must be coalesced, since each represents only one thing, and the elements [Hav] should be coalesced too. This gives the diagram on the right for the meaning of *to lack*. A jolly 'X' it is, and you will recognize it as something like the common schematic diagram for a molecule of methane ($CH_4$), if you have studied chemistry.

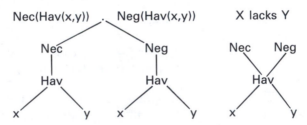

This diagrammatic form is definitely easier to read, and appears moreover to be more accurate than the linear form as there is only one relation of having between x and y.[10] The x and y are still needed in a diagram for word meaning for they relate to the X and Y of the sentence frame and are needed to connect with variables of other words in putting together the meaning of a sentence. These diagrams, then, show much more clearly the structure of word meaning, without the parentheses and repetitions needed to squeeze these relations on to a line. The structure of the meaning of most words is not so symmetrical and beautiful but often simpler.

One other semantic atom is extremely common in the meanings of verbs, in many languages expressed with a **causative** verb suffix. There are a number of verbs in English that differ by this element [Coz], as in the examples below. In such cases the Z is generally called the 'agent' and 'agentive' is another name for this structure. In English, however, an instrumental can generally fill an agentive slot, as we saw in Chapter 11.

| Bcm: | X dies | X gets Y | X learns Y | X | X falls |
|---|---|---|---|---|---|
| Coz-Bcm: | Z kills X | Z gives X Y | Z teaches X Y | Z | Z drops X |

A more common way of adding a causative meaning in English, however, is just to add an agent Z in the subject position pushing what was there into an object position. This can be applied to many verbs that do not have a paired causative form as above. Of course, lexical blocking (Chapter 2) prevents it from applying where there is already a verb with that meaning.

| X Vb | Z Vb X |
|---|---|
| the water is boiling. | he is boiling the water. |
| the dog is walking. | he is walking the dog. |
| corn grows in Kansas. | he grows corn in Kansas. |
| the milk poured on the rug. | she poured the milk on the rug. |

The element [Coz] has two actants, the causer or agent, and what is caused, a proposition that usually includes [Bcm]. Notice how, in the complete meanings for two of these examples, the meaning of the causative verb includes the meanings of inchoative verbs, which themselves may include meanings of still smaller elements. Verb meanings are often like Ukrainian dolls – a smaller one inside, and a still smaller one inside that one, and so on.

Z kills X                                    Z teaches X Y

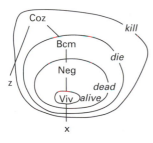
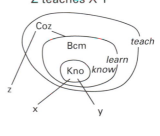

There are many avenues that cry out for exploration from here, but with no more space we will have to leave it to you to walk down them, to see and learn what you will. In any case, if you simply remember that the atoms in this chapter (and their ways of connection) are important in most languages, then when you meet a new word in conversation or in reading you will probably not need a dictionary to find out roughly what it means. As words in most languages are made out of these pieces, if you guess a meaning made from them that fits the context, you have a very good chance of being right. This is perhaps how you learned the meanings of many words when you were a child, and it is a very effective method.

## What counts as a word?

It is a common belief that orthographic words (separated by spaces in writing) or syntactic formatives (elements that function in syntax) are the carriers of meaning. Though such words usually do have some meaning (but few people today know the meaning of *kith* in 'my kith and kin'), in isolation that meaning is too often not the meaning that is expressed when they are combined with other words. The meaning of *to blow*, for example, is expressed by the first *blow* in the examples as [force air from the mouth], while the second can mean either [get angry] or [explode] and the third means only [Coz-explode].

> to blow at a flame    to blow up    to blow up a house
> to look at Y    to look Y up    to look in on Y    to look on

The meaning of *to look* in the first example of the second row is almost totally absent in the second and third examples [to search for Y] and [to pay Y a short visit] and almost incidental in the fourth [to watch an event passively]. In any case, the extra meanings these complexes have cannot possibly be assigned to *on*, *in*, *up*. Rather, the lexicon associates a meaning with one or more words, such as in the lexical items above. The fact that these sequences may include words that have independent meanings is no more than an accident (often with a historical explanation), such as is the fact that *catalogue* contains the words *cat*, *log* and *biological* contains the words *by*, *a*, *logical*, all of which have independent meanings. Using variables and placing the word in a sentence frame, then, forces us to realize that these are three different lexical items above containing *blow*. This prevents us from trying to discover a single meaning for all these *blow*s, or the many other similar examples.

Once we realize that meaning is not a property of orthographic (or syntactic) words but of sequences of them,[11] so-called 'idioms' such as *to kick the bucket* [die], *to work like a horse*, *to look a gift horse in the mouth*, *to look Y (straight) in the eyes*, *to look into Y's eyes* are seen to be unusual only in being strikingly long lexical items, just as single words or parts of words (e.g. the *boy* in *boys*) are the shortest possible lexical items.

## Meanings of words

The semantic elements we have seen are largely the same from language to language; languages differ mostly in how these elements are expressed. What ones are combined into a word commonly varies from language to language, and sometimes what is expressed as parts of a word in one language is expressed with a morphological suffix or a syntactic structure in another, or even left to the addressee to fill in as needed. In fact, a language can be seen to have a 'style' or preference for which atoms are expressed in words and which not. Once this is discovered, learning words in that language becomes much easier.

Of course, knowing the semantic elements out of which the meanings of most words are constructed makes learning the meanings of words in any language far easier, and with a little familiarity one can guess quite accurately the meaning of words one has met only a few times in context. To this end, we have made a collection of common semantic atoms at the beginning of this text.

Here, we have seen not only a number of the most common atoms but also several ways that they are combined together in a word. There is the **conjunction** (like *and*) of several elements, as in *boy*, [Hum(x).Yng(x). Msc(x)], symbolized in linear writing by a dot (.) here but sometimes by an ampersand (&) or a caret (∧). There is also **domination** or subordination of one element by another, as in *to give*, [Coz(x,Bcm-Hav(y,z))], which we can symbolize by a hyphen when there is only one actant, but the general way is with parentheses, (. . .), surrounding the actants. Any notation is adequate so long as it specifies clearly what the relations are, and the graphic notation is no doubt the clearest. In this, the dot for conjunction is not written at all, the conjoined elements being placed side by side, and domination is shown by downward lines.

## Answers and notes

1. We have revised the labels on this chart from the ones used

in Chapter 4, based on what we learned there and in between. We haven't used [Voj] (Visual ObJect) before, but it is a very general element, rather similar to the English noun *thing*, for anything that is (in principle) visible or visualizable, including even acts of speech, as in 'I'll tell you a thing or two!' but excluding movements and colours, for example. By contrast, *it* is not restricted to [Voj].

2. E.g. *stag, doe*; *sire, dam*; *warlock, witch*; *deer, fawn*; *cow, calf.*

3. [Spk(x), Awa(x)]; 'X is close to the speaker', or better, 'X is close to the act of speaking', 'X is away from the act of speaking.'

4. [Fem(x)·Par(z,x)·Par(z,y)].   [Fem(x)·Par(z,x)·Par(z,y)·Sng(z)] or equivalent graphic representation below. ([Sng] for SiNGle or SiNGular of Chapters 4 and 6.)

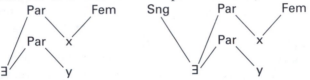

5. 'X is hot', 'X is taller than Y', 'X is like Y', 'X is a boy', 'X is a son of Y' (or 'X is Y's son'), 'X is a secretary', 'X likes Y', 'X lives in Y' and (different meaning) 'X lives', 'X goes to Y.'

6. The general trick is to form up a realistic sentence with as few extra words as possible and combine it with a direct negation of the component linking them with *although, but, however* or the like. It may then be revised till it is a natural sentence with no grammatical or pragmatic problems. One should avoid fuzzy areas (see Chapter 15) such as ? 'Booth assassinated President Lincoln, but he didn't die till the next day.'

7. (p227) 'X is a man', etc.; 'X is a kitten', etc. (p229) 'X is a parent of Y'.

8. Chapter 9 extends the basic contrast between *to* and *at* to many prepositions.

9. [Bcm-Sps(x,y)].  [Bcm-Neg-Sps(x,y)].

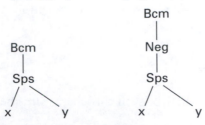

10. This requires a higher-order predicate calculus, which makes a standard logical representation even more difficult to decode. It has evolved to be precise and printable on a line, not to represent natural language effectively. So long as the graphs can be translated into that notation, however, they are as precise.
11. Actually it is more than just sequence, as some syntactic structure must be included. At least some identification of the verbs is needed, for they combine with suffixes, as in 'They were *re*-burying the hatchet yesterday', and are irregular in precisely the same way as the independent verb, e.g. 'he *threw* up', never * 'throwed up'.

## Keywords

conjunctive meaning, domination, inchoative, causative.

## Further reading

Jackson and Cruse are good textbooks. Jackson is more introductory and has an orientation towards practical dictionaries, while Cruse is more theoretical.

Lehrer provides a very readable discussion of various older accounts of lexical structure and illustrates them with various fields of vocabulary. Wierzbicka is also readable, but from a more philosophical and dialectic approach argues for interesting analyses intended to rest on intuitive plausibility. Her 'Japanese . . .' is a ground-breaking application to ethnography.

Cruse, D. A. *Lexical Semantics* (1986) London: CUP.

Jackson, Howard *Words and Their Meaning* (1988) London: Longman.

Lehrer, Adrienne *Semantic Fields and Lexical Structure* (1974) Amsterdam: North Holland.

Kipfer, B. A. *Workbook on Lexicography* (1984) Exeter University: Linguistic Studies, Vol. 8.

Mel'chuk, Igor *et al. Dictionnaire explicatif et combinatoire du français contemporain: Recherches lexico-sémantiques* (1984– ) Montréal: Presses de l'Université de Montréal.

Wierzbicka, Anna *Lexicography and Conceptual Analysis* (1985) Ann Arbor: Karoma.

Wierzbicka, Anna *English Speech Act Verbs: A Semantic Dictionary* (1987) New York: Academic.

—— 'Japanese Key Words and Core Cultural Values' (1991) *Language in Society* **20**: 333–85.

## Exercises with word meaning

1. As was brought out by the Japanese example at the beginning of this chapter, [Yng]-terms for animals contrast with unmarked terms, so that *lamb:sheep* contrast [Yng-Shp]:[Shp]. We skipped over a fact above, that while we can point to a kitten saying 'Get that cat out of my way!', we cannot say 'get that man out of here', pointing to a five-year-old boy. *Man*, then, is not the unmarked counterpart of *boy*; it is also marked, so the additional element [Adt] is needed. It probably means something like [sexually competent], for we can speak of an adolescent as 'a young man/woman'.
   (a) Use this same test to determine which if any other words in the diagram on p.227 are likewise not simply unmarked terms.
   (b) If [Adt] is as we have defined it here, what would be the meaning of *adolescent* (a child in some sense)?
2. Another point we have ignored is that we have terms for human beings that include finer age distinctions, being human ourselves.
   (a) What are the usual terms that classify human beings by age? (Ignore terms that are based on calendar age, such as *teenager*, their meanings pose no serious problems and they are artificial in the sense that they match the calendar rather than the nature of human beings.)
   (b) Which ones count as [Adt] by the definition in (1)?
   (c) Give meanings to all the other words so that each one is different. As *child* can be used for babies and adolescents, those two concepts should be expansions of *child*.
   (d) Can you propose a more careful definition for [Yng] in view of its use with these words and its use with many animals?
3. Until quite recently (this century), we also made many age distinctions in terms for horses.
   (a) What does this imply about the relationship between horses and our English-speaking ancestors?

(b) Make a table for the words *colt, filly, mare, stallion*. Look them up in a dictionary if you don't know their meanings.

(c) We also had the terms *ox, gelding* for castrated bulls and stallions. How can [Prt] (PReTerite, of Chapter 7) combine with [Msc] to capture this notion? Give the meaning of *gelding*, using [Hrs] (HoRSe) to stand for what identifies a horse.

(d) Propose a rough meaning for *to castrate*.

4. (a) Fill in the words missing from this table of inchoative forms.

| wide | long | large | narrow | ____ | big | hot |
|------|------|-------|--------|------|-----|-----|
| widen | __ | __ | __(__) | shrink | __ | __(__) |

(b) Sometimes a preposition-like particle is added to suggest completion as well as to reinforce the inchoative nature. What is added to each of the following?

grow, shrink, dry, warm, cool

5. Sometimes inchoation is expressed with the help of a verb like *to get, to become, to grow*.

(a) Which of the following are normally in a comparative form (e.g. *taller*) when combined with one of these? Why?

(b) Which terms are used to make inchoative forms?

tall  narrow  tired  lazy
ill  dead  in love

6. The copular *to fall* can be used with a few adjectives such as *ill, flat*, and a few prepositional phrases such as *in love, in disrepute*.

(a) Make a list of complements of *to fall*.

(b) What semantic element do these examples have in common?

(c) Note that *ill* is ungradable and has no comparative forms, while *sick* is gradable. What does *to fall* require of its complement?

(d) How might we characterize the meaning of *to fall* when used in this copular way?

7. Give graphs for the descriptive (propositional, cognitive) meanings of the following words. As these are relational words, they must be put in a sentence frame with X and Y, and their meanings will have x and y corresponding. Some may require the existence of a third person, but a variable cannot be used for that as that person cannot be referred to with these words; an inverted E is proper for that person. Also please identify (in English) these 'hidden person(s)'.

(a) mother    (b) daughter    (c) grandmother    (d) sister

Although a person's sister usually shares both parents with that person, a half-sister shares only one and 'full sister' overtly includes that both parents are shared. What, then, are the meanings for:

    (e) half-sister    (f) full sister?

Now, using [Sps(x,y)] for 'X is spouse of Y' or 'X and Y are married', try your hand at the following terms (again identify the hidden person).

    (g) stepfather    (h) father-in-law

8. We saw in Chapter 11 that comparative adjectives have two actants, so:

   (a)  What is the structure of the semantic representation for 'X is bigger than Y' (use [Big])?

   (b)  Now, as the same semantic element must underlie both the absolute (i.e. non–comparative) and comparative forms of an adjective, would you revise your previous answer or admit that a simple adjective as in 'X is big' has a 2–actant meaning?

   (c)  If the latter, to what does the second actant refer when the adjective is used absolutely?

9. We revised the notation and meaning of [Spk, Adr] in the question on page 229, consistent with what we had learned in Chapter 4 and since.

   (a)  Do the same for [Loc] and [Voj] (which we named in Chapter 4 by its syntactic function, Pro).

   (b)  Now, noting that they have different numbers of actants, can you explain why [Voj] forms pronouns while [Loc] forms prepositions (when not combined with a deictic location, as in Chapter 9)? It may help to draw diagrams for 'X is here', 'X is on Y' and 'X is it.'

# CHAPTER 13
# Combining Sentences

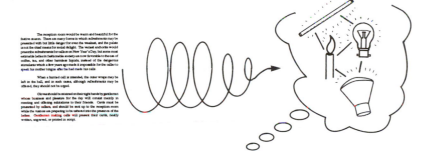

What does *the* mean that makes it strange in sentences like the following?

(1) ★ he found some marbles and put the red one in his pocket.

(2) ★ of all my friends, the longest one is best.

Why can one say, here in this box, 'These are strange sentences' but not ★ 'This is a strange title'? That is, why can't the word *this* point outside this box?

We commonly think that sentences have fixed meanings, and simple sentences do seem to. Most sentences, however, do not stand alone but function as part of a longer unit of discourse, the paragraph. Because of this, most sentences do not have independent meanings that we can point to and say 'This is the meaning of that sentence.' Rather, each sentence adds a small amount to an idea that is being built up. That is why we cannot easily change the order of sentences in a paragraph; revise their arrangement and you are liable to have a different meaning or no meaning at all, even if you straighten out all the pronouns and other referring elements. Consider, for example, how different is the effect of 'I like my car' when it is a response to the following.

- a scooter'll get you anywhere in Bangkok faster.
- Tom's got a new super Zupe that'll do 150 in three seconds.
- your car needs all these repairs; a new car'd be a good idea.
- even Mary thinks your car is weird.
- that's a nice tree you drew, but you can't call that blob a car.
- I'll trade you these three marbles and this dump truck for your car!
- I'm in Car 6; come and sit with me.

A sentence, then, adds a piece of meaning to what is already there, even in conversation where I add a small idea to what you have said, and you add a bit to what I said. Indeed, conversation is largely building an idea together; it is not transmitting and receiving information as many philosophers have imagined. I have often been bored to death by students of English wanting to practise 'conversation' by telling me pointless facts (often information that I already knew, or did not want), and waiting for me to do the same. Real conversation is building ideas together.

In fact, what a sentence adds to its **context** – the sentences or ideas that precede it – is so dependent on that context that there is a strong prohibition, 'Do not quote [somebody] out of context.' Nearly anything a person says can be changed or even reversed in meaning by putting it in a different context. Politicians do it all the time, of course, and tell others not to. We scholars do too, but only by accident of course!

Because sentences ripped out of their contexts seldom have clear and precise meanings, a sentence rarely has a single correct translation. Rather, a sentence may be used to communicate different things depending on the context from which it was taken, and may require different translations. A major Russian linguist calculates that there are some 217,000 different ways of paraphrasing an ordinary sentence of English due to lexical substitution alone. Even when we take into account what a sentence was intended to communicate, there may still be different translations and which one is best depends on what context it will be put into. Ideally, translation is to understand what a sentence adds to its original context, and then to create a new sentence in the other language that adds the same thing in its new context.

The following diagram gives a simple concept of how sentences contribute to the building of the meaning of a paragraph, imagining for the moment that a sentence has an unambiguous and precise meaning. Each sentence ($S_i$) is converted to its 'meaning' which is then combined with the understanding or comprehension ($C_{i-1}$) of the previous sentences (its context). That is, $C_0$ is the context for the first sentence $S_1$; $C_1$ (which includes the meaning of $S_1$) is the context for the second sentence; $C_2$ is the comprehension of the first two sentences together, as well as being the context for the third sentence; and so on until the end, where $C_n$ is the comprehension of the whole paragraph. If $S_1$ is the very first sentence, and $C_0$ is empty, then $C_1$ is just the meaning of $S_1$.

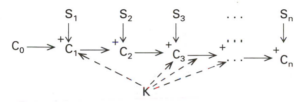

To be sure, not all paragraphs are written so that their meanings can be easily extracted in this way. When they are not, it is not good writing; the reader is left in doubt (at least temporarily) as to what the author wants to be understood. A major goal of writing and speeches, **clarity**, is never to leave the reader in doubt as to what is being said, which means that no sentence can be ambiguous, and no pronoun or other word that points to a referent can be left without identifying that referent. Thus, the general use of *the*, the use of the preterite ('past') tense, and other context-leaning grammatical words that point to something in the context like *else*, *other* (or modifiers like *so*, *such*, *same*, *more*) must each be preceded by a linguistic description of what it points to, technically called its 'antecedent'.

## Background knowledge (K)

One way in which the conception above of how sentences combine their meanings together is a little too simple is that we often take advantage of what the other person knows to escape saying it. Assuming that both people share it, that knowledge has been called 'shared knowledge', but it is really only what the speaker thinks his addressee knows, as in (1a) following, or can observe easily (2a). It has also been called 'encyclopedic' knowledge in studies of scientific and technical texts, where the specific facts used in ordinary conversation are not present. We will call this stock of knowledge simply **background knowledge** and represent it with K as at the bottom of the diagram above. It is available for the interpretation of any sentence, as sketched in Chapter 14. We do not yet know if it is used automatically for every sentence, as some researchers think, or if it is consulted only when a sentence is lacking something for adequate interpretation.

> (1) you missed a great picnic – *the beer* never stopped flowing.
>> (1a) What beer? We assume that a picnic includes beer.
> (2) *the wasp* by your elbow looks like he's tired.
>> (2a) What wasp? Look and see!

It is well known that scientific and technical papers cannot be understood if translated by someone who is not competent in the field. In formal writing, however, this background knowledge is perhaps not so important, for the writer can never know who is going to read it, or what the reader knows. Accordingly, a good writer avoids depending on the reader's knowledge as much as possible. Nevertheless, we are not all perfect writers (not me, anyhow), and in any case it can be extremely boring to read a lot of material you already know, so some and often a lot of background is commonly assumed. To control what it assumed, it is usually necessary for writers to fix in their mind whom they are writing to. This means that background knowledge is far from unimportant even in writing. In talking, or letter writing, of course, what the addressee knows is much more important. We usually dislike being told what we already know,[1] but if the speaker assumes something that the addressee doesn't know, or thinks is not true, it is very easy for the addressee to be confused as to what was being said.

## Clarity – when and why

In conversation, errors of expression are seldom important and are generally forgotten in a few seconds if the idea gets across. Ambiguity and misunderstanding can usually be detected by watching the addressee, and the speaker can add enough until the confusion is removed. Alternatively, a confused listener can ask a question and get straightened out immediately. Sometimes, a little misunderstanding is even a good thing (it is a major source of creativity), and ambiguity is useful when the message is hurtful.

In writing, however, mistakes remain for ever and are very visible. What is worse is that the writer can never know if the reader is confused or misunderstanding something, so cannot add more in case of a confused reader; nor can the reader ask a question. What you write must be clear when it is read, without any possible confusion or mistakes, no matter who reads it. Even if you speak a language well, writing it well is something else again. The need for **clarity** is part of the reason it is so hard to write in English – or any other language. Of all the millions who speak English natively, very few can write it well. You might imagine that clarity is important only for science, and not for ordinary language. In fact, however, there are proverbs and idioms in every language that show clarity to be highly prized; politicians' evasive statements are criticized, and avoiding candid remarks and fudging answers are universally disparaged.

Besides this, the author or speaker often utilizes his addressee's **knowledge** about the world to avoid saying more than is necessary. In speaking, you know whom you are talking to and can usually guess fairly well what they know. If they do not know something you think they do, they may be confused, but if so, you can tell them. In writing, you can never know who will read what you have written, and what they know or believe. Clarity is important so that readers can discover what you think they know; it allows them to make up for what they do not happen to know, and to compensate for what they believe to be different.

Lastly, the writer cannot know what ideas or doubts readers have in their minds that might influence their interpretation. A note to a fellow student can be interpreted very differently by a jealous girlfriend, by the secret police, or by the student. Clarity can then be a life-and-death matter, or worse (the second atomic bomb is said to have been dropped because of ambiguity in the reply to a demand for surrender).

Q. (a) Why is it easier to write an ordinary letter than to write an essay?

(b) However, writing an emotional letter that 'says what you want it to' is often nearly impossible. Why so?[2]

Nevertheless, ambiguity and lack of clarity can be put to good use by a capable writer or speaker. It is very important in science and scholarship, and in politics, to be able to avoid saying what you don't have enough evidence for – to leave yourself uncommitted about things that might not be the way you imagine them to be – yet to be able to state the broad generalizations. It is not such a good style, however, if you mislead people thereby. Vagueness can also be a virtue, for it entices the reader to provide an interpretation from his own experience. It makes reading a creative process, as is found in much good poetry. A really capable writer will even create ambiguities that make good sense in two or more different ways. Some readers may interpret it one way, others another, and some will read it both ways to get some mixture of the two meanings. All said, absolute clarity is not only impossible but not necessarily desirable, and indeed, much creativity comes from understanding something in a way that was not intended or foreseen.

## Ambiguity

It is astonishing how **ambiguous** most sentences are. Most common words are quite ambiguous; look in a good dictionary for any common word and you will usually find two or three meanings, or maybe twenty or thirty if it is really common. Combined together in a sentence, these ambiguities multiply together to make things much worse. If that were not bad enough, even the syntactic structures are themselves ambiguous, as in the following.

> (1) a small girls' school
> (2) the chicken is ready to eat.
> (3) the boy watched the girl in the park with a telescope.

Without looking at the ambiguities of words themselves, the first example may be either [a small school for girls] or [a school for small girls] and the second is likely to mean [the chicken is ready for someone (us?) to eat], but it could also mean [the chicken is ready to eat something (us?)]. It is probably the first because we normally eat chickens and not the reverse, and anyway, chickens are always ready to eat so the second reading is pointless. If we change *chicken* for *alligator*, however, the other is more likely, so it is not just the structure of the sentence that makes one or another more reasonable.

---

Q. Find two ways to understand 'a light house keeper'.[3]

---

In the third example above, it took a mindless computer to find that at least seven different meanings are possible, depending partly on the context in which it is used. Is it that there are two parks, one with a telescope and the other without? That is, is 'with a telescope' being used to identify which park, or is it describing the instrument for watching, or again does it simply identify the girl who carries it? The phrase 'in the park (with a telescope)' may identify the girl, or it may describe the location of the watching. That makes five ways to interpret it, without using *telescope* to identify the girl. There are more, but it is very difficult to know when you have found all the ways a sentence can be understood; each meaning requires creating a setting, and after you have imagined three or so different settings it is not easy to imagine more. In any case, when we add the ambiguities of syntax to all the different meanings of each word in a sentence, it is difficult to see how one person can ever guess what another person means.

(1) [he watched the girl in the park with a telescope, not the girl in the park with a statue]

(2) [he used a telescope (from his window) to watch the girl in the one and only park]

(3) [they were both in the park with a telescope, not the other park, and he watched her]

(4) [they were in the one and only park, and he watched her with a telescope]

(5) [he watched the girl while she was in the park with a telescope, not while she was in the other park]

---

Q. I can think of several more ways to understand this sentence. Can you find two? More?[4]

---

This is a major problem for semantics; how can a person understand the one and only one, and almost invariably the correct meaning that a sentence has in a given context? It clearly involves the context, C, and the knowledge of the listener, K, but how it happens is not yet known for sure. It must be a fairly simple process,[5] for we do it so swiftly that we are usually completely unaware of any other possible way to understand a sentence, and we do it so accurately that we seldom if ever make a mistake in understanding. Simple or not, we are far from understanding it well – it is the very problem that makes computer translation or even just the understanding of human language so difficult for both linguistics and computer science.

## Integration of $S_i$ into $C_i$

Transformational grammars can provide something close to the structural meaning(s) of a sentence by identifying and removing all the superficial irregularities and rearrangements that English grammar and style require. This results in its 'deep' or 'logical' structure, but the words in it may be ambiguous, as well as the structure itself. How does a person know how to interpret it, and the words in it, in the light of its context?

Some part of each sentence is used to tie it down to a specific interpretation by connecting into its context, and the rest of each sentence adds something new. We began with a conception that sentences had identifiable 'meanings' that could be simply added on to previous comprehension, but we know now that that is an oversimplification. The basic way we bypass ambiguity is that we interpret each sentence structure and the words in it so that it adds the least possible to its context – anything that can possibly match the context is interpreted as matching it, and only what is unmatchable is what is being said in that context. This is the 'Principle of Minimum Interpretation'. The easiest way to visualize this process of interpretation is to imagine the meaning of the sentence being overlapped with the comprehension C of what came before. The words and structures of the sentence are automatically interpreted so that as little of it as possible is not already in that earlier C.

To illustrate this, let us start with the sentence 'My friend is helping a young lady learn English' as in (1) below, beginning with the embedded clause on the left. This is repeated on the right, dominated by [Aid], for it is this action that is being aided. The right side, then, is the $C_1$ for a following sentence such as (2) or (3) to be interpreted with.

(1) *My friend is helping a young lady learn English.*

(A young lady is learning English.)   my friend is helping (. . .)

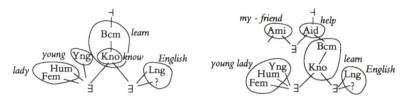

In sentence (2) below, 'She is studying hard', the *she* must **refer** (or point in the world) to the same thing as 'a young lady', not only because (i) that is the only expression that describes something female, but also because (ii) it is the first actant of *to study* which means [Try-Bcm-Kno] and thus overlaps with *to learn* [Bcm-Kno], from $C_1$.

(2) *She is studying hard.*      (3) *She is trying hard.*

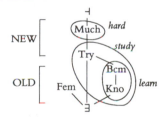   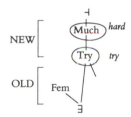

When they are overlapped we get $C_2$, as in diagram (4) below, and we can notice that sentence (2) adds only [Much-Try-. . .] to the *learn* of (1). Indeed, it has the same meaning – in this context – as (3) 'She is trying hard', on the right above. Then *she* in this sentence is still well formed, for reason (i) as above.

(4) *My friend is helping a young lady learn English.*
    *She is studying hard.*      OR: *She is trying hard.*

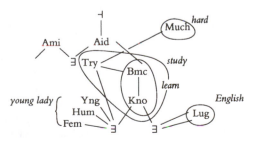

If we were to change the first sentence to 'My girlfriend is helping . . .', the *she* in this last sentence would become ambiguous, for there would then be two female referential elements, things in C that it could match. The *she* in sentence (2) would still be adequate, however, for reason (ii) would still make it clear. Its **redundancy** (repeating information unnecessarily) is useful as it relieves the speaker from checking very closely to be sure there is only one possible referential element that it matches.

---

Q.   Modify the diagram in (4) for 'My girlfriend is helping a young lady learn English. She is studying hard.'[6]

---

The basic rule for using pronouns, then, is that you can and should use one if the resulting sentence fits uniquely when overlapped (i.e. it is not ambiguous), but not otherwise. What to do otherwise? One must add enough descriptive words, a noun and perhaps an adjective or two, to identify which person is being referred to. Then, in English or other west European languages, we add a definite marker like the word *the* (or *this* or *that*) to tell the addressee that she should look in the context to find the person.

Before we continue, notice how the meaning or interpretation of (2) is modified and given substance by its context in (1). By itself, 'She is studying hard' describes some girl, presumably known, as being a good student, perhaps in university, in the sense that she is working hard. In the context of (1), however, it can be used to describe an otherwise poor or lazy student who is hard at work learning English.

There are sometimes several ways of **integrating** a sentence's meaning with what comes before, but human beings consistently choose only one. Which one? Invariably one that adds as little as possible to what has gone before. That is, a sentence is interpreted in the most redundant way possible, i.e. so that it says as little as we can interpret it to say. This may seem a little surprising at first, that we always interpret each sentence so that it says as little as possible, when the whole *raison d'être* of language is to communicate information. It is less surprising when you recall that a sentence commonly has many ways it can be interpreted; this principle chooses the interpretation that is most relevant to the context. Indeed, it is the same principle that guides you when you fit two maps together, or when you interpret an ambiguous diagram. So far, this principle has not gained wide acceptance — it does seem backward to a major use of language, to communicate information – and a more popular direction is to suppose that a person selects the most 'relevant' interpretation. When we get down to measuring relevance, however, it is the overlap between the sentence and its context that counts, so we have nearly the same results.

The unexpected ambiguities of sentences we noted earlier are generally resolved in context because this principle of minimal interpretation almost always selects just one meaning as 'the meaning of the sentence in its context'. Only when the speaker fails to give enough information matching or overlapping the context can there be two equally minimal ways of overlapping. In such a case the sentence is 'ambiguous in context', and the text lacks clarity. Even then, however, readers and listeners normally choose just one interpretation by adding something from their background knowledge (K) so that this principle will still select a unique interpretation. If, for example, one asks for 'the telephone book' to call a friend when there are in fact two telephone directories present, the addressee will no doubt understand this as the alphabetically listed one and not even consider the 'yellow pages' or ask which directory is wanted. Consequently, we seldom recognize ambiguity, and this is the danger of a lack of clarity in writing; by adding a different piece of K, or because one's K may be different from the writer's, the reader can arrive at an interpretation quite different from the one the author intended and may never know it till later, if ever. Fortunately, this principle is not the only factor controlling interpretation.

## Rhetorical markers

Languages commonly have special markers that guide and limit the addressee in integrating the meaning of a sentence with its context. The English definite article *the* is a good example. It tells the addressee that the thing referred to should be searched for in the context C, and if not found, it will be in his background knowledge, K (or, as a last resort, in his immediate environment). In other words, it indicates that this part of the sentence must be overlapped with something and says, in effect, [You know which one I mean – find it!]. As K includes factual knowledge of the context of speaking, *the* may designate something in the world that is described enough to make it unique, as in 'Put it on the table', 'The French government refuses', etc. ('exophoric' uses). As K also includes knowledge about relations between abstract concepts, *the* also has a 'cataphoric' usage, as in 'The comprehension of a sentence is very fast.' K even includes knowledge of the language itself, as seen in the 'generic' usage of *the* in 'The lion is a kingly beast', referring to the concept of lion (Chapter 9) rather than to anything in the world.

Languages that don't use definite markers may instead have a **'topic'** marker like the particle *-wa* in Japanese, but there is usually only one such topic in a sentence while there may be as many definite markers as there are nominals. Like them, a topic marker, such as 'As for (**topic**), . . .', tells the addressee that he should find the thing in the context or in his knowledge, but it may also be used to bring up an entirely new but related topic, 'As for your ex-wife, I was . . .' A topic marker cannot, however, be used with question words like *who*: ⋆ 'As for who, . . .' The referent of *who* cannot have been mentioned before so it cannot be found in the context, but *-wa* says [Find it! in C or K]. Thus topic and definite particles are similar in that they indicate that the addressee should find the thing referred to – in the preceding context, in the situation of speaking, or in his background knowledge.

Quite opposite to these topic and definite particles, languages commonly have another device to tell the addressee not to bother trying to find something in C to match a given element. These are usually called **focus** markers,[7] and the English 'It is (**focus**) that — t —' is one, as in 'It was Tommy that I saw t in the park.' (The 't' here stands for the missing nominal that has been focused on and moved to the front.) This focus of the sentence is normally not to be found in the preceding context and can be considered the 'point' of the predication; most of the rest of the words are said only so that one can 'make this point'. Thus, as we saw in Chapter 3, the force of negation applies to the focus if one is marked. Questions are the same. In spoken English, focus is usually marked by loudness and an abrupt fall (or rise) in intonation, while in spoken French the focus is commonly said first. Other languages may use overt markers, like the suffix *-ga* in Japanese or the words that attract stress in English, e.g. *even, only, all* and the 'strong' prepositions of Chapter 9.

Q. Using this understanding of topic and focus, identify which of the following begins with a topic and which begins with a focus. Paraphrasing them will help. What are their differences in words and intonation?[8]

*Tommy,/* I *saw* him in the park \.     Tommy\I *saw* in the park

Focus marking is quite important in English but it is often not visible in writing because it is the location of the intonation contour, upward or downward, that commonly indicates the focus. In English writing, the general convention is that the last phrase of a sentence is given focus unless there is some indication to the contrary. This sometimes forces the writer of English to twist up a sentence so that the important words end up at the end. This can occasionally be hard to do, so we have other ways to show focus, such as 'It is (**focus**) that — t —', though this device often seems forced or artificial. Other ways are to add small words like *up* to shift the stress pattern, or *own* which attract stress (so in 'with his own car' forces a semantic focus on [his]). A special feature of English is that many prepositions and clause connectors even come in synonymous pairs, one stressed and the other unstressed, e.g. *on to:on* and *although:though*.

When we view the process of understanding a sentence as integrating its meaning with the meaning that precedes it, we see that **topic** markers indicate that some part of the meaning of the marked expression (often much of it) must be in the overlapping part, what is otherwise known as **old information** – the part of the proposition that is already known to the addressee, as was marked in diagrams (2) and (3). If it is not to be found in the preceding discourse (in the C of the preceding context, (1) in this case), then one must search background knowledge (K) or the physical environment for it. Conversely, a focus–marked phrase is normally in the part of the proposition that does not overlap, the **new information**. Definite markers like *the* act a little differently from topic markers, for they can be combined with focus marking, just in the case that the speaker wants to assert or deny the identity of something already mentioned.

The division of the descriptive meaning of a sentence into old and new information corresponds to the part which is overlapped (with C and perhaps parts of K) as opposed to that which is previously unknown. This division, however, is not so systematically indicated as topic marking and focus marking. Topic marking as in Japanese has the effect of forcing the marked element on to some element in the overlapping section (old information), while focus marking may lead to ignoring a potentially matching place in the context. The more visible effect of focus marking, though, is to 'focus' the force of the utterance on to the marked element, which is why that element is usually not in the overlapping part.

Because the old information is needed to interpret the new information, and can be overlapped directly without waiting, most languages tend to express it first, saving the new information for the last. Thus topics usually come first in languages that use topic marking, and pronouns, nearly always old information, tend to appear as far forward in the sentence as the syntax of the language permits, before the verb in most Romance languages, or right after the verb in German. This happens in English, too, except that the only place where it really shows up is in complex verbs such as 'He looked up *your friends in Kashmir*', where a pronoun must be attached to the verb, not *'He looked up *them*' but 'He *looked 'em up*.' In fact, if there is much freedom for arranging nominals in a sentence, they will tend to be arranged in a sequence from the old to the newest and most relevant. This sort of 'activation hierarchy' has been studied most extensively for German.

## Paragraphs

Although we do not yet know very well what a paragraph is, there are several recent discoveries that are useful to know. In referring to something already mentioned, as explained in Chapter 9, one must in principle use a full nominal with a definite determiner, a noun, and perhaps some adjectives or a relative clause – one must give enough of a description to single out the desired referent from all the things that have been mentioned or that are present in the physical context. This could be tedious in long discussions that involve many things, but language provides some short cuts.

We saw above that a pronoun should be used if it is specific enough to refer to something already mentioned. Alternatively, a demonstrative like *this* or *that* may be enough. If an adjective is sufficient to pick out the referent without a noun, a general (i.e. not very descriptive) substitute for a noun will commonly be used in speech, something like *one, thing* or *stuff.* In formal writing the noun can simply be left off, as in the following examples.

> the solution of the second problem depends on your answer for the *first* [one].
> if you take the red car, I'll take the *green* [one].

These short ways of referring to something already mentioned (pronouns, demonstratives alone, noun-substitutes or noun-dropping) are normal and should be used if you do not want to confuse the person you are talking or writing to. They are used when the referent has been mentioned in the same paragraph, and to avoid their use suggests that the thing referred to is not in that paragraph. And except for the case of rhetorical topics, using one of these short ways implies that the antecedent is in that same paragraph. Thus a pronoun cannot have its antecedent inside a preceding paragraph, and a missing noun as in the first example above cannot be filled in from an earlier paragraph. To refer to something mentioned in an earlier paragraph, i.e. to 'bring it into' the present paragraph, one must use a noun with *the* or a demonstrative at least – and complete enough to identify it from among everything that has been mentioned, though *this* or *that* will often identify a noun as referring to the same thing that it did in the preceding paragraph.

---

Q.  What are the two circumstances where one must use a noun (or noun-substitute like *one*) instead of a pronoun?[9]

---

Actually, several paragraphs may develop a topic, and such a topic is in a sense part of each of the paragraphs. This makes a special case for **rhetorical topics**: a pronoun or other short way to referring may be used, in the first sentence of a paragraph even, to refer to a common topic. This is a natural, if not very noticeable way to tie paragraphs together into larger units of organization.

    These facts lead us to conceive of a paragraph as a unit of building ideas. Once the paragraph is finished, the idea is finished and is saved somewhere in memory, not to be modified further. Long paragraphs are difficult to understand, apparently, because all the pieces of the idea must be kept in one's attention, ready for modification. It follows that a complex idea is easier to communicate by explaining part of it in one paragraph, then connecting that with other things in later paragraphs. The part selected for the first paragraph should not need to be modified later on.

If, then, a paragraph is the unit for building up ideas after which they are put away into memory (if worthy enough), then it is like a short conversation, as it allows one to build up an idea from a series of sentences. In a paragraph (or conversation), pronouns and deletions are freely possible and should be used as much as possible. However, they cannot be used to refer to something in an earlier conversation or paragraph. Avoiding a pronoun is thus a way to indicate a change in rhetorical topic.

## Other ideas

There are two other popular conceptions about how sentences are understood, one from logic and the other from computers – two areas where language and meaning are important. From studies in logic we have the idea that each sentence has a specific meaning, so if these meanings are conjoined together with a logical – *and*, we will have the meaning of a paragraph. However, sentences in natural language seldom have meanings as clear and precise as those in logic or mathematics, even though it is a far stronger means of communication, and natural language sentences are commonly ambiguous in more than a few ways. Apparently, this conception cannot help solve the big problem of ambiguity, for conjoining sentences with an *and* only multiplies their ambiguities and lack of clarity!

Moreover, it is clear that sentences are not combined together with *and*, for in fact *and* often breaks a combined idea in two, if it is possible at all, as the following examples show.

> It must be raining. John's umbrella is wet.
> It must be raining and John's umbrella is wet.

> It is cold. Is the window open?
> ? It is cold, and is the window open?

In the first sentence the speaker concludes that it is raining from the fact that the umbrella is wet, but if they are combined with *and* as in the second, the speaker concludes about the rain from something, and then adds that the umbrella is wet (from which we might conclude that John has been out) – quite a different meaning. In the third the speaker suggests that the coldness is due to the window being open, while the fourth, if possible at all, specifically denies any connection between the two ideas. Conjoining sentences with *and* often destroys the connections they would otherwise have by overlapping.

In fact, conjoining facts together with *and* is characteristic of logical arguments, but most use of language is not in logical arguments. Communicating ideas, building ideas, getting people to do things, seeking information are all much more common than arguments, and even those arguments are seldom based on logic. It is not surprising, then, that a model for logical argumentation does not match natural language well. In any case, this conception cannot help solve the big problem of ambiguity, for combining two sentences with a logical *and* multiplies their ambiguity.

The other popular conception comes from ideas about computers. Sentences are like commands in a computer language – actions to be 'executed'. A question is to be answered, a command is to be done, and a statement? Well, they say, a statement is to be believed. But this hardly applies to detective stories, jokes, or half of human discourse.

The problem with this is that more often than not, we talk about things that we know not to be true, or not completely true. Plans, hopes, wishes and schedules are not true yet, and often enough never become true. Stories about the fish that got away, what happened at the party, and in fact all of literature is often not true in detail. Even scientific theories are only ideas about how things would be in ideal and impossible worlds, like Newton's 'crazy' idea that once a body is in motion it will continue for ever in the same direction, or Galileo's heresy that heavy and light things fall at the same speed. They simply aren't true in the ordinary real world! Science most always talks about idealized and simplified approximations of the real world, and it deals only with what might be (or almost surely must be) the underlying and invisible causes for real things we can observe. It seldom talks about real things except in reporting experiments to show that in special (laboratory) circumstances the real world does come close to the idealized world of theory.

Indeed, how can anyone criticize a theory if he has to believe each statement in it? Once he believes it, he cannot criticize it effectively. Rather, just as in reading a detective story, we understand a theory with a 'suspension of disbelief', to build up the complete idea that the author is expressing. Then that idea, not believed but not disbelieved either, can be criticized by comparing it with what one does believe or can observe. One's beliefs are the K in the first diagram, and the $C_i$ is just this idea being built up by the speaker, neither believed nor disbelieved.

## Building ideas sentence by sentence

We see, then, that although sentences are often very **ambiguous** when examined apart from their context, they should never be ambiguous in context. This is possible only because the listener has a rule to interpret each sentence in the most **redundant** way possible, i.e. in the way that adds as little as possible to its context, C. We can visualize this as overlapping the meaning of the sentence with the context so that it fits best. The interpretation that fits best is the one that adds the least **new information**, according to the Principle of Minimal Interpretation. Pieces of **background knowledge**, K, may be added if needed to select just one interpretation. This single interpretation is what we perceive as the meaning of the sentence, and by the way it is constructed it is always the most **relevant** one in that context C, with the right additions from K.

The writer or speaker must construct sentences that the addressee will decode in the desired way. This means he must keep in his head all that he has told the addressee, as well as what his addressee can be assumed to know, so that he knows how the next sentence will be understood. Of course, it is not so easy to do all this, and writing with **clarity** is quite difficult, especially as one also depends on the background knowledge that the reader can be supposed to have. This is why good writers always have a good idea of exactly what sort of people they are writing to. However, they can use rhetorical markers to guide the listener to make the right connections. *Definite* markers like *the* and **topic** markers like 'As for (**topic**), . . .' indicate a location in the overlapping part, the **old** information, and **focus** markers like the intonation contour or 'It is (**focus**) that . . .' suggest a location in the non–overlapping part, the **new** information.

Paragraphs are like small conversations, units of building ideas, which are to be put away in memory and not modified further. Reference into a preceding paragraph usually requires a full description with a noun, for beginning a new paragraph is like a professor erasing the blackboard. After erasing it the professor can no longer refer to some piece of it, though because the students copied it, a piece of it can be referred to with a more complete description.

Also like writing on a blackboard, if too much is squeezed into a paragraph the audience is liable to be confused or annoyed because they can't remember it all. Better to have too little than too much, and a very short paragraph, used occasionally, will communicate forcefully – like an occasional blackboard with only a few words on it.

The meaning that a sentence carries depends very strongly on the context that precedes it, so we will avoid saying that a sentence 'has' such and such a meaning but rather that it adds such and such a meaning to a certain context. This conception of how a complex idea is expressed through a series of sentences in an idealized one-way 'monologue' readily applies to conversation, to the conclusion that each participant adds something of his own to an idea being built in common. This joint-idea often turns out to be more in quantity, quality and any other respect than any of the participants could have created themselves.

## Notes and answers

1. In many Western cultures it is quite annoying to be told something you already know, but there is a polite style, rather common in Japanese, where you avoid saying anything that the other person cannot guess! Instead of criticizing directly, for example, one can state obvious facts that lead the addressee up to the critical conclusion, which then does not even need to be said.

2. (a) You know who will read it, and can be fairly sure of the relevant parts of their background knowledge. (b) You probably do not know what the other is feeling and thinking when he or she receives it, and that will affect their interpretation of the emotions you express. Also, English lacks words that describe emotions well, if indeed one is controlled enough simply to describe them. In my experience it is almost always mis-communication.

3. [one who keeps a light house], [one who keeps a lighthouse], [a light person who keeps house]. There's three – any more?

4. (6) [he watched the girl who was in the park carrying a telescope]

(7) [he watched the girl while they walked through the park that has a telescope in it] (≠ 3)

(8) [using the telescope, he watched the girl while she was in the park] (≠ 2)

5. There are some rather enormous tasks that are similarly done quickly and outside of consciousness, like visual pattern recognition, but we have specialized mechanisms for those (perhaps one-third of the brain for vision alone) and they have been refined by evolution from long before there were mammals. Speech recognition benefits from rather less of both.

6. add [Fem] in the upper left with a line descending from it to the leftmost ∃.

7. Confusingly also called 'topics' in some Russian and some American linguistics. The 't' in the formula indicates a missing nominal in the following clause.

8. The first begins with a topic, the second with a focus. The first has a pronoun in the rest of the sentence that repeats the topic, while a focus has no such reverberation in a pronoun. Further, the second has a focus type of intonation, falling strongly on the focus and remaining low. The topic beginning, on the other hand, has a suspensive or questioning intonation with a pause, with normal intonation on the remainder.

9. For the first reference to it in a new paragraph or a new topic. For introducing a new referent.

## Keywords

context, background knowledge, ambiguity, interpretation, semantic integration, topic, focus, old and new information.

## Further reading

Beyond the sentence.

Brown, Gilian and Yule, G. *Discourse Analysis* (1983) CUP.

Chafe, Wallace *The Pear Stories: Cognitive, Cultural, and Linguistic Aspects of Narrative Production* (1980) Norwood, NJ: Ablex.

Grimes, Joseph E. *The Thread of Discourse* (1975) Mouton.

Hofmann, Th. R. *Description sémantique et dynamique du discours*

(1978) Grenoble: Université Scientifique et Medicale. (1979) Ann Arbor: University Microfilms.

Mel'chuk, I. *Dependency Syntax: Theory and Practice* (1988) Albany: SUNY Press.

Redfern, Walter *Puns* (1984) Oxford: Blackwell.

Seuren, Pieter *Discourse Semantics* (1985) London: Basil Blackwell.

Van Dijk, Teun A. *Text and Context: Explorations in the Semantics and Pragmatics of Discourse* (1977) London: Longman.

Paragraphs and cohesion.

Halliday, M. A. K. and Hasan, R. *Cohesion in English* (1976) London: Longman.

Hofmann, Th. R. 'Paragraphs, and Anaphora' (1989) *Journal of Pragmatics* **13**: 233–44.

Langacre, R. E. 'The Paragraph as a Grammatical Unit' (1979) in Talmy Givon (ed.) *Syntax and Semantics 12: Discourse and Syntax* (1979), New York: Academic Press.

Topic and comment.

Sgall, Petr, Hajičová, Eva and Benešová, Eva *Topic, Focus and Generative Semantics* (1973) Kronberg: Taunus.

## Exercises on combining sentences

1. Explain by paraphrase two meanings of each of the following.
   (a) Sam caught a fly in the outfield. (baseball!)
   (b) Did you see her roast chicken?
   (c) The zebra is ready to eat now.
   (d) Mr Smith told his employees to stop playing mahjong after midnight.
   (e), (f), (g), (h) Add enough context to (a), (b), (c), (d) to prevent them from being ambiguous.
2. Revise the following sentences to remove unnecessary redundancy.
   (a) The President is flying to Tokyo tomorrow and he is flying to Paris next week.
   (b) Did John volunteer or did Bill volunteer?
   (c) Mother will be powdering her face and Father will be shaving.
   (d) Janet will go to Disneyland next week and Nancy might go to Disneyland next week too.

    (e) My father hasn't met my girlfriend yet, but my father will meet my girlfriend soon.

    (f) Pete quit the club this morning, although he didn't want to quit the club.

    (g) This book seems difficult, and that one certainly is difficult. (two ways, please)

    (h) (A) They say you're going to be elected captain.

        (B) Well, I hope I am not going to be elected captain. (three ways)

    (i) Those who prefer to stay home can stay home. (two ways)

3. Use a pronoun like *he/him*, *one*, *so* to remove unpleasant redundancy from the following. Give both ways, if there is more than one way to say it without changing the order of the clauses.

    (a) There's an eraser under the desk if you need an eraser.

    (b) If you need an eraser, there's an eraser under the desk.

    (c) That Professor Evans is unpopular with his students annoys Professor Evans. (two ways)

    (d) It annoys Professor Evans that Professor Evans is unpopular with his students.

    (e) My neighbourhood is quiet now, but I wonder how long it will remain quiet.

    (f) You must taste globefish if you haven't already tasted globefish.

4. English has several ways to show emphasis with phrase order.

    &lt;plain&gt; It was this book that our professor recommended.

    &lt;literary&gt; What our professor recommended was this book.

This latter pattern does not apply to nouns for human beings, so the following is used instead.

    &lt;literary&gt; The one whom/that he saw was Peter.

Give emphatic phrase orders for the following italicized phrases, both ways if both are possible. (Note that the literary patterns apply only to nominal phrases, and be careful of (d) and (f).

    (a) *The squat-type toilets* embarrassed the visitors most.

    (b) The Academy Award Committee nominated *Stephen Spielberg* as the best director that year.

    (c) The local citizens were protesting *in front of the new airport*.

    (d) John wants to be *a movie star*.

    (e) All flights into Hong Kong have been cancelled *due to Typhoon No. 6.*

(f) Japanese don't fully recognize the arrival of spring *until the estimated time for the cherry blossoms to bloom is announced.*

5. English can show the logical connections between propositions using adverbs such as the following.

> *therefore, however, accordingly, incidentally, as a result, nevertheless, in addition, in short, for example, in other words, moreover, on the other hand, consequently, to be brief, still, that is to say, on the contrary, to be sure, in contrast, similarly, by the same token, as a matter of fact*

The logical relations that are expressed are commonly classified as:

(A) addition of (more) examples  (E) intensification
(B) cause-result relation          (F) concession
(C) contrast                       (G) change of topic
(D) summary or conclusion

(a) Which of these relations is expressed by each of these adverbs? (Some adverbs, of course, may be ambiguous, and may express several relations at the same time.)

(b) Make examples illustrating each.

6. Conjunctions (Cj) such as the following are also used to show logical connections.

> *and, because, for, while, as, but, so, for*

Some like *and* are called 'coordinating' (Cjc) and stand between two clauses, and of the others, the 'subordinating' conjunctions', some can be moved (with their clause) to the front of the sentence (call them Cjm, 'M' for movable), as in the example following, while the rest are 'fixed' (Cjf) in that they can appear with their clause only at the end of the sentence as follows:

> Tom came to my house because he was lonely.
> Because he/Tom was lonely, Tom/he came to my house. – Cjm

(a) Determine which syntactic type each of the connectors above is (Cjc, Cjm, Cjf).

(b) Classify them according to logical relation expressed. (Ignore the temporal uses of *while, as.*)

7. Identify the referent of the *she* in each of the possible continuations below, when used after the first sentence, and explain why each is not ambiguous, even though there are three female referents.

> Maria told Liz that Yuko would come in fifteen minutes.

(a) . . . but she didn't arrive until ten o'clock.
(b) . . . but she said it softly.
(c) . . . but she didn't hear her.

8. To illustrate the 'infinitude' of ways to express a meaning, *Saito's Japanese-English Dictionary* (1979, 2nd edn, Tokyo: Meicho-fukyuukai) provides the following translations of an ordinary Japanese sentence:

彼の言う事はさっぱり分からない。(in modern style)

(1) I do not understand him at all.
(2) I cannot understand what he means.
(3) I am at a loss to comprehend his meaning.
(4) I can't make out his meaning.
(5) I can make nothing of what he says.
(6) I do not know what to make of his statement.
(7) I cannot make head or tail of what he says.
(8) I am at a loss to make out what he is driving at.
(9) What he can mean, is more than I can tell.
(10) What he can mean, is above my comprehension.
(11) What he is driving at, is beyond my dull comprehension.
(12) What he aims at, goes clean ahead of me.
(13) I can't see what he aims at.
       etc., etc.

(a) What differences are there between these translations?
(b) Make a few more paraphrases.

9. Sketch a graph for the following sentence:

I can't tell you how I learned the secret, except that John didn't tell me.

(a) Analyse *to tell* as [Coz-Kno], and assume that *John* is sufficient for identifying that referent, and for simplicity use [I,U] for Spk and Adr referents. Easiest is to do the two clauses separately, then join them through *except* and the missing object of *to tell*. (Note that the first, main clause contains an embedded clause too.) Incidentally, if you don't know the analysis of a word, leave it in English spelling; for example, I don't know a good analysis for *except* so just leave it as an unanalysed whole.

(b) Now analyse *secret* too.

(c) Although there are three or four words containing a [Kno], it appears only two or three times. Do the ones that are coalesced represent the same event of knowing? And the ones that remain separate, are they different events?

# CHAPTER 14

# Meaning and Context

Whenever language is used, there is a speaker and his intent, and more often than not, the ultimate intent is hidden behind the literal meaning (i.e. 'between the lines') of what is said. A teacher might say to a twenty-minute-late student, 'My, you're early today!' Does she mean that? What does she mean?

When someone asks you 'Do you have the time?', why can't you simply say, 'Yes, I do.' Or if a Japanese businessman says about your proposal, 'I will think it over', why would it be a waste of time to press him for a favourable reply later? And why do most North Americans ask for the bathroom when they need a toilet?

Gaps such as these between the **literal** meaning of a sentence and what it is used to convey — studied under the broad name of **pragmatics** — are common in everyday life. In non-literal uses of sentences, the idea conveyed is not the same as the meanings of the words. Exaggeration is one very common type, as are metaphor, sarcasm and irony. Politeness is another common reason to avoid speaking too directly or literally.

he's 10 feet tall.                                [extremely tall]
he's built like a brick shit-house.              [extremely solidly]
she's buzzing around like a honey-bee. [busy, preoccupied]

| | |
|---|---|
| a pig wouldn't eat this food. | [it is indescribably bad] |
| that movie was a real winner! | [really bad; wins nothing] |
| your grades were not too good. | [really rather poor] |

What must be explained here is how these non-literal sentences can be understood correctly, especially as they make up a fair proportion of conversation. Often they are used to add force or just pleasant twists to what would otherwise be bland statements, but often enough there is no effective way to say these ideas literally – they 'stretch' the language, as it were, using unusual and even impossible combinations of concepts to say something that could not be said otherwise. Poetry excels in this, but the ability to make new, good expressions is what 'separates the men from the boys' in literature and language use.

Expository or explanatory texts such as this are in principle literal only, so when some non-literal expression is felt really necessary, we must put it in quotes '. . .' to show that it is outside of the normal text, like somebody else's words. It was done twice in the preceding paragraph, the second for effect, but the first (*stretch*) would be hard to say otherwise, and marked there by 'as it were'.

---

Q.  How might you express literally the concepts identified above in quotes?[1]

---

## Conversational maxims

The first step in explaining how these non-literal sorts of sentences can be understood in the way their speaker intended them is to see how a listener can know that they are not to be understood literally. For this, the theory of **conversational maxims**, developed in the last two decades, provides some clues. Although they are phrased as a set of guidelines for how people should choose what to say, the interesting point is that when these maxims or prescriptions for good exchange of information are violated, the listener attempts to find some non-literal meaning.

This theory is based on the realization that communication is a cooperative effort between the speaker and the addressee; the one must 'choose their words' so that the other can understand the intent, and the second must try to figure out what the first meant. The six maxims originally proposed remain essentially undisputed, as below (simplified slightly), but some of them may be derived from more basic principles, and similar maxims of politeness have also been proposed.

Maxims of quantity
 (1) Give as much information as is needed.
 (2) Give no more information than is needed.
Maxims of quality
 (3) Do not say what you believe to be false.
 (4) Do not say what you have no evidence for.
Other maxims
 (5) Be relevant.
 (6) Be perspicuous:
  (a) do not use obscure expressions.
  (b) do not use ambiguous expressions unless necessary.
  (c) be brief.
  (d) be orderly.

Following these rules in talking would make for very boring conversations, if it did not stop them altogether. However, each one of them identifies common errors; they are wise rules for explaining a well-studied subject (in one-way communication), for their accidental violation can be confusing, if not misleading, as we shall see. In conversation, of course, misunderstanding is normally limited by attention to the other participant, as explained in Chapter 13.

The last one (6) is a collection of rules for explaining something and is not much involved in detecting non-literal uses of language, except as the last, orderliness, is related to relevance (5). This relevance, incidentally, is just a maxim for the speaker, based on the principle (Chapter 13) that the listener will use to interpret each sentence; if the speaker says something that is not relevant, the addressee will try to interpret it so that it adds as little as possible – that is, in a relevant way. If it is ambiguous at all, the addressee is liable to get the wrong meaning.

If, for example, in a discussion of syntax, you saw a heron alight on a branch outside and said 'There's a heron in that tree', anyone not watching your eyes would assume you are talking about the structural tree of some sentence under discussion, and would try to understand what *hair-on*, *Hearn*, *hare*, *hair*, or the like meant. To avoid confusion, or worse, misunderstanding if the addressee does find some way to interpret it, the speaker must make each sentence relevant to the previous sentences, or else tell listeners that what comes next is not relevant, with a topic-changing marker like the following.

| | |
|---|---|
| By the way, | [temporary change] |
| Oh, say, | [initial setter] |
| Oh, look, | [break topic, and look where I am indicating] |
| Incidentally, | [short one-sentence change] |

Obvious violations of the other four maxims are good indications of non-literal language. The first two, called the 'quantity maxims', deal with how much to say. If, for instance, you asked in a bar 'Do you serve Heineken Beer?', an answer like 'Only 100 bottles a person' (too much information) or 'We serve beer' (too little information) could not only confuse you for a bit, but this first reply might be taken to mean [we think Heineken is great], [as much as you want] or even [Heineken is very weak beer], while the second might be understood as [Heineken is the only real beer], or, with stress on *beer*, [Heineken is merely called beer; we serve real beer].

Similarly, violations of the 'quality maxims' (third and fourth ones) almost always call for reinterpretation, and all the non-literal examples listed at the beginning of this chapter depend on the listener knowing that the speaker could not possibly believe the literal meaning of what has been said. A violation of these conversational maxims, then, is a good hint that the message is not intended literally. Let us now see how we can discover the speaker's **intent**, what is intended to be understood.

## Reinterpretation rules

How a sentence is reinterpreted is, of course, subject to rules, for we cannot simply give any interpretation we might like. There seem to be many such rules, and they are involved in nearly all language understanding. However, they have not yet been explored well, and in touching this subject we reach one of the frontiers of language study. Here are a few that have been hypothesized.

- Irony RR: If something pleasant but unbelievable is said about someone or something, interpret it as the opposite, i.e. as unpleasant.
- Exaggeration RR: If some impossible amount is predicated, decrease it until it is conceivable.

High-level reinterpretation such as the above is usually open to conscious observation, but lower-level reinterpretation such as in the following is seldom noticed.

- Contents RR: If a container is spoken of, its contents may be the intended referent. For example, 'Which of the pots [on the stove] will start boiling first?' (Pots cannot boil but their contents can.)
- Representation RR: If a physical object is spoken of, it may be only a representation of it that is referred to. For example, it would be normal to say of a child's drawing, 'His sun isn't yellow, and that house doesn't have a door!'

Q.   How would you express the following without depending on reinterpretation rules?[2]
  (a) (in an art gallery) this room is van Gogh; we've seen it already.
  (b) (pointing to a box in a sketch-map of an intersection) this car hit me here.

In fact, in the interaction of aspect and the limitations of actions (Chapter 8) we noted a number of common and unconscious reinterpretations. The progressive aspect with a stative verb or adjective forces it to be temporary, and volitional if the subject is animate ('He is being despondent'). With it or a simple durative like *used to*, however, a punctive verb with a plural subject or object can be reinterpreted as iterative, as in 'The elephants used to die over there by that mountain' (a singular subject is hard to reinterpret this way; *'An elephant used to die over there'). Because these reinterpretations are automatic and effectively instantaneous, they are unconscious and give much trouble to researchers trying to discover what the meaning of the aspectual elements are.

These non-literal reinterpretations are so common that we do not easily realize that they involve finding the right rules and applying them to supply sentences with reasonable meanings. Because there are a great many ways to reinterpret a sentence, it is very difficult to construct a 'semantic impossibility' like the ungrammatical sentences that are used to explore the possibilities of syntax. As soon as a content seems to be inconceivable, the listener immediately searches, and generally finds, a way to reinterpret it to have a reasonable meaning. This not only makes semantic research difficult, especially if the researcher is not aware of it, but because there are often several ways to reinterpret an expression, the context (Chapter 13) of the expression and the background knowledge of the listener are decisive in choosing which interpretation.

## Background knowledge

Another general way in which sentences can carry hidden meaning is by making use of facts that the speaker can presume the addressee to know, sometimes called **shared knowledge**. One common way to do this is to use a definite marker like *the* or a topic marker with no previous mention of the noun, as in 'We went on a picnic yesterday, but there wasn't any ice for *the* beer.' As explained in Chapter 13, this forces the listener to find what the speaker is referring to, but since it was not mentioned, he is forced to search his background knowledge to find a **script** for picnics. An American will find one to the effect that picnics include beer, hot-dogs or hamburgers, and baseball or football. These scripts are pieces of knowledge about a culture, and have been under very active investigation by computer scientists and linguists interested in how to get computers to understand human language.

Connective words can also force the listener to find some piece of knowledge. For example, the conjunction *but* connects two contrasting concepts, as in 'John is smart, but he sure isn't rich', where mentioning intelligence may lead one to expect wealth too. Even humour such as the following depends on this.

**John eats lots of apples, but he's in the hospital anyway.**

Only if we know of the proverb 'An apple a day keeps the doctor away' can we make sense of it. Whether or not we believe that proverb (and few believe it), we can conclude that the speaker is at least pretending to believe it.

---

Q.  How can one understand 'A stitch in time doesn't save nine in America any more'?[3]

---

Similarly, because *and* connects similar things, and *too* indicates something additional, the following sentence can be understood that cooking is somehow like being considerate.

Bill is very considerate and he cooks, too.

This sentence might be interpreted as praise or a compliment, namely that Bill is or will make a good husband. This is because in many Western societies it is accepted that a good husband should help in the domestic chores. This same connotation might be hard to understand, however, in France, Italy and more traditional societies where the husband is expected to stay away from the kitchen. Where one can't conceive of a husband cooking for a family, this sentence may appear scatter-brained for it combines two unrelated facts. Differences in the listener's background knowledge, then, can change the effect or **impact** of a sentence quite radically. Nevertheless, as in this last example, the markers of the relationships between propositions (*and*, *too* here) can allow the listener to infer parts of the speaker's background knowledge, and so to understand him in spite of gross differences.

## Speech acts – utterances involved in social actions

Having come up to the limits of the known in these two directions, let us come back again to the relatively well known in a related direction. Another aspect of language use is that language is not always used to give information. In fact, it is used in an amazing variety of ways, and giving information is not nearly so common as is often thought. In the following examples that have a descriptive meaning (the last two are not clear on this point), the purpose is not to give that meaning, and in the first it is not to give information at all.

| | |
|---|---|
| wake up! | [to awaken someone] |
| can you pass the salt? | [to request the salt] |
| I'm over here. | [to demonstrate one's location, by sound] |
| it's me. | [to show one's identity, by voice quality] |
| (I'm) going now. | [to announce one's departure] |
| come on (now). | [to express disbelief]. |
| all aboard! | [to announce departure of a train] |

bon appétit. (French)  [to wish someone a good meal]
damn it!              [to express frustration (to decrease it)]

These utterances all do something other than simply to give information to someone, and indeed, many of them can be said even though the speaker is not sure whether or not there is someone to hear them. The last might even be used only if the speaker is sure there is no one about.

It was noticed some thirty years ago, again in philosophy, that there are special verbs, and special forms, for utterances that 'do something' other than simply report information about the world. These are called **performative** verbs because they perform something, as in, for instance, saying 'I *promise* to stop soon.' Once this is said, its speaker has a new obligation and the audience the right not to wait very long.

Performative utterances can generally be recognized by the fact that they can include an adverb *hereby, herewith* [by/with this very sentence], as in 'I hereby promise that . . .'. It seemed at first to be a curious fact of English that we use a special form when these verbs are used performatively. Normally, e.g. in reporting information, the progressive (e.g. . . . *-ing*) is required for anything that is true at the moment of speaking but will not continue indefinitely (Chapter 7). Thus we would say of the judge at that moment, 'He *is pronouncing* the prisoner guilty', but if we interrupted him to ask what is happening, he too would say 'I *am pronouncing* him guilty.' The performative utterance, it was discovered, the one that has social consequences (e.g. 'I (hereby) *pronounce* this prisoner guilty'), is never with progressive. This is consistent with the meaning of the progressive that we saw, however, for the effects of the performative utterance do continue indefinitely without fixed end, and progressive is used only when there is a finish point, F.

The English verb *to pronounce* is commonly used in this performative way; a judge pronounces a prisoner guilty, a doctor pronounces a casualty dead, or a minister pronounces a couple married. In each case, after it is said 'I pronounce . . .', the people involved have new rights and obligations. This happens, however, only under certain **preparatory** conditions, for example:

- The speaker is qualified (as a judge, doctor, or whatever).
- The appropriate actions have been taken (evidence observed, certificates and formalities done, etc.).

These preparatory conditions are sometimes, perhaps obligatorily, expressed with a performative authorization such as 'by the powers vested in me by the state, . . .'. All performative utterances can be seen, however, to have preparatory conditions; 'All aboard!' would 'misfire', i.e. have no force, if not shouted loudly by a conductor. If I shouted it, or if the conductor whispered it, it would not function in the way it is supposed to, namely to announce officially the imminent departure of the train. Similarly, a promise not uttered consciously and willingly by someone is not a promise.

---

Q.  When you copy the following sentence, do you feel anything special? 'Whosoever copies this sentence hereby promises to copy it again.'[4]

---

Taken together with the performative utterances, these preparatory conditions can be seen to comprise a ceremony, complex in the case of a marriage but simple in cases like 'I promise . . .', 'I swear that . . .', or children's 'I cross my heart and hope to die.' Simple ceremonies may consist of a verbal act only, as in 'All aboard!' or 'I promise . . .', or of a non-verbal act only, such as a gesture with one's hand to curse someone.

A complex ceremony is much longer and may involve other verbal acts by various people, such as 'Do you accept this person as your lawfully wedded spouse?' with an answer 'Yes', as well as non-verbal acts such as making the sign of the cross, or (in a court) rapping the bench with a gavel, or placing one's hand on the Bible when taking an oath. We attribute special significance to the verbal acts called 'performative' because they are the conclusion of the ceremony, and the reason the performative utterance is always at the end is that the ceremony has force only when completed.

The performative uses of language can thus be seen as simply the vocal parts of ceremonies that have social repercussions. They can be verbal only, as in a promise or a proposal, non-verbal only, such as a wink or a hand sign, or a combination, indefinitely complex, such as a marriage or a trial. These ceremonies, simple and complex, are apparently 'scripts' or 'scenarios' in common (background) knowledge, such as we saw for picnics above. They are special in that they have socially recognized consequences.

## Performative markers and propositional attitudes

Besides these verbs that can be used performatively (always with a first person subject and in the present tense), languages provide for very common performative situations with special markers, sometimes called **performative markers**. In many languages these are sentence–suffixes, and occasionally they are verb–suffixes. Japanese, for example, has both types.

> sentence-suffixes, relating to the proposition [it will be clear tomorrow]

| | |
|---|---|
| asita-wa haremasu-ka | [question] |
| asita-wa haremasu-yo | [assurance] |
| asita-wa haremasu-nee | [agreement] |
| asita-wa haremasu-Q | [statement] |
| asita-wa haremasu-tte | [reported] (someone else said it, not Spk) |

> verb-suffixes, relating to the addressee, [well then, eat!]

| | |
|---|---|
| saa\ tabe-yoo | [suggestion] |
| saa\ tabe-ro\ | [direct command] |
| saa\ tabe-te/ (kudasai) | [request] |

English, like most European languages, has the 'nucleus'[5] at the beginning of the sentence, just the reverse of Japanese, so we might expect sentence–prefixes for performative markers. French does have a sentence–prefix question marker, *est-ce que* (pronounced simply /esk/), but this sort of particle seldom appears as a sentence–prefix in any language. Instead, they are realized as different arrangements of the elements of the nucleus (Sj = subject, Ax = first auxiliary verb (including a contracted negative), VP = 'verb phrase' and the rest), thus for English:

| | | |
|---|---|---|
| Ax Sj VP | *will you* be here tomorrow? | [question] |
| Sj Ax VP | *you will* be here tomorrow. | [statement] |
| (Sj) VP | (*you,*) be here tomorrow! | [command] |

There are, of course, not many arrangements possible, but most languages allow questioning by means of sentence–suffixes, like *-eh/* in British and Canadian, and 'tag questions' in standard English. Along with some special formulas, they provide a few more possibilities. (The slanting lines show the direction of intonation.)

Sj Ax VP\, Ax+n't Sj/?                    [desire for agreement]
         you're coming\, *aren't you*/?
Sj Ax VP\, Ax+n't Sj\?                    [desire for admitting it]
         you're coming\, *aren't you*\?
Sj Ax VP\, Ax Sj/?                        [challenge/threat]
         you're coming\, *are you*/?
If only Sj would VP\.                     [wish]
         *if* you *would only* come\.

Spoken English has a few simple sentence-suffixes, but they go
against the grain of English (having its nucleus at the beginning of
the sentence) so they are written only in informal situations.

| suffix | meaning | where or who |
| --- | --- | --- |
| -eh/? | [question] | Canada, Great Britain |
| no/? | [question] | American immigrants from Italy, southern Europe |
| already\ | [assurance] | New York City, Jewish especially |

The 'tag questions' above may only be this sort of sentence-suffix
surfacing in a grammatical guise. French has a similar tag
structure, '. . ., n'est-ce pas?', that expresses a question. Dialectal
spoken French also has a verb-suffix for questions, -*tu* in Canada
and -*ti* in France, as in 'Cette jolie fille-là, va-ti à la bibliothèque?'
[Is that pretty girl going to the library?] or 'Tu la vois-ti?' [Do
you see her?]

   Thus certain standard actions that are commonly done with
a language are expressed with these performative elements apart
from the propositional content of the rest of the sentence. This
leads us to divide a sentence semantically into two basic parts, the
descriptive part and the performative element. The descriptive
part, a **proposition**, is like a picture or painting; it says nothing
about its truth, falsity, or whether it is a goal, a nightmare, a
danger, a wish, a suggestion or what. The performative element,
called the **propositional attitude**, indicates the relationship
between the speaker, the addressee and that propositional idea,
eliciting action (imperative), eliciting information (interrogative)
or anything else (declarative). It may also relate to the emotional
relationship between the participants.[6]

   Suppose I held up a drawing of myself on an elephant and
said 'Want, want!' The picture is like a proposition; the content
depicted is the propositional content, [Ride(I,x). Elephant(x)].
Then saying 'Want, want!' is supplying the performative element,
which combines to mean [I want to ride an elephant]. Or I could

have said instead, 'True, true!' meaning [I did ride an elephant], or 'Do, do!' meaning [I want you to get me on an elephant]. Thus, with a single proposition (e.g. a picture of an open window) roughly [the window be open] (this is a proposition without any attitude towards it) or [Open(x).Window(x)], we can have many sentences.

> the window's open.
> is the window open?
> open the window.
> could you open the window?
> the window's open, isn't it?
> the window's open, is it?
> if only the window were open.
> they say the window's open.

Q.  Describe the propositional attitude of each of these examples.[7]

Animal languages, and human baby language as well apparently, do not split utterances into propositional and performative parts. Each type of animal cry or baby word seems to have both a performative element and some propositional meaning. Thus a dog's growl means at one and the same time [I am angry] and [I warn you], or a bee's dance is always a report [there is nectar at such and such a place]. However, human babies soon know that rising intonation indicates [desire, want, doubt, etc.], while falling intonation indicates [force, sureness, insistence, etc.].

## Indirect speech acts

Most of the examples above have had but a single direct interpretation but, like ordinary words, performatives can need reinterpretation too. In this case the indirectness of meaning is often obvious, such as using a question to scold, as for example in greeting a late student 'Do you know what time it is?' or 'Have you had a nice sleep?', or using a statement to ask a question, 'I wonder if it isn't time to eat', or even one question to ask another, 'Could you give me the time?', using [are you able to ...] for [what time is it?].

As with non-literal meanings, a sentence is understood to be an **indirect** speech act if it is 'contextually inappropriate', that is, not appropriate to the context. The maxims that we began with apply primarily to descriptive material, so a different set of principles is needed here.

We saw earlier that performative verbs are effective for performing something only under certain conditions, called **felicity** conditions, including the preparatory conditions mentioned above and some sincerity conditions (such as below). Although we could restate these conditions as rules for the speaker like the conversational maxims, or as rules for interpretation, they were first discovered as conditions such as below ('s' for sincerity and 'p' for preparatory conditions) and this form is more general.

### Felicity conditions for a question (incomplete)

- Spk does not know the answer      (s)
- Spk wants to know the answer       (s)
- Adr likely does know the answer    (p)

If one of them is obviously not met, then the speaker must be doing something other than what he seems to be doing. Thus, for example, if a student walked into my lecture forty-five minutes late, I might scold him by asking what appears to be a question:

### Do you know what time it is?

This violates a sincerity condition, however; it cannot be a sincere question for I can be pretty sure (and this is obvious to all) that he does know what time it is. That is, before I ask this 'question' I already know its answer will be 'Yes'. As it violates the first felicity condition given below for questions, it cannot be a question about his knowledge, as it appears to be.

Knowing that a question or other speech act is not really what it appears to be, the only remaining problem is how can we discover what its speaker is actually doing. The reinterpretation rules above may help to some extent, but they also apply only to propositional content. Here, however, the felicity conditions again provide us the way.

Continuing with this example of the very late student, the question I asked was about the preparatory condition for a different question, 'What time is it?' It could be indirectly a question about the time, not about her knowledge, for it is a question one must answer before asking this question. In fact, it is, with rising intonation, a common way to ask the time politely.

In the classroom it could also serve as a means to scold, for it also questions the third felicity condition given below for 'Are you very late?'

- there is a time to begin
- the present time is far past that time
- Adr likely knows the above facts

Many such examples can be given; this is provided only as a simple example of the sort of thinking that goes into interpreting indirect speech acts. There is still a lot of research to do in this area, however, for although the general outlines seem clear, the details are often uncertain. Until they are clarified, we cannot be sure of this approach.

A polite indirect speech act, softer and more deferential than speaking directly, can be made by focusing on the felicity conditions of the act that one is being too polite actually to do. Thus, instead of saying directly 'I want some ice-cream' which might force a blunt refusal, we can politely say 'Is there any ice-cream?', as that is a condition without which the desire cannot be satisfied. Even more politely, we can say 'I wonder if there is any ice-cream.' In any case, if it is clear that we are speaking indirectly, we can be fairly confident that the other will be able to figure out why we said what we did, and will react appropriately, often equally indirectly. Of course, even though most of the common expressions of politeness begin as indirect speech acts, they become conventional, little more than formulas, as in the table in Chapter 5.

## Propositions and people

There are a number of different but related aspects of how sentences are interpreted as something different from the **literal** meanings of the words involved. This normally happens so fast and is so automatic that we are seldom aware of even a hint of the complexity – except when someone mistakes another person's **intent**. Really, though, intent is not even part of linguistics, for any deliberate act, not just a speech act, can have an intent. A wife kicking a husband under the bridge table has a communicative intent, which can be discovered if the receiver is wise enough. The discovery of an intent may involve a lot of guesswork, but when human language is the medium of expression, very clear hints can be given, and should be if the communication is to be unambiguous. We have seen here some of the rules whereby a listener discovers the speaker's intent when it is clothed in words that say something else.

Violations of the **conversational maxims** indicate that speakers are doing something other than simply reporting facts; what they are actually saying may be indicated by the proper **reinterpretation rule**. Of course, language is used for many things other than simply stating facts. A **performative verb** in a proper context can change social realities, but the performative utterance can be seen to be significant verbal parts of the ceremonies that establish the realities.

Languages invariably provide for common performative acts, such as questioning or commanding with special forms, often sentence-suffixes, but verb-suffixes or rearrangements of the elements at the beginning of the sentence. The **propositional attitudes** that they express can also be used in non-literal ways. Understanding another's intent can be a complex process, though there are many expressions (**formulas**) for specific intents. These often have little descriptive meaning or **propositional content**.

## Answers and notes

1. *to stretch* is used there to suggest modifying the language to cover new situations, and in doing so, making strains that could lead to further changes in the language. 'Separating the men from the boys' is only [to distinguish those who are competent from those who are not].

2. (a) This room contains van Gogh paintings and we have seen them/its contents already. (b) The car that this box stands for hit me at this place. If one were pointing to his leg, it means simply that, but when pointing to a place on the sketch-map, it means [at the location represented by the place he is pointing to].
3. It can be understood as the common (background) knowledge; 'A stitch in time saves nine' is not true in America any more, perhaps because it costs more to repair old things than to buy new, and not only clothes.
4. To have stopped copying, you must have broken the promise that you made while copying it, but then I tricked you into making it so perhaps it was not a *bona-fide* (i.e. genuine) promise. Anyway, it was not an important promise and it was made to no particular person, so you needn't feel immoral.
5. I.e. the verb with aspect, negation, tense, modality, moods and performative elements − the things that make a proposition or a description into a sentence, as in Chapter 11. The structures of most languages provide for this either near the beginning of a sentence or near the end. The order of elements here is normal if the nucleus is at the end, but is reversed when the nucleus is by the beginning.
6. Japanese, and to a lesser extent Chinese, seem to split even the performative part in two: a strictly logical part, as in the examples above, and at the very end of the sentence, an emotional part, expressing only the emotions of the speaker and their personal relationship with the addressee. Some Japanese examples are: *-sa -yo -wa -zo -ze*. These are virtually untranslatable, though we might suggest that *-wa* is like speaking softly as it is restricted to women, *-zo* is gruffness (for men mostly), and *-yo* is used in giving assurance (parents use it a lot, as do older children to younger).
7. giving information (statement, assertion), eliciting information (question), eliciting action, same politely, eliciting agreement, challenging (daring), wishing, reporting general belief.

## Keywords

literal meaning, conversational maxim, (re)interpretation, performative, propositional attitude and content, indirect speech act, felicity conditions.

# Further reading

*General*
An excellent introduction to contemporary notions is found in
Leech and Thomas, but for a deeper understanding one should go
on to Levinson. Work on performatives began with Austin and
extended into the speech acts of Searle. Grice led this work into
conversational maxims.

Malinowski studied extensively the nature of ceremonies in
human societies, providing an alternative basis for Searle's work.
Sperber and Wilson provide an account of the background
knowledge used in communicating, but there are many views –
see e.g. Hofmann or Smith.

Austin, John L. *How to Do Things with Words* (1962) Cambridge:
Harvard University Press. *Quand Dire, c'est faire* (1970) Paris:
Seuil.

Gazdar, Gerald *Pragmatics: Implicature, Presupposition, and Logical
Form* (1979) NY: Academic Press.

Grice, H. P. 'Logic and Conversation' (1975) in P. Cole and J. L.
Morgan (eds) *Syntax and Semantics 3: Pragmatics*, New York:
Academic Press.

Hofmann, Th. R. 'Frames in Comprehension, Automatic or Not'
(1985) *Quaderni di semantica* **7**: 78–85.

Leech, Geoffrey *Principles of Pragmatics* (1983) London:
Longman.

Leech, G. and Thomas, J. 'Language, Meaning and Context:
Pragmatics' (1990) in Collinge, Neville E. *An Encyclopaedia
of Language*, London: Routledge.

Levinson, S. *Pragmatics* (1983) London: CUP.

Malinowski, B. *Coral Gardens and Their Magic* (1935) London:
Allen & Unwin. (1965) Bloomington: Indiana University
Press.

Ross, J. R. 'On Declarative Sentences' (1970) in R. A. Jacobs
and P. S. Rosenbaum (eds) *Readings in English Transformational Grammar*, Waltham, Mass.: Blaisdell.

Searle, J. R. *Speech Acts: An Essay in the Philosophy of Language*
(1969) London: CUP.

Smith, Neil V. (ed.) *Mutual Knowledge* (1982) Academic Press.

Sperber, Dan and Wilson, Deirdre *Relevance: Communication and
Cognition* (1986) London: CUP.

## Exercises with context

1. What is the purpose or intent of the following?
   (a) (father to child) What in the world did you do that for?
   (b) (mother to child pulling a cat's tail) I'm sure the cat likes you to pull its tail.
   (c) Well, I'll be a monkey's uncle.
   (d) You can say that again.
   (e) Oh, go jump in the lake.
   (f) Thank God it's Friday. (T.G.I.F.)
   (g) I'll eat my hat if he lives up to his campaign promises.
2. Give three examples (in relaxed, neutral and formal styles) for each of the following actions.
   (a) [thanking]
   (b) [apologizing]
   (c) [parting, leave-taking]
   (d) [beginning a letter]
   (e) [closing a letter]
3. There are a number of ways to reinterpret a noun-form when used as a verb. Paraphrase the following by adding a general verb and returning the noun-form to function as a noun. For example, 'the yellow leaves that carpet autumn's groves' could be paraphrased as 'the yellow leaves that form a carpet for autumn's groves'.
   (a) He garages the car across the street.
   (b) I was going to be boated off to a transport.
   (c) They ferried him across the river.
   (d) He was chained to the stake.
   (e) They saddled me a horse at last.
4. Express the following in idiomatic English.
   (a) This computer is always having trouble. (a metaphor with *lemon*)
   (b) I have been waiting too long. (exaggeration)
   (c) My professor has a large library. (exaggeration)
   (d) The new book is very bad. (sarcasm)
   (e) Many people came to Liz's party. (understatement with *few*)
   (f) Foreign students must take the English examination first. (euphemism to avoid *must* and *foreigner*)
   (g) Buses and trains have special seats for old people. (euphemism)
   (h) That was a good party. (understatement with *some*)

    (i) There is very little chance of that. (exaggeration with *million*)

    (j) It is raining cats and dogs. (irony)

5. Give performative expressions that will fit.

    (a) A: Thank you very much. B: ( )

    (b) (to friend who has just got married) ( )

    (c) A: I'm sorry about that. B: ( )

    (d) (policeman arresting a thief) You're ( )

    (e) (teacher, at end of class) ( )

    (f) (to someone whose father has died) Please accept ( )

6. In which of the following can *please* be used? Say why.

    (a) Will you ( ) get me a martini?

    (b) Are you ( ) going to get me a martini?

    (c) I am ( ) thirsty.

    (d) Could you ( ) move this car out of the way?

    (e) Are you ( ) able to move this car out of the way?

    (f) Is it possible to ( ) move this car out of the way?

    (g) Can someone who isn't busy ( ) move this car out of the way?

7. The italicized adverbs following can be called 'meta-linguistic' as they modify not some overt element in the sentence but something about the act performed in speaking. Show what they mean by making the speech act explicit. For example, 'Okay, you won, *if you insist*' can be made explicit as 'Okay, *if you insist*, I admit (that you won)' where the adverb modifies *to admit*. Often these metalinguistic adverbs are at the end of a sentence and spoken in a specially low intonation.

    (a) What was his name *again*?

    (b) Kaoru's father agrees, *since you wanted to know*.

    (c) Where are you going, *please*?

    (d) I need some water, *if you can catch the waiter's attention*.

    (e) Micky got married, *in case you didn't know*.

    (f) Anyone who goes is a fool, *myself included*.

8. What is the hidden assumption needed to make sense of the following examples?

    (a) Doug is seventeen, and Emily is old enough to have a driving licence too.

    (b) Bill is a Democrat, and you can't rely on Jim either.

    (c) Reuben called Jeanette a virgin and then *she* insulted *him*. (SHE, HIM stressed)

9.  It is a sure sign that reinterpretation is needed when a noun is used as a verb. Give reasonable interpretations of the following italicized verbs by paraphrase using the noun as a noun and then try to re-express it in terms of common semantic atoms (e.g. Coz, Mov, etc.) with the noun.
    (a) A frown *creased* his forehead.
    (b) He *shouldered* his rifle and marched away.
    (c) Can you *peel* this apple?
    (d) When your quinces are clear, *glass* them up, and when they are cold, *paper* them.
    There may be a more descriptive verb that has been replaced by the noun, as in the following examples.
    (e) We were *carted off* to the station.
    (f) The yellow leaves that *carpet* autumn's groves are gone now.

10. In 'to do yesterday's jobs with tomorrow's computers', *yesterday* and *tomorrow* are not meant literally; compare 'to cook tomorrow's meal with yesterday's left-overs'.
    (a) What do they mean?
    (b) How do you know that you should ignore parts of their lexical meanings?
    (c) What parts of the lexical meaning do you reinterpret?

# CHAPTER 15

# Afterwords

意 ? 立 + 日 + 心

> Some people will have these questions: Now that we know lots of facts about meaning, what is meaning anyhow? Is it real?
>
> Some people say that meaning is 'fuzzy'; what do they mean by that and in what way is it true?
>
> If meanings can generally be broken down into semantic atoms that appear in most languages, why don't we make an international language like Esperanto or at least a writing system based on them?

Now that we have seen many facts about meaning or semantic content, we have a basis to stand back and talk about the nature of meaning. Before we do that, however, we should tie up some loose ends and sketch the range of theories of meaning that have been proposed. First, however, let us begin with the intriguing possibility of a writing based on meaning.

The desire for artificial international languages, such as Esperanto and many other less well-known ones, appears to have decreased recently with the wide acceptance of English. However, international systems of symbols are ever increasing in science and some other domains. They are, in a sense, systems of writing based on meaning rather than on the pronunciation in some particular language(s).

A system for writing meaning alone is called a 'pasigraphy'; it is naturally international, for it does not relate to the pronunciation that a language may use for its concepts. Kanji, the characters used in writing Chinese, Japanese and limitedly

Korean, are a sort of pasigraphy, though for historical reasons they do often encode pronunciation in terms of other words in the language. It is the most complete pasigraphy yet devised, but it is complex and not easily learned as an adult (though children have few problems with it).

There are limited pasigraphies near at hand, however, so near that they seem natural and almost unavoidable. The most common, found in nearly every writing system, is the arabic numeral system, *1, 2, 3 . . . 10, 11*, etc. Whether a person writes them in Russian, saying or thinking *odin, dva, tri . . . desyat', odinnadcat'*, or in Japanese saying *ichi, ni, san . . . juu, juuichi*, or in Swahili or whatever, we can read them quite easily and with perfect understanding in English as *one, two, three . . . ten, eleven*. Because they are so absolutely international, they are in great demand in international contexts,[1] such as with aeroplanes (e.g. 'A 707 has just landed'), or in naming flights, as in 'Flight AL 311 is delayed.' Even if you don't understand English, if you are booked on flight AL 311 you can see that you should find out what they are saying about your flight. In other, even purely national contexts, they are hard to avoid; just about the only circumstance that one would write 'November the eighteenth, one thousand nine hundred and ninety seven' is on an engraved invitation. I have the impression even that people are forgetting how to spell the words for *90, 18, 8th*. In fact, some people today, especially students of engineering, are no longer sure how to pronounce some unusual combinations, such as '$\frac{1}{2T}$'.

---

Q.   How does one write 90, 9th, 18, 8th, $\frac{1}{2T}$ in letters?[2]

---

Another partial pasigraphy is the international system of traffic signs, from which natural language words have mostly been abolished today, partly because foreign drivers may not know the local language very well, and partly because one can apparently react more quickly and accurately to a symbol than to a string of words.

The pasigraphy of numbers has been extended recently with the addition of (metric) measures like *Km, cm, m, l* and so on. Again these form a pasigraphy, so together with the numeral pasigraphy they form a more extensive one. Other international pasigraphies tend to be restricted to technical use, such as the chemical notation, e.g. $CH_3(CH_2)_{10}COOH$, or musical notation. Technical pasigraphs are found in nearly all the modern sciences, e.g. mathematics, electrical engineering, computers, and so on. Independent of particular languages, they serve as a medium of communication between specialists throughout the world, but more than that, they provide easily modified yet clear vehicles of thought.

As we have seen, however, languages have quite different concepts, so a kanji-like system does not seem likely to spread. The semantic atoms that compose the meanings of words might provide a better basis, like the letters for sounds that compose the pronunciations of words. However, the peripheral words of a language, like *caribou, moose, bison, buffalo,* are not completely divisible into atoms, at least for an ordinary person. Specialists may know what makes a moose a moose, or the difference between a bison and a buffalo, or a porpoise and a dolphin, but I certainly don't. At best, I have images of them.

Another problem with using atomic concepts for a pasigraphic writing system is that the semantic atoms are not arranged in a row, as sounds follow one another in time, but in three-dimensional structures; we have had to use diagrams to represent concepts like *to lack* (Chapter 12), not to speak of sentences or paragraphs. Writing, however, is normally confined to lines, and where it cannot be confined to a line, as in complex mathematical formulas, chemical equations and the like, it is difficult for printing or typing.

---

Q.   Do these same problems hinder making a spoken language based on semantic elements? What are its problems?[3]

---

If these problems could be overcome, there might be some possibility for an international writing system based on meaning, like the arabic numerals. Of course, kanji were considered to be an impossible burden only fifty years ago, but no longer; word processors can write them as fast as spelled words, and facsimile machines have almost replaced telegraphs, even in non-kanji languages. If it does ever happen that we want to build up a general symbol system without arbitrary symbols for the thousands of concepts represented by words in the lexicon, then semantic theory will have another practical application.

Sign languages are systems of symbols like pasigraphies, and often do express some concepts by their semantic components. In many sign languages there is no sign for [father], for example, such a concept being easily expressed with the signs for [male] and [parent]. In a sense, they were using practical semantic analysis long before there were linguists, but now that semantics has come of age, it may allow further development in sign languages.

## What is meaning?

One of the problems with writing-by-meaning as in a pasigraphy is that the meaning of many words cannot be completely broken down into semantic atoms. In fact, the vast majority of nouns at least, the ones that are used to classify the world, are of this sort. How I recognize a moose is by comparing it with a mental image of mooses and seeing if the thing that is charging me fits the picture well enough. I think I look at the antlers; moose antlers have a flat look. The problem is that only adult male mooses have antlers. If it is female or young, I really would not know what is going to run me down.

This observation makes it seem that the meaning of a peripheral word is at least partly an image of the type of thing that it stands for. This has given rise to theories that say that a word stands for some sort of image. These theories run into problems because images are often too specific. An image of a chair, for example, either has arms or not. If it doesn't, how can you call an armchair a chair? And if it does, how can you call an arm-less chair a chair? For more abstract words, images get harder and harder to construct; try *justice, emotion, thing* for example. Interestingly enough, most people do not perceive images with very abstract words such as *thing, place, action,* while they do see images for very concrete words, e.g. *dachshund, Mercedes, snowman.* This fits, however, with the idea that an image is only part of the meaning of a word.

In fact, the meanings of the central words of a language, e.g. *here, come, may, give, boy* and so on, are often composed entirely of semantic elements that function somewhere else to distinguish other words. These words seldom have images attached to them, or if they do, like *mother,* the image seems to be totally irrelevant to their communicative value, for your image of mother is surely influenced by your mother, as my image is based on my experiences with mothers and is undoubtedly quite different from yours in many details. We can communicate quite well in spite of this differeuce, and will no doubt agree extremely closely on who is the mother of whom. So what image there is with a central word, if any, is not involved in communication.

These observations lead to a view that the meaning of a word has potentially two parts, one part structural as we have been studying, and the other part based on images and remembered experiences. Since children cannot have structural meanings to begin with, their words must be entirely image-based, and in fact very young children do apply words to objects based on superficial similarities. With more and more experience with a word, they can generalize out of its various images some structural elements of meaning, till they may finally arrive at having its total usage explained by structural units.

In such a view, the central words of a language are the ones whose meanings are composed entirely of structural elements, while the usage of peripheral words remains more or less dependent on the non-structural part of their meanings. This is a rather tidy picture of the nature of meanings of words. It accounts for how and when people rely on images associated with words, as well as explaining how children begin with no structural meaning for a word but eventually learn one. It also explains why many people have images associated with many of their words, pictures that may be quite irrelevant in the case of non-peripheral words. However, there is precious little experimental evidence supporting this view yet, though it is consistent with what we know about the application of words to situations, by adult and by child.

## Fuzziness and prototypes

Most concepts or word meanings are a bit 'fuzzy'. While there are clear examples of, say, *red* or *ball*, e.g. the red ball my son is playing with, and equally clear examples that are not red nor a ball, like the black cat that prowls my garden every night, there are also things that are not so clearly red or not red. They may be sort of red or even with just a touch of red. Similarly for balls: an American football is not very much of a ball, nor is a medicine ball. Most concepts do not apply only to a well-defined set of things but to a more or less fuzzy group of things with no clear boundary line between what is in the group and what is not. They can even be said to have fuzzy meanings, which has given rise to doubts, even despair, about whether words really do have structural meanings.

Banish the thought! Fuzziness is a fact of life in the realm of semantics, but that does not imply that meanings of words and phrases cannot be broken apart into semantic primitives, so long as those primitives are themselves fuzzy. They are indeed, as we shall see shortly, and apparently the fuzziness of a word's possible applications is just the combination of the fuzzinesses of its semantic parts, plus perhaps a little more in peripheral words from its non-structural part. Words lacking a significant non-structural part, it seems, are fuzzy only along certain dimensions that correspond to the semantic atoms of which it is composed.

Fuzziness can also be seen as the shading that is inevitable as objects range between different ideal types or 'prototypes'. Draw a typical dog and a typical cat and then range between them drawings that are progressively more cat-like. If you draw a circle around the ones that are drawings of cats, you will discover it is a bit hard to decide how catty a cat must be to be a cat. In the centre of all the cat-like things is the prototypical cat, having all the traits that are possessed by all cats, and other traits to the degree that cats have them. An adequate prototype theory can then assign to any object a degree to which it matches the prototypes in its neighbourhood or semantic field.

A prototype seems at first to be the image or experiential part of the meaning of a word, and this theory should thus work best for children who have not yet abstracted out of that any structural elements of meaning. But those structural elements must also be part of the prototype if they are present, so we may have to refine prototype theory to account for the differences between structural and experiential parts of meaning.

## Field theories of meaning

Because concepts or word meanings are found in the lexicon in hierarchical groupings, the words found under each node form a tight group of contrasts that can be called a 'lexical field', and a 'semantic field' is the corresponding range of possible meanings. For example, *chair* contrasts with *stool*, *bench*, *sofa*, and, together with other words in this semantic domain, forms a lexical field. It is obvious even from a short glance at this field that the respect in which *chair* differs from *stool* is that it has a 'back', and it differs from the others in seating only one person. It is thus a useful research strategy to collect all the words in some semantic field, or of apparently similar meanings if one is not sure of where the field ends, to identify what semantic elements each has. It is not necessarily easy or automatic to find the elements, but it is far easier than trying to find what the significant elements of a single word are.

Isolating meaning elements this way has also been called 'referential analysis', especially when one uses objects or pictures which are classified by the words in the lexical field. Recent studies using pictures of objects varied in small steps not only show clear differences between what things words that are supposedly equivalent can apply to, they show the inherent fuzziness of the range of things each word describes.

## 'Use' theories of meaning

We have been using the notion 'applying words to things and situations' quite a bit, for that is the only ultimate test of what an expression means: to what sort of situations can it apply appropriately? This observation has led some philosophers (especially Wittgenstein and his followers) to propose that the meaning of a word is nothing more than its usage. It is not easy to disagree with this, if it refers to 'all the ways the word might be used'. Discovering the structural part of a word's meaning is simply isolating aspects of usage that are found in all the possible ways to use it, and the experiential part is the aspects of (past) usage that have not been found general enough to isolate as systematic primitives.

The best examples in Wittgenstein's defence are words that are used in specific games or social rituals. The term *run* in baseball is a technical term that has only a historical connection with the English verb *to run*, for one can in fact walk, even crawl around the bases after hitting a ball over the fence, and it is still a home run. Within any social custom or ritual, we need names for the various component actions, and we conveniently adopt common words that come close in meaning. But these are not the normal descriptive uses of the words, only names within the system of that ritual, and we should not expect those usages to have any more in common with general English than common words used as names of people, e.g. *Walker, Smith, North* and so on. Within any specific, well-demarcated activity, then, a word may be used quite at variance with its normal usage and thus be said to have a different meaning. The sciences are full of examples of this, and the words *content, concept* in this book are excellent examples.

Sometimes this notion of usage is restricted to 'all the ways a word has been used (in someone's experience)', which is not so different from 'all the ways it might be used' but it misses the potential uses of a word for things that a person has not yet met. That future usage must be based largely on the structural aspect that was generalized out of these past usages, so we can see this notion of usage as the raw data out of which structural concepts are constructed.

A type of usage theory that has been more popular in linguistics is to take the meaning of a word to be its possibilities of collocation with other words – its possibilities of usage in a language. Few if any words have identical 'distributions' in terms of which other words they can collocate with. An extreme form of this usage orientation (see Further reading) is then to take a word's meaning as all the collocations it partakes in. This looks much more scientific, for we can at least imagine making a computer listing of all the contexts in which a word occurs. Practically, of course, this is not possible, but as a basis for tests to determine which of two theories is correct on some point, it might be feasible as a mental exercise. It was, in fact, the logical basis of a very popular theory of syntax called 'transformational grammar'; a small basic set of simple collocations could be combined and rearranged by transformations into the vast (and infinite) arrangements of words found in a language. This theory is slowly losing ground to more empirical approaches, but it was quite important to semantics; the arrangements of this basic set of collocations were, of course, rather semantic in nature and gave rise to the notions of semantics on the sentence level that we have today.

On a practical level, collecting the collocations of a word is of course very useful in determining its meaning, or its syntactic possibilities. With computer-readable texts widely available, this is becoming a requirement for careful analysis, but it is never to be taken as the meaning or even as definitive of the meaning.

In recent times, usage theories have tended towards identifying a word's meaning with rules governing when it can be used. These rules establish its possibilities of collocation, of course, but they go beyond the narrow usage theories in making allowance for words and expressions such as *hi, by the way* that have virtually no descriptive meaning and little meaning other than the sorts of situations in which they are used. There is nothing much we can say about the meaning of *hi*, for example, other than that it is used upon meeting a person.

## Referential theories

We have noted in Chapters 1 and 10 that the referent of an expression is not the same as its meaning, but on a fundamental level there is something natural about associating the meaning of a word with what it refers to. Especially in the sciences, where meaning is a rather ghostly shadow that has often misled people, a referent is overt and, in principle, open to scientific observation. This orientation was naturally stronger in Latin and ancient Greek where nouns did in fact refer to objects as there were no determiners like *the* to share and control the referential burden. In modern versions of these theories applied to contemporary European languages, the meaning of a word becomes all the things it might refer to, its 'denotation', and the empirical clarity of the original idea is lost to the infinite size and the fuzziness of that group of things.

The word *rabbit*, for example, would refer to or 'denote' the set of all rabbits, and since I expect to be able to use that word thirty years from now, it must include all the rabbits that will exist then, and by such extensions, all the rabbits that have ever been or ever will be. Now that is quite a pile of rabbits, and completely beyond the ken of any human being, yet we do know the meaning of the word *rabbit*, as I can identify things as rabbits and you will agree, or, not seeing them, you will know what I am talking about. The only way, in fact, we can talk about the set of all rabbits is to select certain defining characteristics of rabbits. These defining characteristics are just the structural meaning that we have isolated.

## Semantic differential

Some words are negative in tone, like *dirty, lousy, crazy, fool,* while others are positive, such as *mother, love* and so on. This is

called **affect** in psychology, or 'affective content' in semantics.[4]
By means of statistical analysis of how people rate words and
concepts on scales such as good—bad, far—near, and many
others, three fairly reliable dimensions of affective content were
found.

> good—bad
> warm—cold
> active—passive

In general, mothers were found to be good and warm, fathers
good but cold, snakes bad and cold, and, for the USA at least,
governments were also bad and cold. It was hoped that this sort
of analysis might provide an objective thrust into meaning, but it
went no further than affective content. The technique was called
the 'semantic differential' but further exploration of this avenue
was displaced in the excitement of the sentence semantics that
became possible in the late 1960s. It ought to be possible,
however, to construct a system for predicting the affective value
of a sentence based on the affective values of its component
words.

## The web of semantic relations

In descriptive studies, a recent popular direction has been based
on the fact that each word is enmeshed in a web of semantic
relations, so to give the meaning of a word we must place it in a
'semantic network' of all the words and their relationships to
other words in the language. The hierarchies of concepts that we
saw in Chapter 2 are a significant part of these relations, but in
principle every type of relationship must be included, such as
[primates – have – 2 arms & 2 legs], [chairs – have – legs], [cups –
have – handles] (not ears, as they have in some languages), and
even things like [carnivores – eat – meat] that relates these three
concepts. These theories appeared in the early research on
artificial intelligence but hit against the incredible complexity of
the human conceptual system and did not offer much for
describing the semantic structure of combinations of concepts
such as 'purple carnivore', not to speak of referring expressions
such as 'that green bicycle', or sentences.

A more recent direction, too new to have been adequately
explored, is based on the old notion that the meaning of an

expression is all the facts that follow from it (Chapter 1). Put in a new mathematical–logical dress, it is not too different from the idea of semantic networks above. This sort of 'implicational theory of meaning' must be limited somehow, as the implications one can draw from some act are much broader than meaning in natural language. Not only can clouds imply rain, and rain always implies clouds, though these are surely not anything to do with language, but using a dialectal form such as *wee* for [small] may imply that the speaker belongs to that dialect group, again surely not part of what they are saying. It also runs into trouble from the fact that a contradiction implies anything and everything (which is why contradictions are so damning). So in this theory, all self-contradictory concepts must have precisely the same meaning, namely everything. 'I can imagine a square circle' must have the same meaning as 'I met a man who was a woman', unless this type of theory includes limits to prevent this.

## Theories of meaning

Of course, these thumbnail sketches of various approaches to the nature of meaning are only that, here to help you get a general idea of the variety of thought that abounds in semantics, ever since Plato and even before. They are also meant to help you place a book that you are reading in a larger context and to give you some directions for possible reading or research.

However, any of these approaches represents at least a major portion of the life of some researcher(s), and appears in at least a couple of major books. There is no way to give here more than a few hints of their natures. I have tried to arrange them by their fundamental notions and provide some hint of the limitations of those notions. If you feel that I have been unjust in those comments – and there is usually some way or another to get round a limitation – then please read the real works (see Further reading for references and some personal comments) and prove me wrong!

## Is meaning real?

If you ask for the meaning of a word of French, you will no doubt get some word(s) of English. And if you ask for the meaning of a word of English, you will no doubt get some more words of English – or possibly some other language. A number of brilliant minds, noting the lack of any other valid sort of response to questions about meaning, have argued that meaning is no more than translation into some other language or symbol system (such as the graphs we have been using). Slightly more generous is the proposition that meaning is no more than whatever it is that can be translated: I can try to show you all sorts of things with the same meaning, but I can't, they point out, show you any meaning.

When we take meaning to be everything that is implied by a form, as was suggested in Chapters 1 and 14, then that is certainly real in some sense. However, all the facts that are implied by even a simple form such as 'That is a cat' are so vast that I can't even think of how to start to tell them all to you. Moreover, as we noted above, this is too loose a notion of meaning for what we need. Besides, one might protest that it is in any case a 'mental object', like the number '2'. It has no physical reality.

In this book we have isolated bits of meaning in tables or by other means and have given them three-letter names. We have built graphs out of them, and generally assumed that they are real. Are they? Is this any more than simply translating English into some obscure formal language that we might call 'Semantese'? This Semantese may indeed be useful for it allows us to describe other languages in the same terms, but aren't we still merely translating into it and calling that meaning?

A fundamental goal of semantics is to identify when two forms have the same meaning. That may not happen very often, so a more general goal is to identify when two forms are similar in meaning, and to show how similar they are and, the most exacting goal of all, how any two forms differ in meaning. If we can do this for all the forms of a language, then it would be hard to say that we don't have an adequate account of meaning in that language.

This is just what we have been doing, though we have only scratched the surface of the vast storehouse of concepts that a language provides. The symbols we have introduced sometimes stand directly for differences in meanings, but sometimes replacing one by another accounted for differences in meaning. In all cases we have been working towards this goal of identifying all the differences in meanings between any pair of forms. When we put these elements together, giving the meanings of words and sentences, again we are showing what the differences are between those forms and some other forms.

Thus these elements are symbols for differences or potential differences in the meanings of words or phrases, and their combinations show meanings of complex forms in terms of possible differences. If and when we complete this goal, then we shall know what every form in the language means in terms of its differences with other potential forms. We will have effectively classified every pair of expressions by their differences, small or large, in meaning.

At this point, we can say simply that each symbol stands for or summarizes a (large) number of observations about differences in meaning, or we can say that there is something real behind the symbols that we are using the observations to get at. Except for the conceptual simplicity of the latter, there may not be very much difference between these ways of talking. This situation has been met before in science; the quarks in modern physics for example have never been seen − it is perfectly consistent to say that the notion of the quark is no more than a useful fiction that summarizes the results of many experiments. However, the useful fictions of a well-supported simple theory have almost always turned out to be real, when we later find some means to test their reality. Electrons in 1920 were in quite the same predicament in which quarks find themselves today. Furthermore, scientists who believe that they are working with reality may be more motivated to study it further than those who believe that they are working with mere fictions. So I will take the attitude that these semantic atoms are real enough, though we may be mistaken about some of them. You can make your own choice.

This does not complete an account of structural meaning, however. We have here only an 'uninterpreted' semantic description. It describes only what expressions are similar, or better, what the difference is between any pair of expressions. It doesn't say what those differences, given in terms of symbols, mean in real life. It would allow inter-stellar visitors to make semantically well-formed sentences, and discourses even, but it would not allow them to know what they or you have said − unless of course those symbols were explained in a language they knew.

We need not retreat to a translation theory of meaning, however, waiting for someone to discover a non-existent Rosetta stone that gives parallel translations of some text in their language and our language. One can learn another language as a child does, hypothesizing meanings of words, testing them, and relating the meanings ultimately to potential sensory perceptions.

A complete semantic description must, then, be an 'interpreted' one, where each of the semantic elements is related to some aspect(s) of the world, most easily stated in terms of tests about the world. A semantic atom [Hot(x)], for example, relates to a test something like: if you touch X, you will have a certain characteristic feeling from your skin in the place where you touch X. Or [Red(x)] is a 'feeling' on the retina of your eye, or perhaps in the visual processing areas at the back of your brain, when you look at X. Tests can be complex and operational, as for example [Round(x)] is no doubt something like 'If you turn X, it doesn't change shape.' More complex is a semantic atom like [Ani]mate, including sub-tests such as 'Can it move by itself, other than by outside forces?' and 'Does it avoid some things and seek some things?' or even 'Does it eat? Does it reproduce? Can it be killed?'

---

Q. Some of the attributes of [Ani] are also associated with [Viv] (living, *VIVant*). Which ones? Can you imagine things that are animate but not alive [Neg-Viv]?[5]

---

These tests can assign 'true', 'false', 'inapplicable' and possibly other values when applied to a piece of the world, so a collection of them that a word or an expression relates to can be judged true or otherwise. Thus, when one is told that some piece of the world is 'hot coffee', one can run the test for [Hot] (touch it!) and the tests for [coffee] (smell and taste it, I assume) to determine whether the speaker was correct. More commonly, however, one assumes the speaker is correct, so one can turn the description, 'hot coffee', into the set of tests that the thing passes, in the speaker's opinion. As a result, one can react appropriately to the object even without running any tests on it. Thus we have the simple and basic case of communicating useful information.

Similarly, to find a referent by means of its description, one looks for the piece(s) of the world that pass the tests associated with the description. In this way, all expressions are associated with tests, even though the tests may be hard to perform, as, for example, for 'This building will fall down in March 2016' we will need a time machine or a long wait to test it. Of course, we don't always, or even often, use these direct sensory tests, for we devise other easier ways to determine the results that those direct tests would have. A thermometer, for example, will not only substitute for touching something to ascertain whether it is hot but will also give a fairly precise indication of how hot it is, and it can be used even in a flame or an oven where touching is not to be recommended.

The tests that one person uses may not be entirely identical with those that another uses, as for example the rather important concept of [Hum]an. For me, the sub-test 'Can it talk (or use some form of general communication)?' is rather important, more important than the physical shape of the object, so I would be inclined to afford full human dignity and rights to a monster that differed from me only in its physical shape, and this would also apply in the case of Siamese twins. But other things are important too, for I would not include a computer even though it could discourse beautifully on a wide variety of subjects. Other people take the sub-test 'Does it come from human parents?' as being of prime importance, and they accordingly take abortion to be an act of murder. Yet I can conceive of human beings that are not born of human parents, Adam and Eve for example, and also of non-human beings that are born of human parents. So long as our various tests end up with the same things qualifying as [Hum], there is no problem. This covers just about all of daily, scientific and even philosophical discourse. The current conflict about abortion can be seen as a conflict about just what [Hum] includes, and we are bound to have more such conflicts as science discovers how to make things that differ from ourselves in smaller and smaller ways.

This sort of interpreted semantic theory can be seen as a 'usage' theory, if we understand 'use' in the sense of when a term (or rather a semantic atom) is used *truly and appropriately*. Or it might be seen as a referential theory if we take referents to be those objects that pass well enough the tests for the semantic elements and their combinations. In addition, it can be seen as the important part of an 'implicational theory' of meaning, where the successful passing of the tests is a few crucial implications of an expression. Lastly, for the part of the meaning of a word that is unanalysed, the image or experiential part, we will need prototype theory to match an object in the physical world with the 'images' associated with the nearby words.[6]

In any case, it requires that we do what we have done, break down the meanings of words and more complex expressions into smaller elements that can be related to the world. There are many semantic complexes, e.g. the concept [god], [the ancestor of all human beings] or [a square circle], that cannot be related to sensory data as wholes, for there is nothing in the physical world, apparently, that can be sensed as such.

Whether or not the semantic primitives are physically real is still not to be decided easily, but if we note that anyone who uses English reasonably well must have these elements somewhere in their brain, then we cannot be surprised to find them physically represented somewhere. And if a number of them are found in just about all human languages (e.g. Hot, Round, Ani, Hum, Fem, Coz, Bcm, Neg), as does seem to be the case, then we should be prepared to find some of them represented in the genetic structure of a human being. In any case, they surely have as much reality as the languages in which we find them, and a language has a social reality as well as a mental reality and a means of communication.

## Answers and notes

1. We used to name aeroplanes, as we still do cars, by a model name (e.g. *Tristar, Spitfire, Flying Fortress*), and flights by where they went to, but these customs died out after the Second World War. Only cars and an occasional aeroplane (*Concorde*) get non-numeric names. Buses, coaches and trains are still commonly named by destination, perhaps because they are usually found in a monolingual context, or nearly so.

2. *Ninety* with a silent 'e' in the middle and *ninth* without! *Eighteen, eighth* dropping one 't'. '$\frac{1}{21}$' should be *one twenty-first* or possibly *one-twenty-oneth*, but the first sounds strange and the second worse. Dictionaries often avoid committing themselves on this last point!

3. It is much harder to deviate from linearity (things in a row, or in time) in speech than in writing, which is why it is hard to speak mathematical equations over the telephone, so this problem is more severe, but the problem of decomposing words into elements is the same. There is a further, small problem in choosing a set of sounds that everyone can pronounce and recognize easily.

4. It is also called 'connotation', but that term has no accepted meaning except that it is opposed to denotation, so it may be wise to avoid it.

5. A [Viv] object takes in energy in the form of food and builds (or repairs) its structure, and it has a method for reproduction. Animateness seems to add to this an ability to move about, to seek out its food and 'eat' it. One might imagine a robot that moves about but doesn't have the other attributes needed to call it living. Gods and demons I think are [Hum] in that they can talk, but moving about is not clear, and reproduction and taking in food seem very doubtful.

6. This requires a lot of processing, which may be part of the reason that structural elements are abstracted out of prototypes to form the structural part of the meaning of a word. The more that recognition can be completed using semantic elements, the faster it can be completed.

## Keywords

pasigraphy, fuzziness, prototype, semantic field, 'use' theories, semantic differential, semantic network.

## Further reading

For an account of word meaning having dissimilar parts, Putnam proposed that it has three parts, but the notion that it is part structural and part experiential derives from Chapter 1 of my thesis (in French, sorry).

Putnam, Hilary 'The Meaning of Meaning' (1975) in K. Gunderson (ed.), *Language, Mind and Knowledge*, Minneapolis: University of Minnesota Press.

Hofmann, Th. R. *Description sémantique et dynamique du discours* (1978) Grenoble: Université Scientifique et Medicale, Diss. for Université de Paris IV. (1979), Ann Arbor: University Microfilms.

Fuzzy set theory and fuzzy logic were developed by L. Zadeh, and applied to language by G. Lakoff. He became a strong proponent of prototype theory with special attention to metaphor, and his *Women, Fire and Other Dangerous Things* is excellent reading. Kempton provided an excellent application of prototype theory in an empirical study but Taylor is perhaps the best introduction.

Kempton, Willet *The Folk Classification of Ceramics: A Study of Cognitive Prototypes* (1981) New York: Academic Press.

Lakoff, George *Women, Fire and Other Dangerous Things* (1987) Chicago: University of Chicago Press.

Langacker, Ronald *Foundations of Cognitive Linguistics* (1986) Stanford: Stanford University Press.

Taylor, John R. *Linguistic Categorization: Prototypes and linguistic theory* (1989) Oxford: Clarendon.

The study of lexical fields was developed in Germany between the wars by J. Trier and extended for greater empirical content by Pottier in France. A landmark study on *cup, vase, pitcher, bowl* and so on was done in an anthropological context recently by Kempton, demonstrating the application of prototype theory.

Lehrer, A. *Semantic Fields and Lexical Structure* (1974) Amsterdam: North Holland, and New York: Elsevier.

Pottier, B. 'Champ sémantique, champ d'expérience et structure lexique' (1968) in W. Elwert, *Probleme der Semantik*, Weisbaden: Steiner.

Trier, Jost *Der deutsche Wortschatz im Sinnbezirk des Verstandes* (1931) Heidelberg.

The study of how children use language, and thus how their thinking develops, became respectable early in this century with the works of Vygotsky and Piaget.

Piaget, Jean *The Language and Thought of the Child* (1955) New York: Meredith. *Langage et pensée chez l'enfant* (1923) Neuchatel and Paris.

Vygotsky, Lev *Thought and Language* (1962) Cambridge: MIT Press.

Although Wittgenstein began from a very mechanistic theory of language, he went to the opposite extreme in arguing that a word has no meaning other than how it is used. Ziff restricted the 'usage' of a word to what other words it can be used with, but this was roundly criticized in linguistic circles for being too simple.

Wittgenstein, Ludwig *Philosophical Investigations* (1953) Oxford: Blackwell, and New York: Macmillan.

Ziff, Paul *Semantic Analysis* (1960) Ithaca: Cornell University Press.

The semantic differential was developed by Osgood in the 1950s and was seen at first as a way to get an empirical grasp on semantic phenomena, a popular goal at the time. It is well summarized in Osgood, Suci and Tannenbaum, after which little interest or research has been seen.

Osgood, Charles, Suci, G. and Tannenbaum, P. *The Measurement of Meaning* (1957) Urbana: University of Illinois Press.

Semantic networks were pioneered by R. Schank and his followers, plus others such as David Hays. At first believed to handle all semantic phenomena of note, they have now been abandoned as a useful direction in linguistics but may be seen in the 'relational databases' that have been popular in computer applications. Sperber and Wilson (reference in Chapter 14) provided the modern version that employs implications instead of computer links.

Schank, Roger C. *Conceptual Information Processing* (1975) Amsterdam: North Holland.

Hays, D. 'Types of processes on cognitive networks' (1974) in Antonio Zampolli, *Proceedings of the Conference on Computational Linguistics*, Firenze: Olschki.

Quine worried about the possibility of ever knowing what expressions of a radically different language might mean.

Quine, Willard *Word and Object* (1960) Cambridge: MIT Press, and New York: Wiley.

Of course, there is much work as well as general texts based on views that differ in relatively small ways from what we have seen here. Lyons is probably the deepest, while Leech and the Nilsens are good reads.

Allan, Keith *Linguistic Meaning I and II* (1986) Routledge.

Bach, Emmon *Informal Lectures on Formal Semantics* (1989) Albany: SUNY.

Gordon, W. Terrence *A History of Semantics* (1982) Benjamins.

Kempson, Ruth M. *Semantic Theory* (1977) CUP.

Leech, Geoffrey *Semantics* (1974) Penguin (2nd edition 1981).

Lyons, John *Semantics I* (1977) CUP.

Nilsen, Don L. F. and Nilsen, A. P. *Semantic Theory* (1975) Newbury House.

Pottier, Bernard *Linguistique générale: théorie et description* (1974) Paris: Klincksieck.

# Answers to Exercises

## Chapter 1

1. radio and television broadcasting, especially news reporting and disc-jockeying, or a public lecture. Another is reading a book or a telephone answering machine.
2. (a) Prof X (I don't know his/her name, but you do) (b) yourself, I hope (c) some eating place, probably; only you know which (d) yourself at least
3. (a) if there are several teachers for this course – if your parents have more than one child (b) 'the teachers of this course' – 'the children of your parents'
4. (a) 1 (b) 1 (c) 1 -*s* and -*er* are not *lexical* items (d) 2 (e) 1 (f) 1 (g) 2 (h) 1 (i) 2 (j) 1
5. (a) elephant (b) sparrow (c) neither (d) jack-rabbit (e) saucepan (f) neither (g) house
6.

7. (a) Maybe it is true for chicks and roosters too; try that, and try it for ducks before trying it for eagles, sparrows, and so on. (b) We eat fowls, but seldom other birds.

## Chapter 2

1. (a) (500 metres) high; ★ 'that valley is 600 metres low' (b) (6 metres) deep (c) (2 feet) long (d) (3 cm) thick (e) (2 feet) wide (f) many (g) much (h) often (i) sharp (j) smart (k) large (l) heavy (m) far

2.  (a) height (b) thickness (c) weight (d) width (e) age (f) distance (g) speed (h) intelligence (i) breadth (j) temperature (k) warmth

3.  (a) if the Spk knows that the visits are quite rare (b) if, for example, the Adr has claimed that he can run more slowly than anyone else (c) if one is comparing shallow pools, for children to play in perhaps

4.  (a) *grandchild* (b) *horse* (c) *chicken* (d) *sheep* (e) *spouse* (f) *limb* (g) *sibling/sib* Marked term and label: (h) *bull* (US); sex (i) *warlock*; sex (j) *lioness*; sex (k) *actor, actress*; sex (l) *watch*; portability (m) *kitten*; age

5.  (a) *yesterday* (b) *tonight* (c) *pink, grey* (d) *pork, beef, venison, chicken* (e) *to drive, to fly*

6.  (a) alumna; neither (b) poetess; poet (c) blonde; blond (d) brunette; brunet (e) warlock; witch (f) toastmistress; neither (g) merman; neither

7.  (a) *9th* is a spelling exception only as it is pronounced regularly (adding -th). *5th, 8th, 12th* have phonetic changes (reflected in spelling) that make more easily pronounced forms. The others (*first, second, third*) are independent words that block *oneth, *twoth, *threeth. (b) In expression, the -*th* is added merely to the last digit, as if they were 20(1st), 20(2nd) − if it were added to the whole complex we should have forms like *(21)th, *(22)th which are blocked by the existing forms. NB: we can add -*th* to anything else, as in (100)th, even Nth. (c) The meaning of -*th* applies to the whole complex number, [(20+1)th, (20+2)th ...]. (The mismatch between expression and content in this example is not uncommon.)

8.  (a) *; degree modifiers cannot occur with marked adjectives (b) nothing; there is no other way to describe such an object if we can't use the term *gander*, as to someone who doesn't know that word (c) !; two-headed and unheaded persons are nigh on impossible (d) nothing; it is the normal expression for such a person (e) *; because the modifier cancels out the extra element [Fem] in *policewoman* (f) !; [Msc] is totally pleonastic but might be resorted to for emphasis if the addressee persists in not understanding it.

9.  Adding an element of meaning (ii) makes a hyponym (iv), i.e. a word that is more marked (iii), more specific and less general (i). Or, as a chart:

| (e.g.) | (i) | (ii) | (iii) | (iv) |
|---|---|---|---|---|
| *animal* \| *dog* | \| more general | fewer elements | less marked | general term |
| *dog* | \| *mongrel* \| more specific | more elements | more marked | hyponym |

10.  Adding a meaning element will restrict the applicability (the range of things it describes) of an expression, so it will generally describe fewer things – there are fewer male horses or white horses than horses. (b) If, however, the addition doesn't exclude anything, then adding it makes no difference in this number. In sum, the number of things described will be less than or equal to that of the term without the addition.

11.  The more frequent one would always block the other, which would then drop out of usage and soon be forgotten. It can happen, however, at frontiers between dialects with different forms for the same concept. This happened in the USA when their form *burned* was confronted by the British *burnt*, but instead of dropping out of usage (it was a prestige form, after all) the meaning of the new term was modified based on its most common usage '__ toast', [blackened due to burning].

# Chapter 3

1.  (a) *sweet* (b) *friendly* (c) *tough* (d) *hardcover, hardback* (e) *sober* (f) *harmless* (g) *non-flammable, not inflammable!* (h) *timid, cowardly* (i) *optional* (j) *dissuade* (k) *disentangle* (l) *bill, note*
2.  (a) *medium* (b) *damp, moist, humid* <of air> (c) *so-so* (d) *probably* (e) *pass, fair, satisfactory* (f) *tepid, luke-warm*
3.  (b), (e), (g)
4.  (a) All are degree modifiers; 'slightly open', 'rather open', 'a little bit open'.
    (b)

| (a) G – L | (e) L – G |
|---|---|
| (b) G – G | (f) G – L? |
| (c) G – G | (g) G – G |
| (d) L – L | (h) L – L |

    (c) This *open* has a limit [the wrappings completely removed] and is not an antonym of *shut, closed*.
5.  (a) ir- (b) in- (c) in- (d) il- (e) in- (f) il- (g) ir- (h) im- (i)

im- (j) in- (k) in- (l) L (m) R (n) P, B, M (o) everything else
(p) in- (q) in- (r) in- (s) in- (t) in- (u) in- (v) im- (w) il- (x)
ir-

6.  (a) not having typical British characters − other nationalities
    (b) unlawful − outside of the law or without legal
    consequences (c) outside of morality, without understanding
    of right and wrong − morally wrong.

7.  (a) can't do both − can't do either (b) didn't answer at all −
    answered in a complex way (c) not even allowed to take −
    even allowed not to take (even exempted from) (d) The
    reason that he didn't marry her is that he loved her. − He
    married her for some other reason than love. (e) He was not
    exhausted when he returned. − He was exhausted, so he
    didn't return. (f) only a few can solve it (*not many* is a
    complex quantifier) − many cannot solve it, but (perhaps)
    many can (g) Most (perhaps) can solve it, but not all of
    them. − None can solve it, or, all of them together cannot
    solve it. (But with stress on *all*, (g') can have the same
    meaning as (g).)

8.  (a) If Lucia is Romula's slave then Romula is Lucia's *mistress*,
    not her master. (b) I am a patient of my dentist, but he is not
    my doctor. (c) As one Californian child recently said, 'He is
    my father's husband.'

9.  *Sire* must have the meaning [Msc.Hse.Par], but no revision is
    needed for *father* as lexical blocking will prevent its use for
    horses if the conversants all know the word *sire*. And if they
    don't, as e.g. explaining to a child, one will indeed use the
    word *father*.

10. (a) [Neg-die] (b) [Neg-stop] (c) [Neg-prevent] (d) [Neg-
    leave]

# Chapter 4

1.  (a) *I, we* (and *me, us*) (b) *you, he, she, they* (and objective
    forms) (c) *for this reason* (d) *for that reason* (e) *thus, (in) this way*
    (f) *(in) that way* (g) *what* (h) *which* (it is so not useful to
    distinguish plurality when you don't yet know the answer,
    and anyway, plurality will be shown on a noun if one
    follows) (i) *where* (j) *which place* (k) *I* (l) *we* (m) *you, he, she, it*
    (n) *you, they* and objective forms

2. (b) & (c) express conflicting locations (Spk or Neg-Spk) for the book. (f) is strange as the *here* [Spk] conflicts with *to go* [To-Awa], but it can be reinterpreted (Chapter 14) as [to leave], as in 'I'll go now, and meet you here at 4.30.' (g) is impossible as *to go* cannot include movement towards Spk or Adr, but Adr is to be waiting there. (On the other hand, (e) is quite reasonable if Adr will be there.)

3. The problem in (a) is accepted by the speaker, but in (a') it is outside his domain. So in (b) the speaker is effectively offering to help as he has accepted it as his own. The speaker of (c) is not planning to go, but (c') implies that he believes he will be there. In (d') *to come* implies movement towards Adr, and says that he is at home, so it must have been said on a telephone. A teacher or helper who is involved with the progress of the student would say (e), but someone who is not involved would use (e'). The speaker is on the ground in (f) but (emotionally at least) high above in (f'), so (f') is normally used for plane crashes.

4. (a) this and that (b) come and go (c) now and then (d) here and there: [Spk] before [Neg-Spk] (e) you and I (f) he and I (g) you and he: for politeness, the speaker mentions himself last.

5. (a) A Japanese company has just brought out a pocket-sized word processor. (b) The warm weather this winter will bring the peach trees into blossom a week early. (c) The prime minister's long evening walks bring him into contact with ordinary people. (d) My deplorable test results brought home to me how lazy I had been all year. (e) Their excavation of the tomb at Ixtapetl brought new evidence to light that there was trans-Atlantic commerce even then.

6. (a) Jenkins has gone raving mad. (b) The scheduled went awry yesterday. (c) My predictions have come true again. (d) The electric mains have gone dead. (e) The party finally came alive. (f) Your milk went sour after three hours in the sun. (g) The moon came up at 4 p.m. and went down (set) at noon (*and if you know your astronomy, you will know that it is very cold for this can happen only in winter near the Arctic Circle*).

7. By sub-dividing [Neg-Awa] into [Spk], i.e. [close to the speaker], and [Neg-Spk] giving [close to the addressee].

8.  (a)  Mov.Dir:Neg-Awa      (e)  Mov.Dir:Neg-Awa.Dir:Spk
                                        = Mov.Dir:Spk

    (b)  Mov.Dir:Awa          (f)  Mov.Dir:Neg-Awa.Dir:Neg-Spk
                                        = Mov.Dir:Adr

    (c)  (Loc:)Spk            (g)  Mov.Dir:Awa.Dir:Neg-Spk
                                        = Mov.Dir:Awa

    (d)  (Loc:)Neg-Spk        (h)  Mov.Dir:Awa.Dir:Spk (contradiction)

9.  *To come* implies movement to the speaker or the addressee.
    As Spk is asking where one should go, one is effectively
    asking where the Adr will be. More formally, the question
    has a meaning [Mov.Dir:Neg-Awa.Dir:Qst]. Neg-Awa is
    either Spk or Adr, but we cannot be questioning where Spk
    is, so it reduces to [Mov.Dir:Adr.Dir:Qst].

10. We must conclude that although languages may use the
    same elements, each language subjects them to different
    interpretations. Alternatively, we must accept that Spanish
    sub-divides Neg-Spk with a different element (Visable:Neg-
    Visible, perhaps) than Japanese.

11. I don't know the answer; you will have to criticize yourself.


# Chapter 5

1.  Orientation towards (a) subject: 'Becky put it in her pocket
    secretly' (b) either: 'Tommy answered honestly'/ 'Honestly,
    he answered!' (c) Spk: 'Understandably, he must go to a
    good school' (d) subject: 'Miserably, she put it away' (e)
    either: 'Thankfully, John accepted your offer'/'John accepted
    your offer thankfully' (f) either: 'With a little luck, they will
    finish on time' (g) Spk [the speaker thinks it lucky that . . .]:
    'Luckily, they will finish on time'

2.  Bill was sad to decline in (a'), or he did it in a sad manner,
    while (a) will probably be understood as the speaker
    thinking it sad that Bill declined, though it can be
    understood as (a') in a supportive context. The daughter
    made no mistakes in counting in (b), while (b') is taken to
    mean that counting change was the correct thing to do. In
    (c) the medic was unwilling, but (c') is ambiguous; one or
    the other was unwilling and the context will be needed to
    decide which.

3.  (a) Did Bob have that intention?    describes subject
    (b) Did Pierre have that intention?  describes deep subject
    (c) Did Taro have that intention?    describes main subject

    (d) Spk is frank with Adr          describes speaker
    (e) Request: Adr be serious        describes addressee
    (f) Request: Adr be frank with Spk describes addressee
    (g) It was not intended           describes deep subject
    (h) Spk is hopeful               describes speaker

4. Only (b) is strange, for it is already fact but nevertheless dependent on some good luck. In (c) the prediction is based on some good luck.

5. Here is a table that describes my usage (as a student in the USA), but other people will be more or less polite. '!' marks a shocking response, and '?' a strange one.

| | hands full | | | no reason | | | seems locked | | | |
|---|---|---|---|---|---|---|---|---|---|---|
| | 1A | 2A | 3A | 1B | 2B | 3B | 1C | 2C | 3C | |
| (a) | + | + | +? | −!! | −!! | −? | + | − | − | could ... please |
| (b) | −! | −! | − | −!! | −!! | + | −! | −! | − | 0 |
| (c) | + | − | +? | −! | −! | + | + | −! | −? | please ... \ |
| (d) | − | + | +? | −? | − | − | + | − | −? | please ... / |
| (e) | + | + | + | −! | − | + | + | −! | −? | could ... \ |
| (f) | +! | + | + | −? | | + | + | −? | −? | could ... / |

6. (a) *Please* is used for the benefit of the speaker, but it would be a strange circumstance where using my pen will benefit me. (b) *Shall I* is to offer to do something for Adr, but *please* is a polite way to 'push' Adr to do something. It also implies Spk-benefit, but that cannot explain this impossibility, for some things can be of benefit to both Spk and Adr, like turning on the heat in a cold room, and we still cannot combine these two words. (c) *to have a __* implies pleasure for the subject, but *overcooked* says it cannot give pleasure. (d) *Could, dare to, ask you* mark this as very polite to someone higher and distant, so to add a push, *please*, is incoherent. (e) It is so heavily marked that it is hard to imagine any context in which one could be so polite.

7. (a) *delightful* (b) *troublesome* (c) *regretful* (or simply the noun *regret*) (d) *surprised* (e) *tiring, tiresome* (f) *bored* (g) *pleased*

8. embarrassed → embarrassing (b) unsatisfied → unsatisfactory (unsatisfying? dissatisfying) (c) dangerous girls → endangered girls/girls in danger (d) very painful → in great pain

9. (a) The librarian piled (up) the front desk with huge books. (b) My mother spread her best tablecloth over/on the table. (c) Smoke filled the room. (d) The vast stadium echoed for five minutes with our cheers. (e) Our job is to clear the snow from/off the road as soon as possible. (f) His new book is sprinkled (throughout) with classical citations.

## Chapter 6

1.  (a) Epistemic conclusion based on other facts that it is not yet done, finished. OR: Assertion of the impossibility of doing it, now or ever. (b) Statement that he has permission to go. OR: Epistemic possibility, that his going is entirely consistent with the facts known. (c) Epistemic probability; in view of the facts known, it is likely that Anne is singing. OR: Deontic social obligation that Anne has to be singing. (d) Epistemic conclusion that he is back home. OR: Deontic (authoritative) obligation he has, to be back home immediately. (e) Her capacity to swim is so large that she can last for hours swimming. OR: It is her nature occasionally to go on swimming binges that last for hours. (f) Prediction that Adr not repeat it. OR: (only if *will* is stressed) Insistence that Adr not repeat it. (g) Epistemic conclusion that he will not come before 3.00. OR: He has something that prevents him from coming before then. OR (possibly, in planning): He should stay away until that time.

2.  (a) Spk requests Adr to go. OR: Spk asks if Adr predicts going. (b) Spk offers to open window. OR: Spk asks if Spk has obligation or duty to open it. (c) Spk demands politely that Adr answer the question. OR: Spk asks if Adr managed to answer the question then in the past.

3.  (a) it is not sure, but it is entirely possible that smoking damages your health. / Smoking has the capacity to damage. (b) The nurse's duty includes taking his midnight temperature. / We can conclude that she takes his temperature at midnight. (In older and in non-native English, this *must* may be used with the first meaning.) (c) They have the obligation to start studying now. / We can conclude that they are studying now. (d) The speaker is duty bound to do something that forces her to leave, and has no choice in the matter. (Can be used as a polite way to escape.) / The speaker has an obligation that means that she ought to leave, but she could stay longer if there were a good reason. / The speaker has an obligation but will probably ignore it. (e) The speaker promises that the addressee will not leave till it is finished. / The speaker predicts that the addressee will finish it by then. (If *will* is stressed, it could be that the speaker is insisting on the prediction, or it could take on the threatening nature of *shall*.)

4. (a) could finish → finished/was able to finish (b) could . . . catch → . . . caught / . . . managed to catch (c) OK (d) I like → I'd like (e) you may → please/won't you/you must.

5. (a) 'If you want' conflicts with the promisory nature of *shall*. (b) Capacity modals don't take any mark of future, and *can* doesn't exist as an epistemic modal (except when negated or questioned). (c) *would* is habitual, which requires a repeated event; *used to* is a simple durative past.

6. (a) He couldn't/can't/must not have gone. (b) You can/may sit there. (c) It will surely rain tomorrow. (d) You may not be kidding. (e) They may have got there by now.

7. (a) He might not have gone. (b) You must sit there. (c) It could well rain tomorrow. (d) You can't be kidding. (e) They must have got there by now.

8. (a) don't have to, don't need to (b) should/really ought to (c) should, must, really ought to, had better (d) may not, *cannot (e) of course, certainly you can, *you may (it was *may* of politeness) (f) please, if you could be so kind (g) thank you, that's OK.

9. (a) that is not allowed (b) it is possible (c) it is necessary (d) that is preferable

10. (a) *possibly* (b) *possibly* (c) *certainly* (d) *possibly*, if the epistemic sense; *certainly*, if the deontic prohibition (e) *probably, certainly* (f) *certainly*

11. (a) She never sleeps before midnight. (b) He studies only before exams. (c) They close the road if it snows very much. (d) It rains whenever I forget my umbrella.

12. (a) could (b) would have to (c) can, will have to (d) No addition is needed apparently; these are simply ability modals, focusing on psychological capacity – with the addition of *will* for the necessity case as it is future.

# Chapter 7

1. (a) 2: did (b) 2: has dragged (c) began; dead and finished (d) has taught; still alive, presumably (e) gave; the group dissolved many years ago (f) has been; although some of the earlier presidents have died, the presidency is still alive and well (g) has travelled – is embarking; he is still with us, in spirit at least (h) was; long gone (i) has been; we are taking a longer view here, considering whether it is still potentially

322   Answers to Exercises

alive (j) has visited; Chernobyl is more significant than most
prime ministers and he was probably changed by visiting it
(k) was visited; Chernobyl is not likely to be changed one
whit by visitors (l) visited; my flower-arranging class could
hardly be such a renowned place

2. (a) know → have known; *?knew* possible in USA with 'since
we were children', but difficult here with *childhood* (b) will
come → come (c) don't read → haven't been reading OR:
recently → any more/these days (d) is rising → rises/will rise
(e) for only → in only (f) is raining → will rain/will be
raining.

3. (a) e.g.: He has a test at 4.00 that he hasn't prepared for.
Gen: Getting sick (or rather the pretence of it) can be
controlled. (b) e.g.: 2000 years ago. Gen: when Cleopatra
was alive. (c) e.g.: He has started, but something has come
up and he has decided to put off the rest till next week.
Gen: The act of finishing it has begun, psychologically at
least, and is to be completed next week. (d) e.g.: in a space
station fifty years from now, where they turn on the rain at
certain times. Gen: There is a schedule or plan for periods of
rain. (e) e.g.: some time after Mitterand has died. Gen: The
visit(s) do not share a time frame with Mr M., i.e. either the
place no longer exists (or can be visited) or Mr M. no longer
exists (perhaps as a head of state). (f) e.g.: The dog is
specially trained to detect explosives and we have a tip that
one of the bridges will be bombed. Gen: The dog's action
somehow affects the bridge, in our minds.

4. (a) had already run away (b) falls/?will fall (if long before
and/or enough doubt to warrant a prediction) (c) am going
to take (d) am taking (e) have ended (f) am thinking (g) is
going to start (not a prediction, but inevitable), NOT: will
start; 'is going to rain' is fine, but you changed the verb! (h)
has been losing ('has lost' would be possible with 'a lot of
money')

5. (a) They stayed in Africa for two months. (a') The reason
that they are not here is that they are in Africa (or en route)
and plan to stay for two months. (b) She starts cooking
immediately after I get up. (b') She starts before I get up. (c)
0.36 according to the schedule (c') 0.36 is the expected time
(the schedule is probably not relevant) (c'') 0.36 is almost
certain, as preparations have already begun. (d) New York is
his permanent residence. (d') New York is a temporary

residence. (e) She has a friendly personality. (e') She is acting friendly, by conscious effort. (f) It is predicted that she will have another baby. (f') She is probably already pregnant, but at least decided. (f") She is already pregnant. (g) She is or was here probably, because her perfume is in the air. (g') Spk has opened the bottle and is actively sniffing it. OR: Spk is imagining the scent. (h) is a simple fact. (h') suggests that it is annoying to me; it's always that he is using it. (i) again is a simple fact while (i') expresses annoyance with that behaviour. (j) is a temporary wondering, and will end when you tell me, so it is more tentative than (j') which suggests it is a fundamental emotion. (k) The pilot's choice or intent is to fly at that altitude, while (k') is a prediction of what height we will be at, possibly only a short while. (l) simply predicts a future meeting, perhaps at a specific time, while (l') predicts a meeting with some preparation or perhaps repeated meetings over some period. (l) is thus warmer and more intimate as (l') can be used even if one hopes never to see them again. (m) The orange juice is gone, while there is some (much?) still left in (m'). (n') is a precise prediction made by the pilot or an expert that ten minutes from now we will be in the landing process (i.e. close to the runway), while (n) is a simple prediction, perhaps according to a schedule, and probably not very accurate: only ten minutes more and we will land.

6.
|  | (a) | (b) | (c) |
|---|---|---|---|
| think: | B–F | come:   –F | come:   B–F |
|  | –R————S→ | ————S→ | ——R——S→ |
| refuse: | B' F'? | eat:   B–F | begin:   B' F' |
|  |  | leave:   BF | eat:   B— |

Notes: (a) The thinking (i.e. not being sure) ended (F) when she either refused or not, and is in the past, for otherwise we should say 'I think that she will refuse.' (b) Actually there should be Rs associated with each of the three events, but presented as they are in one collapsed sentence, it feels that there is only one R, i.e. that these three events happened nearly simultaneously. (c) F for *eat* is not shown, as it is not given whether the eating is finished.

7. (a)          noon
          ————————R——S→
       B—drink————?–?–
       B—8*bot*—F

(b)
```
                    arrive
   —S————————R→
   B–?–?–B—show——
            —15mn—F
```
(c) eat —F
```
   ————————R—————————S→
            leave–F
```

# Chapter 8

1.  (a') is strange because its taste is not a temporary thing, but it could be said if we are reviewing its taste over the years. (b) is likewise weird, as beautiful eyes are long-lasting. (c) is definitely strange except in tales where trees can move. (d') is similarly weird, unless reporting illusions. (e) is likewise impossible except in tales of animated buckets or buckets that change their capacity from time to time.

2.  (a) learned → studied (b) wear → put on (c) receive → accept (d) belong to → join OR: when you enter → while you are in (e) putting . . . on → wearing . . . (but we often do say it) (f) drowned → almost drowned/was drowning was just about to drown (g) saw → looked, learn → see/find out (h) have had → have caught/have (i) counted → tried to count/ started counting (j) fed → gave/tried to feed (k) knew → learned/found out (l) get on → ride (on)/am on/take (m) fall . . . → drop . . ./let . . . fall

3.  (a) The sky darkened (gradually). (b) His responses softened (as he got older). (c) My belief strengthened. (d) He got stronger. (e) He got tired out. (f) The weather warmed up/ got warmer/became warmer. (g) She went upstairs. (h) Her problems grew (in time)/got bigger.

4.  (a) They widened this road to ease the traffic. (b) She shortened her skirt to meet the new fashions. (c) I sharpened my knife so that it will cut better. (d) We are enlarging the library to make more room for collections. (e) He simplified the answer to help his students. (f) They legalized gambling in New Jersey to attract more tourists. (g) The foreign exchange rate has been stabilized in order to promote commerce. (h) The boy learned how to read those kanji in order to find his way about Japan. (i) They sent a special envoy to Prague to negotiate the treaty. (j) We convinced/ persuaded Carol to marry the artist.

5.  (a) *for* (b) *in* (c) *in* (d) *for* (e) *in*
6.  The ones that take *for* naturally have no F and the ones that take *in* have an F. An iterative reinterpretation is possible.
7.  (a) A question for the reason for the noise, and possibly intended to shame the addressee if he has no reason. (a') A strong suggestion to be quiet. Often used as a command. In (b) the eating stopped two minutes after it began, and probably not finished (but it continued through the two minutes), while in (b') it was finished, before two minutes had passed. 'Gave a jump' in (c) is an idiomatic way to say [was startled], while 'made a jump' is like *to take a walk*, a deverbalized way to say [jumped]. Similarly, *to give a cry* in (d) refers to a loud noise as if in pain or calling someone, while *to have a cry* in (d') is idiomatic for a period of crying (with tears) from sadness. *To give someone an X look* means roughly [to let the person see an X expression on one's face] in (e), while *to take a close look* in (e') is only to look closely.
8.  It focuses attention at the period between the beginning and the finish, so the finish and thus the completive aspect is overridden. More formally, the completive aspect is that R = F if not otherwise specified (like the presumption that R = S unless otherwise mentioned, see Chapter 7), but progressive specifies that R < F, and therefore destroys this completive presumption.
9.  The perfective verb depicts the event as instantaneous, but an on-going event cannot be perceived as instantaneous so it must not be on-going and is thus yet to come.

## Chapter 9

1.  (a') emphasizes the fact that it was under, not behind or anywhere else, so we expect that she is completely underneath, while by contrast (a) lays more emphasis on crawling and/or the table, and she may well be not completely under it. With stress on *under*, (a) has the same meaning as (a'). (b) suggests that it is a chair without arms, and perhaps a short back, for the *in* of (b') implies that he was surrounded in some sense by the chair. (b') is appropriate for a big stuffed armchair, and to use *on* in that case would imply he sat on it in such a way that the speaker didn't feel him surrounded – perhaps on the back with his

feet in the seat, or perhaps it was upside down. (c) refers to the exact middle of the court, while (c') refers to anywhere near that point, closer to the exact middle than to either end. (d) says that we stopped at the edge of the river, while (d') says that we didn't go any further than the river, though we may have crossed the bridge, or dipped our feet in the river, or even merely got in sight of the river. The speaker of (e') is far away from Singapore, perhaps on the telephone, while (e) does not commit him as to any distance. Note that *over* could be replaced or supplemented with *there* quite naturally, but if *here* is added – 'How's life treating you over here in Singapore?' – the speaker is there too, as if on a vacation, but it is still far away from his usual place.

2.  (a) *on*; a small child in a big armchair, or if the chair had lost its seat (b) *at* (*on* not so good, for there are four corners that she could wait 'on'); difficult! (c) *to* (*in* would require *what*); impossible? (d) *across*; if it is a bridge that doesn't go over anything (e) *near* (or *in* if he was very close to the front); none (f) *in* [into the house], *by* [past the house]; *to walk on* could mean [not pause in walking] or it could be in reference to walking on to a stage, etc.

3.  (a) The cup was upside down. (b) There was a culvert under the street and he crawled into it. (c) Peter was a long way away, at least psychologically, and she walked part way to him. (d) She dropped the penny, aiming at the cup apparently. (e) As they went through the park and on to Harrods, they were primarily talking – probably without stopping or noticing anything else. (f) Apparently Byron and Leech both end at this corner. (g) Either we are very small (like mice) or else the chair is very big, as in an amusement park house built in the shape of a chair.

4.  (a) in, on [on top of] (b) in (idiom!) (c) on (d) in (e) at

5.  In (a) the boy received it, while he didn't in (a') or (a''). In (a'') the ball didn't get as far as the boy, while in (a') it was aimed close to him (with perhaps the intent of threatening or hurting him). (b) is normal, where a dog barks to threaten a person, but (b') is possible if a boy has tried to get the dog to talk to him by barking. In (c) she didn't get to the centre although she walked for three hours, while the three hours in (c') brought her to the centre. (d) emphasizes the aspect of being on, as if it is a dog, while (d') emphasizes the table, appropriate for a mob instigator. (d'') depicts a motion that

passes above the table. (e) describes a location on the surface of a wall, while (e') puts the location vertically above the wall. (e") depicts a position partly above, as 'he leaned over the wall', or a movement, as in (d"), and thus a location on the other side, e.g. 'the path starts over this wall'. (f) and (f') both have him standing all the way, but (f') implies that the movement continued after that point, as the impossibility of ★'the terminal' shows.

6. (a) The part of a [Dir]-preposition that generally drops is its second part, *to*, and dropping it here would leave nothing. (b) 'He crawled there'; the *to* is dropped, but a pronominal element is left. (c) The same reason, presumably. (d) 'It flew from there.' NB: 'It flew away' can often be used for such a situation, but *away* is not equivalent to [from there], and thus does not block it. It is not compatible with [To: Spk] for one cannot say ★ 'It flew away from the telephone pole directly at me.'

7. (a) They are different, for although [not near] implies [not at], [not at] does not imply [not near]. However, they do seem similar, for most cases of [not at] are cases of [not near]. (b) Since we can in fact say 'he was not at the corner/not near the factory when . . .', which lexical blocking would disallow if it meant either of these things, it is probably not correct in either of these cases but is an extended use of the [Apx.Abl], more natural with some distance mentioned: 'he was 3 metres away from the corner'. Distance goes with movement, Dir, Abl or Via, but not with Loc or Neg-Loc.

8. (a) *afterwards* with the *-wards* subject to being dropped. 'Jean left early, and I left shortly after(wards).' (b) Only *since*: 'Annick has not been seen (ever) since.'

# Chapter 10

1. (a) your mother, whatever her name is (b) *Realms of Meaning* (c) Th. R. Hofmann (d) something that was in the past but no longer exists (e) the person that you are facing, if any (f) sentence 1 (f) (g) these three words! (h) no referent; it doesn't exist (i) all the people in the world, or perhaps in some select group

2. (a) always (b) never (c) only if the smartest guy in the room is also the oldest, and the instructor (d) only when Professor Glaston says it

3.  (a) no (b) in, e.g., a seminar where the teacher sits and one of the students talks (c) The concepts in each combine to describe different paths or routes to find the referent. In a typical lecture, both paths arrive at the same person.

4.  Smaller denotations: (a) cat (b) black cat (c) stray black cat (d) mother (e) same (f) same (except in a world where some people have feathers) (g) same, both designate the null set (h) square triangle (the null set is in every set). More detailed meanings: (a) cat (b) black cat (c) stray black cat (d) mother (e) same (by ignoring repetitions of elements such as [Fem] here) (f) featherless person (g) not clear (h) square triangle.

5.  (a) 'the Chinese, who are industrious,' and 'the Chinese who are industrious' (b) the other peoples of the region (who are putatively not so industrious); the lazy Chinese, as well as the other peoples.

6.  (a) 'a chair' (b) 'a golden apple' (c) 'an apple'! (d) uncertain: 'the apple' OR: 'a quarter of the apple' (e) 'an apple' (f) none (g) none (h) 'some fish'

7.  (a) the chair that John built (b) the golden apple that Marie (thinks she) saw (c) the half of the apple that he did NOT eat (I presume!), i.e. the apple that he ate part of (d) either: the quarter of the apple that he cut off OR: the apple less the quarter that he cut off (e) the apple that [each pupil] brought (f) the apples that had been placed on the teacher's desk by the students (g) the apples that she didn't give away (h) the fish that Pete is going to catch, we hope OR: in the anticipated going-to-be world, the fish that Pete catches

8.  (a) specific (b) unspecific (sub-atomic particles are unspecific *par excellence*; they are all identical and have no individuality, according to current theory) (c) ambiguous; future events usually involve non-specific things, but if it is near-future, e.g. if he already has the egg in hand, then it is probably specific (d) unspecific; any apple at all will do (e) specific in that the quantity of water was a certain and identifiable quantity, but the specificity is pointless here and not at all in the speaker's intention (f) unspecific (g) specific (h) specific, whether you know it or not (i) actually unspecific as there are several ways, but [the best way] is intended, and that would be specific (j) unspecific, I presume; it even includes the apples you will eat (k) strictly, this doesn't refer to anything, so it is neither specific nor unspecific, yet it corresponds to a dispute that they agreed to put away for

good, and in that interpretation it is specific. (l) specific (m) unspecific (n) unspecific (while *some* in a question expects the existence of the object, still, which one of that class is not specified)

9.  (a) the existential is dominant [there is a person that everyone loves] in (1) and (2); the universal is dominant [for every single person, there is someone (probably different for each) that they love] in (3) and (4). (b) specific *some* (we might name who it is): (1) and (3); non-specific (identity not knowable): (2) and (4).

# Chapter 11

1.  (a) like *to hit*: (*in*) *strike, kick, shoot, bite*; (*on*) *pat, slap, stroke, kiss, burn*; (*by*) *seize, grab, grasp.* Like *to break*: *bend, fold, shatter, tear.* (b) Largely, the *hit*-verbs deal with surfaces of the patient, while the *break*-verbs deal with its overall structure. However, *to shoot* (and *to stab*) are a little hard to see as surface-affecting verbs. Also, there are limited examples where *break*-type verbs act like *hit*-type: 'I tore the certificate in the corner', 'I folded the paper at the dotted line', 'He broke the pencil in the middle.' Perhaps the truth is that we can use the *hit*-type construction only if (a) the action is localized to a namable part of a larger whole, and (b) the predication is also true of the whole object, so you can 'chip the cup in the rim' but you can't 'break the cup in the handle'.

2.  (a) when the hitting was accidental, as in carrying something that hits a passer-by in the arm. Also, though morbid, if the arm was severed from his body. (b) [the agent intends pain/injury to the patient], but note the use of 'The bullet struck him in the back of the neck.' No doubt there is a better answer; cf. 'I hit him' but not 'The falling brick hit him' is normally interpreted (if no indication to the contrary) as intentional.

3.  (a) their son's → their son on his (b) lost → lost to (c) help → help me with/in (d) to thank all my friends for their generous assistance (e) engaged → got/was engaged with/to (f) to trip → to take a trip/to go on a trip AND university → from university (g) to ask permission to our teacher → to ask permission from our teacher OR ask our teacher for

permission (h) attended to → attended (i) reminded → remembered/ was reminded of (j) was stepped my foot → I got my foot stepped on/My foot was stepped on

4. (a) *ate* (b) *drank* (c) *made* (d) *put* (e) *give, make* (f) *speak* (g) *say* (h) *said* (i) *say* (j) *spoke, talked*

5. (a) 1, 2, 4, 5 (b) *to, for* (c) 1, 3, 6, OK with a recipient but not with a location (d) 1, 3 OK if the verb (not the event) includes that the recipient have something he didn't have (e) OK: *take, make, leave, offer, lend*; not possible: *explain, propose, introduce, attribute, confess*

6. (a) Two: 'X is taller than Y', 'I am taller than you'; 'X is (the) tallest in Y', 'I was the tallest in my class'; also: 'X is the taller of Z' where Z is a group of two, 'John is the taller of my (two) sons.' (b) [X is significantly taller than the average for Ys] (c) Even their meanings are comparative (Sapir) and have two places, but the second place is filled by a noun class.

7. (a) He has been running the water for fifteen minutes. (b) She is no doubt flying your plane over Sicily by now. (c) You are boiling my coffee! (d) Someone is turning that car off the main road.

8. (a) 'He fathered the new recruits' [he acted as a father might], or there is already a standard meaning for *to father*: [he was the father of the new recruits], unlikely in this case as the recruits are probably neither few nor related. (b) 'She daughtered him until he gave in' [she acted to him as a daughter might]. (c) 'She sweet-little-thing'ed him . . .' [. . . acted as a sweet little thing]. (d) 'He chocolate-barred his way into their hearts' [he worked his way into their hearts by using (giving them?) chocolate bars]. (e) 'You are going to coffee yourself to death' [you are going to bring about your death by using (too much) coffee]. (f) 'X R'ed Y' [to act as R(x,y)] where R(x,y) is 'X is R of Y', 'X N'ed Y' [X got to be at Y by using N]. (g) 'sweet little thing' ought to be an intransitive noun but is 'relationalized' in connotation, [she was a 'sweet little thing' TO HIM], and then transitivized as a verb.

9. (a) [a meal] − you can't say this then if he is eating a candy bar (b) [wine, beer or some drinkable alcohol] (c) [money] and [to a charity] (d) [a liquid] (e) [the car] (f) perhaps [the dishes] (in North America where there is no verb *to wash up* for dishes), or perhaps [himself] in some unusual circumstances.

## Chapter 12

1. (a) woman (b) [Hum.Adt.Yng]
2. (a) *baby – child – adolescent – adult.* (b) adolescent, adult (c) [Yng.Neg-Adt.Hum] – [Yng.Hum] – [Yng.Adt. Hum] – [Adt.Hum] (d) [not ready for life as an independent individual] (Note that the age at which childhood stops has been generally going up as society becomes more complex, from the Old Testament twelve years old.)
3. (a) that horses were quite important to them (b) first approximation:

   |         | [∅]   | [Fem]  | [Msc]     |
   |---------|-------|--------|-----------|
   | [Adt]:  | ★     | mare   | stallion  |
   | [∅]:    | horse | ★      | ★         |
   | [Neg-Adt]: | colt | filly | (colt)    |

   However, although many dictionaries have *colt* also under [Msc], this is unnecessary and wrong; it is unmarked for sex but blocked for [Fem] by *filly.* (c) [Prt-Msc.Hrs]. (d) [Coz-Bcm-Neg-Msc].
4. (a) *lengthen, enlarge, narrow (down), small, grow, heat (up)* (b) *up, up, up, up, down*
5. (a) *tall, narrow, lazy;* they are gradable (b):

   |         | taller | narrower | tired | lazier | ill | dead | in love |
   |---------|--------|----------|-------|--------|-----|------|---------|
   | get:    | +      | +        | +     | +      | ?   | –    | –       |
   | become: | +      | +        | +     | +      | +   | –    | –       |
   | grow:   | +      | +        | +     | +      | –   | –    | –       |
   | OTHER:  |        |          |       |        | fall ill | die | fall in love |

6. (a) *asleep, ill, in love, into disuse, silent, victim to nervous exhaustion, into someone's clutches, to pieces, to one's knees, short, by the wayside, flat, foul of someone, apart, back, behind, down, for an idea, in, out, over, through* (b) They mostly describe states that are considered unpleasant or undesirable and outside of the control of the subject, what might be labelled [Bad]. (c) The predicate complement must be ungradable, e.g. ★ 'fall very ill' though 'felt very ill' is fine, so the inchoation must be sudden or punctive (F = B), which we might label [Pnt]. (d) [Pnt(Bcm(P)).Bad(P)].
7. (a) X is Y's mother          (b)   X is Y's daughter

(c)  X is a grandmother of Y        (d) X is a sister of Y

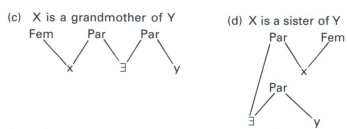

The 'hidden persons' are X's parent(s) in both (c) and (d). (e and f) are the same as (d) but with [1] and with [2] dominating the ∃ for the person or persons that stand in a parent relationship to both X and Y.

(g)     X is Y's step-father      (h)     X is Y's father-in-law

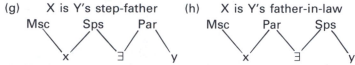

8.  (a) [Big(x,y)] (b) must be [Big(x,z)] also (c) Z is the average range of [Big] for the class that X belongs to (see Chapter 4, double negation).

9.  (a) [Loc(x,y)] 'X is at location Y' or, better, 'X is located by (finding) Y'; [Voj(x)] 'X is a visible object'. (b) [Voj(x)] forms pronouns because it has one actant like other pronouns, nominal phrases and most nouns. [Loc(x,y)] has two actants, so it naturally forms prepositions unless one of the actants is filled, as it commonly is in deictic words as seen below.

X is here            X is on Y          X is it

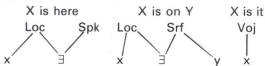

# Chapter 13

1.  (a) Sam caught (a fly ball/a house fly) in the outfield. (b) Did you see (the chicken that she roasted/her roasting a chicken)? (c) It is ready to be eaten. / It is ready to eat something. (d) he told them not to play after 24.00 any more. / He told them that they should stop some time after 24.00 (but to continue until then). / It was after midnight when he told them to stop. (e) The end of the game was when . . . / . . . that had been bothering him all afternoon (f) . . . It was huge. / . . . She does it so well. (g) . . .; it's

been cooking for three hours. / . . . Do you want to feed it? (h) Because he wanted them to get more rest, . . . / He wanted them to learn the game well, so . . . / . . . That's how we know he was here.

2. (a) The President is flying to Tokyo tomorrow and to Paris next week. (b) Did John or Bill volunteer? (c) Mother will be powdering her face and Father shaving. (d) Janet will go to Disneyland next week and Nancy might go too. (e) My father hasn't met my girlfriend yet, but he will soon. (f) Pete quit the club this morning, although he didn't want to. (g) This book seems difficult, that one certainly is. / <literary> This book seems, and that one certainly is, difficult. (h) B: Well, I hope not. / I hope I am not. / I hope that I am not going to be. (i) Those who prefer to stay home can (do so). / Those who prefer (to) can stay home.

3. (a) There's an eraser under the desk if you need one. (b) If you need an eraser, there is one under the desk. / If you need one, there's an eraser under the desk. (c) That Professor Evans is unpopular with his students annoys him. / That he is unpopular with his students annoys Professor Evans. (d) It annoys Professor Evans that he is unpopular with his students. ★It annoys him that Professor Evans is unpopular. (e) My neighbourhood is quiet now, but I wonder how long it will remain so. (f) You must taste globefish if you haven't already. / You must taste globefish if you haven't already done so. / You must taste globefish if you haven't tasted it already.

4. (a) It was the squat-type toilets that embarrassed the visitors most. / What embarrassed the visitors most was the squat-type toilets. (b) It was Stephen Spielberg that the Academy Award Committee nominated as the best director. / The one whom the Committee nominated as the best director that year was Stephen Spielberg. (c) It was in front of the new airport that the local citizens were protesting. (d) What John wants to be is a movie star. / It is a movie star that . . . (e) It is due to Typhoon No. 6 that all flights into Hong Kong have been cancelled. (f) It is not until the estimated time for the cherry trees to bloom is announced that Japanese fully recognize the arrival of spring.

5. (a) *therefore* – B, *however* – C or F, *accordingly* – B, *incidentally* – G, *as a result of* – B, *nevertheless* – F, *in addition to* – A, *in short* – D, *for example* – A, *in other words* – E, *moreover* – A and

E, *on the other hand* – C, *consequently* – B, *to be brief* – D, *still* – F, *that is to say* – E and D, *on the contrary* – C, *to be sure* – E, *in contrast* – C, *similarly* – A, *by the same token* – A, *as a matter of fact* – E.

6.  (a) Cjc: *and* – A or E, *but* – C or F; Cjm: *because* – B, *while* – F, *as* – B; Cjf: *for* – B, *so* – B or D.

7.  (a) Yuko; because *to arrive* overlaps with *to come* (even though it is negative) (b) Maria; because *to say* overlaps with *to tell* (c) Liz (and *her* refers to Maria); because *to understand* overlaps with *to tell* with actants reversed

8.  (a) Some seem to suggest a total lack of comprehension (1, 5, 7) and some suggest that it is the implications, not the immediate (descriptive) meaning, that is not understood (6, 8, 11, 12, 13). Several suggest it is the speaker's fault (9–12, especially 11), a Japanese way to be polite. (b) I can't follow him (at all). Whatever he is saying, it doesn't make any sense to me. I can't guess what we should understand by what he is saying.

9.  I can't tell you – how I learned the secret,

    (a)                                    except – John didn't tell me.

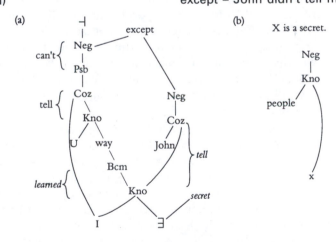

where [people] stands for something
like [people in general], or [everyone except a few]
Actually, there is another component (at least) to *secret*: that someone doesn't want [people] to know it, so 'X is Y's secret' has [Des(y,. . .)] dominating the [Neg], [Des(y,Neg-Kno(people,x))]. Here, however, the Y is not specified, and that would only confuse matters. (c) the [Kno] that derives

from *learned* and the second *tell* are indeed the same knowing, but the one that derives from the first *tell* is different; it describes your knowing how, while the others deal with my knowing a secret. The other possible [Kno] resides inside *secret* and it describes the lack of knowledge that most people have that makes a secret a secret.

## Chapter 14

1. (a) [you should not have done that] (b) [it hurts the cat] and so [you shouldn't do it] (c) [that is impossible], often used when faced with evidence that it is true (d) [Spk completely agrees] (e) [what you say is foolish] (f) [work (this week) is almost finished] (g) [Spk is extremely confident that the person referred to will not carry out his campaign promises].

2. (a) Thanks (a lot). – Thank you (very much). – I (really) appreciate it. (b) Sorry. – I'm really sorry. – I apologize for that. (c) Bye. – So long./(I'll) see you. – Good-bye. (d) Dear John, – Dear Mr Lochman, – Dear Sir, (e) Take care/Love, Ron – Sincerely yours, Thomas R. Hofmann – Respectfully yours/Faithfully yours, Thomas R. Hofmann

3. (a) He keeps the car across the street in a garage. (b) I was going to be taken off in a boat to a transport. (c) They took him across the river in a ferry. (d) He was fixed to the stake with a chain. (e) They put a saddle on a horse for me at last.

4. (a) This computer is a lemon. (b) I've been waiting for ages. / I've been here so long that the dogs thought I was a tree. (c) He's got the whole university library. (d) It's bound to be a best seller. (e) There were a few people there. (f) The English exam will be given to international students first. (g) . . . seats for senior citizens. (h) It was really some party. (i) It's a chance in a million. / There's not one chance in a million. (j) What lovely weather!

5. (a) You're (quite) welcome. (b) Congratulations! (c) That's OK. / Forget it. (d) under arrest. (e) That's all for today. / Class dismissed. (f) my condolences.

6. (a), (a), (d), (g)    (b) because they can be interpreted as requests. Actually, I could say or understand also (b) and (f) with *please* as highly emotional insistent demands. The speaker is interpreted here to be using frames appropriate to his (repressed) anger, and adding *please* in an attempt to

remain polite. However, this interpretation is not possible for (c) or (e).

7. (a) Could you say (what his name is) *again?* (b) *Since you wanted to know,* I will tell you (that he agrees)). (c) *Please* tell me (where you are going). (d) *If you can catch the waiter's attention,* please tell him (that I need some water). (e) *In case you didn't know it already,* I am telling you (that Micky got married). (f) I say (anyone who came today was a fool), with *myself included* in the denotation of *anyone.*

8. (a) Seventeen is old enough to have a driving licence, NOT: Emily is over seventeen. If you can't feel this, try changing 'seventeen' to 'twenty-five'. (b) One can't rely on Democrats. (c) To call a girl a virgin is to insult her.

9. (a) 'a crease came to be on', [Bcm-Hav:crease] (b) 'put on [his] shoulder', [Coz-Bcm-Loc:shoulder] (c) 'remove the peel' [Coz-Neg-Have:peel] (d) 'put them in glass containers', [Coz-Bcm-Loc:Cnt:glass]; 'cover them with paper', [Coz-Bcm-Loc:Cnt:paper] (e) 'carried in a cart', [(Coz-Bcm-Loc:cart).carry] (f) 'cover the ground like a carpet', [(Bcm-Sml:carpet).cover] where [Sml(x,y)] stands for something like 'X is like/similar to Y.'

10. (a) [past] or [outdated], and [future] or [next model] (b) The computers that we have twenty-four hours from now will be essentially indistinguishable from those we have now, so (c) the [day] part of the meaning of *tomorrow* can't be taken literally, and the same for *yesterday.*

# Word/Topic Index

Citations in questions & even in summaries are excluded on the assumption that one is seeking the most detailed explanation, not just occurrences of the word. If it is cited in an important way in the chapter, it will probably also be in the chapter summary in a more general way, & related to other concepts.

Negative prefixes *un-*, *in-*, etc. are not indexed.

For substantive semantic & syntactic concepts, please consult the list of symbols, p.xxii.

To help distinguish the senses intended, countable nouns are cited in their plural forms & verbs in their abstract nominal form.